AMERICAN DISSIDENT
The Political Art of Michael Moore

FRANÇOIS PRIMEAU

Lulu Press
2010

Copyright © 2010 by François Primeau

All rights reserved. No part of this publication may be reproduced, stored in a retrieval system or transmitted, in any form or by any means, without the prior written permission of the author.

This book is printed in the United States of America.

Cover illustration and photograph of the author by Tina Carlisi. ©

Primeau, François, 1969 –
American Dissident: The Political Art of Michael Moore
1st Edition, François Primeau 2007©
2nd Edition, François Primeau 2010©

ISBN: 978-0-9867781-0-0

All experience hath shown that mankind is more disposed to suffer while evils are sufferable, than to right themselves by abolishing the forms to which they are accustomed. But when a long train of abuses and usurpations, begun at a distinguished period, and pursuing invariably the same object evinces a design to [subject] reduce them to arbitrary power, it is their right, it is their duty, to throw off such government, and to provide new guards for their future security.

U.S. Declaration of Independence, 1776

The patriotic ones are the ones who are not afraid to ask questions, who are not afraid to dissent, who are not afraid to say and remind those in Washington that you are there to serve us. 'You are the servants, not the masters.' I mean, that's what real patriotism is.

Michael Moore, 2001

**Dedicated to my favorite rebel,
Tina.**

AMERICAN DISSIDENT:
THE POLITICAL ART OF MICHAEL MOORE
TABLE OF CONTENTS

PROLOGUE: *THE GUNS OF MICHIGAN* xv
Witnesses to History xvii
The Guns of Michigan xviii

INTRODUCTION: *DESPERADO* 21
Searching for Ed Murrow 23
Wanted: Moore-detractors! 27
The Man with the Bullhorn 28
The Age of Unreality 29
Don't Kill the Messenger 32
Radicalizing Hope 33
The Gangster Syndrome 34

CHAPTER ONE: *TAKING OVER THE TUBE* 37
Reagan at Bitburg 39
Living in a TV Nation 40
The Other Michael Jackson 41
Awfully True 43
"We Are Number One!" 44
A Case Made for "Number Two" 45
Green Giant 46
To Mosh or Not to Mosh? 48
Capitalism at its Finest 49
Rich White Guys 51
Let's Move to Turdonia 52
Affirmative Action Plan 54
Beat the Rich 55
White Collar Criminals 56
Cartoon Characters on Welfare 58
Human Resources 59
Temp Nation 60
Armageddon Time 63
Indian Teenage Fall-Out Queen 64
No Go for Kyoto 66
Industrial Disease 67
An Unusual Choir Boy 69
A Nation in Rapture 70
Thou Shall Not Blend Politics and Religion 70
Free at Last 73
Eyesight to the Blind 75

Domestic Slave Labor 76
Buggery on Board 77
Bitch Hunt 80
A Little Politics & A Little Sex 82
Teen Sniper School 83
Feel My Heat 85
Two Sure Things: Death & Texas 88
Out for Trout 94
Help the Dead Guy 96
Republican Solutions 97
Kill the Sick 99
Evil of Two Lessers 102
Saddamized! 102
Tough Love 104
TV is Dead: Long Live TV! 108
Dog Eat Dog 109
The Gangster Culture: Part II 111

CHAPTER TWO: *RENEGADE FILMMAKER* 113
***ROGER & ME* (1989) 115**
Man on a Mission 115
The Truth is Out There 116
Badlands 117
Nice Place to Raise Your Kids 120
How to Destroy a Community without Trying 122
Job Well Done, Now Die! 123
Eye of the Storm 124
Starving in the Belly of the Whale 126
A Factory that Plays Tricks on Your Mind 126
Good Time for a Parade? 127
Exiled on Main Street 128
D. I. Y. 130
Wouldn't It Be Nice? 130
Infiltrator 132
Pet or Meat? 134
The Dawn of a New Era 136
Stranger Than Fiction 136

***CANADIAN BACON* (1995) 137**
Neighbors 137
God Bless America…Again? 138
"You Made It, You Can Own It!" 140
A Typical American Coup 143
Blame Canada 144
Please, Not Anne Murray! 145

Home-Brewed Militia   148
Culture Clash   149
"American Woman (Stay Away From Me)"   151
Sleeping with the Elephant   152

THE BIG ONE (1997)   154
Squeezed   154
Off the Beaten Trail   155
The Call of the "Buck"   156
The Excesses of the Right   157
Voting? For What?   159
Hard Times for an Honest Man   159
Rocking Rockford   160
One Size Fits All   161
Corporate Showdown   162
Turning Lost into a Halo, Turning Crack into Profits   163
Prison Labor   164
Union Maid   166
Racing for It   167
One to Go   169

BOWLING FOR COLUMBINE (2002)   170
Consistency of Convictions   170
Why Columbine?   171
Peace Is Our Profession   172
Membership Has Its Privilege   174
When the Tough Gets Going   176
Wackos   177
Monsters in the Making   181
We Are Columbine   182
What a Wonderful (Ironic) World   184
Teenage Wasteland   185
From His Cold Dead Heart   187
Children of the Damned   189
Burden of Guilt   190
Creative New Ways of Venting Out Anger   191
A Bible and a Smith & Wesson   192
Grey Flannel Suits   194
Paranoid Android   195
Colors   197
Sometimes a Great Notion   199
The 49th Parallel   202
They Were Expendable   204
Behind Poverty   206

Grilling Dick   208
Fear Mongers   209
How K-Mart Was Won (without ever shooting a gun)   211
Thou Shall Not Kill…That Goes for You Too, Moses!   212
"Trees of Green & Red Roses Too…"   220
Getting your *isms* Confused?   221

FAHRENHEIT 9/11 (2004)   224
Into the Fire   224
A Cautionary Tale   225
Send in the Clowns   227
Skull & Bones   229
Endless Vacation   230
Operation Curveball   232
Cantus   234
Reading Makes a Country Great   235
Air bin Laden   238
Black Marker & Angel Investors   239
Yellowcake (the Ultimate Loophole)   240
Screw Habeas Corpus   242
The Visit   243
Freedom Fries   244
Hawk Hunting   245
A Shot in the Face   247
Old Men of (Long-Term) Vision   249
Secret Kingdom   251
Wages of Fear   252
Shades of Orwell   255
Goodnight Baghdad   257
S&M Party at Abu Ghraib   259
Smells like Nazi Spirit   260
America's Broken Backbone   263
When the Lies Are So Big   265
A Matter of Convenience   266
"The facts, ma'm, just the facts!"   267
One More Day (Or Four More Years…)   268

SICKO (2007)   270
This Might Hurt a Little   270
Pray You Don't Get Sick   272
Small Prints   274
Millhouse's Ghost   279
Mother…lovers   283
Looking at You to Find Out Who I Am   284
Street Fighting Man   289

Hoping For the Best   291
Americans in Paris   293
Meanwhile, Back at Home   297
The Last Drop   398
Muchos Gracias, Señor Moore   302
"Me" versus "We"   303

CAPITALISM: A LOVE STORY **(2009)**   304
"Makes Me Wanna Sing 'Louie, Louie'…"   304
Bottom Feeders   306
"Inconceivable!"   308
Turning the Bull Loose   310
Revisiting Roger   312
The Cost of Free Enterprise 313
Dead Peasants   318
Holy Crap   318
Riding the Gravy Train   322
A Novel Idea: Fairness in the Workplace   324
Deregulate This!   326
Dark Days   330
Angelo's Friends   331
The Sky is Falling   333
Here Comes the Flood   334
"Troubled Asset Relief Program" (or how to steal the poor to feed the rich) 337
FDR's Dream   341
Get Off the Dime!   344

EPILOGUE: *REBEL, REBEL*   347
The Art of Turning Kings into Fools   349
Burn, Freedom, Burn!   350
Won't Get Fooled Again?   352
What's wrong with the Left, Anyhow?   354
Rolling Stone Gathers No Moss   356
The Right Side of the Left   357
Louder Than Bombs   359
Spanking the Bully   360
Redeeming the Bully   363
American Dissident   364

MICHAEL MOORE: *WORKING*   367

ABOUT THE AUTHOR   375

PROLOGUE
THE GUNS OF MICHIGAN

Witnesses to History

Sunday, June 27, 2004, 10:35 p.m.

Coming out from the mouth of a moldy subway station near 34th Street my girlfriend and I are wondering how to conclude a perfect day in New York City. Considering the restrictions imposed on us by a limited traveling budget, our minds rapidly set on what is referred to by Manhattan standards as a "modest activity." We gather one last burst of energy and dish out another twenty dollar bill to go sit in an air-conditioned room that would normally amount to buttered popcorn, one-dimensional characters and predictable morality tales. Tonight, however, there is one alternative to the other mediocrity glittering on the Hollywood marquee. Somehow this alternative, this choice, made our perfect day even better, because this is something we search for when we go the cinema and almost never get: diversity. So we kicked-back our heels and started pondering the meaning of this anomaly unfolding in front of our eyes on the big screen.

Five minutes into *Fahrenheit 9/11* we were already feeling through its images, sounds and voice-over properties the importance and gravity of what was being presented to us. Even though the original distributor of the film had dropped it a month before its official North American release, not for commercial reasons but apparently for political ones,[1] this unusual film managed against all odds to find its way in thousands of theaters across the land and illustrate the lack of ethos of the government then sitting in the White House. For some reason it was able to afford dissension, a very expensive commodity in the United States of America in 2004. It was bold, brash, and courageous. It was like nothing we ever saw before.

Throughout its two hour course, *Fahrenheit 9/11* suggested that ethnicity and class are still at the center of the "democratic question" in the United States, regardless of one's opinion about old Karl Marx. It told its domestic audience that war, however necessary it might have seemed to them after the 9/11 tragedy, could never be an acceptable solution to the downfall of American capitalism and an imminent energy crisis. In the end, *Fahrenheit 9/11* left its viewers thirsty for justice and freedom, two precious concepts that should never be taken for granted or left in the hands of cruel and incompetent leaders.

When all was said and done, this powerful film created a strong impression on us, two Canadian cinephiles who don't expect much from Hollywood cinema anymore. Even though the news in it was really bad, it did make our day perfect.

---

[1] Jim Rutenberg, "Disney seeks to block a movie's shot at Bush, Michael Moore is denied distribution", *International Herald Tribune*, May 6, 2004

The Guns of Michigan

> I'm saying that what's great about this form is the communal experience of sitting in the dark with strangers and viewing something that's going to engage us, and that's what I'm thinking about when I'm making a film.[2]

This revised edition of *American Dissident: the Political Art of Michael Moore* is one of the few serious contributions to the study of Michael Moore as a major American film artist. However, it does not entertain the illusion of being exhaustive. It should be read as an attempt at trying to capture the meaning of a "political animal" (Aristotle) unlike any others: a reporter, a filmmaker, an author, a television host and, beyond all of this, a polemicist who uses a hybrid form of storytelling which borrows from the wide vocabulary of journalism, radio, film, and television idioms to stir up political ideas for the masses of film viewers everywhere, especially young film viewers (i.e. under 40).

In the larger scope of things, this book presents itself as a sociological inquiry into the culture that Michael Moore was born and evolves in, as well as a retrospective of the major themes and concerns found within his work over the past 20 years. It is also about the consistency of his style of presentation (what we now refer to as his "trademark," ironically enough). The main contention of this book is that as an American filmmaker Moore is a marginal voice that manages to use mainstream distribution channels to convey dissident political views to large crowds all over the world. In order to prove this important fact about his work, we wish to propose a critical analysis, as well as an interpretation of the work he has produced since the late 1980s for film and for television. It is an attempt at disseminating a body of work that is rich in information and complex in its presentation. This analysis might appear for some to be overly descriptive at times, but this seems necessary to isolate and discuss the elements that are political in his television shows and feature films.

This book is not a biography of Michael Moore, although it does contain some fundamental biographical data about his life. It does not claim to be a character-study of a great man either, although it presents his work in what some would consider being too much of a positive light. Instead it should be read as a cultural studies endeavor which seeks to better understand the American psyche.

Even though we can find American popular culture and its myriad of references in the most remote regions of the world today, because of globalization, there are still many mysteries surrounding it as far as its

---

[2] Michael Moore interviewed by Steven Applebaum, www.bbc.co.uk

meaning and influence are concerned. We feel like a thorough reading of Moore's work would help us achieve a greater knowledge and understanding of this phenomenal and extremely complex culture in that sense. Thus, to set into context a subject of such dimensions seems almost mandatory, because where Michael Moore is from is as important as what he talks about and how he talks about it in his type of political cinema.

The Introduction opens a window on the political and cultural landscape within which Michael Moore has been evolving since he started making movies. His films, books and television shows have always been thematically contemporaneous to the society from which they have emerged and we believe that a basic contextual setup is required to prove if only but a point: that Moore's work is essential in light of the current mainstream media hegemony. This section will serve to introduce him as a political activist and producer of meaning in a culture where these terms are perceived negatively, and will address some of the major social, cultural, and political problems that Americans are faced with today - while a new and more decent President is in office.

Chapter One focuses exclusively on specific episodes of Moore's two television series (*TV Nation* and *The Awful Truth*) that were deemed subversive within mainstream media at the time of their making (the 1990s); while Chapter Two provides a comprehensive analysis of his six nonfiction features and one fiction feature to date (*Roger & Me*, *The Big One*, *Bowling for Columbine*, *Fahrenheit 9/11*, *Sicko*, *Capitalism: A Love Story*, and *Canadian Bacon*). Once again, the analytical parts are intentionally descriptive for those who might not have seen all the work, and will serve to support the idea that Moore is a true anomaly in the American media game (i.e. by today's broadcasting and distribution standards).

The Epilogue will address some of the criticism targeted against Michael Moore and his work. As strange as it may sound, many left-wing viewers do not see the necessity of having at the very least an alternative point-of-view such as Moore's on American politics. It seems to us that, as well as to counter an ever-growing cynical feeling concerning politicians and politics in general, Moore's work stands as a necessary counter-balance to the demagogue and right-wing discourse of media outputs such as Fox News and the *Rush Limbaugh Show*. Since there are so few alternatives to American mainstream media today, Moore's work proves to be articulate and vibrant, but also fundamental to a breathing and working democracy. How anyone can fail to admit this fact defies any rational explanation, as far as we are concerned.

All throughout this book, our main task is to prove that, besides tackling many important issues of contemporary life and revealing many flaws in the "logic" of American state capitalism, Moore is interested in the formal aspects of the mediums he uses to communicate sociopolitical ideas with. We are determined to prove that Moore has great talent for mass communication and that his insights into the world of American politics alone are well-worth the price of admission. It is necessary to specify here that certain sections of this book are highly interpretative in nature, and include comments and opinions which might not necessarily reflect Michael Moore's own opinion on the subject matters at hand. And because his work has an effect on some viewers, at least on this one, it can be considered a study in spectatorship as well.

Finally, this revised edition of *American Dissident: the Political Art of Michael Moore* develops certain theories about Moore's function within American culture, politics and society. These are deeply rooted in the belief that media such as cinema and television are powerful tools which can shape a nation's stance on any given subject. In an ideal world, a media, whether it is the printed word, cinema, television or the Internet, should be a democratic canvas upon which an individual can write his/her heart and mind freely, with figures and sounds taken out of life and, yes, a great part of imagination. In our opinion no one has achieved this with the fervor and the skill with which Michael Moore has in the last two decades.

No matter what one's opinion of his work is, America really could not do without him. And that is a fact.

François Primeau
Montreal, December 2010

INTRODUCTION
DESPERADO

Searching for Ed Murrow

> I was the all-American boy, an Eagle Scout. I won my marksman certificate from the N.R.A. I was religious, attending seminary high school to become a Catholic priest. I obeyed all the rules (to this day, I have yet to smoke a joint) and worked within our political system (at the age of eighteen, I was elected to public office in Michigan). Until the 1990s, I never earned more than $17,000 a year. I have stood in the unemployment line at least three different times in my life and was collecting $98 a week in "benefits" when I decided to make *Roger & Me*.[3]

Born on April 23, 1954, son of Frank and Veronica, along with two sisters, Anne and Veronica, Michael Francis Moore was educated the Irish-American way. Even though this may very well be the cornerstone of his entire body of work, we will address it in a later part of the book. He also developed early on an interest in politics, as well as in larger humanist issues because of this Catholic background. Many of his relatives were involved in the Great Sit-Down strike of 1936-37, and as an Eagle Scout he had won a badge by creating a slide show exposing environmentally unfriendly businesses in his hometown of Davison (a suburb of Flint), Michigan. Around 1972, when 18 year-olds were granted the right to vote, young Michael ran for a seat on the Flint School Board, soon becoming the youngest person to win an election for public office in the United States.[4] He once said that his mother, who passed away just before the stunning success of his book *Stupid White Men* and his film *Bowling for Columbine*, also had a great influence on him.

> She inspired me on so many levels (...) She was the one who educated me. She was taking me to the library when I was four. She taught me and my sisters to read and write before we went to school. She taught us from an early age that knowledge was the dragon-slayer. And the dragon is ignorance and fear, all those things that are caused by a lack of knowledge and information.[5]

---

[3] Michael Moore, *Downsize This!: Random Threats from an Unarmed American*, Crown/ Random House, 1996, p.10
[4] Richard Corliss, Reported by Desa Philadelphia and Jeffrey Ressner, "The World According To Michael; Taking aim at George W., a populist agitator makes noise, news and a new kind of political entertainment," *Time Magazine*, July 12, 2004
[5] Brian Reade, "The Awkward Conscience of a Nation," (www.mirror.co.uk), November 3, 2003

In a 2002 interview with Charlie Rose, after the release of *Bowling for Columbine* in America, Moore told a story about an event that might have been at the root of his social and political consciousness.

> I remember certain things as a child. I remember Holy Thursday mass in 1968, coming out of mass. It's April 4th, 1968 and one of the parents had gone to the car to warm it up, or whatever, and turned the radio on. And a bulletin came on, and he hears the bulletin and he shouts out to the others of us coming out of mass: "[They] just shot Martin Luther King!" and a *cheer* goes up among many of the people coming out of church... As a 13 year-old, I couldn't understand why anybody would cheer the killing of another person. I mean, I was not a political person then, I was not that aware of Civil Rights, but I guess I did not understand. I mean, we were just coming out of mass. Tomorrow is Good Friday, you know? Things like that, I guess, just stuck to my head and through my life. And I guess, what my parents thought me about injustice and doing the right thin, and standing up for what you believe in and following your conscience, so all of that had great impact on me.

Moore also learned throughout the years about the suffering of his family in the Great Depression and all about the sacrifices everyone had to make in order to survive and prosper in this particularly hard land called the United States of America. The Vietnam War and the sociological upheavals of the 1960s had already left their mark on the American psyche before he had reached his twentieth birthday. Like so many Americans, Moore first believed in Johnson's Great Society. But then he also was a witness to the Watergate affair and lived through the cynical climate that followed those terrible years, all the way to Reagan's election and the rebirth of Conservatism in Washington at the dawn of the 1980s. He too was a wide-eyed observer of the major scientific breakthroughs and political events of the 20th century, especially those which rocked the world in the past five decades: from JFK's assassination to Sadat's assassination, from Armstrong on the Moon to the fall of the Berlin Wall, and later, to September 11, 2001 and its irreversible aftermath.

Like most of his contemporaries, he developed a skepticism that allows him to question the actions and policies of American leaders and lawmakers in his work today; even going as far as to question the very President he helped to put in office (Obama). Like millions of others of this post-war generation, Moore had to live with the anxiety which came along with going to bed under Cold War vibes, imagining that his idealistic suburbanite lifestyle would be obliterated within a few seconds by one single and right-on-target Soviet missile. Repeatedly he included images of apocalyptic destruction in his work in order to come to terms with his own fear of a possible nuclear annihilation. Often he will remind us in his work that life on Earth is dangling at the end of a miserable thread, thanks to those "stupid white men" who only believe in instrumental reason, the power of money and ownership, and the law of the financially strong. Moore is against Social Darwinism (which is not the same as Darwinism, in its anthropological definition). He is betting on humanity's capacity to self-determine and emancipate, as we have been doing since we crawled out of our caves and became masters of our destiny.

In the 1970s, after passing on a University education, Moore began a life-long career as an independent journalist. He first worked for the *Flint Voice*, an alternative weekly newspaper in his home state of Michigan. There he soon became the editor, and under his leadership the paper expanded into the *Michigan Voice*, one of the most respected political publications operating in the Midwest at that time. Already in his mid-20s, like some sort of homegrown maverick (more like Orson Welles than John McCain), he was running the newspaper straight out of Flint.

> We came out either twice or once a month, depending on how much money we had. I did everything. It gave me a sense of how to do things *guerrilla-style* with very little money.[6]

In the 1980s, Michael Moore's success at the *Michigan Voice* eventually led to a job offer from *Mother Jones*, where he also became an editor. After a while he believed that the San Francisco-based and leftist journal was going soft, and that it was his goal to bring it closer to "real people." It has been reported that he often clashed with the publishers and was fired by the same people who had hired him a year before, reportedly for refusing to run an article criticizing the Sandinista rebels in Nicaragua.[7] His version of the ordeal can be heard in his first film, *Roger & Me*, wherein he explains in voice-over narration that the magazine had fired him because he wanted to put an unemployed autoworker friend from Flint, Ben Hamper, on the front page of the magazine.

After having worked shortly with Ralph Nader's organization, Moore got the idea to make a film about Flint and how its local economy was collapsing as a direct result of the closure of General

---

[6] Steven Hammer, "A Chat with Mr. TV Nation," *NUVO Newsweekly*, August 1995
[7] Alexander Cockburn, "Michael Meets Mr. Jones", *The Nation*, September, 1986

Motors plants. These assembly-line factories were being closed down in spite of their continuous profitability, something that unsettled Moore to the point where he felt he had to make a film about it. (A film that Nader himself disliked at the time of its release.)[8] He used his settlement fee from *Mother Jones* as seed money, and eventually had to sell his home, ask his parents for a loan and even hold bingo games to raise money to finish it. Nothing could have stopped him, it would seem. It really is the only way one can make a film against the system.

No doubt that Michael Moore had help along the way. His rise to the top of alternative American media was not achieved alone, and it is by no means the goal of this book to edify him as a typical American-style self-made-man. He obviously has a family, a creative/life partner, and a large crew behind him around the clock (including a roomful of attorneys). They are the driving force behind his satirical and poetic diatribe against the excess of corporate America and the crooked politicians and civil servants who support it. Without this tight entourage, and considering that filmmaking and television-making are only possible through good team spirit and team work, he certainly would not have given us all those original and stimulating films and TV shows he did in the last two decades. His name may be on top of the bill, but even he would admit that without a good crew you just cannot produce anything of real value in these forms of mass communication.

For instance, *Roger & Me* would have been a very different picture without the contribution of Kevin Rafferty, Jane Loader and Pierce Rafferty, three independent filmmakers who showed him how to load a 35mm camera, as well as the power of editing through their own films. His television series *TV Nation* and *The Awful Truth* would probably never had seen the light of day if it had not been for the determination of certain key producers at the British Broadcasting Corporation, and his later career has been taken in charge by some of the most powerful people in the business, like Ari Emmanuel and the Weinstein brothers. Hence, through Michael Moore's collaborative efforts and gradual notoriety, we will see in the following chapters how mass media can be used to push dissident political views in the United States today, in spite of a totally controlled media environment.

But before doing so, let us briefly consider the relationship he has been entertaining with his audience, supporters and detractors equally, since it is this very rapport and understanding of it, from both sides of the isle, which makes him for us the quintessential agent provocateur of our times.

---

[8] Doron P. Levin, "Ralph Nader, UAW Unhappy With Film That Attacks GM", *New York Times*, January 20, 1990

Wanted: Moore-detractors!

To begin let us assert that Michael Moore's international recognition has to do with a bond of trust that he has been establishing with his audience since his first feature, *Roger & Me*, produced back in 1989. Since this film's release, many individuals from around the globe perceive him as an *optional* and *reliable* source of information on the topic of America, even though they must consciously know that he "tampers" with his material to prove a point. In other words his supporters and followers want his analysis, interpretation and, therefore, *subjective look* on what America is all about from within. But then again, many others who deem him a bourgeois entertainer and a master-manipulator do not.

But for those who admire and support what Moore is doing, we find ourselves sharing with him a common point-of-view on the state of world political affairs. A lot of us are actually against state-sponsored terrorism, neocolonialism, and preemptive wars which only benefit a few unethical conglomerates. Many of us are also worried that greed and political hypocrisy in the name of profit-making abroad has overshadowed important issues at home in the United States; issues such as the poverty stemming from a totally moribund economy and the non-existing "social security" (a very obscure concept in the U.S., since it is out of government control and into the hands of private business). As fellow women and men who like to travel once in a while, we cannot help but to weep at the sight of inner-city ghettos and poverty-stricken America, especially since the financial meltdown of 2008. Going back home to our reasonably balanced form of socialist-minded market economies, which also have their own share of problems but not on that level, we have a difficult time understanding the reasons why such an opulent nation would leave more than a third of its population in such abject living conditions.

"If America is so great," one might legitimately ask, "why is there so many people merely surviving there?" Or again, "If America is so just and virtuous, why is it not caring for those Americans that are losing their jobs, their homes, and their means for survival?" This line of questioning was particularly intense in the public mind, at least around the world, after the passage of Hurricane Katrina which leveled Louisiana and Mississippi in late August 2005. When the entire world saw how slowly the Republican government reacted to save its most disenfranchised citizens, predominantly African-American and Cajun, it confirmed what its real priorities were. The discrepancy between the magnitude of the tragedy and the absence of relief, because it was busy fighting a useless war elsewhere, was more than plain to see. What those dramatic aerial shots of a completely flooded New Orleans actually confirmed is that there is a great injustice based along classist and ethnic lines at the heart of contemporary American politics. The way in which the tragedy was not dealt with, while Bush was overlooking the tragedy from Air Force One, left us in disbelief and more mistrustful of the American government than ever before. We became even more doubtful regarding the capacity of the Republicans (and the Democrats) to properly govern America (and, by default, the rest of the world). For once, and most probably contrary to the coverage of 9/11, live television was showing us reality, a physical and empirical reality, not an imagined world trying to pass as such.

The Man with the Bullhorn

Moore's greatest contribution to American culture is that he redefines what activism and culture should be like by blending both. Part of a long tradition American dissidents, he often walks the thin line of political correctness to prove a point, especially in his television work. In doing so he always runs the risk of losing at least one part of his American audience: the puritan one. Surely, other entertainers share his penchant for witty derision, dark and disturbing humor aimed at shocking Puritan sensibilities; but contrary to other comedians Michael Moore also succeeds in moving his fans to tears by relying on certain "melodramatic devices," which seems to be one of the traits of his unique style of storytelling, and which will be explored further in the following chapters. Actually, very few in the jaded entertainment world today can make you cry, laugh and think the way Michael Moore does.

In fact, he is not at all what the *South Park* creators made him out to be in their *Team America: World Police* (2004), however politically accurate and technically achieved that film might have been. Even entertainers as detached as Trey Parker and Matt Stone cannot figure out where Moore stands in the political spectrum of things. All they can do is portray him as a radical avenger who is out to destroy the brain police, a very reductive but typical view of his commitment for sociopolitical change.

Unlike most of his contemporaries, Moore is not afraid to sometimes appear emotional, something that his detractors are quick to point to and judge negatively. Along with the more bombastic aspects of his work (gripping credit sequences, fast editing schemes, punk-rock music on his soundtracks, creating a commotion when breaking into headquarters to harass some corporate brass, etc.), comes a certain sense of wonderment regarding the bitter-sweet aspect of American life. In fact, Moore is a romantic and an optimist, and this is usually badly perceived by the western intelligentsia, who prefers to wallow in nihilism to confirm its skewed understanding of the complex world we live in.

The Age of Unreality

As far as we can tell, and implicit to a lot of his work, whether it is in his films, TV shows or books, Michael Moore seems to suggest that a great part of the American public has been brainwashed into believing the myth put on the table by the producers and owners of popular culture. Viewed from the bridge, and for the masses at large, this sort of propaganda often manifests itself in a disdain of any type of music, film, show, play or novel considered to be "too intellectual." For example, this would partly explain why genres like morning shows, talk shows, game shows and daytime soap operas have had such a popular appeal in the U.S.and in other industrialized nations. On top of being quite inoffensive politically, they keep repeating the same predetermined and mindless formulas and turn our brains into pudding. This somehow allows for a kind a familiarity and comfort factor which obviously registers with many Americans and world viewers today, in a harsh world that is to bust at the seams.

Hence, lame situation comedies, overwrought award shows, so-called cable "news" networks and predictable sportive events are all officially considered "culture" by many today. This leaves little doubt as to whether or not mass media influences the way we live and the way we perceive politics and the role it occupies in our lives. In the end, if there is such a thing as an American national identity, it is surely conveyed and cemented by American media more than it is by Washington, D.C. Although, this might have changed with Obama.

Like Moore has often proved, a lot of people in the U.S. lack the necessary information needed to fully comprehend their society, which is based today on production and consumption, and where every individual is first conceived as a consumer part of a monopolized market. This is only one aspect of his work that might be deemed "condescending" by the many who don't like him and/or what he does. Nonetheless Moore's work by its very nature is trying to prove a point: that the current forms of escapism and consumer-control only serve as a smokescreen concealing the truth about the nature of savage capitalism (and the alienation it provokes in a great quantity of Americans). This seems obvious once we read below the surface of his so-called "political farce." That being said, we also have to recognize that there is a double nature to Moore's existence as a popular and iconic figure. On the one hand, he comes from the people and fights for the people. On the other, he became wealthy and famous by using a system which helps to consolidate the status quo, a system meant to keep the Establishment in place and the masses of people subservient to its will.

On top of his implicit stance regarding popular culture, Moore is interested in the nature of American patriotism. He reminds his main audience, which is basically an American one, that the right to question one's country is as fundamental as the right to love this country. Actually, this is the very essence of dissent, according to him. For Moore it is quite simple: Americans could do a lot better than they have since World War II. If only they would allow themselves to be a little more open, curious, and introspective. If only they would agree to listen to alternative point-of-views on America's role within the world community. If only they would not swallow all the lies their leaders and media try to feed them on a daily basis. If they only understood their political system a bit better.

For instance, many Americans are unwilling to admit that their country's early success, their passage into becoming a real empire, was achieved by committing a genocide on Native Americans (when was Wounded Knee mentioned in the media in the last 25 years?), and by enslaving African people, two historical facts which cannot be denied (and that have been perverted a thousand times by Hollywood, the Pentagon's appendage). Even less are probably willing to admit that America's modern success, up until the rise of the new, powerful and highly destructive for the planet Chinese economy, was achieved by exploiting smaller nations and vulnerable cultures around the world, under what Noam Chomsky has described as being the "Kennan Doctrine".[9] Many times over, Moore reminded his home audience of the ways in which American leaders have been perpetrating violence at home and around the world in order to expand this imperialist dominion, lead no doubt by an invisible government which is constituted by extremely rich individuals whose main goal is a New World Order.

One extraordinary example of this is in *Bowling for Columbine*, where he dedicates an entire montage of America's aggressions abroad in rhythmic time to Louis Armstrong's 'What a Wonderful World'. Over a wide variety of stock footage, Moore uses editing, rhythm and some sort of cinematic grace to synthesize half a century of American imperialism (for what might very well be an unsuspecting public...).

1953: U.S. overthrows Prime Minister Mossadeq of Iran and installs Shah as a dictator.

1954: U.S. overthrows democratically-elected President Arbenz of Guatemala. 20,000 civilians were killed.

---

[9] Noam Chomsky, in conversation with Heinz Dieterich, *Latin America: From Colonization to Globalization*, Ocean Press, 1999, p.27

1963: U.S. backs assassination of South Vietnamese President Diem. The Viet-Nam war shortly ensued and went on to last until the fall of Saigon in 1975. 4 million people died in Southeast Asia resulting from this war.

1973: U.S. stages a coup in Chile. Special Forces assassinated Salvator Allende, a democratically-elected President. Augusto Pinochet is installed by CIA-trained covert operations. 5,000 Chileans murdered.

1977: U.S. backs military rulers of El Salvador. 70,000 Salvadorans (and four American nuns) were brutally killed. Not even the murder of the nuns raised uproar in America.

1980's: U.S. trains Osama bin Laden and fellow terrorists against the Soviet invasion of Afghanistan. The CIA gives them $3 billion.

1981: Reagan administration trains and funds "contras;" 30,000 Nicaraguans die.

1982: U.S. provides billions in aid to Saddam Hussein to wage war on Iran. Thousands of Kurds were slaughtered and gassed.

1987: White House secretly gives Iran weapons to kill Iraqis. Oliver North is charged, therefore avoiding Reagan from being impeached.

1989: CIA agent Manuel Noriega (also ruler of Panama) disobeys orders from Washington. Under Bush Sr. U.S. invades Panama (on the day of the Iran hostage crisis) and removes Noriega. 3,000 civilians are killed.

1990: Iraq invades Kuwait with weapons supplied by the U.S. One year later U.S. enters Iraq. Bush reinstates dictator of Kuwait.

1998: Clinton administration bombs "weapons factory" in Sudan thinking it was a training camp for Al-Qaeda. It turned out the factory was producing aspirin (essential to the people and the economy of that country).

1991 to present: American and British planes bomb Iraq on a weekly basis. U.N. estimates 500,000 Iraqi children die from bombing and unfair sanctions.

2000-01: U.S. gives Taliban-ruled Afghanistan $245 million in "aid."

September 11th 2001: Osama bin Laden uses his expert CIA training to murder 3,000 American civilians in New York City.

Don't Kill the Messenger

What might represent an "ideological knot" for some thinkers is the fact that Moore succeeded where left-wing artists from the 1960s have failed. Essentially, he manages to bridge the world of culture with the world of political ideas by subverting mainstream distribution channels like no one else before him. It is quite an accomplishment, especially in this day and age of YouTube culture, and regardless if you are for or against him and what he says. It is also his greatest paradox: to criticize the "System" by turning himself into one of its own commodities. Moore has obviously been undaunted by these types of contradictions and the attacks on him and his work. On the contrary, these only became a springboard for his diatribe against corporate America. For many moderates and civil libertarians around the world he appears to be a giant walking among tiny thinkers who live in a shallow intellectual universe. One way to justify this proposition is to consider how his aesthetics have often been criticized for being too "manipulative" or not "objective" enough at the expense of his messages...More on that later...

Essentially, in its most distilled form, this is the main criticism directed against him: "We know *what* you are saying is right and true, but we just do not like *how* you are saying it."

This snobby attitude amongst intellectuals and cinephiles can only help justify Moore's stylistic orientation to begin with; or his tendency to be "commercial" and "accessible" to a common crowd. Indeed, who can now blame him for avoiding all those techniques of Brechtian pontification that filmmakers were using in the 1960s, back when cinema was political? Why go Jean-Luc Godard's way if you can reach millions of viewers by sending people the same kind of messages, but through different, more contemporary, and therefore more relevant means?

In this sense, trying to define Moore's style may become a difficult and perilous exercise, only because it is so anchored in the fabric of popular culture and its billions of images, sounds and data bits today. It seems to blend smoothly with the uninterrupted daily flow of mediated information across the globe, and this is why it might be undermined in the end. The only way one can get a glimpse of the accuracy and coherence of his style is when one considers the post-modern context within which Moore has been evolving since the late 1980s. By doing so, we can notice how he uses the language of mainstream media and its advertising techniques, a kind of "zapping" style which he relies on to subvert popular culture from within. Without a doubt, there is an element of playful seduction at work in his films and shows; and it is this very quality which makes his work so appealing to young (and not-so-young) people all over the world.

Indeed, Moore gets to the point swiftly, with a certain economy of style. Because as a communicator he knows that, by and large, viewers have no time or sympathy for didactic or pedagogical means. Hence, he uses the shortcuts of popular culture to grab hold of our attention; blending empirical facts with his own analysis and interpretation of newsworthy events, all in a highly "entertaining" way.

As far as we can tell Michael Moore has to engage in what seems to be two simultaneous uphill battles when he produces a movie or a TV show in America. One is made clear by the topics he chooses to deal with, most obviously government and corporate abuse. It often leads among other things to intense confrontation with security personnel, as well as with politicians and various other public officials. The other battle is more implicit and has to do with the intellectual laziness imposed on the public by the conglomeration controlling the hearts and minds of America. This new mass-mystification is a reality which requires Moore to express himself in bold ways, just to be understood by as many people as possible. If flash works, why not?

In addition, he does so without "dumbing down" his discourse, like so many other entertainers and artists do today. It is just the opposite. He uses sarcasm and irony to produce a clever and efficient form of counter-discourse which stirs-up ideas at the grassroots level. Because in the end Moore knows that the best way to be heard in America is to get to a place where you have some form of exposure in a narrow and highly controlled media environment. He knows that you need a bullhorn to be heard amongst the crowd of entertainers out there today.

He also seems to be conscious that, in spite of its obvious vacuity, popular culture is the ideal avenue to promote political understanding and activism, precisely because it is what the majority has been lead to believe to be "culture." Certainly, he must be aware that this constitutes a kind of necessary evil, since it is the only way to reach an audience in the millions and eventually provoke some significant changes in attitude and behavior.

Radicalizing Hope

Undoubtedly, Michael Moore has acquired notoriety by infiltrating the system and by using tools that only a technologically evolved society can provide. Looking back at the kind of progression his career had in the last 20 years, we might be tempted to say that, like a good wine, it blossomed with age. His continuous success appears to have made him more confident and more powerful within the entertainment industry; but it would also seem like this confidence and relative power have never been used for self-serving motives.

In any event, to claim that power corrupts every woman or man once she or he is endowed with it is to adopt a cynical view of the world and its population. Moore's vision of the world and its population may sometimes be bleak, but it is surely not cynical (even if he seems to have a natural aversion to authority and figures of authority to begin with). It would be fair to say that the cynics are the ones who write books about him based on the way he looks, just to reassure themselves, in their own arrogant fashion, that everything is alright the way it is now. These low-budget thinkers would like us to believe that there are no alternative ways of living in this world, no better modes of co-existing than the one we have going on under an imperialist agenda.

Moore simply cannot be accused of being a cynic for two simple reasons. First, he believes that things can change for the better, a fact that makes him an optimist by definition. Second, he has on many occasions shown his faith in *some* American institutions. For instance, his relationship with the N.A.A.C.P. can surely be seen as a positive one (that is, if unlike the Tea Party you believe in civil rights). The same could be said of his involvement in building shelters for battered women or his fight for the rights of prisoners all over America (that is, if unlike the Democrats you are a true liberal). He would not have co-founded the Traverse City Film Festival if he was a cynic, would he? The list goes on and on, and it can certainly be argued that Moore has become an extremely productive and lucid "producer of meaning" in American culture, whether we like it or not.

His films, books, television programs and various public appearances are certainly acts of self-assertion and promotion, but one has to admit they are also acts of courage and communication which truly promote love, peace and understanding; not hate, war and ignorance. Through provocative acts of compassion and a good dose of optimism, Moore wants us to think, feel and act positively upon the world we live in. Beyond these formal interests and sociopolitical motives described above, it would seem like there is really nothing more that can be said about the clarity of his creative intentions.

To doubt that Moore is a genuine egalitarian is to deny the existing facts presented in his work. And to deny these existing facts is to also deny billions of people on this planet a chance at a better life. It is to root for the bad guys, consciously or not.

The Gangster Syndrome (Rooting for the Bad Guys is Cool)

The current version of the American Dream which is still being sold to the American public today is based on the notion that, in order to be truly successful, you must be nothing but "Number One." In fact,

American culture has never been able to reconcile its contradicting precepts: *We versus Me*, something that Moore explores in his film regarding the state of health care in America (*Sicko*, 2007). Even as President Obama enters his third year in office, there is still a growing tension between the individual quest for material wealth and the alleged moral superiority of the American people as a whole, and there probably always will be.

This paradoxical existence is literally illustrated on the United States currency, where we can clearly read "In God We Trust." But it would seem like Americans never bother to care about the contradiction between religion and money. What do spiritual concerns have in common with finance, the most secular of all gods? This philosophical conundrum can be traced back historically to the arrival of the Puritans on Plymouth Rock, when they came with protestant values and a well-defined and functional banking system imported from England. It was then that the first brick of Social Darwinism was laid in the new land, and this in return set the tone for the centuries to come: "To make it in America, you must be Number One, period." In that sense, one only has to go back to the late 19th century, and to moguls like Edison and Hearst, to understand what is going on today.

Cinema and television do not escape these intrinsic values to America, as far as the ultimate message it communicates to the public. In the hands of the new American producer, akin to the Wall Street shark, these two mediums are conveying that you, as an American (or aspiring to be one), do not have to work hard or get an education to achieve in what is really a system of meritocracy. All you need is the personal will and physical stamina to win against your "adversary" and you will no doubt reach the top. Almost every program, show or promotional device on U.S. television today is a form of advocacy for rugged individualism and competition, in one way or another. These are clichés that do not stand for American society as a whole, since what they are truly about is a few individuals chosen to make millions of others dream and consume with a blinded consciousness.

On American television today, we are told that being "Number Two" is not at all to be "the Best Running Mate," but more like being "the First Loser." As a case in point, one show produced by Tinseltown is entitled *The Biggest Loser* and consists in humiliating overweight people on national television. By claiming that this is the right thing to do, meaning that contestants should conform to some kind of American ideal of fitness and beauty, these shows betray their philosophy of eugenics in between the lines. It reveals crypto-fascist streaks between the cracks of its flawed ideological structure. It makes society sick by framing reality a certain way, as to edify the young, rich, famous and beautiful at the expense of everybody else.

Through a symptomatic reading of contemporary American popular culture, nothing can better illustrate these aforementioned notions than the phenomenon of the so-called "reality shows" (which is an oxymoron: if it is a "show," it cannot be "reality"). As trendy commercial products ruled by Nielsen surveys, reality shows are based on the idea that being "Number One" is the only way to go in America. Shows like *Survivor, American Idol, Fear Factor,* and others like it can now be seen on the Internet, and they were made to appeal to the unconscious drive which unites a great part of the highbrow public, not only in the U.S., but in most industrialized countries as well. They attract those who look up to America for prefabricated images of pagan gods and dreams of instant success.[10]

We can only assume that these shows' ultimate goal, besides making enormous profits (because they don't have to pay writers, directors, actors, etc.), is to maintain the illusion of viewer superiority; giving the opportunity to spy on, to evaluate, and then to judge the contestants on a daily basis. These programs are the most watched on television today and their format is now being replicated by every new show produced, in a formulaic way. Their popularity is in part explicable by the fact that they seem to offer a certain level of interactivity with the viewer (the future of media, so we are told). They supply cheap thrills to a population whose mind has already been stultified by the networks and corporate propaganda, advertising and product placement. At the end of the day, these new types of programs are no different than advertisement in America. They *are* advertisement.

And this seems to be the major difference between conventional mainstream television and the shows produced by Dog Eat Dog Films under Michael Moore's guidance. His kind of television programming is asking us to reposition ourselves before opening the tube. It requires us to think outside of that idiot box that we love so much and cannot really live without. In the following section, we will attempt to demonstrate how television can be used to educate viewers in an entertaining way, by relying on tongue-in-cheek humor and a satirical style of presentation. This has been proven by other shows since Michael Moore's *TV Nation* and *The Awful Truth*, as we will see. In hindsight he might even have created a new form of political art with these two original shows, because their influence can now be felt almost everywhere on TV, in movies and on the Net.

---

[10] Actually, the concept is from the Netherlands and was presented to the networks by German producers.

CHAPTER ONE
TAKING OVER THE TUBE

Reagan at Bitburg

In the mid 1980s President Ronald Reagan went to the city of Bitburg in Germany to lay a wreath on the tomb of the "Anonymous SS soldier." When this was announced a much younger and romantic Michael Moore saw, perhaps for the first time in his life, an opportunity to directly target the Republican Party in the public sphere. Moore wanted to remind Reagan of the hypocrisy behind this symbolic gesture. Because while he was remembering a Nazi icon that no one can really forget anyhow, there were a lot of people he was forgetting about in his own country.

In the first season of his second TV series, *The Awful Truth*, Moore told the story of how he went to Germany with a friend of his…"When it happened, I couldn't believe it. I was in Flint at the time," Moore recalls, "and my buddy Garry and I were just sitting around watching TV saying 'Man, this is really messed up, Reagan doing this,'" he adds chuckling. "Garry's parents were both survivors of Auschwitz and I said to him 'They got these cheap airfares for $90 to Germany. Let's get on a plane in Detroit and go over there, just to mess Reagan up!'" Moore's enthusiasm must have been contagious that day, because his friend replied without batting an eye: "Yeah! Let's go do that!"

No doubt, it was Reaganomics time in the U.S., and many had a big chip on their shoulder. Moore and his friend were at least two of them.

Soon they both embarked on a plane and flew to Germany for a showdown with Reagan at the Bitburg cemetery. There were about twenty checkpoints around town at the time of the event, and Moore explained they somehow managed to infiltrate the cemetery grounds where the ceremony would be taking place. Police officers and soldiers with guns, clubs and dogs were surrounding the controversial site where Reagan was awaited. Moore and his friend were scared to be beaten up if they protested too loudly, so they had brought along with them a bed sheet on which it was written: *"We came from Michigan to remind you that they killed my family!"* Expecting trouble, Moore noticed Pierre Salinger from ABC News standing in the crowd and asked him if his camera operator would be willing to cover the demonstration. "I got a feeling that the last thing the Germans want to do today is to beat up a Jew in the Bitburg Cemetery," he said to his audience…

This was a publicity stunt if there ever was one for a redeemed postwar Germany and for Reagan (a man who single-handedly took credit for bringing down Communism in Russia), and perhaps even for Moore himself. Salinger agreed to cover for Moore, and this allowed the latter and his friend to extend their banner under the camera-eye when the President's limousine made its way onto the cemetery grounds.

This event became Michael Moore's first international exposure when it was aired live via satellite television and found its way a month later in *Newsweek* magazine. At the end of his story, he reflects aloud to his audience: "I just thought it was incredible that two guys sitting around could get up and do *something like this*."

Moore had learned right there and then the power of both mass media and political activism at a certain level of intensity and public exposure.

However, this was only the beginning of a difficult journey over what could only be described as an ideological minefield. It seems to have left no scars on him, though.

Living in a TV Nation

In a kind of perverted logic only possible in American culture, Michael Moore was going to find his way to our television sets ten years later in a show appropriately called *TV Nation*. This was his first real experience with expressing himself through the means of electronic journalism, although a short sequel to *Roger & Me*, entitled *Pets or Meat: a Return to Flint*, had been co-produced with the BBC and PBS and aired in 1992. *TV Nation* was a full-hour program and dared to go where no other show went before. As producers of the show Moore and his wife/producer Kathleen Glynn had total control of both form and content. They even wrote a factual account about the making of this original programming two years after it had aired. *Adventures in TV Nation* now serves as memoirs relating to the experience of putting the series on the air, which was apparently easier than they thought it would be; although in the end, and like everything else which is deemed too politically provocative in America, it didn't last for very long.

> *TV Nation* was hailed by the critics as "brilliant" and "subversive" and "the best show on TV in the past thirty years." It had ten million weekly viewers and beat its competition on the other three networks in the twenty-five to fifty-four year-old audience every week it was on the air. It was nominated twice for a primetime Emmy Award and won the Emmy for Outstanding Informational Series for the 1994 season. After seventeen episodes, it was gone.[11]

---

[11] Michael Moore & Kathleen Glynn, *Adventures in a TV Nation*, Harper/Perennial, 1998, pp.ix-x

It is difficult to accept that such a progressive program ran for only two short seasons while idiotic shows like *Home Improvement* or *Married with Children* are still playing in syndication today. Considering the landscape of American television today, even on Comedy Central, chances of ever seeing Moore's series on the air again are pretty slim, mainly because of its political slant. This is very unfortunate, especially if we think about how relevant and influential this TV work is (and in light of his subsequent work, and of shows like *The Daily Show with Jon Stewart* and *The Colbert Report*). Luckily, *TV Nation* has an extremely limited availability on videocassette (see eBay), while *The Awful Truth* series, Moore's best effort for television yet, has been officially released on DVD format for future generations to watch, learn, and enjoy. These two documents belong in every American school, simply because they are reminders that television, as an invention, can be used to other ends than just "selling stuff" to a vegetative public; that it is a powerful and important medium which has the potential to communicate positive ideas and properly inform the masses, as it once did, in the times of Murrow and Cronkite.

The Other Michael Jackson

Back in 1991, after the phenomenal success of *Roger & Me*, Moore and Glynn wanted to produce a fiction film entitled *Canadian Bacon*. He had written a script which was a farce inspired by the first Gulf War, based on the idea that the U.S. government has to fabricated enemies to feed the military-industrial complex. Every studio passed on it until 4 years later, when it was picked up by Polygram Entertainment (and only after the late John Candy and Alan Alda, two "names" at the time, accepted to act in the feature project). The story goes that NBC first offered Moore to do a television series, something he never thought anybody would let him do, especially after his controversial picture about GM and corporate America. According to *Adventures in a TV Nation*, he had met the President of Entertainment at NBC and an executive from TriStar Television with the intention to propose something so outrageous that they would not touch it with a ten-foot pole. As it turned out, they loved Moore's concept of "a cross between *60 Minutes* and Fidel Castro on laughing gas."[12] After all it was now Clinton-time in D.C, and a whole different mind frame was in place. The two executives liked the concept so much that the maverick filmmaker, now TV producer, came out of his Hollywood meeting with

---

[12] *Adventures in a TV Nation*, p.5

a green light and a million dollars to shoot a pilot. Not bad for a guy from Michigan who had only made one "little movie."

The pilot for *TV Nation* was later screened for NBC folks in L.A. and it made everyone in the room laugh non-stop, according to Moore and Glynn. The only question the suits were asking themselves pertained to sponsors and advertising time. They were surely right in their line of reasoning: "Would they (advertisers) buy slots for this kind of show?" Here is one example which can be used to introduce Moore's subversive dimension as an independent journalist, filmmaker, and television producer. First, he was using dark comedy and broadside humor to talk about serious issues, which is already a slap at Puritan sensibility. Second, he was going to great lengths to destroy the image of corporate America and its lap dogs loved it. Moore was given access to one of the greatest mass media of all time and chose to pervert it from within, crucifying vital sponsorship and targeting corporations in and in-between the sketches. No one else could have gotten away with it then, but Moore and Glynn did, for a few seasons only.

The fall schedule for the 1993-94 season didn't allow for TV *Nation* to be aired as planned. It was only a few months later, when Michael Jackson, a producer from the BBC and a very important player in the earlier part of Moore's career, offered NBC and TriStar to buy the show through Channel 4 in London. The second-hand reaction in L.A. was that it must have been a real good show, "if the Brits wanted to buy it." Therefore, they offered Moore the opportunity to air his series in the summer instead. It is only once the BBC appeared to co-produce that American producers recognized the full potential of this concept. In the end, television allowed him to shed some light on America's illnesses with incredible insight and wit. *TV Nation* stands today as a fine and extremely rare example of intelligent and informative television which can be produced within the mainstream in the United States.

> In the battle between art and commerce, commerce virtually always wins. For two summers we were able to dodge most of the bullets and come out with our sense of humor and conscience intact (...) We wonder, as we look back, why more of television does not aspire to something better than shows that reinforce stereotypes, won't question the status quo, or appeal to the severely brain dead.[13]

---

[13] *Adventures in a TV Nation*, p. 202

Awfully True

After *TV Nation* Moore finally got a chance to direct *Canadian Bacon*, his first and only fiction film to date. He also wrote a book entitled *Downsize This! Random Threats from an Unarmed American*, and shot another documentary film, *The Big One* (read following chapter), while promoting it. In 1998 Jackson became head of Channel 4, and when the deal with NBC ran out, he came through once again for the Michigan-born couple. He offered them the chance to produce sixteen more episodes. This satirical series was probably the most revolutionary ever produced for American television and it was called *The Awful Truth*. Moore and Glynn's second television intrusion would turn out to be even more vitriolic than the first one (no small accomplishment). Now a half hour format instead of a full hour, with two major stories per show, and far more incisive than the first series, Moore and associates went on to deal with America's anxieties and neurosis on a weekly basis. From the excesses of capitalism and the failure of American unions to protect its workers, all the way to bashing institutionalized old-time religion and its repressive ideas, no potatoes were too hot to handle.

The first season was taped in front of a live audience at the Illinois Institute of Technology, a place that approximately sits 900. The second season was moved to the original *TV Nation* site, right in the middle of Times Square - a symbolic site for many reasons. Moore was again the host and his introductory words set up the tone for the entire series: *"We all believe in the free press, we just do not own any of the presses,"* referring to the oligarchy in the media world then and now. In essence, he and his crew provided an alternative to this "will of the few" which tends to homogenize the representation of what is in reality a heterogeneous and pluralist society. It is truly a miracle that for awhile, at least, he was able to use these hermetic and restricted structures to communicate ideas and values other than social conservatism to the American public. When compared with what is being produced nowadays on television, we can only remember it as a golden era for a politically intelligent and "uncensored" kind of television. Actually, because TV has now to compete with the Internet for the 18 to 35 viewers, we have witnessed a downward spiral of programming ever since Moore left the air in late 2000. Today, we are still trapped between reruns of *Three's Company* and *Desperate Housewives* and new embodiments of reality TV shows. In fact, it is satirical news shows like *The Daily Show* and some cable news show like *Countdown with Keith Olbermann* that really followed on Moore and Glynn's trail.

"We Are Number One!"

Many topics covered in *TV Nation* and *The Awful Truth* would serve to illustrate Michael Moore's project, but none represents its creative ambition better than the "We're Number One" theme, as it is dealt with in both series. As mentioned in the previous reflection on the state of contemporary cinema and television, being Number One is the quintessential modern American value. Moore has kept satirizing it since his first feature film, *Roger & Me*, but more distinctively in his crusade against savage capitalism and corporate crime, *The Big One*. The saying itself is linked to policy-making in Washington, but also to a blind patriotic feeling which stops Americans from questioning and challenging their government leaders, and which ultimately gets them into all sorts of trouble (at home and especially abroad).

If truth was told, this self-reverential attitude can never really be eradicated from the American psyche because it simply seems to be the ideological kernel around which the nation was born. For Moore, it serves as a Catholic (self-deprecating) joke which reflects on the state of the Union as a whole, as precisely *one* nation under God. Thus, "We Are Number One" is often used in his work as a conceptual thread that pokes fun at America's self-aggrandizing philosophy and warped self-image.

In *TV Nation* for instance it is illustrated by a series of interviews with regular folks from different parts of the country. Farmers, factory workers and homemakers are asked what makes their hometown the best in America. All respondents, while looking straight into the camera-eye, seem to have genuine pride when replying to Moore's question. One man claims that Florida is number one in car jacking, while a woman from Baltimore says her hometown is the best in teenage pregnancy and condom sales. Later in the show, a man from Texas proudly asserts that his state is number one in unemployment, while a middle-aged woman brags that Iowa is number one in Playboy and Penthouse subscriptions. The parallel editing finally culminates with a man from Georgia and another one from Texas fighting it out to determine who the national champion in fruitcake making is. What madness.

"We Are Number One," as an ideological inclination, has also been dealt with in *Stupid White Men* and *Bowling for Columbine*. In this last film, it is carried out through an uneducated kid who is disappointed for not making it as the "Most Wanted Troubled Teenager in Oscoda" after the Columbine shootings. Even being a serial killer can make one proud to be at the top of some list. Any list.

As a journalist, Moore offers a ground-level analysis which deals with facets of a problem, including America's perception of itself. With his scathing and sometimes absurd satirical sketches, he is trying to make his audience crack open a hard philosophical shell. Through one individual he is capable of illustrating the predisposition of an entire people to be competitive and violent toward each other, precisely because he understands that, once framed, all reality becomes representation. In a grander scheme of things, the "We Are Number One" skit mocks the drive which makes American imperialism possible. Read from this angle it becomes both symbolic of a national state of mind and a metaphor for American foreign policies.

A Case Made for "Number Two"

In one of the very first *TV Nation* episodes, Moore experimented with two important but unclear notions in America: democracy and patriotism.

First he notes that at the core of the U.S. Constitution is written that anyone over thirty years of age and born on American soil can run for the presidency. Then he manages to temporarily turn a criminal into a political candidate in the New Hampshire primaries. In fact, Moore allowed for Louis Bruno, a convicted felon, to slide his way next to Bob Dole in the 1996 campaign. For a while, Bruno even ran a parallel race with speeches almost undistinguishable from Dole's: "I'll give you whatever you want as long as you vote for me," seemed to have been their common political platform. In this sketch Moore illustrates the different aspects of demagoguery in contemporary political rhetoric by creating an alternative to the big event. Not only did he allow Bruno to have a tribune, even if he was an ex-convict, but he got across his own point about the workings of democracy through the staged events, the improvisational moments resulting from the interactions between the "characters," and of course editing, the most important aspect of his work.

In Moore's hands, this is not a documentary or reportage *per se*, but more like a kind of traveling political theater.

Because of Moore, candidate Bruno was heard by local media during the race: "I have never run for President before but in a way I've been running all my life," he says modestly on the voice-over. The climax of the campaign, which Bruno would predictably lose, was the moment when he finally admitted that Dole had an edge over him because of his privileged status: "Here it is," he says bitterly, "a day late and a dollar short…Bob Dole." We are then forced to accept with him the most obvious of all American realities: no one without any money has ever been elected President of the United States. It was true for Louis Bruno as it was certainly true for President Barack Obama, who received a lot of money for his campaign from banks and various corporations.

As writer and director, Moore found a way to convey subversive messages about the American electoral system. For awhile he succeeded in transforming a convict into a political candidate in order to discuss the relationship between wealth and political power. For him it was simple enough: in Louis Bruno's hope to one day be President, we also hear the silence of millions of others who will never get a shot at the title. For them, and because they are disenfranchised or just plain unlucky in life, it will always be a one-way ticket to Palooka Ville.

Green Giant

Louis Bruno's race as a mean to express political discontent was just the beginning as far as Moore's subversive agenda was concerned in 1995. The idea that anyone (or anything, for that matter) can be a candidate in a political race will be pursued even further in the much better executed series *The Awful Truth* in 2000. The short film entitled *The Choice* was a clear illustration of the absence of genuine democracy in Uncle Sam's country. Repeating the "Number Two" strategy to conduct a political race, but with more metaphorical weight, this short film foreshadows the coming of another "vegetative" entity onto the American political scene a year later: George Walker Bush. Moore admitted he was committing this stunt because American people were no longer showing up to vote. In *The Big One* he had reminded his viewers that one hundred million Americans didn't bother to vote in the 1996 election; so there was no way he was going to let all these people not show up at the poles in the 2000 election, again (or in 2004, or 2008, or 2012).

The *coup* in question was for Moore to run a three-foot Ficus plant against Republican Congressman Rodney Frelinghuysen in New Jersey's 11th District in the 2000 election. Frelinghuysen had been unchallenged in his riding in the last three elections and just thought he was going to waltz back into office. However, Moore set out to teach him a lesson in the power of real democratic action. How? He simply had 210 New Jersey residents signing a petition to run a potted plant for office, therefore legally opposing Frelinghuysen as a potential congressional representative. Moore himself was to act on behalf of the "will" of the plant, and he chose to bring it everywhere...even inside the Congress.

On April 15, in Morristown, New Jersey, the "Campaign for Ficus" officially started: "This Ficus plant is entering the race because we believe that the American people deserve better. This Ficus will accept no contributions. This Ficus will accept no soft money. Only water, clean air and a little sunshine," Moore stated for the plant in a public release. To his great surprise, the Ficus received a lot of media attention and publicity throughout the campaign. Although, one editorial for *The Daily Record* called Moore's political allegory "an adolescent stunt" and "fluff in content."

At the first official press conference, Moore offered journalists to ask the Ficus any question they wanted. One reporter asked: "Okay, what's your position on tax reform?" (Its answer: silence.) "See, that's the beauty. You're not going to hear anything," he would interpret for them afterwards. The statement was obvious, but it was also true. In the Ficus' silence, there was more substance than in Frelinghuysen's non-existing electoral promises. Hell, the man was not even there! The Ficus would even challenge its opponent to a public debate (which was flatly and predictably refused by Frelinghuysen). The latter did not appreciate Moore's theatrical infiltration of a race that he thought was already won in advance. In the end, the *Daily Record*'s negative editorial had a least one positive effect: the Ficus was polled in Jersey where it was apparently leading. In a second editorial the newspaper again denounced the idea, but admitted that the Ficus had people talking about the issues (such as voter apathy), as well as getting them to question the foundations of the democratic process in America (i.e. the power of money over the will to vote).

Later, while talking to Frelinghyusen's Chief of Staff over the phone, Moore pushed again the question of a possible debate between the two "candidates."

Moore:
We want to challenge him [*Frelinghuysen*] to a debate here in the 11th District. The Ficus vs. Frelinghuysen. No, no, we're very serious about this. We will dog the Congressman until he does face the Ficus and debate the Ficus on the issues that are important to the people here in Jersey. You guys think that you're just gonna go right back into Congress without putting up a campaign? You've got this opponent, as a Democrat *and* a Republican. It's going to challenge you. [*Long pause*] Hello?

Of course, Frelinghuysen refused to be challenged by the Ficus in a public debate, and Moore would later call his tactic a form of "negative campaigning." To answer back to this contemptuous attitude, the Ficus Campaign produced a corrosive campaign ad where we see pictures of the two candidates side by side on a split-screen. A serious voice-over narration clears the choice for the viewer.

Narrator (voice-over):
"Congressman Frelinghuysen doesn't know how to fix our education system. Frelinghuysen doesn't know what to do about taxes. Congressman Frelinghuysen doesn't know how to make health care more affordable. Let's face it, Frelinghuysen doesn't know his ass from a hole in the ground. Vote Ficus! His ass *is* a hole in the ground."

Again to Moore's great surprise people were running plants for office all over the country. As he admits in the show, "This is now completely out of our control." As it turned out, it was not. Because on May 19th, under the recommendation of Jay Martel (one of Moore's talented correspondents), this American dissident brought the Ficus to Congress in order to present it to some of his opponents. Three days later, he officially introduced all 21 plants to the National Convention of Ficus Candidates. When asked by his own crew about the reasons which motivated him to run all this vegetal life form for Congress, Moore rationalized his intentions as followed: "We have a chance to say something very important, and it is that the people of this country are sick and tired of these two political parties posing as two political parties. It's *one* party. So, we've given people a chance to ride in the Ficus on the ballot all over the country. It's our way to say 'None of the above'. This is our way to say: 'I'm sick and tired. I'm not gonna take it anymore'. It's the 'fuck you' vote of this election."

On election day the polls closed around 8:10 p.m. All members from the Campaign for Ficus were awaiting the results at a bar down the street. Frelinghuysen was so confident he was going to win that he did not even bother to show up at headquarters that night. At the end of the day, the clerks did not want to consider all those people who had legally voted for the plant, in spite of Moore's tireless efforts. By 11:00 p.m., Moore paid a visit to the County Clerks to see if democracy was being upheld. As he suspected, it was not, like it would not be in the 2000 presidential election. On the end card we are told Moore's cameras were denied access to the voting tally despite the appearances that the Ficus might have won the first precinct. Who would have thought?

To Mosh or Not to Mosh?

More adventurous than the Ficus skit is the episode where Michael Moore goes on the trail of the 2000 Republican campaign during the primary caucus in Iowa. In the most publicized of all *Awful Truth* episodes, he organized a traveling "mosh-pit" where political candidates were challenged to jump in and ride a human-wave. It was a way for Moore to find out who was "the man of the people" amongst the candidates. The host even got to body-slam during the taping of this weird rally...with candidate Orrin Hatch, of all people. The skit started with Moore telling us that it was simply impossible for him to choose between the candidates because of their common ideological stance. He went on to explain that, not surprisingly, every Republican candidate of the time agreed on the main domestic and foreign policy issues of the race. There was a consensus pertaining to the death penalty, reducing taxes for the rich, Pentagon expenditures, and of course a generous increase in the military budget. It was this political homogenization of the Right that motivated the host of *The Awful Truth* to turn loose the "mosh pit" on the campaign. And it did draw some attention.

Accompanied by a number written and performed by Rage Against the Machine (for whom Moore directed two videos), the host went with a group of adrenaline-pumped 18 year-olds to participate in a weird traveling underground ritual. All of them were standing on a flatbed truck, which only helped to increase the tension whenever they came around at a candidate's headquarters. The first one who dared to *mosh* would get *The Awful Truth*'s vote, Moore promised his viewers. In the end, talk-radio host and candidate Alan Keyes was the only one who agreed to jump in, and "the media finally had something to get excited about," Moore said on the voice-over. Late night television was using it as prime material, while Gail Collins of *The New York Times* claimed it was the highpoint of an otherwise boring campaign. The news of Keyes jumping into the mosh-pit even made it to a televised debate between the Republican candidates, where he had to defend himself against George W. Bush's attacks for having been a victim of Michael Moore's "probing" while campaigning in Iowa.

Implicit here is the idea that all these candidates were men of great wealth and thus alienated from the real world and the real issues. Moore used the ritual of the mosh-pit to bring real folks to politicians, instead of the usual handshake jobs and photo-ops these last ones have become so accustomed to and *blasé* with. The best moment of this segment, which Moore excerpted in *Fahrenheit 9/11*, is when George W. Bush tells him to go get "real work," as if being an artist was not.

Capitalism at its Finest

Another main theme of *The Awful Truth* pertains to a certain trend among right-wingers and money-driven individuals in the conglomerated economy of the 21st century. "Compassionate Conservatism" purports to be a "softer" kind of right-wing attitude, where rich conservative people claim they have "positive feelings" for their fellowmen. According to Michael Moore this is a radically different position than the one held by the old time Tatcherites and Reaganites, whose basic common philosophy was "screw the poor." In reality it is an oxymoron of contemporary parlance, since America is based on the Number One philosophy. At the end of the show, he tells his viewers that if they want to know more about this subject matter they will have to look for it in the fiction section of their local library.

Moore and his collaborators came up with the concept of having two teams of self-proclaimed *compassionate conservatives*, Team Dow and Team NASDAQ, fighting it out through a game whose ultimate goal was to degrade the poor. Correspondent Karen Duffy was hosting the contest and the teams were composed by young and rich white males. They were all stockbrokers and made an average of one million dollars a year. Strangely enough, they agreed to compete in Times Square for the benefit of the show, for everyone to see and judge, and under Moore's scrutinizing camera lens.

The first challenge participants were asked to execute was called "Dunk the Homeless" and, as the title indicates, involved dunking a man whose net worth was zero dollars into a dumpster full of water. In true carnival fashion the man sat on a plank over a small pool and the yuppie contestants all had a shot at him. They threw balls on a target to make him fall and took great pleasure in humiliating him (so much for the compassion part of conservatism). Soon team NASDAQ scored the first point by viciously dunking the homeless in the pool. Later there was a second competition called "Pie the Poor," where the contestants got again a chance to lash-out at their social "inferiors." Karen Duffy explained that "this event combines the wholesome virtues of homemade American pie with the American tradition of stoning." The setup was that two men sharing an income way below the poverty line were standing ready to receive a pie from one of the corporate contestants. When one of them did receive a face-full of custard Duffy sarcastically told him: "It's good and free and it's your favorite!" The man happily replied, "Yeah, apple pie! *I love America!*" All the while, we are implicitly led to believe that none of this abuse of human dignity is really funny.

In one of the last competitions of Compassionate Conservatism Night, Duffy supervised "Pin the Tail on the Illegal Alien," where two Mexicans without visas had tails pinned on their bums by so-called "compassionate" individuals. It was an absurd representation of America's fear of illegal aliens, and perhaps even of immigrants in general (and CNN's Lou Dobbs wet dream). Moore brought this den of inequity to its extremes when in the last round Teams Dow and NASDAQ competed in the final challenge of a "Working Poor Chicken Fight." Workers making less than $25,000 a year had to carry the rich contestants from both teams on their shoulders. Duffy concluded the show by telling us that "This game clearly proves that you can balance the economy on the backs of the poor."

This sketch was essentially a re-enactment of Karl Marx's theories about class struggle on late night television...in America...allegedly the land of the capitalists... No wonder this series was not on the air for long. It was obviously more art than commerce.

Rich White Guys

One of the fundamental democratic values Moore stands for is that America belongs to every American, not only to a few individuals born in wealth, or again lucky enough to have acquired it through inheritance or stock trading, what is often referred to as meritocracy. In his second series he showed concern for the long tradition of rich entrepreneurs in American history. These powerful individuals Moore is often after have confused the notion of free enterprise with state-within-state*ism* (in a political system which allows for this kind of confusion to happen). To this day, rich white men appropriate wealth and land at an ever-increasing rate, creating a new feudal system which will alienate and suffocate the less fortunate even more systematically in the future. These individuals own and exploit essential natural resources such as water and trees, making our very existence vulnerable to the financial trends and whims of the market place. These moguls are the plutocrats of American society, since they represent its only possible outcome: to be alone at the top, to be "Number One." For Moore, a convenient target to illustrate these ideas was Ted Turner, one of the moguls of our time.

Amazingly enough, and one more example of Moore's ability to use the system effectively, Turner was one of the people who helped to conceptualize and develop the cable system within which Moore is able to work and criticize the government and its wealthy friends. The fast proliferation of specialized channels are in large part the result of the many acquisitions and mergers that Turner and other media moguls like him have orchestrated, supervised and benefited from in the last 25 years. Turner becomes therefore a convenient scapegoat because of his symbolic value, if nothing else. He represents for Moore what is wrong with American capitalism: its need to be excessive and overbearing on everybody's life. This kind of high-jacking allows for some individuals to eat out all of the living space (or the *lebensraum*, as the Germans call it) under the auspice of the American government. As stated in the introduction of this book, the subversive element of Moore's playful criticism lies in the fact that he uses and subverts a distribution structure set in place (and owned and controlled) by people like Turner (and old Rupert Murdoch, who Moore stays away from, for some unknown reason). What he does with these kinds of satirical sketches is that he ridicules and undermines the American Dream, its values, and especially its emblems and oversized icons (from Hearst to Gates). He nips that macho American ego right in the bud for a laugh.

Let's Move to Turdonia

"Hail Turdonia" was a skit from the first season of *The Awful Truth*. It mocked the notion of the Self-Made-Man with a wit rarely seen on American television, which usually tends to edify and reinforce the powerful-rich-white-man stereotype (just think of Donald Trump and his prime-time show, *The Apprentice*, for one crystal-clear example). In 2000 it was presumed that Turner might have run for the presidency and Moore decided to go after him with everything he had. This irreverential piece was a corrosive satire against a megalomaniac who is out to buy the country. An eccentric who is branded as a "great American" that everyone should emulate, but who is also one of the people responsible for liquidating America's true potential as a nation, by taking it all, by leaving to others the crumbs.

The sketch starts with a summary of Turner's assets and "accomplishments." While we see shots of different Turner speeches with Moore's voice-over giving cues as to how to read these images (the tampering in question), we soon learn that Turner is worth more than six billion dollars (back then). Moore inserts a shot of the mogul answering a journalist at an unidentified press conference: "It is nice to be rich. Rich is better than poor," he says without blushing. What Turner seems to ignore is that there are rich people and there are RICH people. It is all relative in the end, since a "poor" individual can be "rich" because he or she is healthy or has found happiness. As an aside joke, which is a common stylistic trait in his editing patterns, Moore tells us how Jane Fonda, then married to Turner, would make an exquisite First Lady of Turdonia. He quickly inserts a clip from one of her exercise videos that had incited him to shake it up in the 1980s. The satirical voice-over then goes on to underline some of the billionaire's most obvious contradictions. Turner once proclaimed himself as a misunderstood genius: "Sometimes madness and genius are two sides of the same *coin*," he said without irony. Then, Moore reminds us that Turner was an advocate for world peace who happened to also own a professional wrestling league. Furthermore, as an "animal lover," he is the proprietor of the largest heard of bison in North America. A heard that he eventually transforms into *Beefalo* (a ground meat made out of bison "extractions"). Not that these paradoxical means of earning income matter or distract Turner from his two favorite pastimes, according to Moore: baseball and Jane's rotating hips. What a true American icon.

After this contextual set-up, Moore tells us that Turner owns one and a half million acres of American soil (from Montana to New Mexico, and beyond), which is more land per square mile than Luxemburg. As he deduces cleverly: "He (Turner) is truly the ruler of a country within a country…" So to proclaim Turner's status as ruler of a country within a country the *Awful Truth* reporter decides to help him create an official nation. He takes it upon himself to crown this new king and to christen this new land. He names it "Turdonia" (as in "turd," a slang word to designate a piece of excrement). He has a flag made for this New Kingdom. He prints a new currency: the Ted. Moore even creates post-office stamps where you can chose between Young and Old Ted, just like choosing between Young Bad-Ass Elvis and Old, Fat and Drugged-Out Elvis. Later in the sketch, Moore actually hires a legitimate lawyer to lay down a constitution for Turdonia (where "Cable is a God-given right," he says). After having taken care of all this legal mumbo-jumbo and other constitutional formalities, he visits one of Turner's wranglers and reads him Turdonia's First Amendment:

Moore:
I pledge allegiance to the flag of the United States of Turdonia
and to the Republic for which it stands; one nation under Ted,
with classic movies and *Beefalo* for all.

True to form he goes straight to the United Nations in order to enlist Turdonia as an official member of the world community. In addition, as if all of this was not enough, he even has a pompous national anthem written for this billionaire's empire. This closes the skit with Moore singing along with a choir of altar boys, hand crossed over his chest (N.B. the "tomahawk chop" in this song is in reference to Turner also owning the Atlanta Braves back then…):

Hail, Turdonia,
Land of Turner!
Of your might we sing.
From the Rockies to the Andes,
Ted owns every thing!
Give us Beefalo
And a wrestling show,
With aerobics led by Jane!
With a tomahawk chop,
We'll go straight to the top,
Turdonia long may you reign!

Affirmative Action Plan

In a later episode of *The Awful Truth*, Moore told us about another rich white person who got more than he deserved because of his sex, racial profile, name and social status. Here, Moore inverted the meaning of "affirmative action" in order to show how ethnicity and class are inextricably linked in American society; a fact that conventional media often chooses to ignore. By picking on George Walker Bush, then Governor of Texas, through a very simple staging and compiling of archival footage, Moore had a chance to say something true about success and prosperity based on meritocracy. Looking straight into the camera, he stands in front of an old Georgian-style building, something resembling a New England Ivy-League institution, a directorial decision which visually sets the action on the lawn of the blue-blooded American elite. Over the narration we see shots of Bush behaving silly, cut-in with inserts from his truly unimpressive past. Moore often relies on this technique to ridicule famous political figures. In the case of Junior, he always goes the extra mile. He shows how inadequate the little king really is as a public speaker and how awkward and clumsy he really can be when only given half a chance.

> Moore:
> Affirmative action – Are there two uglier words in the English language? Nothing can be more wrong, more un-American than promoting people who are less qualified simply because of some past injustice. Fortunately, our Supreme Court Justice agrees. They struck down almost all affirmative action laws. Almost. There is still one form of affirmative action that continues to rear its ugly head. So richly rewarding the undeserving that even I decided I had to do something about it. I'm speaking, of course, of *George W. Bush's Affirmative Action…*

Moore's editing was (and still is) merciless in his attack on Bush as a credible politician; often aligning brief shots of him tripping over, looking ridiculous or stuttering in public; taking his words out of context and making him sound like a sub-John Wayne on lithium. And then there is the soundtrack, which usually links him to the shallow culture of the 1950s (e.g. corny instrumentals which sound like shopping mall music). The culmination of Michael Moore's contempt for G.W. Bush is of course *Fahrenheit 9/11*, a brilliant pamphlet that uses him as a funnel for everything that is wrong with the American Right today.

Moore (v.o.):
"This underachiever who had a C average was able to skip over those who were more qualified, simply because he was born-Bush. Friend, are you one of the tragic victims of *George W. Bush Affirmative Action*? As a young boy did you have dreams of attending the prestigious Andover Academy in 1961, but was passed over just so that a little Bush-boy can take your seat? Or are you one of those whose life was ruined because you could not get into Yale University in 1964 because of a Bush quota system that goes back generations?"

Shortly after, Moore introduced a University professor of physics who claimed he was denied access to Yale the same year Bush was accepted. In high school the man had gotten mostly A's and was even awarded a grant to attend the prestigious institution. However, because of "Bush's affirmative action," he was forced to go study at a "lesser university," in Utah. Moore then reiterates that Junior had access to better schools because of his pedigree and shows us more stills from the Bush family vault, blended with some color footage of people snorting cocaine at a tropical resort in the 1970s, quite suggestive if you know Bush's history.

Moore (v.o.):
"Or perhaps you had hoped to go to the world-renowned Harvard Business School in 1973, but that last spot in the class was taken by a man who spent his undergrad years getting C's and D's, and who helped to finance a small village in Columbia? Who was that man? It was little Georgie. Getting that spot that you worked for, that you earned and that you deserved. It's time we stand up to this minority. Who are they to take what is rightfully yours? If you are one of these victims of *George W. Bush's Affirmative Action*, contact us now to join in a class action suit against these institutions and George Junior himself. Put an end to this kind of unconstitutional preference and reversed discrimination that got George Jr. where he is today…"

Beat the Rich

In line with the previous Turner and Bush-bashing sketches, Moore revealed astonishing statistics in one episode from the first season of *The Awful Truth*. He informed us that three men in the Western world were then worth 180 billion dollars when put together. This amounted to the total gross domestic product of 162 countries around the world.

Bill Gates alone was then worth 97 billion dollars, which is still the total net worth of more than 121 million Americans...

The host wanted to prove once again that the "working stiffs" of America are just plain better at life (and at being human) than the rich man ever will be. This time Moore relies on the quiz show format in a classic challenge to "Beat the Rich." The main purpose of this game is to see how smart the "haves" are in relation to the basic functions of daily life, compared to regular and hard-working people. In this number, Moore has well-to-do people from Upper West Side Manhattan against working class people from blue-collar Pittsburgh, Pennsylvania, in a parallel-editing scheme. A series of questions have to be answered by both teams to win the challenge. These range from the price of a bottle of Dom Perignon and Merlot wine, all the way to how to change a bag in a vacuum cleaner. Obviously, the point of this skit was to illustrate how class status influences the way you think and behave. Needless to add that class also affects the way you see yourself, the world, everybody, and everything in it.

White Collar Criminals

When Moore asked people on the street who were the worst criminals they could think of, most dished out the canonized version of American psychos: Ed Gein, Charles Manson, Ted Kaczynski, Albert DeSalvo, Ted Bundy, Jeffrey Dahmer, etc. Indeed, America has had its share of wackos, but Moore reminded us that these were "lightweights" in comparison to the real American criminals...The quick and on the spot interviews in the middle of Times Square then give way to a reportage which will reveal who the true sickos of our age really are. (What the host usually does after he interviews a passerby is to draw his/her attention to the camera lens by pointing at it; as if the story we were about to watch was unfolding in American homes, where everyone should feel concerned). In a montage sequence of television and archival footage, sustained by elaborate charts, graphics and a mock newsreel voice-over, we are reminded by Moore of a legal system which allows for a few rich people to get richer on the back of the working majority.

Narrator (v.o.):
"There is a crime problem in America! But thanks to tougher laws, tougher judges, and the mass round-ups of undesirables, the streets of America are safer. Murder: down! Robbery: down! Crimes against property: down! Yet, America still cannot sleep soundly at night, for there lurks among us a terrifying group of hoodlums who prey upon the innocent and

the unsuspecting. Their crime costs the taxpayer more than three trillion dollars a year, and each year they steal more than all burglaries combined. They kill more people than all the murderers in America. Who are these thugs? these punks? these low-lives? They are the corporate criminals! Their weapon is not a gun but a pen. They run loose, not on the streets but in the suites. And although those charged with catching them can talk the talk, they cannot walk the walk. And as the corporate crooks roam free throughout the land, polluting the air, defrauding the senior citizens, embezzling, price-fixing...dangerous products, yet, the evening news ignores their activities, Congress passes no laws to stop them, cops make no arrests..."

While we are being told about the current state of ethics in the business world today by a bombastic narrator, we are simultaneously shown pictures of individuals who have been arrested and convicted on charges of illegal business practices, as well as Moore dressed up as a special agent walking the beat. On the soundtrack there is the theme song from the exploitative television show *Cops*, giving a rastafarian rythmn to the sequence in a very different way than its original intent. We also find ourselves laughing because of Moore's ridiculous allure as a law enforcement officer who is out to kick some corporate butt.

In one particular episode of "Corporate Cops," goes after C.R. Bard Inc., a company which had already pleaded guilty to 391 counts of criminal fraud and conspiracy of conducting illegal experiments with non-approved by the F.D.A heart catheters. The company had been fined 60 millions dollars and its executives were sentenced to jail terms. However, not one of them ever served a second or paid for damages resulting from these illegal experiments. Ten years after their sentence, even after the F.D.A. had sent them enforcement reports, Bard was still putting public safety at risk. Moore first wants to prove that corporate crime is not a priority for government and local judiciary systems alike. He goes to have a talk with county prosecutors concerning the indictment, but winds up being ostracized by them instead. He then hires a private parole officer, sets up a neighborhood-watch program, and replaces the company sign with another one which reads "Corporate Criminals." Soon the police arrives but only to tell him that they couldn't care less about Bard's illegal activities, and that he has to leave the grounds immediately.

His effort to put these criminals where they belong had failed. Although, he was able to denounce Bard's illegal activities on national television for a few minutes, and this means something in the end. On the final card of the report we learn that from the time Clinton took office in 1992 to the time the show was aired in 1999, corporate-crime prosecution had gone down 27% in the United States. This particular piece of information allows us to assume that Clinton and Bush have a lot of friends in common and that they both worked for the same people in the end: American industrialists and the invisible world government.

Cartoon Characters on Welfare

Back in the 1980s the Reagans instituted different programs to ensure Americans would "just say no to drugs." In conjunction with federal and state offices, the administration came up with the brilliant idea to have a mascot called McGruff the Crime-Fighting Dog to promote its national program then known as *Take a Bite out of Crime*. But while petty offenses related to small possession of light narcotics were being investigated by McGruff and his minions at the Drug Enforcement Agency, and while the American government was busy taking control of the international drug trade with the CIA's help in Afghanistan and in South America, another type of criminality, way more disastrous for the social fabric of America, started to increase dramatically all over the country. Soon enough, though, a seven foot-chicken came to the rescue...

Crackers the Crime-Fighting Chicken was one of the better creations of the first series, *TV Nation*. Back by popular demand the gregarious and intrepid mascot was to reappear twice in Moore's second TV series.[14] In one particular episode of *The Awful Truth* the chicken was sent to investigate a labor dispute between ABC/Disney and its technical personnel. The corporation had locked-out its engineers because they wanted a better contract. Most of these workers had temporarily been employed and precarious for more than two decades. Their union had been weakened by mergers and had basically abandoned them in their quest for job equity– but what else is new in a country known for its anti-union streak and strike-breaking power? Even though Moore had done business with Disney for *The Big One*, he didn't mind going after this corporation when it proved to be dishonest and too greedy for its own good. In his inquiry about this case, Crackers found out that Disney treats its employees unfairly and that it even owns sweatshops in China. This information compels him to manifest in front of Disney headquarters in New York and to lend a voice to the locked-out technical workers. At one point Crackers tries to infiltrate the building but gets trapped in a revolving door by security personnel. He decides to go directly to Disney World in order to ask for Mickey's help instead.

---

[14] In order to know more about the origins and evolution of Crackers the Crime-Fighting Chicken, we recommend reading *Adventures in a TV Nation*, pp. 46-59

Crackers drives down Highway 95 to meet with the mouse himself, but before doing so, he has a talk with a cast of character-actors who explain to him that Disney has been cruel, not only in foreign lands, but to its own local employees as well. The man who use to embody Trumpet the Elephant Man on the kingdom's grounds describes how the heat was unbearable in his ex-mascot costume. The performer who use to played Chip and Dale says that his chipmunk costume had been so badly washed that he once developed "crotch fungus" from it. (Here, Moore perverts a corporate video produced by Disney by having Chip's crotch area examined with an intrusive iris.) Finally one of the performers playing the part of one of the Seven Dwarves recalls that some employees did faint from heat and exhaustion in their heavy corporate gear. You would think that Disney made enough profit to afford lighter and more comfortable materials for their mascots, the true spirit of its artificial world, but apparently not.

Next, Crackers started searching all around for Mickey but the giant mouse is too busy in the twelve o'clock parade to answer his labor questions. The chicken is finally caught by security personnel, body-searched and then quickly ejected from Disney's premises. He decides to go "where money talks the loudest" and gets involved at the grassroots level instead. In Washington, Crackers goes to a grade school where he asks children (Disney's first customers) to back up a boycott of Disney products. He proposes to write a letter addressed to Michael Eisner: "Do you all know how to spell the word *exploitation*?" he asks them. When all was said and done, the pressures on Disney must have been so great that the corporation decided to let its employees go back to work and discuss a settlement (not that we are ever told that this outcome is resulting from Cracker's efforts, mind you). What this reportage is really telling us is that Disney, like the American Dream itself, is a mirage. Moore portrays this corporation as a greedy player in the world economy; one which cannot even treat its smallest heroes in a decent way. Let's not kid ourselves, when a corporation puts chipmunks on welfare, forces princesses and dwarves to live in their cars and elephants to shower in a locker-room, it certainly has an image problem.

Human Resources

A more dramatic case that Crackers decided to follow on was the one involving Harrison Research Laboratories, located in New Jersey. This company had been accused of violating the Federal Insecticide, Fungicide, and Rodenticide Act many years in a row, according to reports Moore found in the archives. In another episode from "Corporate Cops," Moore told the viewer that Harrison had allegedly paid 390 human subjects five dollars a piece for testing highly concentrated DEET products on them. DEET is a cancer-inducing pesticide found in very small dosage in insect repellent, but which can become lethal to humans when used in highly concentrated form. Even after being accused by the Supreme Court, Harrison's CEO posted bail and continued testing on human subjects, unpunished and unfazed by matters of legality and ethics. With his Crime Unit, Moore decides to go after the President of Harrison Research Lab, a woman who thinks herself above the law simply because she is "incorporated."

When Moore pays her a visit he brings along a relevant gift: the biography of boxer Ruben Carter (a.k.a. The Hurricane, a man who served an extremely long jail sentence for a crime he had not committed, just because he was black). Over-reacting to this necessary act of provocation, Harrison's personnel first throws Moore out of the building and then stops the Corporate Crime vehicle from exiting the parking lot. He even has to call the police to release himself from the grips of these vindictive (and humorless) corporate criminals. Here is probably one time when he was glad to see the red, white and blue flash in front of his eyes! Quite fortunately, Crackers is called-in to save the day, and since the chicken happens to be desperately in need of the 5 dollars offered by Harrison Inc., Moore proceeds to spray it with a big insecticide gun (filled with "play-DEET"), right in front of Harrison's headquarters, as another form of his political theater. After a long psychedelic trip set to a variation of Hendrix's 'Purple Haze', the morning after, Crackers winds up in the bushes somewhere but, as always, a very trustworthy chicken. Somehow the viewer knows that Crackers will still go on fighting for all those underdogs who are trying to make a honest living out there, in this real and dog-eat-dog world.

Temp Nation

One of the things which the Crime-Fighting Chicken has taught us in *TV Nation* and *The Awful Truth* is that few corporations should ever be trusted when it comes to respecting the human rights of its employees. Even the most seemingly sweet one on the surface, like Disney, has something truly rotten lying at its core (i.e. the never-ending quest for ever-growing profits or, as they put it, the "need to stay competitive" on the world's market…that they've created). As we are so often reminded by Michael Moore's work, American corporations have kept their employees precarious for years while they have grossly overpaid their executive staff and made outrageous profits. He keeps pointing to the fact that corporations have understood that the best way to stay competitive is to exploit their own workers, among other things, and getting paid handsomely for cutting that "red tape" around what they call the "human resources." For many blue chip companies, this exploitation has become as normal as screwing over a customer or backstabbing a business competitor. By keeping workers without a contract and at part-time status, these conglomerates finally found a way to squeeze the last drop out of the lemon. These policies created a "temp(orary) nation," a country made out of the working-poor.

As a result of these unethical and reckless business practices the economy has become more unstable, since it is difficult (if not impossible) to consume and buy things when you can't pay for your rent and bills (and when your credit line has reached its limit). In fact, before like after the huge meltdown of 2008, America is a land where regular working folks wake up every morning not knowing if they will still have their part-time job by lunchtime or even own their house by supper time. So much for equal opportunity.

It is in this line of corporate thinking that Moore and his staff came up with a special contest entitled "Mind that Memo," a challenge between himself and the "Number One" employer in America: Manpower Inc. This corporation specializes in finding people temporary jobs or, as Moore puts it, it is "The biggest supplier of jobs-for-a-day in the country." As an American institution, Manpower was founded in the late 1940s but only became a major player during Reagonomics, a time of great distress for the middle and working classes (due to extensive privatization and a more lenient tax-bracket for big business). By the mid-1980s, when the "big crunch" against the middle-class was taking effect, it had over a thousand offices worldwide and many interests in various sectors of the economy. When someone gets a job through Manpower, you can almost bet that it entails no job security, no social benefit and no protection from any form of corporate or managerial abuse. It is an "in-between" corporation which has seized and capitalized on the reality of an unsteady workplace composed of temporary employees, and where computer technology has replaced conventional human labor. (In this sense, technology does play against humanity.)

The idea for "Mind That Memo" came to Moore when he was shooting *The Big One* back in 1996. There is even a segment in this movie where he goes to Manpower in order to help a man who has just been laid-off by Johnson Controls, another titan of corporate America. Since that day Manpower executives had issued a "special memorandum" warning its employees about Moore's subversive doings. It contained a few easy instructions to follow in case anyone had to deal with him personally. The document was called *"The Michael Moore Alert"* and included the following recommendations for its employees across the country:

- *Be polite but firm;*
- *Ask him to leave;*
- *Call headquarters;*
- *Do not respond to questions;*
- *Do not call the police!*

The purpose of the game was for Moore to go to branches across the country and see if Manpower employees minded the memo faxed by head office. If they minded, they scored; if they did not, Michael scored. A voice-over explained the show's conceptual thread: "*Mind that Memo* is the game show that tests corporate efficiency in the age of the new global economics." The game show aesthetics are utilized here as a mean to subvert television culture, because Moore is aware that it is a popular format which extols the virtues of individualism. These shows willfully keep viewers in the dark as far as active political thinking is concerned. It numbs down political consciousness by feeding guilty pleasures and entertaining narcissism.

At one point in the game, Moore goes to a Manpower branch in Madison, Wisconsin. There, he winds up talking to an employee for nearly an hour. He asks him: "Have you received the *Michael Moore Memo*? There have been two or three of them at this point." The naive employee then goes through faxed documents which have recently been sent by head office, and Moore takes this moment as an opportunity to make a sign which says "Time Out" flash over the poor guy. The voice-over comes in again to tell us: "Let us enjoy a brief time out as this Manpower employee tries to find the *Michael Moore Memo*." After discussing every topic under the sun, from corporate memos to time sharing and underwater diving in Hawaii, Moore finally gets tired of the hospitality and concludes that, "Of course, according to the memos, this is a complete failure. But as a *human being*, he is a complete success," which is what really counts in the end. The last branch to be visited by Moore was the one based in England.

Moore:
It seems as if you could use a few temps in here.

Manpower Employee:
We totally could, yes.

Moore:
I noticed that there is a homeless guy out there. Uh, is he sleeping in that cardboard box?

Manpower Employee:
Yes.

> Moore:
> So England has our tin companies, now you're importing our homeless too?
>
> Manpower Employee:
> He's been here for about 7 years.
>
> Moore:
> About 7 years?
>
> Manpower Employee:
> About 7 years. And we received memos for him too.
>
> Moore:
> Have you thought about giving him a temp job?
>
> Manpower Employee:
> We tend to not get too involved in social interaction…

At this point, the voice-over comes in to declare Moore the winner.

> Announcer (v.o.):
> "Ouch! This chap ignored the memo and answered one too many question. So this week's winner is Michael Moore! Michael wins the Grand Prize: a $7/h temp job doing data entry for Channel 4 in London. Congratulations Michael! And we'll see you all here next week on 'Mind that Memo'! Hotel accommodations for 'Mind That Memo' were provided by Carlton International…"

While the voice-over turns the outcome of the challenge into derision, and even poking fun at the show's producing channel in England, the camera pans up and reveals that the homeless man is indeed sleeping on a corporate box, but with the logo of Carlton Hotels on it. This idea of mocking corporate icons is consistent with his overall themes. In one of the following episodes of that same season, "Advertiser-Friendly Night," Moore went as far as to use real convicts and criminals to promote the products of major corporations like Johnson & Johnson, Coke, American Express and Budweiser.

Armageddon Time

So far one could be lead to believe that Michael Moore is only interested in challenging figures of authority and wealth, as well as faceless corporate entities (at ground level). But there are many other issues covered in his work besides stupid rich white men, cruel politicians, white-collar criminals, and the social inequities these people help to create and foster on a daily basis. Most of the topics he chooses to address concern all of us in the end. World security, environmental policies, public and psychological health are only some of the themes found in his two television series. Moore never did shy away from the big issues, even on a small screen. Unorthodox in this day and age he seems to flock to them with uncommon courage instead.

For instance, he often shows scenes of nuclear destruction in his films and television shows. The introductory credits for *TV Nation* includes images of nuclear catastrophe and bombing of Levittown-type suburbs.[15] Like most Americans born after WW II, Moore has been lied to about the chances of surviving a nuclear attack and the radioactive fallout which would result from it. He has also been brainwashed by governmental propaganda, such as the one inherent to *Duck & Cover*, a short "instructional" film produced by the Civil Air Defense in the early 1950s. With the help of a goofy turtle character, this short animation was created to illustrate what to do in the eventuality of Armageddon. Essentially, it goes something like this: When you see a bright flashing light over your city and hear a big bang, just "duck and cover" to avoid molecular vaporization.

This government document has also been used elsewhere, like in the compilation film *The Atomic Café* (Loader, et al., 1982), and it seems to have had a great influence on a whole generation of Americans. It obviously still affects Moore to this day. As a matter-of-fact, when we see how these disturbing images function within his work, we can read them as part of a greater mosaic created to exorcise the demons unleashed by Fat Man and Little Boy in 1945. In Moore's oeuvre, they produce an aesthetic of paranoia and sinister contemplation; something that he does not necessarily use for nihilistic ends, but that sometimes borders on hysteria and desire, like some sort of revisionist Kubrickian tale.

Indian Teenage Fall-Out Queen

In one *Awful Truth* episode he tried to clarify the ideological warfare which is still going on between India and Pakistan, two nations who have been fighting for years over the propriety of the Kashmir region.

---

[15] Moore even went to the ex-Soviet Union to ask the military to point in a different direction the missile that was designed for his hometown of Flint (in the first episode of *TV Nation* "Mike's Missile": read *Adventures in a TV Nation*, pp.125-133 to know more).

Having enough to worry about as it is, with all the terrorist attacks, natural and ecological catastrophes, oil catastrophes and wars, and ethnic genocide around the globe, people could surely use a bit of humor to unwind these two fighting parties. This is when Moore comes in. For him the only way to proceed is to rely on the famous turtle to convey to the Indian and Pakistani ambassadors the feeling of dread he felt as a kid growing up in the 1950s. For this skit, Moore goes out of his way to teach what *duck and cover* really means to groups of Pakistani and Indian adult students.

First, he stages a debate at a local school. After both parties quarrel as to which nation is "Number One," Moore screens the *Duck & Cover* film for them, distributes gas masks, and hands out "sunscreen against radiation" to them. Later he brings some of his "advanced students" on a field trip, where they get to visit a traditional American fallout shelter. In the bunker they learn all about the effects of radiation, how to use a chemical toilet (a large plastic can), preliminary lessons in self-defense (a .38 caliber gun), and tips about cannibalism (how to cook your dead radiated neighbor).

Despite Moore attempts at trying to make them understand the implications of nuclear weapons, the students cannot help themselves but to be excited about the "unlimited value" of the bomb, especially regarding its possibilities in terrorizing the enemy with absolute fear. Obviously, these people were under the spell. They had learned how not to worry and love the bomb, like all those crackpots at the Pentagon after WW II, the Hawks, and Dr. Strangelove himself.[16] In the end, there was unfortunately no way for Moore to deprogram these people from such a powerful and cataclysmic turn-on.

Much like the U.S., India and Pakistan are two phallocentric, military and caste-based society which spend more time, energy and money on developing nuclear weapons (and nagging each other) than on their own underfed populations. Moore is trying to get a point across through a dark humor which many people have problems with, mainly because of political correctness issues and/or personal hang-ups. Nevertheless, the idea that some nations use 1/3 of their budget to produce bombs which will serve to kill their close neighbor instead of feeding their own starved population is a shameful one, no matter where you stand politically or who you vote for. There is no other way but extreme forms of satire to convey the nonsensical aspect of it all. And Moore does it better than anybody else.

---

[16] Moore challenged the American double-standard regarding weapons of mass destruction in another episode of the first season of *The Awful Truth*. In the skit "Weapons Inspectors," he went to the Umatilla Chemical Depot of the United States Army with an Iraqi man to inspect his own country's arsenal. The two men even went to the National Committee to deposit an official report of their inquiry.

No Go for Kyoto

Beyond the worries of a possible destruction of the world, expressed clearly within Moore's work, there are more concrete concerns about the state of our global ecology and the way business and religion have been intertwined into the perception and conception of nature over the last 30 years. Many scientists, ecologists, environmentalists and oceanographers with great credentials have already warned us against the Greenhouse Effect and the possible catastrophe(s) which will result from it (within the next century, they say). Organizations such as Greenpeace and the World Wildlife Federation have already tried different means to make the world's leaders and policy-makers change their minds about the issue, but to no avail. In January 2007, an important convention held in France and reuniting over 500 leading experts in various fields of natural sciences gave birth to a report proving that the consequences of global warming are real, catastrophic, and not too far ahead. Still, from an American standpoint, it would seem like there are no profits to be made from trying to preserve and protect nature. It is just the opposite. American politicians and industrialists are much better served by exploiting it to the fullest, which is the story of the "stupid white man" in the end.

In an attempt at creating some eco-security for all, an agreement was signed in 1997 by many countries to participate in a collective effort to reduce low-gas emissions in the atmosphere. The Kyoto Protocol was signed and agreed on by fifty countries, except the United States of America, no doubt the biggest consumer and polluter in world terms. Over a decade later, during the 2009 Copenhagen Conference, only the U.S. and China backed again from signing an agreement with the rest of the conscious nations of the world, on the basis of some derogatory clause. The fact that the American government (under Clinton, Bush and even Obama) backed-out of a necessary and concrete action to save the planet is truly overwhelming to anyone who understands the ultimate power that our environment has over all of us, rich or poor. The only possible explanation for this refractory attitude is that America's financial interests would be at a loss if it ever decreased production and consumption for the sake of Mother Nature and her children. Even though we are in the realms of speculation here, we can very well imagine that the American economy, notwithstanding the great competition coming from China and India, and following the great meltdown of 2008 on Wall Street, would no doubt suffer even more from a reduction of mass-production and mass-consumption. American leaders know this too well, so what they propose is *more* mass-production and mass-consumption, completed by a warped right-wing rhetoric concerning the so-called "natural cycles" of global warming (as if the last 200 years of Industrial Revolution had not taken their toll yet). In all this political small-mindedness, President Barack Obama has at least given us some a glimpse of hope when he first took office by clearly stating that clean energy is the way to go for America.[17] But up until the day when he actually will take the lead on this issue, either by developing a new energy grid or by fully subsidizing clean energy companies, we will assume that America is not ready to change its industrial, 20th century way of dealing with energy consumption. (Even the monumental 2010 ecological disaster of the BP oil spill in the Gulf of Mexico did not have an effect on their perception of problem. Wait until cancers from the Corexit 9500 dispersant chemicals start acting up as a mass phenomenon, then it might have a real effect on their consciousness regarding the problem.)

Industrial Disease

Michael Moore has tackled the relationship between environmental policies, public health and corporate greed in many different ways over the last 20 years. In one episode of *The Awful Truth*, he gave the "Man of the Year Award" to one of America's greatest polluter of all time: Leon Ira Rennert. Rennert is a mega-millionaire industrialist who owns Renco Group Inc. and who is known to have strong lobbying powers in Washington, D.C. This reportage blends many of the aforementioned themes: stupid rich white men, rootless corporations and the state of our environment. For Moore giving the award was a way to make people realize that the world is not ran by governments but by greedy and carefree CEOs. Yet very few of us know who these people are and how much they are aware of the consequences of their actions. By presenting highlights of Rennert's career in hommage format, Moore encapsulated all dishonest capitalists who are polluting our lives and slowly giving us cancer on a daily basis.

In effect, according to reports from the Environment Protection Agency, Rennert had an astounding record around the states of Ohio, Missouri and Utah at the time the show was made. Using profits from his steel, lead and magnesium factories, which together in a one year measure of their regular combined output, released more than 73 million pounds of toxins in the atmosphere. He even built himself a San Simeon-like castle on Long Island, and this villa has more bathrooms than all the resorts of the area put together, according to a municipality official interviewed in the *Awful Truth*. At some point in the editing, Moore shows us an image of a toilet bowl flushing under Rennert's picture, while a voice-over tells us about the effect of the Magnesium

---

[17] "Statement on President Obama's Announcement to Fight Global Warming and Move to Clean Energy," *Targeted News Service*, January 26, 2009

Corporation of America on Utah's Great Salt Lake and vicinity. Denizens of this region reported stories of widespread cancer, birth defects and cows being born without teeth. In the piece, they tell us how the smell of burning sulfuric acid was/is constantly dangling in the air, affecting the taste of food, water, breast milk and bodily odors. The local barber even recounts seeing many of his customers developing green hair! This stuff seems to be straight out of a science-fiction novel, but it is not... In fact, it just keeps getting weirder as the hommage progresses.

At another point the voice-over mentions that one of Rennert's companies was sentenced to a 20 million dollar-fine for polluting the environment, and it ends that part of the statement in exclamation by saying: "Way to go, Ira!," as if it was so tragic that we could only but laugh at it in despair. But the viewer gets a chance to become even more enraged when he finds out that Rennert didn't have to pay the fine, and that he will keep on getting more tax breaks from Washington as he continues to destroy the planet. Moore also discloses that another one of Rennert's companies [was] manufacturing the Hummer, the gas-guzzling monstro-truck of them all and proudly driven by Hollywood's muscleman and Governor of California Arnold Schwarzenegger. When you break it down and as the years go by, it seems like the full portrait of the stupid rich white man is more clearly defined in Moore's oeuvre.

At the end of the sketch, it is up to Moore to present Rennert with his Man of the Year award in person. He goes to his New York City penthouse but is greeted with hostility by a door attendant and a bellhop. It is true that the six-foot statue made out of unknown chemical crap, which also has to be handled carefully with rubber gloves, is a bit obtrusive on the sidewalk of Rennert's Upper East Side home. Therefore, Moore decides to go to his Rockefeller Center office to give him a more modest award instead (actually, it looks like a melted-down post-apocalyptic Oscar). There, he is greeted by a smiling employee who finally accepts the prize on behalf of Rennert (with a pair of rubber gloves on).

A week later, the Man of the Year himself files for a restraining order against Michael Moore at the New York State Supreme Court. Charges of harassment are laid against the television host who can't come within 150 feet of Rennert. In failing to comply with the ruling Moore explains that he can face up to six months jail. The host turns the ordeal into a gag on his show by requiring the services of a certified surveyor to measure exactly 151 feet (one extra foot to be sure) from the Rockefeller Center. He also hires a security guard to stop himself from getting close to the building. Recognizing that he is used to be unwelcome at certain given places – General Motors, Nike headquarters, high school prom – Moore nevertheless becomes emotional when it comes to being excluded from this "Art Deco masterpiece, center of his artistic and social life," as he put it. Later on, he also complains about the fact that he [was] not allow to go to his favorite church, St. Patrick's Cathedral, because of its proximity to the Rockefeller Center. No doubt, he must have been one unhappy Catholic boy on that day; unable to confess all the shenanigans he had done since last week's show. It must have been like not being able to go through with a sketch entitled "The Confessional" in the pilot for *TV Nation*, years before.[18]

An Unusual Choir Boy

As one of the most politically incorrect moment to ever be aired on American television, "The Voice-Box Choir" has lost none of its punch over the years. It shows us handicapped men and women with voice boxes singing Christmas carols in the lobbies of Philip-Morris and R.J. Reynolds, decorating a Christmas tree with cigarettes on the front lawn of a corporate CEO, and expressing their good wishes for the season through their robotic voices. The corporate personnel who they meet along the way are so troubled that it cannot even push Moore and his "merry" band out of the door. Security agents and police officers alike just stand there, covering their mouths or scratching their heads. Nonetheless, the irony created by Moore and his choir is not all lost on the tobacco industry people. Some are actually shocked by the spectacle put on by these cancer patients. It is a shameful sight that is still today very painful to watch. Moore even has the nerve to cast himself as the conductor of the choir with a baton in his hand. In one moment from the skit, Moore and his choir pay a visit to ex-Senate Leader Howard Baker's law firm, which is well known for representing big tobacco companies. Baker had a wife who died from lung cancer years before, but this still didn't stop him from lobbying for tobacco products in D.C. Moore even claims that Baker's firm had made two million dollars representing cigarette companies in those years.

Another lawyer from Baker's office tells Moore not to be cynical with this kind of sick stunt. Moore replies that "What is cynical is telling people that cigarettes won't give you cancer…" The dramatic highpoint of this episode come when a woman afflicted by throat cancer asked the lawyer: "Have you ever heard a laryngectomy talk?" The man, who started out cocky, finally escapes through the back door, obviously affected by the moral turpitude this scene is provoking in him. Moore can sure be shocking at times. Here is a case to be made

---

[18] *Adventures in a TV Nation*, pp. 5 -13

against the lobbyists and he pretends to wish them a happy holiday season with his unusually pathetic choir.

This controversial piece ends with a dynamic montage of the respective members of the choir singing 'The First Day of Christmas' in front of a luxurious CEO home at night. In the middle of the song, one of the cancer patients, disguised as Santa Claus, has to stop singing to cough-out a piece of his lung. All of it is captured by Moore's camera for propagandistic and humanistic purposes...of course.

A Nation in Rapture

In the trauma following the Columbine shootings, religious fundamentalists and their politician friends found a way to bring old-time religion once again into the classrooms and public offices of the nation. It is a well-known fact that religious fanatics, very much like in certain parts of the Middle East, have been controlling that great country we call the United States of America since the Reagan era. Even though the U.S. Constitution clearly states that State and Church are two different entities, and have to remain as such, some politicians somewhere inside Congress always find a way to merge these two institutions in a lethal cocktail of ideology, morality and legislation. The Bible-Belt crowd, from which George W. Bush (a self-proclaimed born-again Christian) emerged, has denied evolutionary theory and went on to suggest that God created the world in only seven days, just like it is written in the Old Testament. These retrograde dogmas about "intelligent design" are enforced in schools all across the U.S., propagating a romanticized and counter-scientific vision of life. As antiquated beliefs, it also serves to conceal the interest of the ruling elite, since this one profits immensely from abusing natural resources and from people's ignorance about pollution, global warming, and its links to industrialization and exploitation of resources. All it takes is a few religious loonies, a handful of greedy industrialists and shameless politicians to repudiate all that science has taught us since the Enlightenment. In the end, these people think that "freedom of religion" means the freedom to impose their beliefs on everybody else.

Thou Shall Not Blend Politics and Religion

In one *Awful Truth* episode Moore decided to tackle the embarrassing issue of religion in politics by going to Capitol Hill, where metaphysical beliefs have replaced political ideas for a cleaner and safer America. As he put it in the piece, "Some politicians found out that passing a bill for the Ten Commandments to be posted in classrooms and public offices are a good way to get votes." He added that "It is also a good way to kill any gun control laws which might eventually try to be passed in Congress." Instead of supporting secular politics, which could have been cleared of religious prejudices and preconceptions in regards to the origins of life, the institution voted for a bill which allowed teachers to post God's orders to Moses in public schools all across the nation. As one Republican Congressman puts it in the episode: "If either of the boys [*who shot up Columbine*] had taken the Ten Commandments into their hearts, I'm convinced that there wouldn't have been a Columbine," to which Moore answers on the voice-over: "Hallelujah! Praise the Lord! A solution to school shootings that even the National Rifle Association could love!" He then goes on by explaining that 41 congressmen posted the Commandments on their own office walls in symbolic support of the bill...and that he has to do something about it.

Since everyone in Washington had turned to mysticism instead of good old pragmatics, Moore decided to make a pilgrimage of his own. He actually went to visit some of the congressional representatives who had hung the Commandments on their office walls and gave them plaques with proverbial sayings, personalized to suit their respective deed. For Kansas Representative Jim Ryun, who was one of the men responsible for passing the bill, Moore offered the following inscription: "No man can serve two masters, for either he will hate the one, and love the other, or else he will hold on to the one, and despise the other, *you cannot serve God and Man.*" (Matthew 6:24) For Florida Representative Dave Weldon, the plaque quoted Luke in one of his most famous parabolic stance: "Again I tell you. It is easier for a camel to pass through the eye of the needle than for a rich man to enter the Kingdom of Heaven." (16:11) Upon reading it, Weldon said: "That's one of my favorite verses of the scriptures." Moore then went on to ask him a trick question: "When you support a flat-tax and cutting the capital-gain tax, and taking P.A.C. (Political Action Committee) money, are you worried that you're not following this particular Commandment from the New Testament?" Weldon replied: "No. I do not see any conflict there at all."

For his part, North Carolina Representative Robin Hayes found a better way to remember God's main points to humanity by creating an abridged version: "Giving the Ten Commandments, even way back when, got a bit complicated for folks. So we reduced them to two: Love God and love your neighbor." For him, Moore had brought a special gift. It was a trophy with an ecclesiastic inscription: "For what is Man profited if he should gain the whole world and loseth his own soul." Moore asked him if it was possible to make a good profit and not lose your soul. Hayes had this to say: "Absolutely. Again, referring back to the Bible, money is not the root of all evil. The *love of money* is the root of all evil." Like so many of his "brothers" in Congress, we learned from Moore that this man was worth over 35 million U.S dollars. Finally, the fourth representative was Ronnie Shows from the state of Missouri. The host presented him with a quilted pillow that bore God's following advice: "I do not sit with deceitful men, nor do I consort with hypocrites." (Psalms 26:4) This congressman told Moore that he would put it where "they" can see it, as if this hat didn't fit on him.

One of the purposes of this last episode was certainly to confront the religious hypocrisy that has overtaken the American political life since the 1980s. In order to do so Moore has often pitted the precepts of the New Testament against the ones found in the Old Testament, because it is an effective way to illustrate the ideological factions at work in America today. The Old Testament's version of religious faith is relying on a dark and apocalyptic imagery which conceives an angry and vengeful God, and where the unbelievers are left in a state of divine retribution. This opposes the New Testament's version, which is epitomized by Jesus Christ's sermon on the mountain, and in which he tells us that God loves everyone (and to love one another, even as flawed human beings). It is up to individuals to decide for themselves which version is more suitable as a philosophy or as a way of life for them. No one should be allowed to impose their beliefs on someone else, especially religious ones. By playing missionary and blending both of these distinctive fields, one physical, the other metaphysical, you can eventually wind-up blurring the line which separates life and afterlife. In this sense, fundamentalists Christians are no different than the fundamentalists Muslims they so despise, because both groups cannot conceive that the universe functions whether we understand it or not, whether we are all here or not, whether there is a God or not. Moreover, they cannot accept plurality and diversity, which goes against two of nature's fundamental laws (and Man is part of nature).

Although, for Moore, what is paramount in all of these issues is that religious beliefs influence how you understand politics, a truly human preoccupation. It also influences who you vote for and why you voted for them in the first place. It just simply affects everything and everyone, believers and unbelievers alike, in the same way in the end. Religious faith, like ethnicity or sexual orientation, or the right to die, should lie in the realms of the *private* sphere, not in the public one. It should certainly not be a factor in policy-making today, in a modern world which has been explained in great details by both political and natural sciences.

Free at Last

> To our reproach it must be said that, though for a century and a half we have had under our eyes the races of black and of red men, they have never yet been viewed by us as subjects of natural history. (Thomas Jefferson, *On Slavery*, 1774)

The United States of America have changed since the first edition of this book was published in 2007. And it changed in ways which very few people could have predicted, even the most educated and well-informed ones. Who could have seriously conceived that, within the space of a few years, a black man from the working class would become President of the country and one of the most recognizable man in the world? Needless to say that the election of Barack Hussein Obama in 2008 opened up a brand new conception of what America is and, most importantly, of what America *could be* if people got politically involved (even if it is just to "tweet" a message regarding a given political candidate). But this is only a surface reading, because the reality of black America has not changed since Obama is in office. The idea that an African-American family is currently in the White House does not diminish the fact that being African-American constitutes an impediment on a daily basis. Obama might have changed the paradigm for everyone and gave strength to people of color all over the world, but there is still a lot of racism regarding non-whites in the United States today, and this affects the dynamics and the inner-workings of that potentially great society, no doubt.

In that sense some of the most provocative *TV Nation* episodes will serve here as a bridge to discuss a topic which is clearly central to Michael Moore's work: civil rights. Like his quote regarding the assassination of Martin Luther King indicated (see Introduction), Moore never hid the fact that he was ultra-sensitive to the African-American cause. On many occasions he used his camera and the power which comes along with it to lend a hand to this continuous collective struggle. This has been the case since *Roger & Me*, when he forced into the distribution deal with Warner Bros. a financial compensation for the (mainly black) families evicted from their homes in the film. For Moore, ethnicity and class are closely related from a socioeconomic point of view.

In the reportage "Apartheid, American-Style" from the first season of *The Awful Truth*, he addressed himself to the white people of South Africa who became "disenfranchised" because of the break-up of the Apartheid system. Like in the case of the "George W. Bush Affirmative Action" report, Moore is relying on an explicit reverse-psychology tactic to break down the myth of equality and justice for all in his own country. In this piece he told this minority of African whites to leave their continent and to come to America, where "the appearances of racial harmony reign" and where black people are kept politically inoffensive and in economic shackles. One of the stunning statistics Moore gave his audience is that 1/4 of African-American men are either in prison, on their way to prison, or getting out of prison. He added that the 14% of them who are in prison are also denied the right to vote, which like the religious vote generally makes a substantial difference when comes the time to decide who will actually run the country.[19]

In an earlier episode from *TV Nation*, Moore had sent independent filmmaker Rusty Cundieff to Mississippi, the one state which had yet to legally abolish slavery (circa 1995). Cundieff, even as a black man, was able to buy six "honkey slaves," as he called them. He even strolled them through town for a couple of days, gave them names (i.e. his), forced them to work for no wages, and cruelly drove golf balls at them. Sometimes he allowed his slaves for a bit of fun at the Friday evening dance (achy-breaky-heart style). He even wondered about their "natural ability for rhythm," a comment on the way blacks have been exploited by the entertainment industry in the last century, and on many white people's inability to really be loose and funky on the dance floor.

In the resolution, and not after creating some commotion at City Hall, Cundieff decided to set all his slaves free. The final satirical punch came when the (black) master had to literally chase his (white) slaves away, since their love for him was so strong they did not wish to part (an extremely provocative concept here). In effect, this last piece is a subversion of the standards and practices of American television. It is also miles away from the stereotypical characters of black America created by the Semitic-American imagination in Hollywood. It goes way beyond what *The Cosby Show* might have done to help the black cause in America; that is, if this sitcom ever helped to change the image and the reality of African-Americans at all. It is also light years ahead of all those clichés entertained by a part of the black population itself: the pusher, the pimp, the gang-banger, etc. Moore has been accused of perpetuating racist stereotypes, but one misses the point in thinking so literally. After all, he does often use satire to prove a point. What he is looking for is some answer pertaining to the nature of the American psyche, and this endeavor must necessary include a reflection on ethnicity and the role it plays in the construction of the overall social fabric.

---

[19] According to an August 2003 Bureau of Justice Statistics analysis, 32 % of black males born in 2001 can expect to spend some time in prison over the course of their lifetime. That is up from 13.4% in 1974 and 29.4% in 1991. By contrast, 17.2% of Hispanics and 5.9% of whites born in 2001 are likely to end up in prison. Source: www.washingtonpost.com (consulted in June 2010)

Eyesight to the Blind

Emancipate yourselves from mental slavery.[20]

Two other examples of Moore's commitment to the study of racism are the "Taxi" episodes from *TV Nation* and *The Awful Truth*. In the first instance, Moore proved his theory of tacit bigotry by opposing convicted killer (and political candidate) Louis Bruno with one of the few leading black men in Hollywood (albeit, in the 1970s), the talented Yaphet Kotto (*Across 110th Street, Blue Collar, Alien*), on a search for a New York City cab. Almost all of the taxis first hailed by Kotto decided to stop for Bruno, a dangerous white man far behind him on the curb. When asked about it afterwards, the cabbies (who themselves had dark skin, coming from Middle-Eastern countries) obviously lied, claiming they first saw Bruno and that it was the sole reason why they had decided to picked him up in the first place. Again hosted by Rusty Cundieff, this reportage proved that many Manhattan cabbies are not color-blind. Although Cundieff still managed to catch a ride for two members of Run DMC at the end of the show.

The second episode of the "taxi experiment" came as a conceptual thread in one episode of the second season of *The Awful Truth*. In true reverse-discrimination fashion Moore posed as a driver who only took in the "colored folks" of Manhattan. The reactions ranged from disbelief to anger among the white customers when they were refused access on the basis of skin color (therefore becoming Yaphet Kotto for that brief moment, through a perverted twist of identification). This sketch is still probably one of the better known of the series and illustrates Moore's deep affection for this particularly unpopular cause among white people.

A few years later, while the trend of shooting black men for no reason was growing, Moore tackled the issue of racism on *The Awful Truth* one more time. In a segment entitled "Don't Shoot, It's Only a Wallet!" he gave his white audience another glimpse of what it is like for black people living in America. In this episode, he told us in a sarcastic way that being a police officer is not easy because being overworked can make one see things that are not there in reality. He went on to enumerate a series of "incidents" involving unmotivated shootings of African-Americans in those years. As it turned out, in various reported cases, the police "misidentified" a remote control, a hair clip, a kitchen spatula, a candy bar and a cell phone...for a gun, just because the handler had dark skin. He also reminded us of the Amadou Diallo case. Diallo was an immigrant who had recently

---

[20] Bob Marley, *Redemption Song*, from *Uprising*, Island/Tuff Gong, 1980

arrived from Liberia when the plain clothed N.Y.P.D. fired *forty-one times* at him for holding...a wallet. One of Moore's heroes, legendary singer-songwriter Bruce Springsteen, even commemorated the meaningful *fait divers* with his controversial song '41 Shots (American Skin)'.[21]

So to counter trigger-happy police officers walking the New York streets, Moore went to Harlem for a day. Standing on a sidewalk he offered a group of African-American men "Day-Glow Orange" wallets so that the police would not confuse it with anything bearing the resemblance of a gun, or at least they would not have this alibi to invoke whenever they happened to shoot for the wrong reasons. Moore encouraged passersby to hand-in their black and brown wallets, just to give them some form of protection against police bigotry. He also asked a black man to cover himself with fake rubber bullet wounds and play dead on the sidewalk, as if he had already been shot by a cop. He even asked another one to hide under a specially made garbage bag used to conceal black people whenever "law-enforcement" officers are around.

When the police did show up, he taught them the difference between a wallet and a gun with the help of a big graphic chart divided into two distinct images: a wallet and a gun (that he pointed to alternately with a ruler, in a very didactic and sarcastic way). The cops did not have to think too long to figure out what he was referring to with his spontaneous "happening" on a Harlem sidewalk. All they could do was stand there and grin...with a twitch in their eye and an itch in their finger.

Domestic Slave Labor

In the "Dixie Night" episode of *The Awful Truth* Moore explained how racism and exploitation have been distilled into the capitalist structure itself: with its minimum wage-jobs created to keep black and Hispanic people poor and, consequently, politically impotent. As a theme for the whole show, he explained to us how southern values, if not the confederated states themselves, had won the Civil War.[22] Apart from the fact that by then all American presidents of the last 50 years had originated from the South, we can see how slavery has been propagated in subtler ways than slave ownership, according to him. In this particular episode he even raised the Confederation flag over Times Square, a subversive act unto itself; especially if we consider that most

---

[21] *Bruce Springsteen & the E Street Band Live in New York City*, Columbia, 2000

[22] Moore even went as far as recreating a battle from the Civil War in order to commemorate the L.A. Riots: to know more read *Adventures in TV Nation*, "Reenacting the L.A. Riots," pp. 197-199

New Yorkers are allegedly more "liberal" than the rest of Americans, and that New York City is supposed to represent the idea of the American "melting pot." For this special celebration in honor of southern values winning over Yankee ones, Moore hired black people to stand handcuffed in the middle of Times Square and had them speak straight into the camera. One man says: "Hi. My name is Elliot Rosborough, I'm a Welfare-to-Work recipient, and I work for approximately 22 hours a week. I make $476 a month and I receive no benefits. Congratulations Confederacy! Take my ass back to the plantation." A second man explains that "I work for McDonald's for $5.25 an hour, no benefits," and that "the South has risen again in the 21st century."

So many testimonies and scientifically-based studies have revealed that skin color, much like gender and class, does have something to do with the kind of job you occupy and your integration into the United States economy.[23] It also obviously determines if you will catch a New York cab or not. Moore is out to understand prejudice in all its forms, and he is particularly interested in the effects that racist-based policies, conscious or unconscious, have on the socioeconomic status of individuals. To confirm this, just consider the thematic recurrence in his film work: *Roger & Me* ends with a black family being evicted on Christmas Eve because of corporate decisions and bad business ethics. *Bowling for Columbine* deals with White America's fear of black men, even relying on exploitative TV shows like *Cops* to make a point. *Fahrenheit 9/11* reveals information concerning the high-jacking of the 2000 elections at the expense of black constituents in a Florida county, and it illustrates how black soldiers abound in the army and are being used as cannon-fodder for the war in Iraq. In fact, when this last film was screened at a N.A.A.C.P. special event in July of 2004, African-American leaders received it with great enthusiasm. Finally, *Capitalism: A Love Story* ends with the victims of Katrina, mostly African-Americans and poor.

Buggery on Board

In one of the most elaborate and provocative *Awful Truth* episodes of the first season Moore tried to convince Conservatives that gay rights is good for them. He told Neocons in the audience (probably a minority)

---

[23] To know the details of these studies, consult the web page of the U.S. Bureau of Labor Statistics. There is a section concerning earnings by demographics.

that "The more gay men there are, the more women for you!"[24] He suggested they put their homophobic tendencies aside and try to see things the other way around: how it can benefit *them*, as conservatives. However, reality is still quite different than the humor presented on stage by Moore, as he is most certainly aware of. Many conservative and narrow-minded people would like to see a quick solution to the "Gay Question," even if it means to trample the Bill of Rights to carry out this solution. Moore put it clearly in his show: "Gay rights are the last frontier of civil rights in this country." Thus, the host of the *Awful Truth* decided to go preach some sanity in the land of Matthew Shepard's killers, down to the southern borders of the Divided States of America.

After telling us about the increasing rate in homophobic crimes and stricter sodomy laws in many southern states throughout the 1990s, Moore introduced "The *Awful Truth* Gay Team of Freedom Fighters," a dozen gays and lesbians on the road to spread some basic common sense to all those rednecks who still believe in medieval remedies. He and his fighters boarded an outrageously pink Winnebago and headed out for "Queen City, USA!" On the vehicle's sides, Moore had suggestive inscriptions describing the journey's subterranean intentions: "Sodom is For Lovers," "U.S. Out of My Anus," "If the Sodomobile is a-Rockin' Do not Come a-Knockin'," "Buggery on Board" and "Please Tailgate!," it bravely affirmed on dangerous grounds.

The first stop of the tour was in Topeca, Kansas, for an interview with a man who had been prosecuted under strict laws banning the act of sodomy. He told Moore about how he was forced to reveal private details of a homosexual encounter he had one night, and how the prosecutor humiliated him in the courtroom because of his sexual orientation. When the Freedom Fighters started being friendly and affectionate with each other on the front steps of the Court House, the man asked Moore: "Is there room for one more?," proving that no one can really stop the urge to love and be loved. Then, Moore went to confront one of the most vicious homophobic preachers the United States has ever known: Pastor Fred W. Phelps, a gung-ho Baptist who enjoys picketing at the funerals of people who died from AIDS. According to Phelps, God gave him the mandate to inject a "little sanity" and to spread "Bible truth" into that "insane orgy of homosexual propaganda and lies which exists in America today." Phelps chastised leaders of the homosexual community for making Shepard a "poster boy to promote their filth," and for "holding him up as somebody to emulate." As if this part of the rhetoric was not enough,

---

[24] Yet another example of this kind of reversed-psychology is in his book *Dude Where's My Country?* At Chapter 10: "How to Talk to Your Conservative Brother-in-law," pp. 183-201

the pastor also said to Moore with frustration: "He [Shepard] was not a good man. He is in hell now...You are like dogs eating your own vomit, wake up!" Moore answered calmly, "Yes, but they do that. My dog eats his own vomit," pointing to the fact that all tastes are in nature, defying the very notion of "normality" on national television.

Afterward, Moore invited his Freedom Fighters to join in on the "discussion" about freedom in America with the demented Phelps. The Sodomobile pulled over and out came a group of gay men determined to confront the preacher man, his family, and their homophobic friends. While Phelps repeated the same mantra against "fags" and "queers," the Sodomobile started rocking and shaking with the song 'Funky Beat', blasting from the RV radio. Revolted by what he imagined was happening inside the vehicle, Phelps had no choice but to retreat to his lair. There will be a second encounter between these two groups later in the segment.

Going back on the road Moore made sure to let us know (as a gag) that "These long days and nights of traveling offered nothing else than sodomy to pass the time." This is also the moment when the Sodomobile makes a stop at the intersection of three states where sodomy is illegal, and where homosexuals are persecuted with so-called "fag-drags:" Missouri, Arkansas, and Oklahoma. This part of the sequence ended with a freeze-frame picture of three half-naked men from the Gay Team making out on a historical monument, in a blasphemous snapshot that would offend any conservative sensibility. It said in postcard-fashion: "Greetings from Three Corners!" No doubt, this sketch is like a campy masterpiece that might as well have been directed by John Waters. Next, it was southbound to Pascagoula, Mississippi, in order to confront Republican Senator Trent Lott, a rabid conservative who sees homosexuality as "a disease like kleptomania," Moore said. After finding out that homophobic Lott was once a cheerleader, Moore organized a spectacle with gay cheerleaders who spell rhythmically the word "Q.U.E.E.R." in front of his home. Soon enough, the cops came to put an end to this political theater performed right there in the middle of arch conservative America.

With this segment, Moore wanted to shock Puritan sensibilities for whom sex is only used for procreating and keeping women prisoners in traditional and submissive roles. Moreover, this colorful and dynamic skit foreshadows the struggles that the country will be faced with in the future. Freedom of sexual orientation and rights of sexual minorities, freedom of a woman to choose (even after Roe v. Wade, if we can believe it), freedom in the bedroom and, most certainly, in light of the Patriot Act, and even under Obama, unfortunately, privacy issues in general.

Bitch Hunt

> And I continued to perform oral sex and then he pushed me away, kind of as he always did before he came, and then I stood up and I said...I care about you so much; I do not understand why you won't let me...make you come; it's important to me; I mean, it just does not feel complete, it does not seem right...[25]

While rotten-rich moguls like Turner were buying the country at an alarming rate; while people like Rennert were polluting the world with impunity; while civil rights were still being trampled on every day in the streets of big cities like Chicago, New York and Los Angeles; while homosexuals were getting murdered almost monthly in the South; the Republicans were once again diverting people's attention to the most ridiculous and inflated scandal in modern American history: the so-called "Zippergate Affair." This political melodrama originated from the sexual hang-ups of the Moral Majority, which are still determined by its Puritan heritage, a large constituency founded by Jerry Falwell in the late 1970s. The details concerning oral sex and the creepy fascination with Clinton's "cum stains" on Monica Lewinsky's navy blue dress are only some of the elements which are symptomatic of America's dislike of real sexual freedom (that is, beyond the false sexual freedom promulgated by pornography).

That being said, it seemed obvious even then that the impeachment trial was a travesty of the American judiciary apparatus. Anyone who remembered the Gary Hart/Donna Rice controversy which had happened back in 1988 knew the Clinton-Lewinsky Oral Office scandal was just another chapter in this sick book written by the American Far Right. It was not only a blow below the belt to the Democrats (no pun intended), but also a cheap attempt at removing Clinton from the White House and affecting the chances of any Democratic candidate to win the 2000 Election. And it sort of worked.

Everyone in Washington knows that sexual scandals have always played an intrinsic part of the American political life and landscape. These are as inextricable as the relationship between politics, money, and corruption is. Thus, on the very first episode of *The Awful Truth*, Michael Moore decided to tackle the *scandal du jour* in his own inimitable way. Before the segment started, he had warned his audience that a "puritan fever [is] sweeping the nation." He explained how Ken Starr, the infamous prosecutor responsible for Clinton's near-

---

[25] Excerpt from Monica Lewinsky's testimony as it appears in Kenneth Starr's *The Starr Report: The Official Report of the Independent Council's Investigation of the President*, Prima Lifestyles, 1998

impeachment, spent more than 50 million dollars to uncover what most adults already knew: that some middle-aged men have affairs with younger women (in his *Starr Report*, 500 pages of hardcore political porn). How ridiculous all of this sounds today in the post 9/11 world.

Being familiar with U.S. history, Moore decided to use a format which proved to be quite efficient in the early days of the colony (and in the post-WW II context): the witch-hunt. In this instance, he had to come up with a portable witch-hunt, much like a traveling "mosh pit," which was to be taken all over Capitol Hill to look for "fornicating Congressmen."

To conduct this cleansing of the sinners, Moore required the help of correspondent Jay Martel - disguised here as a pilgrim clergyman. They had brought along with them a group of hysterical and puritanical women to help them curse sex-loving politicians in Washington. First, they went after Ken Starr himself, who was just coming out of his home in the morning with a big cup of coffee in his hand, ready for another day of destroying the Union. He laughed at the portable witch-hunt and then proceeded to go do just that. Then, the hunt moved straight to Capitol Hill with the aim to inject some old-time religion sense into the folks up there (screaming such insults as "ejaculating whore mongers" at innocent bystanders and so on). The women for their part went around looking for a cheating senator, a libidinous Congressman, or anyone that could allow them to exercise their sexually repressive theater. After having touched the plaque on Newt Gingrich's office door, they started throwing fits on the Capitol's floor and speaking in tongues. As Moore put it in the sketch, "People got so turned on by the [Starr] Report that, even if they weren't having sex, they were sure thinking about it." In other words, petty politics had paved the way for total mass-titillation.

Moore then went on to have a chat with Congressman Bob Barr, one of Clinton's "impeachment trial managers." Barr told Moore that Clinton was "abusing" the Office, to which he replied that "[He] was not abusing the Office, he abused the *hallway down* the Office!" The Flint journalist also reminded the Congressman that in 1982 there had been a reported incident where he had licked off whipped cream from the breast of a young woman in public. Barr did not deny these allegations but told Moore that "People should not be persecuted for mistakes committed in the past," obviously not practicing what he was preaching right there on the Congress floor, day after day, for months on end. Right after his encounter with Barr, Moore went inside the House of the Judiciary Committee where discussions about oral sex kept dragging on and on. As he observed Starr doing his destructive work, Moore used a graphic-effect in post-production, morphing the former into a red-eye devil with his pornographic report catching on fire in front him. It is a wonderful TV moment which only digital software can produce. It is like the collage work on the advertising poster for *Fahrenheit 9/11*, where we see Moore holding hands with George W. Bush on the White House back lawn (instead of a Saudi prince), or like on the cover of *The Fahrenheit 9/11 Reader*, where he sits in a film theater casually sharing popcorn with the Commander-in-Thief, both watching a film that bashes the latter relentlessly.

Later in the segment, Martel walked down Washington streets accusing anyone in sight, coercing people into repentance and conveying the sense of randomness inherent to such kangaroo-court activities. The Puritan priest punished people right there on the street, even forcing one man to slip his head inside a small guillotine brought along by the *Awful Truth* grips. Moore finally admitted in voice-over that "Once you get it going, it kind of takes care of itself," referring to both the hysteria that followed the news of Clinton's affair with Lewinsky and the way a witch-hunt should be conducted to be effective. Essentially, it should be led in an arbitrary fashion...and then it should just snowball.

A Little Politics & A Little Sex

In light of the *disneyfication* of 42nd Street in the mid to late 1990s, Moore wanted to illustrate the hypocrisy of people like then Mayor Rudy Giuliani who claimed that sex stores are "unclean" for a city while having wild sexual affairs themselves (which most probably included wide paraphernalia of sexual products). This political double-standard regarding the commercialization of sexual products and accessories in NYC was legalized by a ruling which allowed for only 40% of sexual material to be sold on the shelves of Manhattan stores; while the other 60% had to be of "non-sexual nature" (which is ridiculous, since any deviant animist and fetishist will tell you that *most* objects can be used for sexual purposes and gratification). In failing to respect this bylaw, merchants could have face up accusations of gross indecency and even jail terms.[26] One storeowner decided to fight this ruling by bringing it to its logical extreme, and Moore was more than willing to help him out.

In one *Awful Truth* episode Moore christened a new store opening in honor of New York's "Number One Casanova." It was called "The Mayor Giuliani Gift Shop & Sex Emporium" and was configured as to ridicule a bureaucratic conception of human sexuality and natural urges. Inside, scantily clad women greeted customers and introduced

---

[26] To know more about this process of cleaning up Manhattan of the sex industry, read Todd Seavey's article "Erogenous Zones, New York porn shops say goodbye to Broadway," *Reason Magazine*, March 1997

them to a wide variety of Giuliani products. Moore was standing at the door, and welcomed customers by asking them if "Anyone [is] interested in politics here?" He also took the viewer around the shop with the help of a montage cut to a techno track. On one side of the Emporium was good wholesome tourist products, like ashtrays with a picture of the Empire State Building or mini-replicas of the Statue of Liberty; while on the other were smut products blessed with the effigy of Mayor Giuliani. In fact, the Emporium had it all: Giuliani-approved blow-up dolls; Giuliani vibrators; Giuliani T-shirts which said 'Tough Enough for Love - Tough Enough for Gay Sex?', Giuliani butt-plugs, and of course Giuliani clitoral stimulators. As Moore puts it at the end of the segment, "It's sometimes hard to know where the Giuliani stuff stops and where the sex begins," evoking the close ties which exists (and will always exist) between politics, power and sexual repression.

Teen Sniper School

Another correlation which must be made if one wishes to understand the American psyche, just as much as the one between politics and sexuality, is the existing link between sexuality and violence. This seems to be at the heart of the American social problem. Moore has never really touched upon it, because for him violence is not born out of sexual repression or the Protestant ethos, but out of fear, as we shall see in the analysis of *Bowling for Columbine*. Americans are violent because they are afraid, according to him. This is one of the reasons why so many choose to be armed. Actually, Second Amendment defenders say they are afraid for their children. They say they carry guns because they want to protect, not only their lives, but their virtue as well (in a neoliberal society which seems to be eroding by the minute). The sad irony of this attitude is that, in the process of wanting to protect your child by owning a gun, you also increase the chances that he or she will be killed by that very same gun. The extension of this flawed logic would be to fully equip your child with guns and ammunitions, according to *The Awful Truth* creators.

Presented as a mock-infomercial, the "Teen Sniper School" segment was an extremely controversial sketch and one of the two preliminary attempts at understanding a terrifying phenomenon such as high school shootings. According to the *Washington Post*, Bravo! Network pulled this segment out when it aired the episode of *The Awful Truth* after the Columbine massacre.[27] In what concerns us, the satire foreshadowed Moore's masterpiece *Bowling for Columbine*, with its

---

[27] Lisa de Moraes, " Bravo! Pulls Gun Segment From Michael Moore Show," *The Washington Post*, June 10, 1999

sarcastic use of voice-over and shocking images of children handling firearms. This is an instance where Moore created a *mise en scène* to depict children behaving like disturbed American adults. There is one scene where we see a group of them practicing their aim with semi-automatic weapons at a firing range. Even if they are not really firing their weapons, it is still a scary sight to behold; considering that the fictional setting established by Moore only re-enacts what is really happening outside of our TV screens, in schools all over the United States. For him, to raise the issue in satirical form is the best way to recognize that there is a problem.

In this segment he tells us in voice-over that, "This institution is more than just a total immersion course in firearms proficiency, it's also fun," upon which we see a group of kids "fishing" by firing their handgun in a pond and having humiliating contests that punishes the "loser." More shocking is the following part of the sequence which shows a fictitious child-sniper shooting a group of younger children playing in a field. We hear a shot and see one of them fall to the ground, while the others run for cover. It is a dramatic moment treated with a vicious sense of the understatement. The aim is to provoke and shock an audience that has been numbed by TV violence for the last forty years, and it surely achieved what it set out to do in this particular number. Moore continued to provoke thoughts by emphasizing the perverted nature of a child operating a gun. We were shown a young teenager disguised as a militiaman and standing with an automatic weapon in a high school cafeteria. He was aiming at multiple targets representing various student types. On the voice-over, Moore asked candidly: "Who do you take out first? the quarterback? the popular girl? or the honor student? Well, the quarterback of course, before he tackles you! Then, take your time and clear the rest of the cafeteria." The teen then started shooting targets laid out across the room, blowing things to smithereens. Right after this violent eruption of violence, Moore abruptly cut to an interview with Charlton Heston, the spokesperson for the National Rifle Association, where he claims that training children for safer weapon manipulation is a "good thing."

Next in the sequence we were presented with some kids who were attending the fictitious Teen Sniper School. One little girl said to the camera: "My brother better watch out when I get home!," while another kid proudly claimed that "I'm going to be on TV for sure." Moore's voice-over explained that accidents are [now] being avoided because "Students have to wait at least five weeks after their most recent incident of animal torture before they can enroll." The sketch closed in a grotesque climax where a group of children is bathing in their own blood after a (mock) shoot-out. The very last shot is a close-up of a small infant awkwardly holding up a gun to her face in freeze frame, while the sound of a shot is being heard and it quickly cuts to black.

Up front, no one is lead to believe that this should be interpreted as being funny, even for the biggest moron of this world. In many ways, this sketch proved that sometimes only a satirical mode of discourse can get the job done. In this particular scenario, we were witnessing a form of inverted propaganda fighting against the mishandling of the Second Amendment by private interest groups like the National Rifle Association. Moore and his crew brought us to a place where our worst nightmares have come true. He presented a world where children have easy access to guns and used them on each other, and where schools have become a battleground because of certain socioeconomic realities. He often relies on these *grand-guignol* re-enactments to make us think about the ultimate consequences of a flawed understanding of the Bill of Rights. In the end, he tells us that these claims of individual freedom must also come with social responsibilities. It is sort of a package deal in any civilized society, but seemingly not in the United States.

Feel My Heat

In the second season of *The Awful Truth*, Moore returned to the topic of gun-control, but this time he let filmmaker Jay Martel, a subversive kindred-spirit of his, do the work. Very much like Moore, Martel uses a specific tone to convey his humanist point-of-view on the world. The journalist has a particularly effective method to get the reactions he wants from people that he interviews. Most of the time, he just plays dumb and lets them talk, since he knows that it is the editing which will bring out the true essence of the filmed interaction in the end. However, Martel is also a natural actor; something that he proved in the aforementioned episode about the witch-hunt. The reportage entitled "Gun Crazy" also relies on a mascot to satirize America's fascination with self-defense, self-righteousness and gun violence. The mascot concocted by Moore, Martel and associates was a big purple .38 caliber revolver bearing a giant Mark Twain mustache which hung from both sides of its barrel/nose (obviously targeted at children in a sinister way).

Once again, the episode was a precursor to *Bowling for Columbine*, insofar as it tried to get a point across about gun control by relying on dark humor and disturbing imagery. It began with a quick montage rhythmically cut to the 'Star Spangled Banner', harmonious with the sounds of various guns fired at different pitches. Then, Martel's voice-over narration explained the situation over the images of various armed Americans, shooting left and right with different types of guns.

> Martel (v.o.):
> "As long as we've been Americans, we've loved our guns. But sometimes, the gun-haters have tried to take them away. That's when the National Rifle Association, the organization headed by Charlton Heston, takes a firm stand…"

It cut to a shot of Heston at a N.R.A. meeting, victoriously hollering "Guns!" while members of his association applaud and cheer in the background.

> Martel (v.o.):
> "Thanks to the N.R.A., we are well protected from…gun-control."

We cut back to the same shot of Heston but this time saying "Thank you!" to his fellows members, and then to another montage of recent high school shootings, including Columbine. "But now the stakes are higher," Martel told us, "Now kids are using guns to shoot…kids." While he went on to discuss the case of six year-old Kayla Rolland, a first grader who had just been shot by another six year-old classmate in Flint (read the section pertaining to *Bowling for Columbine*), the editing repeated the previous shot of Heston at the N.R.A. convention saying "Thank you!" - with applause and cheers to support his right to bear arms. Stylistically speaking, this is an example of associative montage. This type of editing has to do with a certain organizational logic where the juxtaposition of different shots from various sources, supplemented by the ironic "voice of God" narration and sound bridges, help to create a third level of meaning in the viewer's mind. It basically orients the reading of the images for the viewer.

> Martel (v.o.):
> "But once more, the NRA has the answers…"

In the next sequence we were shown a television-ad sponsored by the N.R.A., where its official mascot Eddie Eagle warned a group of grade school kids about guns. Eddie told them that if they should ever get near one, they have to "Stop! Do not touch! Leave the area!" and "Tell an adult!" Martel wondered out loud on the narration: "It seems like Eddie Eagle was not dealing with the real issues. Eddie thinks that all you have to do is to tell kids to walk away whenever they see a gun and everything will be okay. But in a country with 250 million guns, where are they supposed to walk to?"

Here, while the grade school kids say goodbye to the N.R.A. mascot, the editing includes stock footage of hunters shooting down birds, as if they were shooting Eddie himself. Soon after this visual joke, we saw Martel and Pete singing along with a group of children in a classroom. The tone of the song emphasized the ludicrous aspect of the N.R.A. trying to tell kids that guns are bad. With reverse-psychology tactics, the *Awful Truth* provocateurs winded-up singing that guns are good:

> *Pistol Pete, Pistol Pete,*
> *I'm a son-of-a-gun who's really neat!*
> *Pistol Pete, Pistol Pete,*
> *Pull my trigger and feel my heat!*

Pete then asked the children in the classroom: "Who wants to show me they know how to beg for their lives?" And, in typical western outlaw fashion, said to one little girl: 'How about you?" upon which we saw her quickly get up from her seat and plea "Do not shoot me!" A few seconds later, a group of children is exercising with Pistol Pete and Martel. They hung from monkey bars and Pete "shot" them down with one giant bullet. Martel explained that Pete was a "big hit" with the kids, and that the time had come to take him on the road. First, they went to Las Vegas, home of the world's largest gun show. As it is usually the case with Moore and his team of correspondents, it represented an intrusive act, the infiltration of an event which was endorsed and sponsored by corporations or powerful pro-gun associations. Inside the convention, Pete was ecstatic. He screamed "I'm home!" to the visitors. In relation to the mascot, one man told Martel "This is a good idea, cos' it gives kids something to relate to. A gun is not any different than a typewriter or anything else, it's just a *tool*."

All the while, other conventioneers were also enjoying Pete's presence. Some of them hugged him and even had their pictures taken with him. Actually, no one seem to question his presence nor meaning in this particular context.

Later, Martel and Pete stopped by the Hi-Point kiosk at the convention. As chance (or research) would have it, Hi-Point is the company which manufactured the guns that were used by the two teenagers who shot-out Columbine. Three sales representatives there tried to convince Martel that firearms can be safer with the help of the new polymer locks available on the market. For one of these men, this piece of plastic proved that there was no real reason to have better gun-control laws.

Soon after Pete's presence was detected as being subversive by security, and both *Awful Truth* provocateurs were thrown out of the building. Outside the main door, the mascot lamented: "You would not do this to Eddie Eagle! I'm a tool! Like a Xerox machine or a waffle-iron!" Next thing we knew, Martel and Pete headed out to the N.R.A.

headquarters. There, they showed a P.R. man excerpts from a video pertaining to bullet-damage, and this one admitted that there [is] a "serious problem with violence in this country." Still he did not want to acknowledge that guns played a huge part in it. Martel even brought a clinical plate with a blood-soaked sponge where one could practice the art of removing slugs from scar tissue...When the man finally had enough and fled back inside the N.R.A. bunker, the *Awful Truth* trouble-makers followed him inside, tailgating him in Moore-fashion. They were rapidly told to leave the building by security personnel, and this is when Pete rightly claimed: "It is my home here!"

Discouraged by this non-responsive attitude from the N.R.A., Martel then suggested they both go up to Capitol Hill to have a talk with Congressman John Dingell, a powerful friend of the aforementioned association; a man who had been "killing" gun-control bills on the Senate floor for years. Inside Congress they created quite a commotion with Dingell's staff running for cover, dismayed at the Dada coup being perpetrated on them by Martel and his purple friend. Both of them were once more evicted from the building by security, and they decided then to return to the children to sing happily together that "Pistol Pete is not a bad guy," that "(he)'s just a *tool*," and that "(he) does not kill people, but that "people killed people..." In the end we learned that, in the 10 weeks following Kayla Rolland's death, 936 children were killed with a handgun in the United States. We understand that this is not a joke, but a tragic fact that should (but will not) make gun-lovers of America seriously think about the implications of what they are defending.

Two Sure Things: Death & Texas

Along with gun control, the death penalty, euthanasia, and abortion are some of the most controversial issues in America today. These divide the country in half and underline the ideological schism existing between liberal and neoconservative agendas. In the most "electrifying" episodes of his second TV series, Moore and his crew set up a contest to see which one of the Bush brothers was the meanest when it came down to the death penalty. At that time George W. was Governor of Texas, while his younger brother, Jeb, was Governor of Florida. Actually, these two states still have a reputation for having the toughest laws concerning the death penalty, as well as having the highest rate of executing convicts. Once again, Moore required the help of Jay Martel to travel south and report back on any instances of killing killers.

> Martel (v.o.):
> "Here in America, we've always had a soft spot for violence; whether it is football, baseball, hockey or…the death penalty. Me, I've never been a big fan of the death penalty, but it was getting so popular that I wanted to find out more."

On a map of the States different states are "popping-up" from having received electric shocks: "Turns out that states all over the country are executing prisoners like crazy…and why not?" There is then a montage of archival footage of Clinton, Bush and Reagan stating their support for the death penalty, with a big rowdy cheer after Reagan says it gruesomely: "*The death penalty!*"

> Martel (v.o.):
> "Politicians who support the death penalty are elected, like George W. Bush of Texas and Jeb Bush of Florida; two brothers who are going at it, *mano e mano*. Who's the toughest Bush? Let's take a look."

Moore and his team relied once more on the game show aesthetics to subvert meaning and to generate empathy from the viewer by offering him/her a recognizable format. We are shown a score board with a graphic representing the Bush brothers and the title of this silly, inhuman contest: "Death Penalty 2000."

> W.W.E.-type announcer (v.o.):
> "Since taking office, big brother George has executed more prisoners than any governor in history (*116 executions*). And with no public defender system and a limited appeal process, we understand why they say: There are only two sure things in life: Death and *Texas*."

This previous pun is then cut with a clip from a press conference where W. was being his usual moronic and inarticulate self: "If you're asking me whether or not I feel like, that everybody who's been executed is guilty of the crime to wish they, to wish they, uh, to, uh, to wish they've been made convicted of, uh, my answer is 'yes.'"

> W.W.E.-type announcer (v.o.):
> "But here comes Florida! When Jeb took office, Florida had only executed a dismal 7 prisoners in 3 years. The electric chair, fan favorite Old Sparky, was experiencing one mishap after another…"

While the lowbrow and bombastic voice-over is still ranting on, we are shown television news reports of sloppy executions where inmates caught on fire or were only "half-baked" by the death chair.

> W.W.E.-type announcer (v.o.):
> "Jeb fixed the chair and brought-in a lethal injection machine, along with a confidence that Florida could challenge Texas for the title."

There is a short clip of Jeb Bush being apologetic with the media concerning the inefficiency of Florida's system.

> Jeb Bush:
> We're ready, I mean, *there's no problem with the chair* or anything like that. *We're ready to go.*

But in comes Martel driving a convertible which has a plastic pink flamingo on the back seat. He explained that he too "was ready to go."

> Martel (v.o.):
> "Florida was about to execute their first inmate of the year and I was not going to miss it. The day before the big execution, I stopped by the State Capitol to meet some pro-death penalty legislators... Star members of Jeb's team."

After Jay has penetrated Florida's House of Representatives, the editing cut back to the interview with Senator Victor Crist.

> Martel:
> Texas has a great program; they're doing really well with the death penalty. Do you think Florida can learn anything from them?

> Crist:
> I do not see any reason why Florida couldn't execute two inmates a month. *If Texas can, why can't we?*

A few seconds later, Jay interviews Randy Ball, another strong advocate of the death penalty within the "House of Bush."

> Martel:
> Do you have any nostalgia for Old Sparky? Do you think that lethal injections may be letting these guys off a little too easy?

> Ball:
> It *is* letting them off a little too easy. There's something *aesthetically appealing* to see someone have a quick sudden death. That seems more like punishment than quietly and gently drifting off into slumber land.

With a whimsical music playing in the background, Martel attended his first "big home opener," as he called it: the well-publicized execution of convicted killer Terry Sims. The wacky *Awful Truth* correspondent was dressed up as a baseball fan and pretended he was rooting for the executioner.

> Martel (v.o.):
> "Florida officials really go the extra mile. They even wrote off separate sections for opponents and fans."

While everyone was anticipating the prison's siren to confirm Sims had indeed "been punished," Martel had a one-on-one interview with a reporter from a local TV station in Orlando. This one explained with a white chalk on a blackboard that "If you get rid of all those lawyers who are filing for all those frivolous appeals, you are going to send more people to the chair and to the gas chamber." Over a military drum-roll, Martel asked him if Florida had a chance to "keep up" with Texas. The reporter replied, "Well, there's the big brother-little brother rivalry, but *the overwhelming majority* of people in Florida support capital punishment and they want to see *a lot of people* put to death." Martel, astonished at the man's coldness, acted as though he was in agreement with him: "Yeah," he replied in a laconic way. An uncomfortable silence sustained by the shot's length, leads to Martel standing with two spectators in the middle of a field, holding a small Florida flag, a coffee, and a donut, as if he was Homer Simpson at a baseball game. When we heard the siren signaling Sim's death, he started clapping and cheering: "Alright! It's over. One for Florida!" The sarcasm of this scene is disturbing because it makes us realize that executions, like everything else, are a spectacle in this culture. We can see how anything can become a "sporting event" like in ancient times, even the death of a fellow citizen who may have been eventually exonerated from the crimes he/she was accused of in the first place.

At another point in the sketch Jeb Bush is coming down the stairs of a luxurious reception hall, apparently on his way to give a press conference regarding Sim's execution, and Martel does not wait and jumps in to confront him face to face.

Martel:
Governor Bush, hi! I'm a big fan of Florida. I just wanted to know: Your brother George has had a lot of…

Jeb Bush:
Hey…Wait with the others for the press conference. I'll talk to you in a second, ok?

Martel:
No, but I just had to tell you…

Jeb Bush:
Can you move out of the way?

Martel:
No, sir… George has had a lot of success with the… death penalty over in Texas…

Bodyguards came in and carried Martel down the hall, but he was still screaming at Bush from afar. He is then body searched and questioned by Bush's security. Incredibly enough he is allowed to go back to the press conference afterward. There, he confronts the Republican governor for a second time.

Martel:
Hey, Governor Bush? I'm telling you, if you just get rid of the public defender system, you'd be whooping Texas…

Jeb Bush:
Chill out, man. Just chill out!

Martel:
I'm chillin'…I just want to help you win. George is kicking your ass, sir.

The agent provocateur is again led outside by Bush's security.

Martel (*on his way out*):
I mean, are you jealous? I mean, he's a hundred prisoners ahead of you!

Outside, Jay keeps talking to one of the security guard, all in good spirit.

Martel:
I mean, the coach gets fired if a team does not do well... And Florida is really hurting' right now... I'm hoping that tomorrow things will start moving along...

He is dragged outside of the main building into the parking lot, body-searched once more, and then pushed into a police car.

Martel:
You know, I *am* just a fan. I really just wanted to...uh, ya' know...The way you guys are treating me... I just want to go root for the state of Texas now...

In the car, he speaks directly to the viewer.

Martel:
That does it, man. I'm a Texas fan now.

In the next shot, we see him driving a pickup truck to Huntsville, Texas. He has a cowboy hat and plays the tough Texan with *savoir faire*. We soon learn that Huntsville [is] a place known for executing more inmates than any other in America. Walking through the prison graveyard, he tells us that this town took great pride in building a monument for every W. victory (i.e. a cross for every execution), and that it was "serious about the game," contrary to Florida... He then interviews a spokesperson from the Texas Department of Criminal Justice who winds up telling him: "We had an execution on Tuesday, Wednesday and Friday of last week, and then we are going to have one on Monday, Tuesday and Thursday of this week." Jay asks the man if "This is a new record?" This former answers "Yeah, it's a lot." Now we understand why Junior was Number One in his home state. People really appreciate a man of action down there.

One of the aforementioned executions was of Karla Faye Tucker, the first woman to be put to death in over a century in the United States. The editing showed us a series of shots of jubilating citizens in favor of the death penalty. Some were holding signs on which it was written: "Bye Bye Karla Faye" or "Forget Injection, Use a Pickax" or "Kill the Bitch Anyway!" Martel claims to know the reason why Texas is Number One: "It is because of the fans," he says sardonically. We then meet yet another supporter of the death penalty at the execution of Billy Hughes. It is a woman who says that "It is *awesome* to know that a man is actually being put to death, I mean, justice [is] being served and you're grateful for that, and you're glad that we have a system that allows for this..." Of course, there is indeed a system, but how sure are we regarding its accuracy and efficiency in deterring criminal behavior? Considering Huntsville's record, it seems like this system of killing killers is not working at all, the show tells us.

Jay stands now with a crowd of supporters who are respectful of the "Death Penalty Pre-Game Prayer." The prayer is brief and goes like this: "Let's hope that *this* gets done properly. Amen." The *Awful Truth* correspondent punctuates it by exclaiming out loud: "Alright! It's execution time!" Next thing we know he is holding a sign that says "Go George!" and supporters do not yet suspect that he is a liberal infiltrator. At least, not until he brings down a marching band and a couple of cheerleaders with a scoreboard that pits George against his brother Jeb! As the satirical piece concludes, the announcer's voice describes the pre-execution energy found in Texas.

> W.W.E.-type announcer (v.o.):
> "The excitement built as the killing hour approach. Every breath was held in anticipation. The prisoner was strapped to the gurney and a needle was inserted into his arm. He coughed once and at 6:18 p.m. was declared dead…George W. Bush had done it again: Execution number 117."

There is then stock footage of people getting hanged or shot in the head, followed by shots of W. laughing like a dim-wit and tripping over the patterned floor of a conference room.

> W.W.E.-type announcer (v.o.):
> "In the annals of execution history, the Governor [*George W. Bush*] stands as a great champion. And even though the discoveries of innocent people on death row caused weaker or more timid men to abandon the death penalty, deep in the heart of Texas, a true winner continues unbound. Not for glory, not for truth or justice, but for the love of the game."

Out for Trout

Another theme dear to Moore is the idea of personal freedom versus the rules of a police state; subjects that he will revisit in the post 9/11 world. In the "Stop & Frisk Night" episode of *The Awful Truth*, Moore had a report on Nevada County, California, which could be seen as a fine example of micro-totalitarianism within the United States territory. In this mainly white and rich community, which boasts for being the "Hometown of the Constitutional Parade," there is no real apparent justice for the poor. We learned through Anne and Michael Moore's investigation that Nevada County forced more than 900 people into a guilty plea without ever allowing them a fair trial. Moore's sister, who had previously worked as a public defender for the minority of poor people in that community, noticed that only one out of nine hundred people arrested ever went to trial. She blew the whistle on this dysfunctional use of the law apparatus and lost her job for it. From all of this other investigations were launched and the Moores and their team of researchers unveiled once gain the awful truth about a certain America: low-income individuals were actually railroaded into jail. As one county lawyer puts it in the segment: "There are a lot of people in jail right now who should not be there right now..."

According to the 6th Amendment of the Bill of Rights, every American citizen has a right to be defended by an attorney-at-law and has a right to a fair trial, but the Nevada County Courthouse was "mysteriously empty," as Moore remarked on the voice-over. Empty because the low-income people who had been arrested never actually saw the color of the walls of the trial room. No judges, no juries, no public defenders, no district attorneys, no one in sight... Another lawyer at the Public Defender's Office claimed that he went to trial two or three times in the last 5 years. In most instances, the accused was "suggested" (i.e. coerced) into making a quick "pre-trial deal" in order to avoid a harsh sentence (i.e. even before a jury could hear the testimonies or see any evidence). He was judged guilty by class-association, if not by class-suspicion. In a first case, Moore presents Brian Corin, father of five and victim of the Public Defender's Office. Corin was told that if he did not make a deal, he would go to jail for 16 years. Under pressure, the man was obviously going to sign along the dotted line. Fortunately, a clause allowed him to prove his innocence against his public defender's will. The second case that Moore got interested in concerned Peter Mazon, a man who had been accused of killing his baby. The infant had actually died from suffocation resulting from a medical condition, and the way the police reacted to his grief was to accuse him of having participated in his death. Since Mazon couldn't afford an attorney, he was assigned a "defender" instead. Like Corin, Mazon was coerced into pleading guilty not only because he was poor but also because county officials wanted to take a permanent vacation at the expense of justice.

Another employee of the County Office reported that the accused were "huddled through reports like cattle." They weren't seeing their attorney or were simply told that a deal with the D.A. had already been made for them. Once in court the accused were immediately sentenced and sent to jail without what we usually consider normal standard procedures. As it turned out, every public defender, judge, and administrator was too busy fishing on those days of trial... Moore decided to make a point about this legal system by cutting the intermediary and sentencing everyone in town to jail. He read the townspeople their rights, had a banner trailing behind a helicopter telling them to go to jail, he went to public places and on local radio and television stations to tell people that they were under arrest. He also had pre-plea bargains signed by hundreds of County residents... even infants and dogs, and distributed prison jump-suits to everyone passing on the street; all in a great awareness-raising operation. In one last absurd moment, Moore even went to the Public Defender's Office with a book of pictures of various penal institutions. He met up with a County judge and made him choose the best prison for his next guilty plea. Amazingly enough, even with a camera in his face, the judge selected his ideal prison with a smirk on his face. Obviously, he was already gone fishing in his small but degenerate mind.[28]

Help the Dead Guy

The episode entitled "Help the Dead Guy" was a conceptual follow-up to the previous one. It also came in the second season of *The Awful Truth*, perhaps the strongest of all of Michael Moore's television work. As a matter-of-fact, there is a lot of thematic consistency throughout both series. This leads us to believe that Moore is an artist with a very specific set of preoccupations and particular formal means of exploring them. The theme for this episode was inspired by the story of a man who died while riding the New York subway. It had taken 5 hours before someone noticed his death and reported it to the authorities. The incident made a small column in the paper on the following day, and it got Moore to think about the notion of empathy and its absence in American culture. As a national reality check, Moore decided to pit America against England and Canada, the two other countries where the show was being aired, to see which one would be more empathetic and more civilized when it came to respecting human life and dignity. In the show's direction, Moore had three actors playing dead people on the streets of Manhattan, Toronto, and London, late at night. In every one of these cities there was a candid camera set up to observe people's behavior as they walked by and, most of the time, ignored the fictitious dead guy. In the end, a woman from Toronto won the contest when she came to help the "Dead Canadian Guy." She received a medal from *The*

---

[28] Luckily, the Nevada County public defender system has been subjected to reform since this segment was aired in 1999. For more information, read Alan Maimon article "Panel Endorses Limiting Public Defender Cases," *Las Vegas Review Journal*, July 25, 2007

Awful Truth team and Moore took that as an opportunity to end the show with a rendition of the Canadian national anthem.

Republican Solutions

The main question asked by Moore in this next *Awful Truth* episode was: "How do you get rid of the 600,000 homeless people in America?" (It is probably more as you read these lines.) Moore had a special way to deal with this "Republican problem" and to get these homeless people out of public view. For the challenge "Out of Sight/ Out of Mind," he decided to put his three best correspondents on the case. First, correspondent Karen Duffy met a homeless woman who had already learned how to survive by sleeping in her car, inside bus and train stations, and in New York's subterranean transit system. She explained how she had found the best deal in town: a $30 monthly storage space at Manhattan Mini-Storage. There in that narrow space made for objects, she found shelter and warmth on cold winter nights, without having to worry about being evicted the morning after. Later in the episode, Duffy interviewed a member of the City Council, a Republican, and proposed the homeless woman's idea to him.

> Karen Duffy:
> At Manhattan Mini-Storage, you can get a storage room for 30 dollars a month. Then, rather than spending 130 million dollars on those 25,000 homeless in New York, we can put them in Manhattan Mini-Storage for 30 dollars a month...

The Republican does a double-take. He wants to be sure he heard Karen well.

> City Council Member:
> Where?

> Karen Duffy:
> At Manhattan Mini-Storage. It's a *private sector solution* for a *public sector problem*...

Following this strange interview Duffy invited a dozen homeless people in a storage space and asked them if they appreciated the concept. Assuming that if you do not have any roof over your head any type of shelter would be considered a good one, they all seemed to appreciate the idea (if only in support of the satire). She then called an interior designer to jazz up the place and eventually they all gathered to chat and sip exotic cocktails. At the end of her reportage, she told us:

"It was a great deal. The homeless were safely stored away. Just the way we like them: *out of sight and out of mind.*"

Later in the show, it was up to correspondent Jay Martel to find a proposal to solve the New York homelessness issue. In a back alley of Manhattan's Lower West Side, he interviewed a young black woman who called herself Midnight. She had been sleeping on the streets for 5 years before the show started airing. Martel explained that in Holland the government offers its homeless population weatherproof mini-shelters to make sure that they sleep safely at night (a basic human right). According to Martel, the best thing to do was to actually "crate and ship" the American homeless people into more "homeless-friendly countries." He asked Midnight to penetrate a huge crate that he had filled with small Styrofoam peanuts, gave her a few sandwiches for the road and closed the lid on her. He told her: "Alright Midnight, next thing you know you will be sniffing tulips and dodging windmills..." She said goodbye to the camera, and then a FedEx employee came to scan the crate and took it away (while corny island music played on the soundtrack to suggest exoticism).

The last proposition found correspondent Ben Hamper (*Roger & Me*) telling the viewer that a good way to get rid of homeless people is to either use large garbage cans or the spacious trunks of cars parked on the curb at night. He asked one homeless man if he was comfortable in the trunk of a large American-made car. As the man answered in the positive and yawned loudly, Hamper closed the hatch on him and said to the camera: "Snug as a bug in a rug." After all of this, Moore decided to conclude the episode by having picture cutouts of some of the homeless people seen in the sketch on advertising panels in Times Square.

Once again, he perverted the usual iconography of American sponsorship which usually requires images of famous, wealthy, healthy, and/or young people for corporate endorsement. One may get offended at the tone of this sketch, but again, it would be to ignore the redeeming values of Juvenalian satire.[29] Moore is using sordid humor in order to make us think about the seriousness of these issues. We catch ourselves saying: "Hey, I should not really be laughing at this," which is at least a first step toward self-analysis and introspection, two things Americans are desperately in need of today. This is also a sure way to make us think about the reasons why we should not be laughing at other people's misery in the first place, which is a first concrete step towards real empathy.

---

[29] Refers to "A bitter and ironic criticism of contemporary persons and institutions that is filled with personal and invective, angry moral indignation, and pessimism. "(*Encyclopedia Britannica*)

Kill the Sick

> My conscience started bothering me. It does that from time to time.[30]

There exists a precursor to Michael Moore's "horror" film *Sicko* (2007). In one *Awful Truth* episode from the first season, after reminding us that 43 million Americans lived without health insurance, he criticized the concept of "Work Care" put forth by some executives at the Jamaica Hospital in Queens, New York, by opening up his very own guerilla hospital. The idea behind this program was to have patients who had been treated and who did not have any insurance or money to work for the hospital as a way to pay back their medical bill. To illustrate the inhumanity of this loony right-wing concept, Moore picked up individuals in need of treatment from the street and, in exchange for a professional consultation with a certified M.D., made them work for their bill.

One pregnant woman suffering from laryngitis had to iron Moore's pants, while another was asked to peel potatoes for the emergency staff's meal. One patient who could barely walk had to fix a pothole in the parking lot, and another one, walking with crutches, was forced to repair the *Awful Truth* ambulance. Again this is meant to provoke the viewer and to ask serious questions about a certain ideological position; something that will eventually become the cornerstone of *Sicko*.

In another episode from the same series a spectator from the audience screamed that HMOs (Health Maintenance Organizations) are "pure evil" and Moore started explaining to his viewers that someone had suggested that "It is better to kill the sick than to heal them." A sinister concept probably already implemented by the Nazis in the 1930s, when they "neutralized" people with diseases and disabilities to "purify the social body" of the German nation. After showing us stock footage of old black and white movies where actors die in histrionic fashion, and reminding us that one day death comes to us all, Moore introduced 34 year-old Chris Donahue from the state of Florida. Chris was a father of two and suffering from extreme diabetes. We learn in the segment that he is desperately in need of a pancreas transplant or else he would die. Even if he had paid his HMO for 7 years (i.e. for full coverage), it denied his claim and refused to pay for an essential transplant. Ironically enough, the company in question is called "Humana..."

According to this corporation, Chris was not covered as far as vital organ transplants were concerned. There were two conflicting clauses

---

[30] Michael Moore in *The Awful Truth*, First season, 1999

in his contract with Humana. On the one hand, the policy was covering all problems related to his diabetes; on the other, it stated that it did not cover pancreas transplants. Needless to point to the one the corporation decided to honor. In the meantime, the man was worrying about his kids, who could have become fatherless at any moment. This was no joke but a matter of life and death. Moore just had to fight the bureaucracy (and greed) that was going to stop Chris from having a necessary operation. As a way to further contextualize the story, Moore explained that in 1997 Humana had revenues of over 8 billion dollars. Its chairperson, David Jones, was getting paid 4 million dollars plus stock options while people like Chris had to beg a few thousand dollars to save their lives. According to Moore, the company had a reputation for rewarding employees who denied coverage to their clients, and it was rewarding even more generously doctors who delayed or withheld care. These unethical practices have since then been confirmed by Linda Peeno in *Sicko*, wherein she explained that herself, as a medical reviewer, was richly rewarded for denying coverage to needy, dying patients. Moore also told us that the salaries and stock options of Humana's top five executives totaled over 28 million dollars that year. Enough to pay for 473 pancreases transplants…The question begged to be asked: Who's really sick here?

Under Moore's suggestion, Chris played like he was already dead. He went to the *Palm Beach Post* to place his own obituary in the paper. "Cause of death?" the typist asked him, "[He] died because of the lack of quality care from his HMO, Humana," he answered calmly. Then Moore and Chris met with the then Head of Worldwide Public Relations for Humana, Greg Donaldson. The latter told them that the executive-brass decided to postpone the interview, but that he was personally willing to look into the case (i.e. later on in the show). But Moore insisted by reminding him that Chris could die at any moment. Donaldson's hands were obviously tied and he suggested they both came back later, as if this made any sense under the circumstances. Moore then brought out the heavy-artillery… He asked the man to help him choose a coffin for Chris in a funeral home brochure: "What do you say, mahogany or oak? I prefer the oak myself," he said to the man. Moore followed him around like a leech, pestering him.

Many times Donaldson showed him the door, but Moore was adamant and refused to leave. He told Donaldson: "Everyday that goes by, while you are investigating the facts, is one day closer to his funeral." The man tried to stay emotionless, like a good corporate robot, but could barely make it. On the soundtrack, Moore used Rossini's 'Thieving Magpie' while we saw him tailgating relentlessly Humana's representative inside the headquarters' hallways and main lobby. Chris even showed Donaldson his T-shirt on which it was written: "*I signed with Humana and all I got was this lousy T-shirt…but no pancreas.*" Moore warned Donaldson once more: "We're not going to stop until you guys let him live. It's that simple. We're going to be all over you, man." Then, he grabbed his right hand in order to shake it and looked into the camera and said: "This is Greg Donaldson (...), he'll be with us all season here on *The Awful Truth*...We'll check back with you from week to week to see how you're doing checking the facts, and maybe Chris will still be alive by the end of our series."

Later, Moore and Donahue were standing in Humana's lobby handing-out invitations to employees. An exasperated Donaldson further pleaded with Moore, "As a courtesy to us, leave." Moore retorted loudly, "As a courtesy to *you*?" Donaldson reasserts, "Yes. This is just disruptive." Moore finally nailed him with "As a courtesy to *me*, why do not you pay for *his* pancreas?" Soon thereafter, Moore is asking Chris to show Donaldson the catheter hanging out of his left side... Next thing we know, Moore is drawing Donaldson's attention outside the window which gives on the entrance of the building: "Do you see that, Greg? It's Chris' hearse." As suspected, a hearse pulled over in front of Humana, and it is at this moment that Donaldson realized the scope of Moore's dedication to the cause. *The Awful Truth* host had actually brought Chris' funerals to Humana's HQ that night, as a kind of "dressed rehearsal."

In his fictitious eulogy dedicated to Chris' memory, Moore said, "I did not know Chris for too long. He was a great guy with a lot of integrity, a rich sense of humor. In fact, I remember something he often used to say, uh..." then he turned around to Chris, who was standing next to his own casket, and asked him, "What is it that you used to say?" Chris answered, "I just want a pancreas..." Moore continued addressing the small crowd gathered for the occasion, "He used to say 'I just want a pancreas'...that's it. He was a good man."

In the last minute of the segment, we saw Chris discussing with a Humana employee. She told him "I sympathize with you," and he told her "I'm not looking for sympathy. I just want a pancreas transplant." It was that simple for him: he just wanted to live. It seems like this is too much to ask these days in *dog-eat-dog* America. Finally, with a bagpipe version of 'Amazing Grace' playing on the soundtrack, we saw Chris' casket being taken away to its final repose. We learned in the end titles that, less than a week after Moore's visit, Humana reversed its decision and agreed to pay for his transplant. After all of this, the corporation who had felt threatened by Moore's disturbing political theater decided that Chris could live... In the weeks which followed the settlement, the company changed its policy and started covering all pancreas transplants...thanks to Moore and Chris' persistence.

This was left-wing activism at its most courageous and effective. The reality of personal and political action had once again paid off for Moore and his crew of misfits. The most touching part in all of this is that Chris was in the audience at the Illinois Institute of Technology during the taping of the show, along with his two children. In a moving gesture, after Moore presented him to the rest of his audience, he actually blew a kiss to Moore across the room onto the stage; acknowledging that, without this American dissident, perhaps his children would have by then spoken of him in the past tense.

Evil of Two Lessers

After he explained that the Bravo! Network was 25% owned by the General Electric Corporation, Moore told his TV viewers that for a season closer he originally wanted to have a special show dedicated to the "genius" of Jack Welsh (then CEO of GE). Welsh was about to retire after personally having made millions in profits, downsizing the company 50% of its work force, and allowed for the dumping of vast quantity of chemicals into the Hudson River. At that time he was making an astronomical 94 million dollars a year, with an expected retirement salary of 8 million dollars a year. Just for comparative purposes: most retired workers at GE received at the time a 500 dollar-monthly pension. It appeared like he was the perfect subject for a final *Awful Truth* episode, conflating all the thematics previously dealt with. The embodiment of everything that is wrong with America today: Turner, Bush and Rennert all wrapped into one powerful symbol of merciless capitalism.

Almost in the same breath, Moore also told us that the show's producers came to the realization that it was [then] the 10th Year Anniversary of the beginning of the first Gulf War, "A very special time when the love of the Kuwaiti people rose deep in the American heart and gave us the will to go and bomb the crap out of Iraq," Moore sarcastically told the camera-eye. Conflicted but not confused, the crew decided to simultaneously do a show about both these important topics; meaning that the interludes between the official reports were to be dedicated to that "genius" Jack Welsh, while one of the reports reminded us that the Iraq War was not yet over.

Saddamized!

Moore began one of his boldest and most accomplished reportage by telling us that the prices at the gas pump went up again. He explained that some people attributed this inflation to OPEC's decision to limit oil production, while others were blaming the evil (and late) Saddam Hussein (then dictator of Iraq). Moore also reminded us that "Even though CNN told us that the Gulf War ended 10 years ago, it is still going on today," which will be later corroborated by the second American occupation of Iraq. In fact, we know now that, in direct violation to the U.N. humanitarian mandate, illegal bombings of essential installations dedicated to electricity, food and water, as well as unjustified economic sanctions against Iraq, only exacerbated the oil crisis throughout that particular decade. Moore was reminding us that the real culprits for this crisis were in fact both the American government and American consumers.

In order to grasp why so many United Nations workers resigned "in protest against Anglo-American tyranny," he said, Moore started the sketch by interviewing a former Assistant Secretary General to the United Nations. The man explained how thousands of Iraqi children were dying each month as a direct consequence of the American/U.N. embargo. He goes as far as calling it genocide, a word even the Clinton administration was reluctant to use in Rwanda (where 800,000 people were murdered with machetes in less than 100 days). On the voice-over, Moore illustrated the dilemma for his American audience as clearly as he possibly could: "Dying kids? genocide? How about: 'It cost me forty bucks to fill up my mini-van last week!'?"

As a temporary solution to these high gas prices, Michael Moore set out to operate an independent gas station in Upper State New York. It was a gas station offering Iraqi petroleum purchased straight from Hussein's refineries for 60 cents a gallon (all in exchange for food to the children of Iraq). The mock-gas station was named "Saddam Gas" with its motto being *Undercutting the infidel since 1999.*" In one shot from the segment Moore stood on the curb next to a life-size cardboard cutout of the ex-dictator saluting American drivers with a mechanical arm, yelling: "I buy all my gas from the Wacky-Iraqi!"

Soon enough, people started flocking to the gas station, bringing along with them canned goods for the needy people that their taxpayers' money helped oppress on a daily basis. One ad next to the gas pumps even said "Our Misery = Savings for You," while another one stated that Saddam Gas had the "Lowest Prices…and that's No Shiite." Our rebel journalist then interviewed customers and asked them which one was more important to them: patriotism or a good bargain. Most of them did not care the oil came from Hussein's country, as long as they were able to save a buck on that day. It was almost as if they had all forgotten about Bush Sr.'s "line in the sand." To the ones who bravely answered his questions, Moore had a special gift: coffee mugs to the effigies of Scud missiles, General Schwarzkopf, Hussein, and even Bernard Shaw (the reporter from CNN) hiding under a table in his Baghdad hotel room.

Moore even had the audacity to use some of his customers to advertise his strange gimmick. In one shot from the segment we see an American family waving Iraqi flags and screaming "Saddam has gone crazy!" in typical advertising gusto. Only in America can we witness such blatant contradictions...and Moore is keen on playing with them to prove a political point. As an added bonus to this *mise en scène*, he had hired three Arab-Americans to attend the pumps for him. He even allowed his Muslim staff to stop working to pray to Mecca four times a day, which created a huge back-up line overflowing unto the streets.

After a day of filling up American tanks for cheap, Moore finally met with Chris Douceaux, then a representative of Voices In The Wilderness, a humanitarian association which helped Iraqi people survive the harsh U.S. sanctions (and Hussein's obliviousness) throughout the 1990s and up to this day. Like Moore, Douceaux was a very brave man. Especially if we consider that he could have faced up to 12 years in prison and a $500,000 fine for having fed the impoverished children of Iraq under the embargo.[31] Moore asked him if he was worried about the government coming down on him for these charitable acts, and Douceaux answered that being Catholic made him more worried to be in trouble with God than with his government. No doubt, Moore probably related to this kind of fear. At the end of the sketch, we saw Douceaux flying over Iraq in a helicopter and holding a box of *The Awful Truth Oil for Food Program*. He explained that distribution was done monthly all over the country. Back in America, Moore explained for his part that "As long as the Americans' love of a bargain continues to be greater than who the media and the President tell them to hate, we'll always be open for business."

In the ten years after the first Gulf War "ended," from 1991 to 2001, over 1 ½ million Iraqi civilians died as a direct consequence of the American/United Nations embargo. 5,000 Iraqi children were also dying each month as a direct consequence of these sanctions.[32]

Tough Love

The second report of the "Gulf War" episode related to the fate which had been reserved to the veterans of that war. Not unlike the thousands

---

[31] It is interesting to note here that he probably would not had fallen under those terms if he had been at the head of a major American corporation, such as the one then ran by Dick Cheney.

[32] Or course these numbers do not take into account the second Iraq War. According to the Brookings Institution's Iraq Index, as late as August 2010, it is estimated that 650,000 Iraqi civilians had lost their lives as a direct result of the American invasion (since 2003).

of Vietnam veterans who after being shipped back home were left for dead by their ingrate leaders, the Clintons, Gores, Bushes and Cheneys of this world have seriously neglected the Gulf War Veterans after the Desert Storm Operation. To this day, an increasing amount of these vets suffer from what has been called the Gulf War Syndrome.[33] Along with racism towards African-Americans, this topic seems to occupy a very special place in Moore's work. As a matter of fact, the heart of *Fahrenheit 9/11* is constituted by the spirit of soldiers and veterans, and Moore even followed that film with yet another book entitled *Will They Ever Trust Us Again?*, an anthology of letters written by the soldiers themselves.

Clearly, the mistreatment of war veterans is only one of the most shameful aspects of contemporary American politics. The consensus among conservatives is that "War is a soldier's job. That is what they are paid for: to fight, suffer, and die if necessary. And, if they ever survive combat and manage to come back home, well, just ignore them and they will eventually go away." To counter this right-wing attitude, Moore relied again on the trusty Jay Martel.

> Martel (v.o.):
> "In 1990, the U.S. government came to the men and women of our Armed Forces with a great deal: "Kick Saddam Hussein's ass and we'll pay you money to do it. Sure, you may have to kill a few hundred Iraqi soldiers and civilians while you're at it, but when you get home, we'll give you a big parade." What a deal! But then, these men and women who came back from the Gulf War, according to the government, do nothing but complain."

Over images of sick and disgruntled veterans, the sarcastic narrator continues.

> Martel (v.o.):
> "Over 100,000 of them say they got a bunch of illnesses from being in the Gulf War, which they call 'Gulf War Syndrome.'"

In one testimony at a Town Hall Meeting of the Office of the Special Assistant for Gulf War Illnesses, a veteran explained that his back, spinal fluid, kidneys and bladder are all "screwed up." As if this was not enough misery for one ex-soldier, he tells Martel that he has been bleeding from the brain as well.

---

[33] Scott Shane, "Chemicals Sickened '91 Gulf War Veterans, Latest Study Finds," *The New York Times*, October 15, 2004

Martel (v.o.):
"The U.S. government has refused to pay any of their medical bills, claiming that the Gulf War had nothing to do with their getting sick. And we all know that the U.S. government never lies, right?"

Next we are thrown in an interview with another sick veteran: Fabian Moody. This one explains how he has been suffering from sore throat, memory lost, nervous behavior, sleeping disorder, extreme headaches, nausea, and sinus pains ever since that war ended. But Washington did not care about his predicament.

Martel (v.o.):
"Instead, the government has created a new office to deal with Gulf War illnesses."

The following shot of the sequence is of Bernard Rostker, then Director of the Office, sleeping during a commission about the veterans' fate.

Martel (v.o.):
"Rostker's department has spent two years and 50 million dollars finding bold new ways to ignore the problem. You'd think those whiny veterans would be impressed by such an expensive public relations display. But no, they still won't shut up."

We then go back to the interview with Moody where we learn that he went all the way to convince the government of his sickness. The fact that he had lost huge amounts of weight and several jobs, and that both he and his wife had to declare bankruptcy, did not impress the V.A. either. Moody claimed he was poisoned in Desert Storm and that all he wants is some form of compensation which would give him a certain quality of life back.

Martel (v.o.):
"I knew exactly what Fabian and his supposedly sick soldier friends needed: a little tough love! If these sick vets really needed to make some money, they were gonna have to earn it. How? That was easy. How do all victims of disease make bundles of cash? Two words: charity race."

In a clever narrative twist, Martel stands in Central Park where a banner of the *1st Annual Gulf War Syndrome Fun Run* has been installed. The banner has the icon of a gas mask on it to symbolize what originally motivated the race. Martel then sets up a dozen veterans at the starting line, while an *Awful Truth* foreign correspondent already had aligned (in the editing) another group of runners to compete with the sick veterans: about 20 Iraqi children in the middle of a derelict Baghdad street.

> Martel (v.o.):
> "That's right, the enemy. These boys and girls were part of the menace that the U.S. government sent our soldiers to crush. Now, with food and medicine shortages, and the continued bombing of their country, they needed some quick cash too."

Impersonating a drill-instructor, Martel asks a U.S. Army Sergeant who spent 9 months in the Persian Gulf (and who is tied to a wheelchair) to get up and start racing. She replies matter-of-factly: "I do not think so." Next he tells a Staff Sergeant who spent 40 days in the Persian Gulf: "According to the government, you guys are healthy?" Her reply is also quite evocative of the treatment veterans must endure because of the invisible nature and insidious aspects of their illness: "Yeah. I know. I look fine, right?" Before the race begins, Martel fills out a health questionnaire for every contestant. To the questions "Are you suffering from open sores? uncontrollable blood pressure? joint pains? sleeping disorder? heart palpitations? night sweats?," all veterans answer positively. He gives the last person interviewed a pat on the back and rallies all of them to start the race. The veterans, like the children of Baghdad, are now ready to run a charity race to get their health back.

> Martel (v.o.):
> "Yes, it was stacking up as a race between the conquered and the conquerors."

In a quick parallel editing sequence, we see the children of Iraq running as fast as they could while the veterans can barely move forward.

> Martel (v.o.):
> "And it looks to me as if the conquerors could have used a little more stretching. But look at those kids go! It's going to take more than a little dirty water and constant bombing to keep those wacky Persians down!"

More than simple sarcasm, the dark undertone of the piece is powered by the contrast between the high energy of Martel's performance (as drill instructor and narrator) and the obvious physical malaise and strenuous efforts of the sick veterans. Along the way one young female veteran even had to stop because she could no longer feel one of her feet. Another veteran sitting on a bench complained to Martel, "I can't even walk for the rest of the way." To which the latter clapped his hands and went, "Ok, alright! The rest of you let's keep going!," in a tone reminiscent of the "Death Race 2000" and "Pistol Pete" pieces. Since the race was taking so long to unfold, Martel decided to try to get more donations from the folks at the V.A., located just a few blocks down Central Park.

Soon enough, he meets with the Director of Media Relation. After asking him to sponsor the 25 mile-run, the man replied, "I do not think you should have them running?" Martel retorts, "Well, what else can they do? They're not getting any help from you guys." Later on, Jay is still stirring important business in front of the V.A. He is now personally asking Rostker for a contribution, "Cos' you know, they went to fight for oil, at least we can give them a few bucks." Rostker tells him that they are doing whatever they can for veterans, all the while trying to get into his private limousine. Frustrated by the man's nonchalance, Martel tells him, "I guess the short-term memory lost those veterans have from the symptoms is really helping you guys out, uh?"

By checkpoint three, most exhausted veterans have to stop and be fed with an oxygen mask. The race painstakingly culminates in a cemetery for the veterans (decorated with a finishing line ribbon that said "Caution Bio Hazard"), while the children of Iraq are still running the streets of Baghdad, "thanks to the shortage of finishing lines in their country," Martel says in voice-over. After handing out medals to the "losers," he explained that for American veterans "Glory had to be enough."

In the end titles, we are told that 147 American soldiers died during the first Gulf War and that more than 9,600 Gulf War veterans have died since they returned home (statistics from 2000). Assuming that a percentage of them died of natural causes, it still leaves an unusually high amount of people dying *after* the war, for no apparent reason... For the viewer, though, Vietnam and Agent Orange obviously come to mind. After watching this segment, we can assume that the second Iraq War will reserve the same fate to its veterans. McNamara, Cheney or Rumsfeld, it is all the same at the end of the day. Cannon-fodder is not meant to last and hang around. Just have a talk with Gulf War and Iraq War veterans to be convinced of it.

TV is Dead: Long Live TV!

As this chapter has been illustrating with the help of many textual and descriptive examples, Moore and his co-conspirators not only had the *moxy*, but also the intelligence and the heart to pull this left-wing television project off the ground. And they did. While most shows on the tube are about rich, powerful and well-to-do individuals (or the opposite, the "nobody" who becomes "Number One" in reality shows), *TV Nation* and *The Awful Truth* managed for four seasons to give a voice to the working class and even to people on the fringe of society, like ex-prisoners, homeless people, sick veterans and dying people. Moore's television project was essentially subversive because it proposed altruism instead of individualism, tolerance instead of discrimination, and understanding instead of confusion. It was for awhile an alternative to the lowest common denominator.

Few shows in the history of American television have ever achieved what *TV Nation* and *The Awful Truth* did in four short seasons. Even programs such as *60 Minutes* or *20/20*, with all their combined years on the air, have never went where Moore and his correspondents have been. These investigative TV journals, although of high quality, are hiding behind the illusion of "objective reporting," as well as constantly concealing the fact that networks are part of conglomerates ruled by specific private interests groups (making them more influential and dangerous than one may be lead to believe). Yet, through the power of private ownership and a centralized form of distribution, these become America's main source of information, and they chose to focus on issues that do not always matter that much (or that do not have any real political bearing).

Recently, we have even witnessed a merging of investigative reporting and actual law enforcement on television, as it is the case with the NBC show *Dateline: To Catch a Predator*, which is fixated on framing adults who solicit sexual encounters with minors on the Internet (a pathetic freak show). One exception to this "faits divers as real information" paradigm could actually be some of the prime-time programs on MSNBC, like *Countdown with Keith Olbermann* and *The Rachel Maddow Show*. These shows dared to challenge the Bush/Cheney regime while it was in power and questioned the awful and caper-like McCain/Palin presidential campaign of 2008. They are even hard on President Obama, as they should be. Their type of political theater is obviously influenced by Moore, and he is often invited on these shows to comment on topics such as the ones found within his own work.

Dog Eat Dog

Moore and his collaborators personalized their journalistic work through performance, tongue-in-cheek humor, irony, and experimental techniques that went way beyond what any non-fiction show was able to do since the advent of television. They presented a fresh perspective on social problems by interacting with reality, and even by re-enacting elements of this reality for the sake of the camera, a big no-no in conventional journalism and documentary filmmaking. Sometimes the tactics of reverse-psychology and satire were highly effective and led to actual results. (Moore actually helped to save a man's life, as we have seen.) Other times, the whole thing remained at the level of witty and sharp criticism in expressive form, which is not a bad thing either, since it still managed to raise awareness regarding important social issues that most take for granted. By subverting the conventions of broadcasting, Moore was asking his viewers to be more aware of their system's flaws and foibles and, moreover, to reflect on their own capacity (or incapacity) to empathize with the less fortunate. To this day, he wants Americans to stop being so self-reverential and to start questioning the political reality behind the facade of their materialistic world, and he succeeded on a certain level in influencing a large group of individuals in Western society, especially young people, leading them to believe that things can change for the better. This had not happened since the 1960s. For a lot of people, he was in fact the face of hope before Barack Obama came crashing into the scene; as a beautiful orator, full of intelligence, empathy, grace and depth, but still defending the ruling elite and its goals for a New World Order. *Plus ça change...*

Michael Moore and his crew also went to places where few of us would dare to venture, either out of disinterest, laziness or just plain fear. One could argue that other journalists and correspondents have accomplished far more difficult tasks before or since, like these 141 journalists who got killed in Iraq during the war, but none were ever allowed to report with a sensibility such as Moore's and the expressivity found in the TV shows described in the previous pages. This certainly requires some courage as well: the courage to be exposed, to be criticized, to be ostracized or even dismissed as a lunatic. In that sense, his work is more akin to art than to actual news or electronic journalism. As it is now more generally accepted, compared to when the first edition of this book came out, Moore has a certain artistic temperament which distinguishes him from other "news people," a fact that we do not feel necessary to emphasize from now on. However, Moore has been devalued in the eyes of some of his longtime fans. It would seem like the model of American manhood that he represents does not fit the bill, because it is too "soft." In fact, it is not uncommon to meet film people who actually believe that his work is inferior to what you can find on the Internet today. What a sad reality this is for all of us who expect a bit more from movies than just sex, blood and guts.

The Gangster Culture Part II (Rooting for the Bad Guys Isn't Cool)

While most American journalists prefer to hide behind the illusion of objectivity in reporting the news, Michael Moore proposes a kind of investigation which foregrounds involvement and subjectivity, something that requires courage, as we have just discussed. His method of acquiring knowledge is to live through daily experiences at ground level, which disrupts the line between journalism and activism in many people's minds. Moore's mandate is about action. His work would serve no purpose if it was not outside of the office, on the street, with real people. It would be everything his detractors claim it is: biased, narcissistic, and whiny. Luckily the work speaks for itself and proves that this kind of criticism does not apply to what he does.

In it we can clearly see him interacting with its subject matter, which was considered pretty unusual before he started doing it. That way he not only exposes the apparatus but he also exposes himself, as being part of both the problem and the solution. This unusual, self-questioning process leads him to numerous discoveries about the nature of the American psyche, and probably about his own psyche as well; something that conventional journalism and documentary filmmaking are rarely able to achieve. It is an understanding carried-out through the reality of *being there* and *doing it*, not from the mind's view of an armchair reporter or seen through the distorting effect of a zoom lens or virtually through a web site. It is in fact much closer to the artistic process, which allows for a certain margin of trial and error.

But what is most obvious to us is that Moore's signature truly emerges with his film work, on the big screen. To offer a brief introduction to his film style, let us propose this introductory portrait: Moore's art is *embryonic* in preproduction, when he comes up with a subject matter and a concept; *organic* in production, when he actually interacts with people through his trek; and *synthetic* when it fully blooms in post-production, writing his voice-over narration and shaping his rushes into a coherent and meaningful whole. No doubt about it, many years from now we will look at what he produced for television and realize how original and meaningful it really was. But what he will be mostly remembered for are his amazing and, yes, beautiful motion pictures. As we will see in the following sections dedicated to his feature films, Michael Moore achieves quite a lot with very little at times. What many consider "fluff entertainment" is actually a masterful and thought-provoking form of political art. To claim otherwise is really to root for the bad guys, anyway.

CHAPTER TWO
RENEGADE FILMMAKER

ROGER & ME (1989)

> When I make a film, I'm not doing it purely for political reasons. If I wanted to do that, I would have run for office. I love to go see a good movie... Try to remember when was the last great film that you saw and when you left the theatre it was like a religious experience; you have tears in your eyes because this art form was honored by what you just saw on the screen. And it's so rare these days. It's been that way for the last decade or so, and so I think as a filmmaker, my first contribution would just be to make a good movie that people would love to go see and leave the theatre charged with that sense of excitement that we've all had.[34]

Man on a Mission

Without a doubt, *Roger & Me* is a milestone in American independent cinema. It marked the rebirth of the nonfiction form that had then been waning since its heyday in the 1960s, mainly because of the broad commercialization of television and its made-for-TV documentaries (or feature-length reportages), and it most certainly achieved the status of a success story within the mainstream film industry. Michael Moore did not just slipped in through the door of the executive suite uninvited: he crashed it in with a powerful 2 hour-statement about the reality of corporate decisions made over three Martini-lunch breaks or at the golf course. This film is a relentless attack on the narrow-minded vision and greed of technocrats, bureaucrats and administrators, and it delves deep into the catastrophic consequences of a nation ran like a corporation. Moore once described *Roger & Me* as being the "portrait of a town, a corporation and a decade." For him it was clear that television was not properly covering the layoffs at General Motors since they started happening in the early 1980s; because it would have meant to get into embarrassing details about a systematic social genocide, which is what was happening at that time. Obviously, Washington and its sponsors who owned stocks in General Motors, and other of its affiliate companies, were clearly gagging the networks. After all, G.M. was not just another company. It was a major institution that made America what it is today. It was a pillar of industrial society. It was a sacred cow, so to speak.

Thus, Moore took it upon himself to provide an alternative point-of-view on these unfortunate events, not expecting much as far as distribution was concerned. What happened afterwards was just the

---

[34] Michael Moore interviewed by Andrew Collins, Monday November 11, 2002, *Film Guardian* Online Exclusive, 2002

opposite: the film made him famous and allowed him to pursue a prolific career in the world of electronic journalism, trade publishing, media communication, and filmmaking. It was in fact the dawn of a new era. Until *The Big One*, *Bowling for Columbine*, and *Fahrenheit 911* came along, *Roger & Me* was the most lucrative nonfiction film ever produced in the United States. He must have done something right in this first effort. Perhaps it was that a relatively unknown person was taking hold of the medium and was saying something true with it for the first time in a long while. Actually, when it was first released on American screens, it rattled the cage of the American Establishment to the point where the President of the United States himself had to request a print for private viewing. Surely, George H. W. Bush could not have suspected that his offspring was to be standing in the middle of Moore's target range, fifteen years down the line. He probably did not suspect that the heritage of his (and Reagan's) policies would be so well-documented in the following decade either. Chances are that Moore's subjective accounts of this era are what will be remembered in the future, not the empty rhetoric of speeches written by the likes of David Frum.

The Truth is Out There

In the years of Candid-Eye, Cinema-Vérité and Direct Cinema, three relatively different approaches to filmmaking, there had been an explosion of vibrant documentaries independently produced to inform people on important social issues. Political documentaries such as *Primary* (Drew, 1960) and *Point of Order* (De Antonio, 1964), or again work criticizing institutionalization such as *High School*, *Titticut Follies*, *Law & Order* and *Hospital* (Wiseman, 1966; 1967; 1969; 1970), proved to be an effective alternative to conventional television news. It was back at a time when filmmakers were more politically committed and dedicated to use film as a tool for social change. Most of these underground figures were left-wingers and had strongly been influenced by the British social documentaries of the 1930s (*Housing Problems*, 1935; *Coal Face*, 1936, etc.). Now, Moore strays away from this long tradition of documentary filmmakers who captured reality as it unfolded. Not politically, or even thematically, since the fight against the excesses of capitalism and the resurgence of fascism remains pretty much the same today, but stylistically speaking. Like so many filmmakers who managed to make a lot out of nothing, Moore was only armed with a good concept, a 16mm camera and a tape recorder when he made *Roger & Me*. Although, what he decided to do with it turned out to be quite different than his precursors' work. There was something in Moore's films which distinguished him from his fellow left-wing filmmakers from the start. This difference was at the time the total assertion of the director's personality in the frame, the immediate presence of what would become a persona and an icon: "Michael Moore." This is something which never would have been accepted at a time when "observational" was a methodological keyword to be followed like a religious dogma in English-speaking documentaries.

As mentioned before, Moore's films are not objective. They fully embrace the subjective aspects of what is specific to filmmaking (basically, framing and recording of moving images, recording of sounds, and editing images and sound together). His camera is not following the "fly-on-the-wall" technique, but is immersed in its subject matter, much more like the cinema made by Quebecois filmmakers in the late 1950s, early 1960s (Pierre Perrault, Gilles Groulx, Michel Brault, etc.). Moore's style is very involved and rarely contemplative, except in cases where it fits the argument. It is the documentary of the wide angle lens, full of life and close to its subject matter.

Besides occupying an unusual position in film history, *Roger & Me* is a good example one can present to illustrate how the documentary form has evolved and been rejuvenated over the years. It can also be used to explain how context always influences the making of a film and informs how the film is received by a public. *Roger & Me* shook the industry, winded-up winning many international awards and put Michael Moore at the forefront of the new American cinema. It was a major accomplishment by someone who had never touched a camera before.

Badlands

The story goes that Warner Bros. not only made the best offer to buy *Roger & Me* from Dog Eat Dog Films but also accepted Moore's demands surrounding its theatrical release. According to the filmmaker, Warner agreed to screen it in over 1300 of its theaters across America. The major also agreed to a compensatory fund for the people who had been evicted from their homes in the film. As if this was not enough charity from one corporation, Moore requested a quarter of a million free tickets for any jobless person who wanted to see it upon its initial run. Moreover, the studio went to great lengths to promote the film by pouring another quarter of a million dollars into marketing and advertising it to the desperate masses.[35] Perhaps that all that money being put into such a frivolous thing as a movie seems ridiculous, or

---

[35] Listen to the director's commentary in the supplement of the *Roger & Me* (DVD, Warner Bros., 2003).

even outrageous, considering how it could have been used to feed needy Flint citizens, for instance. However, seen from a cultural perspective, it was done with good intentions and to alert people about the state of corporate crime in America (a concept that did not even exist in the public mind before Moore started filming it around 1986). *Roger & Me* had a greater role than to heal locally and temporarily. It was aiming at a higher plain, aspiring to be a visual record of the times instead.

Its production started at the end of 1986, when Moore himself did not even know how to make a film. He was a great cinephile but had no formal training in film-making. Early on, he admitted not knowing how to put film stock in a camera and had to request the help of certain people who would eventually become important figures in the earlier part of his career. Among them, Kevin Rafferty, Jane Loader and Pierce Rafferty, the collective who had made *The Atomic Café* (1982), a chilling compilation film about nuclear weapons and American military propaganda after WW II. Rafferty had previously asked Moore to join him in the production of *Blood in the Face*, an award-winning documentary about hate groups in Michigan (released in 1991). Moore's off-screen appearance as an interviewer of hate mongers is the first significant one to ever be recorded on film, and it could certainly not have foreshadowed what would soon thereafter become his trademark of interactive, on-screen method of interviewing people.

Moore started *Roger & Me* with clear intentions. His task was not only to report certain facts about corporate America and to connect the dots for the viewer, but also to illustrate the dramatic side effects of the layoffs on the city's infrastructure. It seems quite clear that there is no claim to objectivity in the presentation of the material. It also seems obvious that Moore wanted to foreground the subjective treatment of the film by inserting 8mm home movies and a voice-over narration describing who he is, where he is from, and what his relation to the General Motors Corporation is. One of the home footage shows him with his dad, Frank. The latter had worked for G.M.A.C. building spark plugs for thirty-three years and we actually get to meet him in Moore's *Capitalism: A Love Story*, released in 2009. Moore tells us in voice-over that his entire family had worked for G.M. at some point in their lives...everyone but him. This family bond (or lack thereof in case of Michael) has in fact propelled the making of *Roger & Me* at a time when his own financial situation did not allow him to afford one reel of film stock. At the preproduction stage, Moore was unemployed and broke. The *Michigan Voice* had ceased to exist and he found himself with a 400 dollar-monthly income and substantial debts.[36] In a sense,

---

[36] Commentary by the director about *Roger & Me* (DVD, Warner Bros., 2003)

this film is motivated by a personal understanding of the socioeconomic problem, since Moore was also living it indirectly through his family, as well as directly through his own meager earnings, barely surviving in Davison.

Originally he wanted to interview Roger E. Smith, then Chairman of G.M. and responsible for the laying-off which had been going on since the early 1980s. His ultimate goal was to make Smith aware of the havoc created in the wake of his decisions and, hopefully, to have him reconsider the plant closings in Flint (wishful thinking, no doubt). When Smith shunned him, the filmmaker changed course and turned his amateur camera on the effects of the plant closings instead. In his mind it was a much more effective way to bring the problem to public attention. In the process he also targeted the municipal government whose response to the factory closings was to promote an inefficient form of tourism (e.g. opening shopping malls when no one had power of purchase, recreating a factory line in an "amusement park" just to remind people of their prosperous past and miserable present, etc.). As we can clearly see it in the film, all endeavors created by the municipality soon proved to be embarrassing failures, and these provided the "comedy relief" of *Roger & Me*, an otherwise pretty grim portrait of America in those years.

In parallel to these ludicrous development projects, Moore also exposed what he believed to be the condescending attitude of the rich population and the consequences of big business' cupidity on the community, two of his major themes. He was equally harsh towards the union leadership and the federal government which had helped to create the tragic situation in his hometown and elsewhere in America. As this wedding between government, business, and union is exposed on screen, Moore takes time to chat with common Flint folks who were stripped of their livelihood by unscrupulous politicians, industrialist, and scabs. A good part of town, nearly 25%, had followed President Reagan's advice and left to find work elsewhere in the country. What we were actually witnessing at the time was the beginning of a great exodus linked to the emerging post-industrial world and the fully automated, computer age. It was a time when workers left the assembly line and were asked to recycle as computer technicians. It was a time when CEOs understood how to maximize profits and defecated all over the working-class. Moore himself put everything he owned, time, energy and money into the financing of *Roger & Me*. For him it seemed like a small price to pay in comparison to the suffering he had witnessed all over his hometown. People around him were going through extreme hard times because of these Draconian downsizing measures. Relatives and friends all had a story to tell about how they were proposed a rotten deal by their employer, and about how their pension was being mishandled or robbed by management or, worst, by their union representatives. Autoworkers had accepted substantial pay-cuts in the 10 years previous to the downsizing, and by the late 1980s they felt they had sacrificed themselves for nothing. For a bunch of *corporate monsters* who in the end stole their money, their future and their life away from them.

Among the people who felt terrible was Moore's friend, Ben Hamper. The latter had been laid-off four times from the factory line in the past decade and when Moore interviewed him, he was coming out of a mental health center. Before being a correspondent for *The Awful Truth*, Hamper appears for the first time here in *Roger & Me*. He explains the way in which he reacted upon learning the news of the last and final layoff. He describes how he felt listening to 'Wouldn't It Be Nice' playing on the car radio on the way back home from work, and tries not to get too emotional in front of the camera. Hamper is also the author of *Rivethead*, a book about the circumstances around his job termination from the biggest and richest corporation in America (at that time). Like Moore, he was witness to this economic tragedy unfolding at the time.

> A miniature Auschwitz had been assembled far behind the clicking of the cashier's keys, far removed from the lazy shuffle of the fresh claimant's feet, off in the back where you now only waited for the pellets to drop and the air to get red. Oh, I guess it could have been worse. You could have been burned to death in a Pinto. You could have snagged in a plane prop. You could have been fatally trampled at a Paul Anka concert. You could have had to go out and find a job.[37]

Nice Place to Raise Your Kids

It is implied in *Roger & Me* that Flint stands as a microcosm of most post-industrial American towns. The city's history needs to be understood in order for Moore's earlier work to be fully appreciated, and for us to link it to his overall artistic project. It is also essential to add details about the past and present of this city to fully grasp why Flint, once a major car production center, has been so affected by the G.M. downsizing.

Flint was founded in 1819 by fur trader Jacob Smith, and was incorporated into the Union in 1855. It has been host to various industries in its relatively short history: trading/trapping, lumber, carriages, and automobiles. Obviously, the landscape and culture of the

---

[37] Ben Hamper, *Rivethead: Tales from the Assembly Line*, Warner Books, 1992

city is dominated by the auto industry. Flint was the host of the Sit-Down strike of 1936-1937 which turned the fledgling United Automobile Workers into a labor union of note (read further down in this chapter). During WWII, it was a major contributor of tanks and other war material due to its heavy manufacturing facilities and competent labor force. The city and vicinity also hosts a large cultural center funded by revenues from the auto industry. It boasts of having many institutions which now seem disproportionate to its current economical stature: the Whiting Auditorium, a beautiful two thousand-seat auditorium; the Sloan Museum, a large portion of which is dedicated to rare automobiles; the Longway Planetarium, the largest planetarium in Michigan; and the Flint Institute of Arts, a well-stocked art museum and learning facility. It is also home to the Bower Theater, the Flint Institute of Music and the Pierce Cultural Center, all set on a 30-acre site near downtown; as well as being host to the University of Michigan's Flint campus and Kettering University.[38]

Up until now, nothing can lead us to believe that it would one day become a Third World landscape.

As we can observe for ourselves in *Roger & Me*, as well as in *Capitalism: A Love Story*, Flint is the most notorious illustration of the effects of the 1970s collapse of the U.S. auto industry. The film does not stick to a precise timeline of those events. Rather, it highlights the failure of city officials to reverse economical trends with entertainment options all throughout the 1980s (just like Hollywood did in the Great Depression). According to Moore, the 1990s were even more difficult than the previous decade for the people of Flint. They kept on struggling under the heavy foot of Corporate America, and, overall, the conditions only got worst there under the Clinton/Gore administration. In the early years of the 21st century, Flint predictably stands as an empty shell of its former self. The auto industry continued its exodus from the city, as did the population and sources of revenue. It has now the highest crime rate in Michigan and the 45th highest crime rate in the United States. The unemployment rate in Flint is nearly 50% and the city has been unable to pay its debts to the federal government.

As a dire consequence of G.M. pulling out of its territory, Flint was placed into receivership by the state of Michigan in 2002, thirteen years after *Roger & Me* had rang the high alert.[39]

---

[38] www.flint.com
[39] Ibid.

How to Destroy a Community without Trying

> Mexicans did not take your job. Americans took your job, and they took it to Mexico.[40]

General Motors argued that the main reason for downsizing throughout those years was fierce competition from Japanese auto manufacturers. The corporation claimed that the only alternative to these closures would have been major government handouts or the abolishment of Free Trade with other car-making nations. Moore jumped on these issues, remarking that G.M. factories were even more profitable once they had moved production to Mexico. (He later produced a *TV Nation* episode about the very same topic.[41]) In 1986 alone G.M.'s top brass shut down eleven of their older plants located in and around Detroit, Pontiac, and Flint. While the two first cities may have been able to survive the closings, thanks to other commercial outputs, the results for Flint were utterly disastrous, as we can see in the movie. Flint underwent a total transformation throughout the decade. It went on from being just a typical American town to become a catastrophe zone. The city even made it to the 300th position in the *Money Magazine* listing of "The 300 Best Places to Live in America," which is something we are told midway through the film. How did all of this happen? Moore provides many (if not all) of the answers here in his filmic manifesto.

Factories which had been running for almost 60 years were shut down and moved to Mexico, where workers were paid 70 cents an hour. In return, the corporate brass used the profits made from home-downsizing and cheap labor in foreign countries to buy into other companies involved in dubious activities (weapon manufacturers, "consultation firms," etc.), or into bankrupted companies (for a dollar), therefore multiplying the profits exponentially. They dealt with the union, one of the most powerful in the U.S. at the time, by telling its soft representation that the company was broke; even forcing employees to take wage cuts and work half-shifts, putting them in a situation of partial-employment. Then, bosses laid-off thousands of workers, took great chunks of what should have been retirement money, and opened other factories in underdeveloped countries (where, again, they used cheap labor and started the vicious circle one again). Like Moore says on the voice-over track: "Roger Smith was a true genius"…of some kind.

---

[40] Michael Moore, *The Awful Truth*, 1999-2000
[41] *TV Nation*, "NAFTA Mike," originally aired on NBC July 19, 1994

Job Well Done, Now Die!

The renegade filmmaker also brought to our attention Roger Smith's opulent lifestyle to prove his point about corporate abuse. For instance, he followed him at the Waldorf Astoria in New York City, through the path of private yacht clubs and a gymnasium restricted to the elite. After laying-off thousands of workers, Smith had given himself a lofty 2 million dollar raise while being totally oblivious to the tragedy unfolding down below at his royal feet. As disturbing as the layoffs were in themselves, it is all the covering up by G.M. executives and their lobbying friends in Washington which bothered Moore the most. Limiting the informational output to the public was part of the tactic at G.M. under Roger E. Smith, and as the film progresses, Moore is having more difficulty filming on G.M.'s premises. In an attempt to do some damage control, one spokesperson for the corporation told Moore that it was "not a plant closing but the *lost of one product line*" earlier on in the narrative. Moore used the same manipulative tactics when it came down to get the footage he needed to put his argument across on film. In order to shoot the last truck going down the assembly line, the film's production team posed as a TV crew from Toledo, Ohio. While the last car was finished being assembled by workers, many of them started cheering, but one man told Moore's camera: "I don't know what everybody's cheering about, *we just lost our jobs…*"

It would not be the last time that Moore and his crew used deceiving tactics to infiltrate a place or an event either. As briefly discussed in the chapter pertaining to his television series, infiltration is the crux of Moore's methodology. He usually does a "symbolic sit-down strike" on enemy grounds. The idea is to not leave until somebody relevant in the echelon starts giving serious answers to serious questions. There is a limit to tolerance and good will, especially when you are dealing with money-driven entities and their hypocritical representatives in the lobby. Doors do have to be knocked down occasionally, and Moore has the intellectual, emotional, and physical stature to accomplish such a difficult task for some of the disenfranchised and voiceless people of America. In this instance, somebody had to stand up and let these corporate criminals know that workers will never forget what happened in those years of Reaganomics. In certain ways, the film immortalizes the excesses of government and corporate greed in the 1980s, as well as showing us how the corporate mind really works. How does it work? Just follow on Michael Moore's trail to find out…

At the beginning of *Roger & Me*, G.M. spokesman Tom Kaye tries to defend Smith by saying: "I'm sure that Roger Smith has a social conscience as strong as anybody else I know… He has as much concern about these people as you do… He's a very warm man…"

Moore emphasizes the discrepancy between what the man is (hesitantly) telling us and what actually happened as a result of some of Smith's executive decisions. Over a still shot of Smith, he tells us: "A *warm* man? Did I have Roger Smith judged all wrong simply because he was eliminating 30,000 jobs from my hometown?" This line of questioning will serve to launch the search for the General Motors Chairman. Again, and like it will later be the case for Bush, Turner, and Rennert in his TV shows, Moore uses Smith as a paradigm of American capitalism. For him, he was a symbol of the decaying corporate ethos. He was another soul-less executive who only responded to his shareholders' demands and who did not recognize his social role within the community. This figure of wealth, power, and authority had to stand trial, according to Moore. And he did.

Eye of the Storm

Michael Moore always structures his films as personal and revealing journeys. In fact, these are constantly framed as "narratives" which allow him to seek out the answers or to open up new ways of looking at a problem. This Homeric structure helps to cement the drive of his films, as well as allowing him to personalize his work through formal manipulations and stylistic choices, such as the use of voice-over, home footage, and stock-footage. Moreover, confrontational dynamics between Moore and those he believes have to respond for their actions are at the center of these journeys, acting as structuring agents to his films. These have changed quite a lot since his first film. At the time *Roger & Me* was being made he was virtually *persona non grata*. Nowadays most people in America know who "Michael Moore" is and those with power tend to fear him (consider the case of Senators running away from him at the end of *Fahrenheit 9/11*). Back then the corporate brass did not give him the time of day for different reasons. They would often base their opinion of him on the way he looks (i.e. like a regular, rather inoffensive kind of guy, scruffy looking and with a naïve look in his eyes), and since he was putting himself in front of the camera the subjects interviewed were probably thinking that what he was doing was not professional enough to be taken seriously. They were probably thinking that it would not be aired on television, never mind that it would eventually be distributed in cinemas around the world and make film history! Beyond this deceiving facade, though, Moore has his greatest weapon: his tongue-in-cheek and sarcastic humor. He uses it to disarm people who are giving him a hard time and phony alibis, such as "staying competitive in the world's free-market economy," while outrageously increasing executive salaries into the tens of millions of dollars. As we came to realize over the years, Moore uses humor to diffuse confrontation and to exhaust the frustration of a subject. Sometimes this results in his expulsion from corporate grounds. These expulsions are often polite and moderated, but other times they are violently awkward and the cops are called in to escort Moore out the front door.

As one example of a polite and funny exchange with a corporate entity, Moore goes to the G.M. headquarters in Detroit for the first time in *Roger & Me* and a security guard asks him for his business card. Moore hands him his Chuck E Cheese discount card and on the voice-over he tells us that "He [*the security agent*] said that the card would not let me in to see Mr. Smith," as if any other card would have done the job, anyway. After being refused entry into Smith's office, Moore goes back (in the editing – since there is no real temporal linearity in the film) to see Tom Kaye (who will reappear 20 years later, in *Capitalism: A Love Story*). The man tries to rationalize the reasons why Smith gave himself a raise after putting all those people on unemployment and, eventually, on welfare. He explains that "a corporation does not have a responsibility to its workers but only to its shareholders," and that "it has to do what it has to do in order to stay competitive." The main goal of any company is essentially to make a profit, even if it means firing all the workers, according to Kaye (who ironically lost his job before the film was released).

Later, while Flint is having a surreal and quite inappropriate parade, a man clears up the situation for Moore. He explains how the union is getting weaker and how too many people in it are "friends with management." Unfortunately, this seems to have been a trend throughout the 1980s and 1990s all over North America. We just have to recall how the late-great composer/musician Frank Zappa once described American unions to understand what the nature of the problem really is. More than two decades ago, Zappa was one of the first to tell us that the labor movement had the 'Mafia curse." In *Roger & Me*, Moore uses an old G.M. promotional film to establish the tense relationship between management and its workers. Stock footage shows a G.M. executive saying to the camera: "Most of our employees, *even those who at times cause problems*…are conscientious and hard-working men and women." It was as clear then as it is now: management is always going to have the last word in relation to working conditions, pay equity, grievances, and social benefits, because they are hired to keep the shareholders happy and the workers in line. Top level management was going to somehow find a way to get rid of American workers and replace them by Mexican ones or by Japanese hydraulic robots. But the worst in all of this is that it was all done with government approval and support, through deregulation and contempt for Civil Rights.

Starving in the Belly of the Whale

One element which has rarely been discussed in relation to *Roger & Me* is its sense of history. Moore often refers to an important event in his work: the Great Flint Sit-Down Strike. This puts the layoffs in real perspective for the viewer. It also illustrates the forces of socialism which are at work in the United States, as well as pointing to a long tradition of left-wing thinking. In late December 1936, G.M. workers barricaded themselves inside the factory for 44 days with the hope that the standoff would give them their rights. At that time, the city of Flint, G.M. executives and the police were apprehending an insurrection and started roughing up strikers. Roosevelt sent in the National Guards to oversee the strike and to protect workers against violence and police brutality, the film tells us. In February of 1937, G.M. finally gave in to the workers' demands and the United Auto Workers was born.

The Sit-Down Strike changed the UAW from a collection of isolated locals on the fringes of the industry into a major force, and eventually led to the unionization of the entire American automobile industry. It had understood that it could not survive by piecemeal organizing campaigns at smaller plants, but that it could only truly organize the automobile industry by going after its biggest and most powerful employer: General Motors. The Union focused on the production complex in Flint, which eventually became a symbolic ground for all the other plants across the country. It remained one of the most powerful unions up until the mergers of the corporate era in the 1980s. Hence, one of Moore's main lines of reasoning in *Roger & Me* regards the failure of unionization in America. He shows that not only were the corporate bosses corrupted and greedy but that union bosses were expandable and could be bought like any bureaucrat or politician.

A Factory that Plays Tricks on Your Mind

> We shall begin from a contemporary economic fact. The worker becomes poorer the more wealth he produces and the more his production increases in power and extent. The worker becomes an ever cheaper commodity the more goods he creates. The devaluation of the human world increases in direct relation to the increase in value of the world of things. Labor does not only create goods; it also produces itself and the workers as a commodity, and indeed in the same proportion as it produces goods.[42]

---

[42] Karl Marx, *The Economic and Philosophic Manuscripts*, New York: International Publishers, 1964, p.13

Later in the film, Moore tells us about those who managed to "escape" Flint and the assembly line for which it was known. He goes on to enumerate the guitar player from the defunct rock group Grand Funk Railroad, host Casey Kasem, the woman who married conductor Zubin Mehta, actor Don Knotts and Bob Ubanks (the host of the game show *The Newlywed Game*). Ubanks even allowed Moore a brief interview. His presence in the film allows Moore to integrate comments on the state of American mainstream culture, which serves as a kind of backdrop tapestry to the film's main discourse. Right from the start, Moore's editorial choices include archival footage of G.M.'s promotional puppets, such as Anita Bryant and Pat Boone; two icons of the 1950s who participated in the propaganda of car culture. Back then, Boone was promoting G.M. cars and spark plugs and making a living being on its payroll. Here the footage from the 1950s and the one from the performances given by Boone and Bryant, while Flint was dying a slow death, serve to remind the viewer of the intrinsic commercialism in American culture.

In *Roger & Me*, Moore implies that white culture and product placement are inextricably linked in his country. This goes all the way back to traveling sideshows, where entertainers were also salesmen. Everything is an incentive to sell "stuff" in America. Everything can be boiled down to a philosophy of materialism and consumption, even in times of recession and depression. As he is presented in the film, Pat Boone embodies the shallowness of Americana. He, like so many crooners and cute faces of his days, served to brainwash society into believing the great American lie. People like Boone are just corporate representatives without a political will or opinion of their own. As it was in the 1980s, and up to this day, very few people who ever (really) worked for General Motors could or can afford a sports car like the one Boone drove his happy family with, or the luxurious sedan that Roger E. Smith was being driven in.

Good Time for a Parade?

Moore also chose to include footage from a parade that was commemorating the Sit-Down Strike. Against boarded-up stores and apartment buildings, hundreds of people watched unaware of this great right-wing conspiracy to keep them poor and oppressed. The parade was a reminder of the disparity between what Boone advertised for years and what reality is for the common people of Flint, on a daily basis. Moore inserted it right in the middle of the film to introduce the section about the "reconstruction" of Flint's economy. At some point in the parade we can even see Ronald McDonald standing in a convertible

car. He cynically asks the out-of-work denizens if it is "a great time for a parade?" Moore cuts-in reaction shots into the scene and gives us a sense of the derelict aspect of the downtown portion of Flint, so we gather that the answer to Ronald's question would probably be "no". Clearly this fanfare was used by municipal leaders to mystify the population. These empty rituals were obviously trying to impose phony optimism on a totally depressed and barely redeemable environment.
There is also a lot of coverage as far as reaction shots from the parade are concerned. It confirms that his editing patterns are built around a scene, making it often less static and highly expressive.

In *Roger & Me*, Moore tells us that, in light of all these problems created by the layoffs, the only thing Flint officials could do was entertain people with diving donkeys and TV evangelists like Robert Schuller (who was paid $20,000 by the mayor to rid Flint of its "unemployment plague"). The idiotic content of shows like *The Newlywed Game* or the *Miss America Pageant* also helped to re-enforce the strength of escapism in Flint at the time, like the interview with Miss Michigan revealed. One of the people interviewed in the film was working for the Star Theatre (funded by G.M. money). He implied that the Flint show business frenzy was created in order to keep people entertained (i.e. out of touch with economical and political reality). It worked during the Great Depression, why not in Reagan's America? And is it the case today, at the dawn of the fall of capitalism?

Exiled on Main Street

One of the most absurd topics covered in *Roger & Me* regards Flint's administrators trying to rebuild the town with commercial and unsustainable projects. Obviously, those who came up with these gimmicks never learned anything about the inner workings and dynamics of capitalist society. The reality they were missing on goes as follow (and it is truer today than it was then): *If people do not have money because they are unemployed, they do not go around buying a bunch of useless stuff. Before anything else, they have to eat and pay rent!* This should be clear to anyone with half a brain, but it was not for Flint officials at the time. Or maybe these impossible projects were really about getting the last penny out of an already squeezed-dry and "lemon-like" economy. Could it have all been done, once again, for the benefit of corporations, banks, and credit card companies?

Local politicians and businessmen alike were pretty quick to answer to G.M. closings by developing huge (un) real estate projects, such as the Hyatt Regency, a luxurious hotel in Downtown Flint, and the Water Street Pavilion, a totally obsolete piece of architecture which included expensive stores where no one could buy anything - they could look at it, window-shop it, dream about it, but never buy it. The city also had to rely on tourists and visiting associations in order to survive, which obviously was not enough. You need a permanent 12-month-a-year-economy to make a city run smoothly. You also need jobs to keep people consuming and spending around the clock, which is the foundation of modern American society. Without this process of selling and buying around the clock, American capitalism runs the risk of becoming…unaffordable.

Moore tells us in voice-over that conventions such as the Michigan Ready Mix Concrete Association and the Statewide Organization of Scrabble Players did not succeed in saving Flint from its tragic downfall. Both the Hyatt and the Water Street Pavilion went bankrupt, and only a few people really benefited from such "fraught-with-peril" business ventures. Flint administrators went as far as to build an even more outrageous attraction to distract its desperate populace. Some genius on the Board (in the same sense that Jack Welsh and Roger Smith were geniuses) called upon Six-Flags Inc. to construct Auto World, a monument and tribute to mismanagement and human stupidity. Auto World was designed as an attraction site based on the concept that "the automobile made America possible," Moore says in the film. Six-Flags went to great lengths to recreate a small decor of Downtown Flint the way it was before the massive layoffs (all based on a Disneyland template). He underlines the absurdity of these projects by telling us that "People had to pay $8.50 to ride the city's only escalator and the world's only indoor Ferris-wheel."

But Moore, who has an exceptional flair for making conceptual connections while shooting, insists on an exhibition sponsored by G.M. This one had a mechanical puppet autoworker singing a love song to the robot replacing him on the assembly line: 'Me & My Buddy"… The final irony was that AutoWorld closed after only six months for lack of visitors. Moore reminds us that "Some people just do not like to celebrate human tragedy while on vacation." He even shows us the building for AutoWorld being destroyed by a wrecking ball in the end credits. What a shitty deal this has been for Flint citizens. Nobody really deserves to be treated like that.

D. I. Y.

Another segment in the film detailed how some Flint residents were still delusional concerning the possibilities and merit of hardcore State capitalism. Just like that quick insert of young workers picking up horse dung at the parade, the inclusion of the lint-roller and the "Am-Way Lady" in the film are all comments on the jobs now available in the post-industrial economy of Flint. The Am-Way phenomenon was supposed to save Flint from its economic downfall by putting people back to work; selling and distributing detergent and home products and receiving a small commission on every account in return. It was door-to-door sales disguised as Tupperware parties. Moore ridicules these attempts at rebuilding the Flint economy (and society) by having his "color analyzed" by a friendly and desperate woman. He knows that these kinds of jobs will not be effective as far as reinvesting life in a region built on steel and wheels. China leads the way in useless services and plastic products, anyhow. No one can ever come close to that level of planned obsolescence.

Moore's absurd humor makes the viewer shake his head in disbelief. He is asking us to look at the bigger picture and reflect on it. He also tells us to cheer up, that everything is not yet lost, that there are still good people out there, and that they will always find a way to survive, somehow. For some, these humorous scenes may feel like digressions from the main concern of the film, or an excuse for Moore to ingratiate in his love for comedy, but for us it essentially remains on target as far as exposing the effects of job lost on individuals. Losing your job at G.M and finding another type of work meant in most cases to lose on job quality and, most certainly, on job security. The argument made by these moments is subtle, but gets its point across when perceived within the film as a conceptual whole.

Wouldn't It Be Nice?

One of the great uses of ironic juxtaposition of sound in Moore's career comes after Ben Hamper talks about the Beach Boys single, 'Wouldn't It Be Nice?' We see a series of tracking shots showing us derelict houses around Flint and hear a report about a booming rat population overtaking the city. Excerpts from other news reports explain how Flint had been unable to cope with these sanitation problems, while Moore plays up to the pathos inherent to the shots by combining them with a popular song. The scene is difficult to watch because of its negative dialectics. Moore distorts the common take of image and sound by using a famous feel good song over images of human misery. Another, more humorous example of this tactic is in *TV Nation*, where he used 'Lovin' You' by Minnie Ripperton to taunt hate mongers in the "Love Night" episode.[43] Actually, it is hard not to notice how he got very agile at manipulating images, sound, and music over the years, as we will see in *Bowling for Columbine, Fahrenheit 9/11, Sicko* and *Capitalism*.

---

[43] *Adventures in a TV Nation*, pp.14-21

Moore also uses leitmotivs that will become part of his trademark. For instance, he inserts stock footage of antiquated modes of communication, such as the telegraph and old telephone operating boards to explain how he tried to get in touch with Smith (but to no avail). These shots are playful and entertain a certain rapport we all have with popular culture iconography. Today, in an age of laptops, Blackberry, iPhones and iPads, a medium such as the telegraph seems obsolete and therefore funny to us.

Without a doubt, Moore's style of inserting stock footage and cutting evokes the compilation film, which was the domain of Emile De Antonio, a filmmaker/political satirist at the head of the New York avant-garde in the 1960s-70s. De Antonio was an expert at using archival footage to mock politicians and politics in general. His films about the Vietnam War (*In the Year of the Pig*, 1969) and the one about Richard Nixon (*Millhouse, a White Comedy*, 1971) are still considered two of the best and most revealing nonfiction films ever made about those topics. In the first instance, De Antonio used music to satirical ends: a version of 'La Marseillaise' played by traditional Vietnamese instruments over shots illustrating the devastating effects of French colonization in Indochina. In the second film, he used an off-key version of 'Hail to the Chief' to ridicule Nixon; a satirical tactic that Moore often relies on.

In relation to other kinds of formal manipulations, the idea of letting the camera run "no-matter-what" often expresses itself in the form of long takes. Even though the average shot length of both his films and TV shows is pretty short, Moore still manages to make the most out of his material by inserting other footage inside a wide master shot. The most expressive use of long-take, moving camera and sound in *Roger & Me* is the lateral tracking shot on a series of abandoned houses while we hear dogs barking on the soundtrack. This slowly gives way to the well-preserved Buick Headquarters building in Flint with a fade-in of birds chirping in the background. Through camera movement and sound mixing, the filmmaker makes it clear that the problem has to do with the corporate mind running amok and class struggle at the end of the 20th century. In fact, Moore will use excerpts from *Roger & Me* two decades later, in *Capitalism: A Love Story* to address the very same issues. No one can ever accuse him of being inconsistent in that sense. Especially if we consider that his presentation style has only gotten more refined in the two decades that followed. Anyone who denies Moore the title of filmmaker should only compare these two films. It will automatically reveal that they are part of a long continuum, and that he is a true author of nonfiction cinema, like De Antonio was before him.

Infiltrator

Michael Moore does not only rely on formal manipulations, humor, and interactive forms of journalism to probe the ever-changing American society. He relies on infiltration as well. His tactics of crashing in certain social affairs and political events have only gotten more refined over the years. *Roger & Me* has many early and fascinating moments where Moore seems totally out of place and way too inquisitive for his own good. We sometimes have to wonder how he achieved such intrusive moments, even if a small production unit of only two or three people accompanied him. As mentioned before, most opponents know who Moore is nowadays, but back in the days of shooting his first feature, he must have appeared like a welfare recipient just walking around with a bunch of amateur-filmmakers, doodling around with non-professional equipment and concocting an amateurish "flicker." It is perhaps this low-budget quality and Moore's anonymity that allowed him to enter the wealthier quarters of Flint at the time.

Infiltration #1 is entitled "The Great Gatsby Party" and is set on the back lawn of a rich Flint industrialist. Moore not only wants to show us how the elite lives, but he also needs to understand why some wealthy people do not have any social conscience (he since then stopped demystifying the rich and started focusing beyond wealth, to issues of power, authority and social order). Here, the event he infiltrates is crowded with bourgeois Flint citizens who do not see anything wrong with hiring poor people (mainly young and/or black) to pose as "statues" in order to decorate their lame cocktail party. It must be that objectifying the other is so much part of their everyday life (since they already "own" businesses and workers) that using real people to decorate their lawn is a totally acceptable idea to them; they become like Marx had said: commodities.

At one point one of the guests tells him "We started something and we're gonna finish it. We're gonna be the leaders." When Moore asks him what is it that he and his "race" have invented and are "Number One" at, the man replies, "We have invented the wheel again," referring to the Industrial Revolution and the inventions that propelled it for 200 years. This wealthy man, who obviously never suffered a day in his life or missed anything essential (like food, shelter, and clothes), gives the people of Flint some good advice: "Get up in the morning and *do something*." He seems to believe that most poor people are in this predicament because they are lazy and unimaginative, not because they have perhaps been fired by one of his lackeys the month before. When asked by Moore about the positive aspects of Flint, another rich white man replies, "Ballet, hockey... It's a great place to live," as if anyone unemployed or underemployed could afford leisure activities. The editing then swiftly cuts to Deputy Fred Roos ("the only man in Flint with a secure job," the filmmaker tells us) evicting a black woman from her home, which makes the previous scene even more indecent for conscientious observers.

Throughout *Roger & Me*, the director infiltrates many other environments where he would not have normally been caught dead in. Infiltration # 2 is set at the Grosse Point Yacht Club, where Smith had been hanging out on weekends. At this restricted boating club, Moore encounters a secretary from whom he gets relevant data about the lifestyle of the rich and not-so-famous. The secretary tells him that exclusive members are usually fond of hunting animals for their meal. She points out that some of the animals hunted are "exotic," things like snakes, alligators, and other on-the-verge-of-extinction furry animals never brought to a rich man's plate before. Moore manages to stroll around the large dining room with his cameraman, while the receptionist calls someone to inquire "if anyone knows anything about this" (Moore lied and told her that Smith had agreed to see him there). While the scene is unfolding, Moore establishes certain links *in absentia* between the new financial aristocracy and the rituals of past aristocracies.

Infiltration #3 is quick but serves the point that Smith is part of this new kind of elite. Moore goes to the Detroit Athletic Club where the CEO is usually hanging out (after having fired thousands of people) to again establish links with history (the history of class behavior, perhaps). There, an obnoxious clerk tells him "If you can't get inside G.M. you can't get in here either," making it clear that it is all the same segregationist environment: wherever Roger hangs out is sure to be restricted to *his* kind of people. Soon thereafter, Moore infiltrates yet another bourgeois environment: the Country Golf Course. There, he encounters four women part of the financial elite of Flint. One of them, dressed in pastel plaid and driving a wedge, tells him that "Some people just do not want to work," that they are "lazy, taking the easy way out, I guess." When asked by Moore about the reasons why they like Flint, considering its desolated landscape and unappealing economic situation, their response is not very surprising either: "We like the stores, what's left of them...We like our friends..." The parallel editing between the effects of the plant closing and the wealthy relaxing, playing golf or having parties is not innocent on Moore's part. It obviously serves to reinforce the fact that one's wealth is always made on somebody else's back; a Marxist theme that will reappear again in his future work.

Pet or Meat?

But one of the most fascinating and unusual aspects of *Roger & Me* is the way in which its discourse intertwines the personal and the social almost indistinguishably. The story of each individual interviewed in the film is linked through a greater awareness of the problem in question. For instance, halfway through, Moore interviewed a young man who had to give blood just so that he could eat. The few dollars he made draining his life essence away barely allowed him to survive. Still, in spite of the drama inherent to the scene, and definitely out of Moore's control, it is all bathed in tenderness and affection as a moment of cinema, because Moore decided to not cut and insert this moment in the film. The humanity of the scene comes through when the young man's friend helps him to take off his coat in order to show the needle marks on his forearms. Moore gives the viewer time to think and to feel; feel that these young men stand for thousand of others who have to give blood and plasma daily in order to survive. Like in *Capitalism*, with its underpaid commercial airline pilots, Moore seems to be saying to the viewer: "If this is not an outrage to democracy, then what is?"

At another point in the film, Moore cuts-in a series of TV reports concerning criminality in Flint, already considered one of the most unsafe places to live in America. The voice-over of a television reporter claims that "The problem is that there are not enough jail cells for all the criminals," which denies the possibility of asking about the reasons why there is such a high level of criminality in the first place (i.e. to trace it back to its source: unemployment and economic instability). These kinds of deceiving tactics are often used by network television to diffuse viewer-involvement regarding what he or she is being presented with on screen. Moore pursues further this denial, just to emphasize it, by cutting directly to a shot of three men firing at a target range. After noticing that he had missed a shot, one of the men said to the other one, "I'll tell you, your biggest problem is your barrel length," as if this was the best solution to the social problems surrounding them: a bigger gun.

Standing as a precursor to two *Awful Truth* episodes described in the previous chapter, as well as to *Bowling for Columbine*, the following scene is an interview with two gun-store owners. They tell Moore that the mere sound of a shotgun racking is enough to scare-off any potential burglar or aggressor. While we hear the racking of the gun, Moore abruptly inserts a shot of a child waiting for her father to purchase a gun. The effect is jarring and creates a tension between what we saw before, what we are hearing in the sound bridge, and what is shown to us in the following shot. As discussed earlier, he uses this type of editorial manipulations to create an ironic distance and to make people think about the issues by creating links with peripheral but seemingly related events.

Ironically, the most talked-about scene in *Roger & Me* has to do with its explicit content that shocked animal-lovers everywhere. It is the scene where we see a desperate Flint woman butchering a pet rabbit so that she can eat. This moment is often pointed out to as being exploitative, but then again, one who believes this should be reminded that, on top of being something quite normal for a lot of rural people, Moore did not ask her to slaughter that animal. No one else did either. She did it on her own will, even before Moore came into the picture, in order to survive, which says a lot about the inhumanity of the current American system (allegedly the richest and most opulent in the world). To think that some people have to breed small animals (or even kill pets) to feed their families is truly disturbing in today's context, to say the least. It is way up there with senior citizens eating cat food. It shows that there is no more space for unpretentious individuals to prosper in a conglomerated world where monopolies are crushing everyone around them. All of it is arranged to make poor people even poorer and more indebted, by stepping on them, by not allowing them to start their own small business, or even have the bare necessities of life, such as a decent shelter and a balanced diet.

Another example of expressive editing in *Roger & Me* comes with the juxtaposition of the question being asked by a member of the crew to the aforementioned Bunny-Lady: "What happened to your brother?" the off-screen voice asks; the editing jump-cuts to the woman bashing the rabbit on the head with a club, after the question is being asked. This makes the transition evocative of the principal themes of the film. Her brother has been "hammered" by the corporation; workers are nothing but "meat"; executive decisions and profit-oriented obsessions will eventually lead America to Third World conditions, etc. The messy ritual of slaughtering and skinning the rabbit becomes therefore a hyperbolic representation of the suffering masses under extreme forms of capitalism.

But the most disturbing scenes of Moore's first film come towards the end, when well-to-do Flint citizens rent out prison cells for a night in order to party, or again when we find out that unemployed autoworkers have been recycled as prison guards who now have to take care of some of their ex-colleagues on the assembly line. These moments are truly disturbing because it reveals the flawed logic of State capitalism and its ramifications on social structures.

The Dawn of a New Era

Roger & Me was a critical and commercial success, but in the end it was perceived as entertainment for the masses. That is the reason why Moore believed he failed with his first feature,[44] since it did not manage to raise social consciousness concerning corporate abuse, and did not lead workers to concrete political action or social revolt either. However, the film did make people who saw it discuss the real issues, and brought to the foreground some of the major problems that America will have to deal with in the next century, such as a greater economic disparity between rich and poor, and the ever-increasing corporate abuse of public gullibility. For the more pessimistic viewer, though, the end of the film leaves you with the impression that nothing will ever change under the American dollar. As a matter-of-fact, Flint suffered even more under the Democrats in the 1990s, and it is still one of the most destitute places in the United States, as we can see in Moore's most recent film, *Capitalism: A Love Story*.

This being said, Moore's first major film serves today as a pedagogical tool for teachers of history, economics, sociology, and cinema. Not because of its "objectivity," but precisely because it is subjective. Almost two decades after its release and the controversy it created in its wake, a lot of people are still regarding it as a great piece of humanist filmmaking, as well as a brilliant analysis of how the corporate mind really works, through the negation of basic human dignity.

Stranger Than Fiction

Soon after *Roger & Me*, Michael Moore decided to give a shot at the conventional fiction film format that he so admires as a cinephile. His first attempt at creating an official work of fiction was received with mixed reviews upon its release, and he has yet to write or direct another one. Maybe was he aware that nonfiction allowed him to be more experimental, which is one of the most interesting aspects of his work? In comparison to films like *Bowling for Columbine* and *Fahrenheit 9/11*, his only fiction film to date, *Canadian Bacon*, seems classical and contrived. Although, in hindsight, we cannot help but to notice how accurate and prophetic its thematics really were.

---

[44] Michael Moore, director commentary, *Roger & Me* DVD, Warner Bros, 2003

CANADIAN BACON (1995)

> Canadians will tell you they have a lot of problems, and they do. But from our viewpoint, it looks like nirvana. They somehow get to have a similar culture but with a hell of a lot less problems of the kind that we have. And I encourage people to think about how well it's worked in Canada: they have national health care, they have these things that we should be able to have, and they attempt to deal with their racial problems in a different way than we do, and they're not always in a rush to get behind us to go to war and drop bombs on people.[45]

Neighbors

Canadian Bacon was the next project in line after Moore completed his pamphlet against G.M. and corporate America in late 1988. The film was produced by Propaganda Films in 1993, but its release got delayed for two long years because of a conflict between Moore and producers at the studio.

> They were very much in my face and tried to interfere in the process from beginning to end. Ya' know, these money guys are around and they're extremely nervous. Here I was: I finished this film on time, on budget, shot it in 38 days, and they just couldn't leave it alone. In some ways, what has delayed the release is my insistence that the film be the way it is, as opposed to the way they wanted it to be. They wanted more of *Uncle Buck*.[46]

Considering what is found in *Canadian Bacon*, it is fair to say that the mere fact that it was made and released is in itself amazing. Moore wanted to create a "serious comedy" about America's need to fuel on political aggression and expand its imperialist dominion. He had come up with a cinematic concept that uses a distinct society up the 49th parallel for comparative purposes. In fact, Moore often compares his homeland to Canada to frame the former with a different ideological positioning, and to oppose it to a more functional and relatively less violent society.

---

[45] Michael Moore interviewed by Andrew Collins, Monday November 11, 2002, *Film Guardian* Online Exclusive, 2002
[46] Michael Moore interviewed by Bob Strauss for *Pulse Magazine*, 1995

The United States and Canada, although geographically close, are fundamentally different in spirit. Their differences and aspirations can be traced back to 1776, when English-Canadians sided with Britain and French-Canadians with Americans in their revolutionary war. To this day, most Canadians wish to keep a distinctive identity and a more or less different set of values. They probably lean more to the left than their southern neighbors do, but Canada always did have a strong backbone of social conservatism as well (partly because of American pilgrims that came to colonize its western territories at the turn of the last century). If truth was told, as much as they want to preserve a distinct identity, a majority of Canadians cannot help themselves but to be totally immersed in, and utterly fascinated with American culture. For instance, most Canadians consume American films, television shows, and music, not their own indigenous productions. In many ways, this book is also symptomatic of this fascination described above. It offers a view on American politics and culture which is atypical and foreign, literally outside of the box, but not without having some form of contemplative qualities either. In fact, whatever admiration Michael Moore might have for Canada truly finds its equivalence in the admiration Canadians have for him, as a true American original with a heart.

God Bless America...Again?

> Most films in America are dumb and stupid and make a lot of money. Then you have a few art-house films that do not make much money. I think there's a big middle ground. People who live in the Pittsburghs and the Milwaukees and the Flint, Michigans, have a brain and would like to see a film that has all the normal movie conventions but is also about something. Why do these things have to be incompatible?[47]

Although classical in form and in style, *Canadian Bacon* contains many themes which are more relevant today than when it was made. This film also stands as a prototype for a kind of political filmmaking that can be produced within the studio system. Moore does not reinvent cinema at the level of narrative structure, which is predictable here, or even at the level of cinematography, acting, or editing, which are not very bold or expressive in this case either. The major bug with *Canadian Bacon* concerns the lack of finesse in some of the performances, which might be attributable to Moore's inexperience

---

[47] Michael Moore interviewed by David Sterritt, "One Filmmaker's Answer to Apathy," *The Christian Science Monitor*, October 2, 1995

with directing dramatic actors, and its slapstick elements, which sometimes defeat their own purpose. Although, this criticism seems minor when compared with what the film actually says about politicians and contemporary politics in general. Judging it from a formal angle does not seem appropriate. Rather, it should be assessed by the validity of the thesis that Moore puts forth concerning America's expertise at creating an economy based on lies and war. No doubt, his script is filled with awful truths regarding the workings of American politics.

While Tex Ritter's version of 'God Bless America Again' is heard on the soundtrack, Moore's camera flies over Niagara Falls on the Canadian side of the border, then quickly switch-pans over to the American side. From Olympian heights we follow the American President (Alan Alda) in his limousine. He is on his way to an auction of unused military arsenal from the Cold War era. We will soon find out that the company putting up these weapons for sale is Hacker Dynamics, and that it has a real conservative maniac for CEO. A local television reporter admits that the turnout for the President's visit is pretty low, but that this is not surprising, considering that the last President to visit Niagara Falls was William McKinley (who was assassinated there in 1901). We keep tracking the President's constituency making its way to the auction as the director mixes-in a deliberately pompous score composed by the late Elmer Bernstein. Quickly we are introduced to the idea that terrorism often comes from within the American borders (six months later, Timothy McVeigh was on his way to Oklahoma City). Roy Boy (Brad Sullivan), a desperate man who has just been laid-off from Hacker Dynamics, is trying to commit suicide by jumping into the falls. As he is about the commit the ultimate sacrifice, the presidential cortege passes right by him, unimpressed by the statement he's trying to make about corporate America and the way it treats its human resources.

The reporter indirectly introduces Sheriff Bud Boomer (the late Canadian actor John Candy), who also serves as Moore's unstable alter ego in this instance, as well as his wife, Deputy Honey (Rita Moreno), a wacky caricature of American womanhood. Both are simple-minded police officers from a small town on the American side of the border. The way Moore sets it up, we could be in any small town, including Flint. The two are standing at the bottom of the falls looking up. They are equipped with all the right gear to retrieve dead bodies from the turbulent waters. They both scream in harmony to Roy Boy: "Jump! Jump! Jump!" as if it was some kind of lucrative spectacle for them. Soon, the dialogue reveals that it is not the first time they've been retrieving bodies from these waters, since a lot of people have been desperate in the aftermath of the plant closings. We also learn that both used to work at Hacker before they were laid off and recycled as law enforcement agents, a self-referential wink to the recycled prison guards of *Roger & Me*.

From the onset, Moore tells us that some are profiting from other people's misery in America. Some individuals would actually do anything for a buck, even wishing at times for their neighbor's complete peril. This feeling usually stems from economic instability and social despair. Watching Roy Boy literally hanging by a thread of duct tape, Bud says to Honey: "It's a free country. If he does not like it here, he can swim across the river to Canada; a lot of work there!" Luckily for Roy Boy, the Sheriff suddenly realizes that he is a guy they both know from the neighborhood. Unfazed, Honey continues to scream "Jump!" anyway, but Bud brings her to reason, "No, let's help him out!" She then runs off-screen, leading us to believe that she will get the unemployed man out of his unfortunate position, but returns with a rifle and proceeds to shoot him in the shoulder (to "immobilize" him). Moore is making sure to let us know that Honey is one feisty and trigger-happy woman. She is just like all those outrageous militia babes in *Bowling for Columbine*: as alienated as her masculine counterpart.

"You Made It, You Can Own It!"

As the opening credits come to an end, Bud, Honey, and Roy Boy are now in a police car singing 'High Hopes' and driving through a post-industrial landscape reminiscent of the "Love Canal" episode in *TV Nation*.[48] They are on their way to the Hacker warehouse to buy some weapons for the local police force. After being ridiculed at the door by two *state* police officers, they finally enter the auction. Inside the military compound, the image composition emphasizes the ridiculous situation of sophisticated weapons being sold to the public. All around banners are hung on which it is written "Hacker Dynamics: Peace through Fear Since 1947!" There are also two symmetrical lines of rocket launchers displayed as to show their phallic properties. The idea behind this scene is close to the one found in *Bowling for Columbine*, when Moore proposes that the American government is keeping its subjects armed, dangerous and divided so that it can better rule over them. In this scene, an auctioneer is calling out for chemical and nuclear bombs, but no one dares to bet on them. Exasperated, he finally tells the curious people gathered for the occasion, "C'mon ladies and gentlemen, built right here in Niagara Falls, New York. This is your chance to own one. You built it you can own it now!" This might seem irrelevant to the narrative, but on a grander scale of things, it most

---

[48] *TV Nation*, first episode, originally aired on July 19th 1994

definitely conceals a Marxist undertone. Moore tells us that, for lack of being able to afford a nice home and a fancy car, you can always compensate by buying yourself some weapons for cheap. It illustrates once again the links between socioeconomic despair and social violence.

This is the moment when we are introduced to Kabral, an African-American municipal cop played by Bill Nunn (Radio Raheem of *Do the Right Thing* fame) and friend of Bud and Honey. At one point, he asks Bud permission to leave the warehouse, because "white people buying bombs make [him] nervous." Soon enough, one of the bombs is finally sold to Roy Boy for 25 dollars. He seems happy to own one and perhaps he will finally take revenge on the corporate world after all (if not by making grand statements where he self-destructs, then by taking a shot at the President). Next we are introduced to R.J. Hacker (G.D. Spradlin), the mad CEO of Hacker Dynamics, and the most dangerous character in the movie. This self-important man, who is obviously the quintessential Republican figure, pushes himself through the auction crowd and interrupts the proceedings.

Hacker:
I reckon that some of you folks don't know me, and if you don't, I'm R.J. Hacker and I own Hacker Dynamics, Hacker Aerospace, Time Hacker…and a bunch of others that I don't even remember their names, and you don't care! You're upset because I closed this plant and I put you all out on the street. But I want you to know that I'm upset too. In fact, I get kinda choked up thinking about it…

Hacker is not even done with his speech that we see the President of the United States arriving outside the warehouse. He is greeted by angry citizens who are holding picket signs saying: 'No Jobs - No Justice' and "Throw the Bum Out!' The President is also accompanied by two of his dangerous spin-doctors: National Defense Advisor Stu Smiley (Kevin Pollack) and General Dick Panzer (Rip Torn). These characters are composite ones and seem to have been inspired by some of the loonies working at the Pentagon after WW II and the Hawks in the Bush administration. They are the fear mongers who see world politics as a game that America will eventually win, and who make up the rules as they go along. They are the people who create and promote civil wars and who subsidize *coups d'état* in underdeveloped countries. They are the criminals who use tax-money to get richer and who send young people to die in useless wars for their benefit. At one point, before entering the military compound, Panzer draws Smiley's attention to the protestors outside the fence, "Look at that! That's what we get for kicking butt in every goddamn corner of the world!" Inside the compound, Hacker is still ranting through a large amplifier, obviously nostalgic for the good old days of the Cold War.

> Hacker:
> It used to be that you had your Russian-Red, you had your Cuban-Red, Hollywood-Red, Here-Red, There-Red, Everywhere-Red-Red, E-Hi-E-Hi-O! But it kept us on our toes! We didn't know who to mistrust but we had to defend ourselves! And you had good jobs to put meat on the table. But today we find ourselves being destroyed, not by the Reds, but by a bunch of short-sighted, bleeding-heart, penny-pinching Washington wimps!"

The President finally enters the auction and asks Panzer about Hacker.

> U.S. President:
> Who is this guy?

> General Panzer:
> R.J. Hacker, sir.

> U.S. President:
> R.J.? How' bout a little credit? I'm the only President who has not gotten us into a war!

> General Panzer:
> I think that's his point, sir. You have yet to send our boys into battle.

> U.S. President:
> But send them where? Nobody's bothering us.

> Stu Smiley:
> Send them *anywhere*, sir. Guaranteed 30 point boosts in the poll.

> U.S. President:
> Well, I'm not gonna start a war just to increase my popularity…What can I do for twenty points?

When the President steps on stage accompanied by an off-key version of 'Hail to the Chief' and various booing from the crowd, Hacker takes the opportunity to join Smiley backstage. The businessman strongly suggests to the latter that the government should force the Russians to go back into "Cold War mode," meaning that his likes could once again profit from imminent war and the fear it would induce in the American collective mind. Bud and Honey also meet up with Smiley but to acquire guns, while we hear the President rambling in the background. He is quoting unconvincingly from Dylan's 'Blowin' in the Wind' before being accidentally shot by Rob Boy. Bud saves the day by jumping on the President, allowing him to dodge the bullet, but everyone feels let down, somehow.

A Typical American Coup

The morning following the auction, Smiley and Panzer announce to the President that the accidental shooting at Hacker's plant helped his popularity rating, as well as the Dow Jones index. Panzer tells him that "Rumors that you were clinically dead for 5 minutes and returned to life boosted your rating with the Religious Right." Smiley seems happy to report that "Most of the voters felt that the President being dead or alive had no real bearing on their daily lives." Panzer finishes the naïve President off by telling him, "With all due respect, sir, enjoy your single term," to which the President nervously jumps out of bed and starts complaining like a spoiled brat, "That's not fair! Every other President had the Russians to blame for everything. What do I have?" Moore makes his fictitious President a "soft" Republican, a man willing to do almost anything for a second term in office; even creating a fictitious war with a friendly neighbor like Canada. In many obvious ways, Alda's character foreshadows George W. Bush sitting in the White House, precisely because he is presented as being immature. Moore has had clear premonitions about Bush Jr., six years before he came into office. Many references in the film remind us of Bush and Cheney's shenanigans to keep power in the second term, the influence of Rumsfeld on the conduct of the war, the manipulations of the Christian Right by Paul Wolfowitz and Karl Rove, etc. It is all here at the core of *Canadian Bacon*, an extremely clever film in its own right.

In the following scene, Smiley and Panzer suggest to the President that he should do a "summit thing" with the Russian Premier (Richard Council, who is well known for playing gangsters). Soon, a desperate American President is eating Kentucky Fried Chicken with the Russian Premier and asking him to participate in a mock Cold War. Unconvinced, the Russian Premier puts on his coat and leaves. Desperate for an enemy, the Americans go after him in the White House hallways. They insult, provoke, and finally attack him physically, in a slapstick moment that evokes *Dr. Strangelove* (1964).

As he enters his private helicopter, refusing to support the U.S. government's idea of a fake ideological warfare, he looks at the U.S. President straight in the eyes and tells him: "Goodbye, Mr. President. And good luck," again foreshadowing what Bush Jr. would have to prove in his second term in office: that unjust wars can be initiated, fought, and "won."

Blame Canada

Later, the President and his entourage are screening slides of old-time enemies in the war room. Most are already dead: Khomeni, Mao, and Brezhnev... Manuel Noriega comes in on a slide and Panzer tells the President, "This guy's is still alive, but he's down in Florida making license plates now," referring to the ex-CIA agent's fate after he had shafted the American government in Panama and it had blown up in Poppa Bush's face. When Jane Fonda comes on the slide-show, Panzer says, "She's reformed," referring to her dissident past during the Vietnam War. Another "defense consultant" ridiculously proposes an invasion of aliens from outer space, evoking a certain 1950s understanding of the world, America, and its share of problems. Then, the President starts whining, "Jesus, is that the best you can come up with? How about, you know, international terrorism?" Panzer replies, "We are not going to re-open missile factories just to fight some creep who's running around and exploding rail cars, are we, sir?" (Note to the reader: pre-9/11 humor). Desperate to solve his image problem, the President says jokingly, "How about Canada?" Moore cuts the previous scene with an insert of the Canadian flag at a hockey game. While a crowd sings the Canadian national anthem, we see individual close-ups of Bud, Honey, Roy Boy, and Kabral getting restless as they wait for the game to begin. Bud mocks the national anthem and makes fun of the maple leaf situated at the center of the flag. He wonders aloud if it is "a piece of weed or something." Honey tells Bud that "Canadians do not have a care in the world," while Roy Boy insults the game by claiming that hockey is an American invention. For his part, Kabral complains that there are not any "brothers" in hockey, that it is mainly "a white guy sport." They are all portrayed as being loud, unrefined, and obnoxious. All of the insults do not mean a thing to Canadians until Bud actually screams that "Canadian beer sucks." A fight between hockey players and crowd follows right there and then. In a parallel editing scheme, Moore cuts back to Smiley and Panzer watching footage from "precision-target missiles" that were used during the first Gulf War, or so we are told by Panzer. Excited, the latter yells, "Look at that! That's footage you've never seen on TV!" Moore is reminding us that politicians and generals are running the war at a distance and without a care. Like overgrown children, they treat it as a meta-video game without any real consequences.[49] Smiley changes the channel with a converter to keep up with what is going on in ill-stricken America, and his attention is suddenly drawn to a report about the fighting going on between American and Canadian hockey-lovers at the border. It is at this moment that he gets the idea to declare war on Canada, one of the most pacifist countries in the world.

Please, Not Anne Murray!

Soon after this local incident, Smiley meets up with a secret agent assigned to the "Canadian file" in Washington (we are made aware that he has just been demoted from the "Cuban file"). He reminds Smiley that Canada has been undermining capitalism for decades.

> Secret Agent:
> I've been telling you all along, they've always had these tendencies! They're a little strange with this socialized medicine stuff.... Did you know that they provide free college? To anyone! Free trains! Free eyeglasses! Free condoms!

Then, we see Smiley (whose name evokes the saying "The assassin comes with a smile") hosting an emergency Security Council with the President at his side. He exposes the situation to the Pentagon staff.

> U.S. President
> Canada? Did you say Canada? The American people, Mr. Smiley, would never buy this.

> Stu Smiley:
> Mr. President, the American people will buy whatever we tell them to. You know that.

---

[49] Consider Bush's decision to send 21,500 more soldiers to Iraq in January of 2007. This was done at a time when even Republican hard-liners were begging for a total recall, and in spite of the recommendations of the bipartisan Baker-Hamilton study group. Moore wrote an open letter to Bush on January 11th of that year wherein he suggested sending all 64 million Americans who had voted for him in 2004. He also told Bush that he, himself, should be the first one in the line of fire in Iraq.

Council Member #1:
Are not you overlooking one major obstacle? Like how to get the average American to hate and *fear* Canadians?

Council Member #2:
Hell, they're whiter than we are!

Stu Smiley:
Gentlemen, please. Allow me to clue you in to a few rude awakenings. For those of you who think that Canada is a "mom and pop" operation, it's time to wake up and smell the snow. Fact: Canada is now the second largest country in the world. Fact: Canadians freely cross over our border, walking among us, undetected… How many of you knew that they've eliminated the *Miss Canada* contest?

General Panzer:
I think you're on to something here, Smiley. Remember the air force C-130 that crashed mysteriously a few years ago? It happened over Canada, Mr. President.

U.S. President:
My God, that's, that's shocking! How… When did they get rid of *Miss Canada*?

Stu Smiley:
A year ago.

U.S. President:
Jesus! Suppose something like that caught on down here?

Stu Smiley:
One week, Mr. President. Give me one week and I'll have Americans burning maple leaves so fast that they won't have time to think about their smog-filled lungs, rising interest-rates or their dwindling savings accounts. One week sir…

Following Smiley's proposition to make an enemy out of Canada, NBS announces in typical American propaganda-style that the northern country has been developing military build-up.

NBS Anchorman:
NBS News has obtained Pentagon documents that show that our neighbor to the North, the sovereign nation of Canada, has embarked on a military program aimed at the U.S.

Moore inserts some vintage footage of people skating and taking snow baths, two clichés of Canadian life.

> NBS Anchorman (v.o.):
> "Canada, known for ages as a polite and clean country has, under a socialist majority, undertaken a massive military build-up on its border with the United States...."

Again, we cut to Smiley at a press conference. He is now trying to convince Americans of a "Canadian threat" by totally perverting the statistics. "Canada owns more of the U.S. than any other country," he wrongfully claims. A reporter is also telling us about "who the Canadians really are." Moore has a corny graphic that says "Canadians" with headshots of famous Canucks over a crowd walking American streets. All the while, Sheriff Boomer is watching this news report in his living room, in classic couch-potato mode. The sequence is interrupted with friction like channels changing on a TV set, a technique often used since then. It cuts to a *Sally*-kind of show where the host asks the wrong questions as usual, "Is Canadian Prime Minister Clark MacDonald part of a satanic cult?" and then to some old footage of charging Mounties and a man sharpening a skate. Meanwhile, Honey is watching the report and cleaning one of her biggest *rocket launchers*. Moore emphasizes the idea that American media needs to create drama and spectacle when reporting the news, and that this has an influence on the way Americans usually react to situations of conflict (or fictitious conflict).

> NBS Anchorman (v.o.):
> "Most of Canada's vast military technology has been built and supplied by the United States. The Canadian National Tower in Toronto, erected to transmit nuclear attack warnings from radar stations in Northern Canada, is now solely in Canadian hands. It is the height of six American football fields. Or five Canadian football fields...as if Canadian football really counts. What would be the psychological motivation for erecting such a huge, long, rigid shaft...?"

Moore cuts back again to the main architect of the lie at a *Meet the Press*-type morning show.

> Stu Smiley:
> First of all, there is no Canadian culture. I've never read any Canadian literature. And when have you heard anyone say "Honey, let's stay in and order some Canadian food?"

Roy Boy and Kabral are sitting in a bar watching this show. The NBS anchor resumes as the camera tracks-in to his dramatic facial expression.

> NBS Anchorman:
> Congress is also asking intelligence agencies to investigate why the Canadians maintain a threatening lead in Zamboni technology. Think of your children pledging allegiance to the Maple Leaf. Mayonnaise on everything... Winter, eleven months out of the year... Anne Murray, all day...everyday....

Home-Brewed Militia

Michael Moore often mocks the reactionary quality of Americans with amusing and revealing montage sequences. In *Canadian Bacon*, he does so by letting the paranoia percolate through the grassroots, and by having the nutty sheriff taking control of the situation. Along with Honey, Roy Boy, and Kabral, Sheriff Bud Boomer organizes a vigilante defense unit modeled after the Minutemen. Over the theme song for *The Green Berets*, Moore creates a montage of armed and barricaded Americans guarding the local bowling alley and the Niagara Falls Visitor Center. They are putting up signs that say "Bomb Canada" on various walls and trees of the community. In a moment pre-dating *Bowling for Columbine*, the director pushes the gag further by having a line-up of various American citizens waiting to be handed free guns for a mortal combat with Canuck. Later, in the same montage sequence, a man destroys a road sign giving directions to Canada, and a homeless man is arrested for drinking Molson beer out of a brown paper bag. People even have to hand-in their ice skates to Bud's militia. In the final moment of the sequence, Moore's *mise en scène* has a group of Native Americans on the back of a pick-up truck, waving guns and a U.S. flag. This inclusion is relevant here, because the U.S./Canada border in the northeast region has many reservations representing, not only a legal constitutional body, a parallel people and culture that somehow managed to avoid extinction, but also a ground where local and vigilante warfare could possibly occur.

In the following sequence, Smiley meets up again with the sinister R.J. Hacker. The latter tells him that Americans *really* have to believe the scare concocted by the government. He gives the example of Vietnam, where people believed, for a short while at least, the threat of communist proliferation in the West, evoking the so-called "domino theory." Like the Hawks (Cheney, Rumsfeld, Wolfowitz et al.), Hacker believes that America has a mission in the world: to defeat "evil." Any evil. If it does not exist, you can invent it at your convenience. Here,

Moore inserts a mockumentary of the "Canadian Threat" that mimics the propaganda newsreels of the Cold War. Instead of having red blood dripping over a map of the Soviet Union with a grim voice-over commentary, he just has maple syrup dripping over a map of Canada with a grim voice-over commentary! After having screened it, the President calls the audiovisual document "stunning." Smiley then comes up with the brilliant idea to create a Canadian hit squad which could sabotage American installations and infrastructures along the border. There are obviously not limits to his Machiavellian schemes.

Next thing we know, a Niagara Falls hydro station is being raided by a fictitious Canadian commando. Before they can blow it up, Bud and his Militia manage to stop them. The event makes it to the NBS evening news where a reporter (Jim Belushi) explains that "Canada has amassed 90% of its population along its border with the United States, the longest unprotected border in the world, stretching from the Atlantic Ocean…to the other one," therefore putting more oil in the Republican's propaganda machine. Moore cuts back to Smiley playing chess with Hacker (they are supposed to be the two smartest characters in the movie, which is a scary thought). He tells the latter that the "Hacker's Hell-Storm" was delivered to Canada the day before. From now on, anything can happen. Here again, and much like in *Fahrenheit 9/11*, Moore links the CEO of a weapon-making corporation to the National Security Advisor, suggesting that American politics are fueled by war mongers who profit from perpetual conflicts and human misery. Hacker's character is one who makes a living from the war industry and from war itself. He is the new version of General Ripper. Moore makes it clear that Hacker used to be an army man who made the switch to corporate life while keeping the ethos of warfare. This character announces the coming (back) of people like Cheney and Rumsfeld in the White House. They are just your typical American byproducts of the post WW II years. Individuals afflicted by the illusion of grandeur that came along with winning that war, still high from the beneficial effects of the Marshall Plan.

Culture Clash

After having set the dramatic build-up in place, Moore leaves it to the actions of his characters (and unfortunately to characterization) to carry the ideological messages of the film. Honey becomes obsessed with the CN Tower where the climax will be held. At one point, we see her carving the tower out of mashed-potatoes like Richard Dreyfuss in *Close Encounter of the Third Kind* (1977). For his part, Bud manages to reorganize his militia and cross over the Niagara River to "pollute Canada." Of course, Honey hops along with them (actually, she seems to be leading the commando). Once in Canada they encounter two Mounties who politely ask them not to pollute and who wind up arguing about proper English grammar because of it. In the confusion that follows, Bud, Roy Boy, and Kabral flee, forgetting all about Honey who remains stuck on the Canadian side of the border. The plot device is a ploy which will serve to have the boys deliver her later in the film.

In the following moments, the President goes on national television to announce that Canadians are holding Deputy Honey hostage (how convenient for him). He warns the Canadian Prime Minister by looking straight into the camera, even appearing mature for a short while, "Surrender her pronto, or we'll level Toronto. God Bless America," he says gloriously. After seeing an amateur video of Honey calling on him to save her from the clutches of the evil Canadian government, Bud promptly reacts. Moore cuts to a TV set announcing the official start of "Operation Canadian Bacon: A Line in the Snow" (mocking the patriotic jingoism that Americans use in times of crisis). In the final act of *Canadian Bacon*, Bud's militia again crosses over the border to save Deputy Honey. As they storm into a power station in Southern Ontario, they are greeted by an elderly couple eating cookies, having tea, and watching a documentary about elks on television (that's Canada alright...in Moore's eyes). They seem harmless quite enough, except that Bud is suspicious by nature, and so he decides to tie them up anyhow. Bud eats their cookies, drinks their tea, and then asks the couple about the "switch" that would allow to "pull the plug" on the Canadian Mounted Police Headquarters (represented by a log cabin in the film, deliberately in a low-budget way). Bud soon pulls a lever that blacks-out Toronto and proceeds to leave with his brothers in arm.

Next, Bud's militia is erupting at the R.C.M.P. headquarters, which is guarded by one single Mountie (Steven Wright). The latter is in the midst of writing a Christmas card to a criminal ("Thank you for keeping your cell clean," it says). The Mountie is peacefully eating homemade fudge and writing good wishes to all when the Americans come crashing in through the front door. Bud threatens him right away with the barrel of his gun, "I'm your worst nightmare. I'm a citizen with the constitutional right to bear arms," he says to him. Kabral mocks the Canadian accent ("aboot" instead of "about," the Mountie says), while Roy Boy threatens him verbally at gunpoint, "We have ways to make you pronounce the letter "O," he says grinning with all of his bad teeth. Pressured by the Americans, the Mountie shows them the only three cells of the headquarters to prove that Honey is not occupying one of them. Bud asks him about Honey's whereabouts, to which he replies that she is being detained in the nation's capital. Bud gives his orders, "Okay men, let's go to Toronto!" The Wright character reminds him that the Canadian capital is Ottawa, not Toronto. Suspicious as usual, Bud's militia storms out anyway in direction of

Toronto. They highjack the Mountie's truck and graffiti some profanities against Canada on its sides.

The parallel editing Moore designed takes us back to the war room in the Pentagon, where the President, Smiley, Panzer, and other Security Council members are reunited to plan the next big step in this new type of cold war against Canada. The President proposes a nuclear bomb to resolve the conflict, an idea to which Panzer is opposed (because war has to be perpetual for him to have a job). The latter proposes instead that Bud Boomer, now made famous from the hockey-night incident, should be perceived as a national hero by the American public (because heroes are essential to a country built on myth and self-reverence). Another council member interrupts the discussion to draw the President's attention towards a television set in the Oval Office's main room. On one screen, we see shots of Americans harassing other Americans, vandalizing property with Canadian signs on them, and burning Toronto Blue Jays paraphernalia and Bryan Adams pictures (among other "Canadian things"). This sequence also includes cameos from Moore and his friend, *Roger & Me* star and *Awful Truth* correspondent, Ben Hamper. They both play unstable Americans idolizing Sheriff Bud Boomer and imitating his loony vigilante actions against Canada.

"American Woman (Stay Away From Me)"

In the less-inspired resolution of *Canadian Bacon*, hostage Honey manages to escape from a candy-colored hospital where she was being held (because of a self-inflicted wound), while Bud and his militia are discussing around a campfire site on their way to Toronto, "Canada's National Capital," according to him. The men are also talking about the importance of heroes in American culture, for Kabral explains, with no great surprise, that black characters always die first in Hollywood movies. Later on up the road, they even try to sing the Boss' 'Born in the U.S.A' together. The song is well known for being a criticism of the American government regarding the way it had treated Vietnam veterans upon their return, but for Bud's militia, like it was for President Reagan, it seems to mean something entirely different. It becomes an idiotic anthem for shallow and empty patriotism.

Meanwhile, there are worst problems on the home front. R.J. Hacker is connected to a remote activation system that will allow him to detonate a nuclear bomb from Canada unto Russia. This would entail a retaliatory response from the Russians unto U.S. territory within minutes, as well as ending civilization as we know it. The bomb is predictably located inside the CN Tower where Honey is now stuck.

This final line of action propels the ending of the film, an ending that seems a bit awkward, like most American film endings usually are. Honey is at the top of the tower in sniper-mode and Bud has come to rescue her. From a chopper hovering next to the tower, the police pleads with her, "Attention please, attention please, this is the Royal Canadian Mounted Police. Would you come down from the tower, please?" Honey screams at them, "If you say 'please' one more time, I'm gonna let you have it!"

Moore's first fiction concludes with a convoluted climax where a nuclear showdown is aborted *in extremis* by Deputy Honey. There is a shoot-out that messes up the motherboard located inside the tower, and the world is thus saved from total destruction. At the same time, Smiley inadvertently kills Hacker in the war room, while Panzer takes control of the situation by ordering his arrest (in other words, they turn on each other). The latter tells the President that he's ready to nuke Canada, just so that it will give him the opportunity to finally fight the Soviets (the real nemesis of Americans). The President, regaining reason and personal will, tries to talk the Canadian Prime Minister out of a nuclear war, even though he was the one who initiated it. The final pandemonium gives way to a kind of happy ending where Bud Boomer and Honey are seen navigating a small boat on top of Niagara Falls…at the threshold of their sanity. In the end credits, there is a dedication to Moore's grandfather, William J. Wall, "a Canadian who came to America and who loved going to the movies." Overall, the real interest in *Canadian Bacon* lies in the fact that it addresses again in satirical form many issues that are central to Moore's entire work.

Sleeping with the Elephant

The fact that he is interested in those matters of mutual interest between North American countries is not very surprising, since it relates to other themes present in his films and TV shows. For him, to study these friendly neighbors up North seems to be one way to understand what is wrong with the United States today. It gives him something to oppose insanity to. Although, the film is more about what America is than about what Canada is not. Therefore, it remains only half-efficient as a full-blown satirical piece. The plot would have certainly gained from showing the Canadian side of things to the American viewer, which is not exactly like Moore's point-of-view either. There were rumors for a while that he had to cut the original ending with the Canadian Premier character (Wallace Shawn, who will reappear in *Capitalism: A Love Story*), mainly because it left things too "open-ended" for the general American audience. Considering the problems Moore had releasing the film, there is little doubt that *Canadian Bacon* will never be re-released in director's cut format in the future.

As far as the depiction of Canadians and Quebecois people in his film is concerned, it is not difficult to imagine that some of them might be offended by being reduced to such an outline of a culture. But this would be to miss the entire point of Moore's political satire (which is often aimed at understanding and accepting diversity and difference). In order to address many issues simultaneously, satire requires that a creator narrow things down to the contours of a subject matter. The caricaturing dimension of Moore's humor necessitates a stylization of content. By and large, Moore's interest in Canada is flattering and serves as an example of possible openness of the American mind. Canada itself is the paradigm of a democracy that can work, having successfully balanced capitalism with "socialist tendencies" for years. Moore wants to remind Americans that there is still space for an understanding of every culture in this world, even of the smallest ones. He acknowledges the limitations of ethnic stereotyping by using it himself, so as to short-circuit it. He often relies on derision in order to sublimate a reality or to freeze-frame it for analytical purposes, something that seems quite clear in *Canadian Bacon*. Beyond this, Moore's mode of discourse is apologetic. He wants to illustrate that even Americans are inherently good people, that they are just easily manipulated by their leaders.

Lastly, the forces of demography have made Canada a satellite of the United States as far as politics, economy, and culture are concerned. This will probably never change because, although Canadians never wanted to be participants in the Americanization process, the riptide of popular culture sucked them into it. By controlling every aspect of the economy, American policies define, not only its own culture, but foreign ones as well. Canada is certainly no exception in that way. Actually, it probably is the first victim of the American expansionist attitude. It is hard to get some rest when you are "sleeping with the elephant," as ex-Canadian Premier Pierre Elliot Trudeau once remarked to a group of American journalists. On the day this pachyderm decides to roll over to its side, its bed-partner will surely be crushed forever by its outrageous and ever-expanding girth. *Canadian Bacon* is only one illustration of this uneven and rarely discussed partnership. (In the 2006 Canadian elections, Moore chastised Canadians for re-electing Stephen Harper, a right-wing conservative not too far politically from George W. Bush. This may very well prove that the gap between U.S. and Canadian cultures might not be as wide as we believe after all.)[50]

---

[50] "Michael Moore Disappointed by Harper Victory," *Resource News International*, January 24, 2006

THE BIG ONE (1997)

> I don't think we live in better times. I think a lot of people are doing much better, but what seems to be forgotten, what's not being reported in the media, is that a lot of other people are not doing well right now. If they have jobs, they're working longer hours for less pay, less benefits, and no job security. A lot of people I know are working two jobs just to pay the bills. Credit card debts are at an all time high, bankruptcies are at an all-time high. These are the statistics that rarely get reported when they are talking about the "Great Economic Miracle."[51]

Squeezed

Following the late release of *Canadian Bacon* and the airing of the second season of *TV Nation*, Michael Moore went back to nonfiction mode with *The Big One*. This title refers to the big earthquake scheduled to destroy California (and by extension, America), to the "We're Number One" skit of *TV Nation*, produced two years earlier, as well as to Moore's proposition to rename the country in his book *Downsize This! Random Threats from an Unarmed American*. Shot on video, and transferred to film, it was produced and directed while he was busy touring the country to promote this first book. Not surprisingly, he barely managed to remain on schedule during his book tour, since he also took every opportunity he could find to shoot a "road movie" on the side. With his small crew, he winded up visiting 47 cities all over the U.S., while shooting what became a pretty informative and entertaining picture along the way. No doubt, it must have been a way to combine business with pleasure.

Although *The Big One* is not Moore's best effort, it still contains enough quintessential moments to make it a mandatory viewing for any fan. The film is in logical continuity with *Roger & Me*, made 7 years earlier, since it has the same political goal: to confront giant corporations, expose their bad labor practices and, ultimately, give voice to those directly affected by the downsizing. In many ways, both films are structured, developed, and resolved in the same fashion. Both are shaped as a journey made up of discoveries and conflicts between filmmaker and security personnel (at lobby level), as well as including many other humorous moments where Moore meets with fellow entertainers or regular folks struggling to get by on a daily basis.

---

[51] Michael Moore interview on *The Arlene Bynon Show*, Canadian television (Global Television), 1997

Moore has truly developed his style with this particular film. The whole exercise made it clear that he is not only a propagandist interested in politics and human rights, as if this was not enough, but also a producer of meaning with a sensibility for form and aesthetics (two words foreign to American mainstream culture). Both films are non-linear in their storytelling structure and multi-layered in the presentation of the material gathered, organized, and included in the final cut. Moore often steps out of his main narrative drive in order to comment on peripheral events surrounding corporate downsizing, which always relates to consumerism and capitalism as a whole. As noted in the previous chapters, corporate crime became a regular trend in the 1980s and grew wildly out of proportions in the 1990s. In fact, the whole corporate over-indulgence Moore has been criticizing for two decades culminated with first the Enron scandal, then again with the subprime mortgage crisis and the financial meltdown of Wall Street in 2008.

The Enron scandal was a shameful affair that has since been buried under the 9/11 tragedy, the "war on terrorism," the Afghanistan War, the capturing, "trial" and execution of Saddam Hussein (if not of bin Laden, the so-called culprit of 9/11) and the occupation of Iraq. The subprime crisis was/is the result of banks and insurance companies creating, over a period of just a few years, a financial system where anyone could borrow money, even to those who knew from the start that they couldn't pay it back. It was triggered by the rise in mortgage delinquencies and foreclosures in the U.S. and had incredibly damaging consequences on the biggest banks in America (Bank of America, Freddie Mac & Fanny Mae, Goldman Sachs, etc.). In fact, and as we will see in Moore's *Capitalism: A Love Story*, it is the closest that we have come to a total obliteration of the entire capitalist structure as we know it. This was avoided *in extremis* by a newly-elected President Obama, who pushed Bush's 700 billion dollar bailout to Wall Street even before he officially took office (something never seen before in American political life), bringing along in his new administration members of the Federal Reserve Bank (a private entity) and the Bush regime, like Timothy Geithner and Robert Gates.

Off the Beaten Trail

Random House had proposed Moore a conventional book tour to promote *Downsize This!*, but he chose to go to cities that "serious" authors are not usually interested in instead. Needless to say that places like Flint and Des Moines, or even medium-size cities like Milwaukee and Baltimore are almost never on the agenda of famous writers or TV personalities, unless it is to make a point about the importance of regions on book sales. But generally speaking, American media does not venture much into the belly of the nation unless it has a good lead or a dramatic story-line (e.g. a little girl trapped in a well or kidnapped by one of her parents; a serial killer or sniper on the loose; a natural catastrophe that will allow human resilience to triumph over adversity in the end, etc.). We can almost break it down into 4 or 5 genres of investigative reporting, but they all boil down to the same thing: sensationalism at the expense of the American heartland. Moore beats his own trail. He is not interested in genres (and even less interested in sensationalism, which is not the same as controversy). When he does use these prefabricated forms of storytelling, it is only to dismantle them with the idioms of satire, an area that conventional journalism necessarily avoids. Furthermore, his choice of beating a different trail for the promotion of his book proves that he is more interested in content than in presentation, something that eludes most popular authors living in the United States today.

Moore uses aesthetics in a populist way and with a kind of intelligence that surpasses most so-called "independent films" out there on the market. Through quick and jagged editing that messes-up temporality and reinvents the nonfiction form, he offers multi-angular point-of-views that often explodes into a vibrant and meaningful mosaic of contemporary society. The people he interviews all throughout *The Big One* greet him as both, a champion and a troublemaker. He also gets into trouble with his "media escorts" along the way, something that his detractors are quick to point to, suggesting all the while that Moore is a mean-spirited man by nature.

The Call of the "Buck"

The film opens with a stand-up routine given by Moore while on tour. He explains to a crowd how he sent fake 100 dollar-donation checks to political candidates running in the 1996 elections, and how they all cashed these without taking under consideration the identity of the donors. This is comes directly from the book (*Downsize This!* pp. 22-26) and shows how far the political elite are willing to go to fuel their climb to the top. Moore reminds his public that "We live in sick, sick times" after explaining that Pat Buchanan had cashed a check signed by the "Abortionists for Buchanan," that Clinton had cashed-in a hemp growers check, and that Ross Perot had cashed his, which was endorsed by the "Pedophiles for Free-Trade Association." In effect, Moore is telling us that, since the Nixon campaign of 1968, we haven't yet been able to differentiate between campaign funding and the campaign itself. Partly because American politics have become part of the entertainment industry: the bigger the promotional budget, the more chances to be voted Number One. We should admire Moore for taking the time to commit these subversive stunts, however prankish or insignificant some may believe they are. Most of us already know that many politicians are crooked and have no morality, but few would go to those lengths to prove it.

People who criticize Moore should try to do something about these kinds of political shenanigans themselves. They should stand-up and make their own convictions be heard in the public arena, in whatever positive way they can. They should voice their own ideas in a constructive manner. They should try to make their philosophy concrete by acting it out in their everyday life. If they are not prepared to do this, then, they should get on with his program, which is about liberating the full potential of a world that could eventually be freed from the excesses of the Right.

The Excesses of the Right

In an interview for KMOX in St. Louis, Missouri, Moore explains the "logic" of corporate America in the mid-1990s.

> Moore:
> Most of this welfare we give corporations comes in the form of things like a million dollars to McDonald's to help them promote Chicken McNuggets in Singapore, that's our tax dollars. Or the Pillsbury Company gets 11 million dollars that goes to the Pillsbury Doughboy to be promoted in Third World countries…

Later, upon paying a visit to Pillsbury's HQ in Minneapolis, he asks the then-CEO the following question: "Why does Pillsbury need 11 millions dollars in welfare money for the Doughboy?" That few in the electronic media criticize such mishandling of public funds is a scary thought. It only goes to show that the knowledge of a problem is a very different thing than the understanding of that problem, since most investigative reporting lays out the facts but rarely bring the casual viewer to a full grasp of the consequences of such administrative policies.

The case of Pay Day employees is another example of serious mismanagement and corporate greed in Clinton's America. Some employees had worked there for over 50 years and got laid-off with no benefit whatsoever. The Centralia factory we see in the film made 20 million dollars in profit the year that *The Big One* came out. Yet the corporation downsized its work force without batting an eye or shedding a tear. One frustrated employee encapsulates Moore's philosophy about this new version of capitalism: "Tell me something. I wanna know what is gonna happen to the United States of America when they downsize everything and we get down to where everybody is making minimum wage? Who's gonna buy 30,000 dollar-cars? Who's gonna buy homes? Who's gonna buy this stuff? I wanna know! And it's just gonna be like a snowball effect, because then auto-makers are gonna be out of work, the construction people are gonna be out of work...Who's got the money to buy this if we're all downsized to $4.75 an hour? When is it gonna end?" Later in this segment, Moore goes inside the Centralia factory in order to talk with the foreman. The camera stays at distance, since the latter does not want to be caught lying on camera. As it turned out, he winded-up telling Moore the truth.

Moore:
What is the message to the American worker, that if they come here, work hard and do well...because of their hard work the company does well, their reward is unemployment?

Pay Day Manager (off):
You know, if this place would have done better and would have made more profit there would have been a quicker payback...

Moore:
You're saying that if you had made a bigger profit here, the move would have been even quicker to get out of here? If the workers had done a worst job, if the candy bar hadn't done as well, there might still be a candy bar plant here?

Pay Day Manager (off):
That's true.

Moore:
That's insane!

What Moore is after since *Roger & Me* are life-lessons in corporate ethos. Why do these companies lay-off their workers after they had just made record profits (we are sometimes talking in the billions here)? Why do they use the excuse of "staying competitive" in order to move their plants outside of the country and put their fellow Americans in misery (therefore creating more social problems that will wind-up affecting everyone, perhaps even them)? Why does the Federal Government give tax breaks and hand-outs to big companies who do not need them, instead of distributing wealth more fairly among its working (and consuming) population? Is that all free enterprise can offer? Those are the questions almost never asked in American media. Those are the questions that Moore has been consistently asking in his work for over two decades.

Voting? For What?

A few scenes later, Moore goes to a Hearty Platter coffee shop where he interviews regular folks concerning the upcoming election. When asked about which candidate he will vote for, a middle-aged man replies, "I wish we had a better choice, but we have to pick between two evils." The man goes on to admit that he works harder than he ever did, and that he doubts there will be any money left for his retirement fund. Another young female customer explains that "You gotta pay your rent, your electricity, your water, your gas, your food and your clothes for your kids…There's no money left at the end of the month." In a close-up shot, Moore makes sure to let us know that this woman has two jobs and cannot even see her kids on a daily basis. She only gets to see them on the weekend, "like someone whose been divorced or sentenced to a jail term," as he points out in the movie. What kind of advice does this woman have for her fellow Americans? "Don't vote!" she says bitterly. The American Dream seems to be unattainable for most common people, and this is only one of the things the film is constantly hinting at.

Ironically, while shooting *The Big One*, Moore learned that *Downsize This!* made the #1 Best Seller position of the *New York Times*. After one of his assistants underlined the fact that himself now works for big corporations, the filmmaker said mockingly, "Now that I made the *Times*, I do not think corporations are such a bad idea after all…Flat tax is not such a bad idea either, come to think of it." Of course, he is being sarcastic (it seems all too clear when he adds what was to become the mantra of all 2000 election candidates: "flat tax" was the common platform of the "Republicrats," as he used to call them). The author/filmmaker is making fun of himself. He knows all too well that he needs the system as much as it needs him. Moore *does* believe that American capitalism could work. If only it was more like Canadian capitalism…with its "socialist tendencies."

Hard Times for an Honest Man

As mentioned before, Michael Moore is combining business with pleasure in *The Big One*. An example of this is while he is signing books at a Borders store in Des Moines. There, he is handed out an anonymous (and typical) note that reads:

> Hey Michael, we're organizing here in Borders in Des Moines. There's a secret meeting statewide tomorrow night. We thought you should know that we, the rag-tag employees at Borders, are not allowed to do book tables for your reading. Only *management* is here tonight selling your book to these people. Borders headquarters and Ann Harbor say that they're protecting us…from you. Ah, well, you know the *schtick*. Take care.

Moore had problems with Borders before (and after) the movie came out. In Philadelphia, he had previously refused to cross a picket line for a book signing and reading session. Instead, he brought the protesters inside along with him. Consequently, Borders had stopped him from doing a public reading at their New York store on the following week. (Random has since broken all relationship with the artist.) In spite of these pressure tactics put onto him by his own publisher, the renegade filmmaker continued to support part-time workers for their rights, something that he deemed more important than his own reputation within the publishing world. In *The Big One*, he answers that letter written by the part-time employees by meeting three of them behind a so-called "power mall." In this scene the young workers explain that they make $6/h, and that most Border employees also have a second (and even a third) job in order to make ends meet. One employee says she makes 600 dollars a month, which adds up to a meager 7,000 dollars a year. Moore includes the footage of these young, precarious people in the film to prove a point about America's fear of unions, and to illustrate that the country has permanently become a "temp nation."[52]

Rocking Rockford

In 1996, Rockford, Illinois, was occupying the last spot in *Money Magazine*'s "Best Places to Live Now!" edition. Like Flint a decade before, it was considered rock bottom by the magazine and was victim of an unexpected, rapid, and brutal de-industrialization. Moore emphasizes these links with his hometown by describing how much Rockford and Flint have in common, as far as being examples of American midtowns that have been screwed over by Reaganomics and sleazy corporations. Flint had Bob Ubanks, while Rockford had actress Susan St. James. The former city boasts of being the hometown of

---

[52] Watch the sketch "Strikebreakers" from Season One of *The Awful Truth* to find out what Moore really thinks about this "fear of unionization" in America.

Grand Funk Railroad, while the latter could do the same by claiming Cheap Trick. Actually, one of the best moments in the film happens when Moore pays a visit to Rick Nielson, the guitar player from the Rockford band. On Nielson's living room sofa, Moore does a convincing impression of Dylan singing 'The Times They Are A-Changing', a relevant song in this case, if only taken with a small dose of irony. If they were changing, it seems like it was for the worst.

Before leaving town, Rick gave the creator of *Roger & Me* an advice on how to get rid of a media escort (something that Moore will follow on later in his journey across the country). It is a running gag, not a mean-spirited prank. Moore uses it to prove a point about authority, conditioning, and repression. Later in the film, he tells a security agent to stop his own escort from re-entering the building after he had sent her to get coffee. This was done to see if law or security enforcement personnel arbitrarily execute orders. Moore shows the young security agent a picture of his escort and convincingly tells him that she's a stalker. When she returns with coffee, the guard escorts her outside under Moore's mischievous eye and the escort's disbelief. Of course, it is all done in good fun and no more harmful than a candid camera number.

One Size Fits All

Twenty-five minutes into the movie, Moore describes his experience at a book signing at Media Play, a giant surface that sells entertainment by quantity, if not by quality. Media Play is like the Future Shop and Best Buy phenomenon. They are all stores where electronics, books, CDs, and DVDs are sold *en masse*, therefore monopolizing the market of entertainment products and killing smaller electronic stores, bookstores, record stores, and video stores in the process. The emergence of these large chains, for which Wal-Mart represents the quintessence, signaled the end of the mom and pop-operated store era (in the mid to late 1980s). Controlled by conglomerates, these major outlets have taken hostage the consumer who does not have a choice but to shop there. It is a form of market-control meant to appeal to the common suburbanite, and this one quickly becomes a prisoner of a consumer-based environment. While signing copies for fans, Moore encounters a woman who tells him that she has just lost her job selling cars for the Ford Company. He consoles her and writes in her copy of the book: "Downsized, but not out!" The woman is obviously shaken by the news and, in many ways, stands for all those desperate people Moore talks about in his work. This unemployed worker, who just spend some of her precious savings on *Downsize This!*, represents the fallacy of the American Dream: only a few can afford to really dream it. This unfortunate woman probably gave 15 years of her life to a company that just left her out in the cold with nowhere to go. Her hopes for herself and her family have just been shattered by a few decisions made by a couple of suits. This is never much fun to hear, but it is nonetheless the truth. Moore does not rub it in. He just decides to give time to it in his film.

Later, when he is interviewed by a reporter from WNIJ, he explains the whole purpose of *Downsize This!* (and of *The Big One*) to the viewer. "I've been to 20 cities so far on this tour and the entire country has seen the effects of what it is like to be downsized, while these companies have gotten filthy rich and lots of people lost their jobs…" In a later interview for Channel 4 in Milwaukee, he continued his thinking about this failure to encourage those who invest themselves in a company that they do not own: "The union leaders have hopped into bed with management in the last two decades, and every time management snapped its fingers unions would jump." Like the man in *Roger & Me* said so eloquently: "Some people know what time it is, some do not." Moore is definitely one who knows what time it is. He's also trying to fix the clock.

Corporate Showdown

The company Johnson Controls is a major supplier of parts for the auto industry in America. In spite of this reputation, some executives there decided to move the Milwaukee production to Mexico and lay-off thousands of American workers at the same time. Being in Milwaukee, Moore decided to hand out the "Downsizer of the Year Award" and a symbolic 80 cent-check to the powerful company (i.e. so that it can pay one Mexican worker for his first hour of work on the assembly line). The filmmaker's presence at the company's HQ is obviously disturbing for the Public Relation people there. They weren't aware that the filmmaker and his crew were going to show up on that day. This is another characteristic of Moore's infiltration tactics: the element of surprise. After all, why should he let these corporations know that he's coming when they do not even have the decency to warn their employees before laying them off?

> Moore:
> You know, we wish you would have called and told all the workers so that they would have been better prepared.
>
> P.R. Woman:
> They were.

Moore:
Yeah?

P.R. Woman:
We've been talking with our employees... They knew it...

Moore:
Yeah, they've known this for years, right? That you're gonna be leaving. Each year, as you made a bigger and bigger profit, they knew that you would leave Milwaukee because they did such a good job here and you made so much money...

P.R. Woman:
I think our employees have a much better understanding of what's happening than you do.

Following this corporate showdown Moore cuts to a Johnson Controls employee who dedicated twenty years of his life to the company (coming in on Friday nights and all). The forty-something man had recently been downsized and tells Moore that the news of the move to Mexico was given on a short notice, contrary to what the P.R. woman had previously told Moore. The filmmaker brings the man to Manpower Inc., the famous company against which Michael will pit himself three years later in *The Awful Truth*. The whole point of the aforementioned sequence from *The Big One* is to prove that there is no more job security in the United States and that unions are weak, useless even (a point stressed out in his first feature and, later on, in many segments from both of his television series). Beyond this fact lies another awful truth: Some companies benefit from the void created by corporate downsizing and the misery that results from it.

Turning Lost into a Halo, Turning Crack into Profits

In his first three films, Moore depicts a society where the work force has been used as an expendable mass, stretched beyond the limit of its elasticity, and left broken to die. This is one of the main arguments made about contemporary business and politics. The idea that the social fabric is decomposing because of bad labor laws is often reiterated in his work. It is perhaps his most cherished theme. Implicit to this discourse, the viewer must understand that business people prefer to conceive economy as an abstract matter which can be toyed with in the executive suite. Indeed, it would be truly difficult to imagine a disturbed and violent society if everyone in that society was employed and treated fairly. The links between corporate behavior, unemployment, poverty, and criminality are certainly not tenuous ones, as Moore proved repeatedly in his films. In another one of the stand-up segments from the film, he talks about being on a plane with a corporate person sitting next to him. After a couple of bourbons, the man recognizes him because of the success of *Roger & Me* ("Roger Moore," he calls him).

Moore:
"I know you! You made that movie! Whaddaya got against profit?" That's what they have to say, right? *"Whaddaya got against profit? A company's got responsibility to its shareholders. That's our system! The shareholders!"* That's not our system. Our system is a democracy. I've read the U.S. Constitution. The word "shareholder" does not appear once in that document. I've seen the word "People," "of, by and for the People," I've seen that, but I've never seen the word "shareholder." If it's just about making profit, now why does not General Motors sell crack? They can make a huge profit selling crack. A 2,000 pound car makes G.M. about 1,000 dollar-profit, so 2,000 pounds of crack, lemme tell ya, there's a million bucks there!!!

Prison Labor

In another sequence concerning the state of the workplace and corporate ethics in America in the 1990s, Moore explains to a small crowd that he went to the Mall of America and encountered a young man who had just came out of Ventura Prison. Actually, he was a distressed youth dressed-up as a punk who told him he had been working for TWA while he was inside; booking flights over the phone, earning next to nothing (of course).

Moore:
So you're in prison and you're taking airline reservations, and your sending people to the Bahamas and you can't even walk outside?

Punk Kid:
I think it's like a "corporational" thing so TWA does not have to hire people. And they can pay less. Because if you go under a job at TWA, they're gonna pay you seven, eight, nine bucks an hour.

Moore:
Have you heard of any funny stories about people calling up for reservations?

Punk Kid:
Ah yeah. There are all kinds. Like people getting phone numbers and stuff like that, and get hook-ups, you know. Like, girls would be calling and we'd be, like: "Hey what's your name?" and this and that…Y' know, your normal stuff that would probably happen if you had been working at TWA, y' know. But they don't realize that they are really talking to a rapist or murderers or, y' know? People that are just, like, y' know? I came out as a murderer. I don't give a fuck about you, you, you, you…anybody in here. Ya' know?

Moore:
You don't give a shit?

Punk Kid:
No.

Moore then tells his audience to remember this story next time they try to book a flight over the telephone. He explains that this is just the tip of the iceberg as far as prison slave labor is concerned. Well-known corporations are using those methods of employment in America to this very day. Moore tells us that Spalding packages their golf balls in a prison in Hawaii, that Microsoft packages their software in prison in Washington, and that Eddie Bauer makes clothes in Washington State jails. In Colorado, AT&T uses prison inmates to do their telemarketing, etc. In the same line as the "G.M. selling crack" reasoning, Moore has another suggestion for the already ethically flawed American work place.

Moore:
Why do not we close down all the factories, throw everyone out of work. A number of them will obviously turn to crime because they'll be unemployed. We can then ship them back into the factory, which can now be a prison, and we can give them their old jobs back, which they are already trained to do and get paid two dollars an hour for it, and the company can make a huge profit! What a great idea, uh? Then the Dow can hit ten thousand!!!

Union Maid

The last half-hour of *The Big One* focuses on the idea that, a) America has been poorly prepared to move from industrial to post-industrial society, b) the union dream is now a thing of the past, and c) new American entrepreneurs do not give much consideration to their contemporaries. First, Moore meets up with activist, author, radio host and left-wing legend Studs Terkel to discuss these issues. Terkel is positively a kindred spirit to Moore. He became a familiar voice on radio working as a news commentator and disc-jockey in the 1940s. He also acted and appeared on several television programs. In 1949, Terkel began his own television show, *Studs' Place*, an improvised sitcom where he played himself as a restaurant owner. After being investigated by H.U.A.C. in 1953, his contract was cancelled. Unlike Elia Kazan, Terkel refused to give evidence against other left-wing activists and members of the American Communist Party. Consequently, he was blacklisted and prevented from appearing on network television for a long time.

In 1958, Terkel started his long-running daily radio program and, in the 1960s, became interested in oral history. His first book on the subject, *Division Street: America* (1967) contained interviews with 70 people who had lived, worked, and suffered in and around Chicago. This was followed by *Hard Times* (1970), which featured interviews with Americans talking about their experiences in the Depression, and *Working* (1974), an account of working lives. He has been described as a historian and a sociologist, but he prefers to described himself as a "guerrilla journalist with a tape recorder" (does this sound familiar?). In any case, in the interview with Moore, he points to two pictures and captions concerning terrorism at the beginning of *Downsize This!* One is of the Alfred P. Murrah Building in Oklahoma City after it had been bombed, the other is of a derelict factory in Flint after the G.M. downsizing. He then asks the author what, in his opinion, is "terrorism."

Moore:
Obviously, if you park a Ryder truck in front of a building filled with explosives and blow up that building and kill 168 people, that's an act of terrorism. There's no question about that. But what do you call it, Studs, when you politely remove the people from the building first, and then blow it up? But then, in the ensuing years, people who used to work in that building, because their livelihood has been stripped from them, the people who used to work there, a number of them will die. They'll die from suicide. They'll die from spousal abuse. They'll die from drugs and alcoholism, all the social

problems that surround people when they become unemployed. Those people are just as dead as the people in Oklahoma City are, but we don't call the actions of the company "terrorism," do we? We don't call the company a "murderer." But I do consider this an act of economic terrorism. When, at a time when you are making a record profit, you would throw people out of work just so that you can make a little bit more.

Moore is a populist but also a strong defender of the U.S. Constitution and a reverse-psychology expert. He constantly reminds people that the government is at their service, not the other way around. Many times over he used a kind of inverted logic to talk about perverted issues, such as greed, dens of inequities, and forms of exploitation of all kinds. His true gift is that he manages to make us laugh about things that should normally make us extremely depressed.

Racing for It

The Big One echoes *Roger & Me* through its final moments, when Moore encounters a well-known corporate egghead. Here, he goes after Nike founder Phil Knight, who had the privilege to grace the title of "Corporate Crook #3" in the book the author was then promoting (*Downsize*, pp. 127-28). Akin to Roger Smith and Ted Turner, Phil Knight is the embodiment of the Self-Made-Man and exemplifies the "corporate soul" in America. In Moore's frame, he becomes an icon for the Right much like Heston will be in his following feature documentary. The Nike Chairman officially invited Moore to his San Francisco headquarters so that, for once, the latter did not have to impose or play the role of the infiltrator. Analyzing the "acting" in this movie, it seems evident that Knight is aware of his own image when he meets up with Moore. We can also notice that the mogul admires the filmmaker's courage and determination to challenge him on his own turf. Knight had obviously seen *Roger & Me*, and his wife had already given him a copy of *Downsize This!* (with his face circled in red) for their wedding anniversary. Essentially, he seems flattered by Moore's interest in him, even though he's being perceived as the bad guy.

Moore:
How much is enough? If you are a billionaire, would not it be okay to be just half a billionaire? Wouldn't it be okay for your company to make a little less money if it meant providing some jobs here in this country.

Knight:
No, but, I mean...

Moore:
No, just think about it...

Knight:
I've thought about it, a lot. And I'll give you the answer that, basically, what drives me is not money...I'm not in this for the money anymore.

Moore:
I wouldn't think so.

Knight:
...and basically, what I want to do before I go to that "Great Shoe Factory in the Sky" is to make this as good a company as I can make it. I simply have the basic belief, having been burnt-out once, and really believing this very strongly, that Americans do not want to make shoes. They do not want to make shoes...

After Knight says that he would consider opening up a factory in the U.S., but only if Moore could demonstrate an American will to make shoes, the filmmaker goes back to Flint to assemble a group of people seeking a job in the shoe-making business. They create a video message of their willingness that Moore eventually shows to Knight. One man in his thirties tells the camera-eye (which stands for Knight here) that he has been wearing Nike shoes for over 20 years. He adds, "If Nike means that much to me, Flint should mean that much to you." Another one says, "If you do not make them here, we should not buy them here." A third man holding his son tells Knight, "If I can buy my son these Air Jordans, and he can wear 'em, you better believe that I will help you make 'em! Come to Flint."

Moore then cuts to a shot of a TV set in Knight's office playing back the video message. Unimpressed (although he said that he was), Knight refuses to open a Nike factory in Flint and gives Moore a pair of "American-made" Nike shoes instead. Depressed by the outcome, the latter then proposes that they race for the Flint factory. The Chairman refuses the offer but plays along with Moore's rascal-like attitude, giving the impression that he's still a "good guy" who is simply out to defend his own private interests (nothing un-American about that). Moore finally proposes to arm wrestle for it, on which Knight replies, "You *would* win that one!"

The whole effort did not turn out to be in vain. Even though Moore did not get Knight to close down his factories in the dictatorial state of Indonesia, nor to reopen them in Flint, he still managed to get $10,000 for Flint schools (and only after himself offered to make an equivalent donation). Losing ten grand on that day actually appeared painful for Knight, even if it constitutes a tiny, tiny fraction of his fortune. And, equally important, the Nike Corporation raised its minimum age for its Indonesian factory employees after it had been suggested by Michael Moore during the shooting of the film that 14 years of age is too young to be working in a factory...

Here is another example of a positive political action which came about through Moore's artistic journey.

One to Go

Jürgen Habermas once wrote that "fascism is capitalism in crisis."[53] Nothing could be closer to that truth than when we look at how American economy and politics have been working since the early 1980s. Michael Moore summarizes this thesis brilliantly in the conclusion of *The Big One*. He tells his American audience that, as long as they accept the collusion of their government with corporations, democracy will always be undermined in one form or another.

> Moore:
> These companies, big business, right? They had us talking that talk for so long: *"Free Enterprise!" "Free market!" "Capitalism!"* when they were the last ones to believe in it. It's all so weird, is not it? Now, we're at a point in our history where we have *one* candidate, *one* party, *one* company... I'd like to say: "One evil empire down, one to go."

---

[53] Jürgen Habermas, *Legitimation Crisis*, Polity Press, 1988

BOWLING FOR COLUMBINE (2002)

I want to make a movie that's going to challenge my assumptions. I want to make a movie that is going to be surprising and shocking and take different twists and turns, all the reasons why we like to go to a good movie. The road we ended up on was looking at the "why." Why are we such a violent people? Why do we want to kill first and ask questions later? How is our way of violence connected, whether it's locally or globally? I wanted to paint a picture of this country at the beginning of the 21st century that was on a larger canvas than just "Let's make a movie about guns," in the hopes that we would take a look at our ethic, our American ethos, the way we truly are.[54]

Consistency of Convictions

For his third feature documentary, Michael Moore decided to tackle the controversial issues of gun-control and fear in contemporary American society. For him, these two notions are inextricably linked because guns induce (consciously or not) fear, but also because fear is responsible for their presence in our daily lives. This seems to be a conundrum which only a reflexive and poetic cinema can shed a light on. Like *Roger & Me* and *Fahrenheit 9/11*, *Bowling for Columbine* seems to stand out at a time when "documentaries" look more like television reportages. For instance, a movie like *Super Size Me!* (Spurlock, 2004) does not exploit the audiovisual language the way *Bowling for Columbine* does. From a stylistic point-of-view, it is extremely flat and with no expressive use of framing, sound or editing. Its director does not experiment with film time beyond the basic elliptical cutting required for a public screening. He obviously tries to imitate Moore's approach and style, but only winds up with a recorded subject, constrained within the limitations of the frame, that does all the talking instead. The camera's sole reason for existing is to catch what is in front of it and not much else.

Thus, by experimenting with the language of cinema, as well as by having a style of his own, Moore distinguishes himself from most contemporary filmmakers. Even from those who claim to follow on his example by being "socially involved" with a camera and a microphone. In that sense, *Bowling for Columbine* should not be assessed on the same level as most "documentaries" out there today, because it is so much more controlled and stylized. It is in fact on par with

---

[54] Michael Moore interviewed by Bill Maher at *Bowling for Columbine*'s premiere at the Writers Guild of America Theater, October 2002.

masterworks such as *Fog of War: Eleven Lessons from the Life of Robert S. McNamara* (Morris, 2004), *A Social Genocide* (Solanas, 2004), and even Werner Herzog's more recent and truly amazing nonfiction films, *Grizzly Man* (2005) and *Encounters at the End of the World* (2007). Although, the themes found in *Bowling for Columbine* are not as specific as the ones found within these aforementioned films, and they leave no one indifferent. Yet, some critics were quick at dismissing it, even going as far as asking the Academy of Motion Picture Arts and Science to revoke the Oscar it had given Moore. This was of course in reaction to his speech where he accused, in front of an estimated billion people, George W. Bush of being a "fictitious President" creating a "fictitious war" in Iraq. What these critics missed out on is the fact that *Bowling for Columbine* is a personal film and an *impression* of an era. Furthermore, the controversy on Academy Awards night proved that Moore is a man who acts on his convictions and who is not afraid to speak his mind, even in the most formal of occasions. It also showed that he is an artist who has found a way to create meaning in an industry corrupted by finance and polluted by advertisement.

Why Columbine?

More than a journalist's job or an "experiment in the extremes," *Bowling for Columbine* stems from both, Moore's deep-thinking about these coexisting social problems, and his need to hold a mirror to America's face. The film illustrates the dramatic consequences of a blind faith in the 2nd Amendment of the U.S. Constitution and, as usual, is marked by his idiosyncratic style of storytelling. Moore decided that he was again going to use cinema to challenge our preconceived notions about America, its ideological paradoxes, and alienated population. After the Columbine shootings in April 1999, he felt he ought to confront head-on this creepy fascination that many Americans have with their guns (and with violence in general). He was going to initiate a public debate about a disturbingly new concept: children killing each other. Like G.M. shutting down his hometown through the terrorist act that is downsizing, Moore couldn't just stand by and be a mere witness to the tragedy. He had to investigate and to understand this event through a personal immersion, from inside the problem.

Bowling for Columbine announces itself as being about guns, but is in fact about violence and fear in their various forms. Violence and fear are used here in their conceptual sense, not strictly as a socio-cultural phenomenon. Moore analyzes a *state of mind* more than he whines over a state of fact. With a surface reading perhaps that he seems to be rambling at times. However, when looked at more closely, we realize that what he does is the opposite: the film delves ever-deeply into its topic as it progresses, only to unwind in the last two minutes. One example of this rigor found in Moore's discourse is the correlation he draws between the Columbine shootings and American foreign policies. These are no superficial correlations, by any means. Links, albeit abstract ones, have to be made between these two kinds of human destructiveness, if only to grasp the breadth of the problem in question. For Moore, this culture of violence seems to be about fundamental values and beliefs at the end of the day. His quest is about finding out how Americans perceive themselves, as a people with a common history and a shared consciousness.

Peace Is Our Profession

The filmmaker opted to introduce his subject matter with an excerpt from a short film produced by the U.S. Army in the 1950s. This inclusion is telling us from the start that the problem is rooted in a specific culture that dates back to the immediate post-war era and the prosperous decade that followed. As mentioned earlier, it also relates to a certain conception of what America is supposed to be about at its core (Number One). Pentagon generals such as Curtis LeMay and Thomas Power, politicians like Richard Nixon or movie actors like Ronald Reagan were all byproducts of this culture of fear which Moore investigates in his film. The 1950s were a time when Americans were afraid of invading entities, whether they were ideological, cultural or from other planets. This fear could in fact be held responsible for America's insular and paranoid attitude towards the *Other*. It is most conducive to cultural isolationism, when we get right down to it. Very much like his previous features, Moore frames his narrative with an authorial voice. For instance, at the beginning of the film, we get helicopter shots of American landscapes, and his voice-over joyously notes how everything seems "normal" on the surface of things. He describes a typical day in the country, blending banal and daily events with worldly affairs, while an instrumental version of 'The Battle of the Republic Hymn' is heard on the soundtrack.

Moore (v.o.):
"It was the morning of April 20th 1999, and it was pretty much like any other morning in America. The farmer did his chores. The milkman made his deliveries. The President bombed another country whose name we couldn't pronounce. Out in Fargo, North Dakota, Kerry McWilliams went on his morning walk. Back in Michigan, Ms. Hughes welcomed her students for another day of school. And out in a little town in

Colorado, two boys went bowling at six in the morning. Yes, it was a typical day in the United States of America."

Moore is again using a voice-over marked by irony and sarcasm. He gradually weaves its many different points in one single paragraph. He conceptually links the bombings in Eastern Europe by the Clinton administration and the two boys who ravaged Columbine High School at roughly the same time. The writing sets up all of the film's thematics, as well announcing its stylistic quirks. Through a bird's eye point-of-view it claims to be a survey of the American mental landscape, while the pompous musical score underlines the fact that Moore will allow us a directorial, if not an omnipotent look at the problem in question. His strongest critics keep saying that he manipulates situations (and people) in the frame, which rarely seems to be the case. As a performer, he sometimes plays up to a situation or a character trait of the person he interviews, but as a journalist, he observes, listens, questions, and lives through his subject matter. Later on in the process, as an editor, he uses the best footage to support his overall thesis. In fact, Moore's films seems to be the result of intense post-production work, since he and his crew select the best moments from a vast quantity of rushes and shape them later into a cohesive structure that questions, moves, and chocks the viewer.

In the introductory sequence, we follow the filmmaker walking into a bank to open an account and coming out with a free gun. Moore did not invent any of this. He simply was answering a newspaper-ad promoting this weird offer by a known Michigan institution. In the bank, Moore is first subjected to a quick background check by a clerk and the usual filing out of forms. After the clerk made some disgraceful innuendos regarding ethnicity and gun-crime, still a pervasive preconception in the U.S., he easily managed to leave with both a savings account and a brand new shotgun. On his way out he asked one the bank's consultants: "Don't you think it's a bit dangerous handing guns in a bank?" and then pretended to shoot in the camera lens. This provocation on the viewer's senses triggers the opening credits with a cover of the song 'Take the Skinheads Bowling' on the soundtrack. It puts the viewer in a position of discomfort by directly targeting and then grabbing her/him by the collar. Moore reminds us that we can all be potential victims or/and perpetrators of gun-violence, simply because these are so easily available to anyone. In the credits he also uses black and white stock footage of bowling alleys in slow motion, creating a nightmarish aura around the presentation of the filmmakers. As mentioned before, these kinds of images evoke postwar America and the perception the country has been having of itself since 1945: as an idyllic playground with no apparent social problems.

From a formal point-of-view, Moore's ability to create purely cinematic moments has never been the object of serious analysis until now. This cinematic virtuosity, developed over a relative short period of time, is obvious when we look at how brilliantly some of his credit sequences are conceived. He pays as much attention to these as to the rest of his films, encapsulating the concept visually in less than a minute. The opening credits of *Capitalism: A Love Story* are a case in point. Often in the end credits he uses a simple white font unrolling as a sharp and dry rhythmic sequencing to ironic music. The end credits of *Bowling for Columbine*, for instance, recall the ones from Scorsese's *Goodfellas* (1990), except that it is not Sid Vicious' decadent version of 'My Way' that is played over the names but Joey Ramone's upbeat version of 'What a Wonderful World'. In both instances we have two modern versions of classic ballads used to comment on the degeneration of the American Dream. It's audio political commentary with an edge.

Membership Has Its Privilege

Bowling's opening credits are abruptly interrupted by a vintage TV-ad for a toy rifle manufactured by a company called Marx... This footage from the late 1950s indicates that Moore is initiating an inquiry into a mindset that has now been evolving for decades. He explains that, as a youth, he couldn't wait to "go outside and shoot up the neighborhood," not excluding himself from the problem, as we can see. He also informs us that as a teenager he had won the National Rifle Association Marksman Award, Junior Diploma (to his great pride). Like he did in *Roger & Me*, the director uses Super-8 home movies, and over these images he lays Irving Berlin's 'I Want To Go Back To Michigan' to contextualize his discourse. Moore never disconnected himself from where he is from. He always proudly claims his roots by anchoring almost all of his films' narratives in Michigan soil at a given time in history. In this historical perspective, he makes us understand that Americans are still carrying the ideological remnants of a certain way of life, namely, the one that allowed them to exterminate the First Nations and acquire their independence from England and bring in slaves from Africa. For him the attitude of gun-defenders is anachronistic because we live in an age of relative social order and in a highly evolved technologically-based civilization: so why need guns then? As a way to live, it seems quite primitive.

Indeed, the idea that millions of Americans feel like they have to carry guns for survival or self-defense might appear like a throwback to cultures that have a more sophisticated understanding of the "social contract". Considering that most of America is one big shopping mall, characterized by abundance and diversity of products and merchandise (all neatly organized on a shelf near you), we might be in fact led to ask about the reasons *why* Americans so desperately need their firearms after all. In suburbia, or even in places where hospitals and schools are in terrible conditions, you're almost certain to find at the very least a Dollar Store, a Burger King or a Wal-Mart. Why then do people feel like guns are essential to their lifestyle and well-being, if they do not have to kill each other in order to survive?

One explanation, quickly dismissed by Moore, is the long tradition of hunting in the U.S., which could justify why so many people own guns. However, this fact does not solve the question regarding their usage in every day life and in acts of aggression all across the board. This is the very first trail that Moore goes on to follow. He describes Michigan as being a "gun lovers' paradise" and reminds us that Charlton Heston, the famous actor and spokesperson for the N.R.A., is also a homeboy fond of hunting. "We come from a state where *everyone* loves to go hunting," Moore brags sarcastically on the voice-over. Here, the editing pattern creates a false shot-counter shot between Heston and Moore from two different visual sources. The way it works out in the sequence makes it appear as if the two men are actually shooting each other (because of the 180-degree rule in visual continuity, a basic convention of classical cinema perverted here by Moore and his editor, Kurt Engfehr). Clearly, manipulation of prerecorded visual sources and collage characterize part of Moore's style. His images, voice-over, and sounds collide with impeccable logic at times, creating dialectics of evocative associations and provocative suggestions.

This last segment about Heston and the N.R.A. leads into an absurd story about an incident involving two hunters and a dog in Michigan. Right from the start, Moore keeps it simple for the viewer: "Guns do not kill people, people kill people." The two hunters had apparently strapped a rifle to the back of a small dog and it inadvertently went off, seriously wounding one of them. It is difficult to say if the scene was really captured on a video camera by one of the hunters or if it has been recreated by Moore and his gifted accomplices *post facto*. The camera is obviously on a tripod, and we see a medium-high-angle shot of a beagle dressed in hunter gear with a shotgun tied to its back. We can also notice the leg of the hunter lying on the forest floor protruding from off-screen left. The camera only pans to the left when the dog starts moving off-screen left, which leads the viewer to ask why the hunter/camera operator did not come to the rescue of his wounded friend instead of reframing the "action" led by the dog. Moore pushes the gag as far as to asking a Michigan State Trooper "if it [is] possible that the dog knew what it was doing..."

When the Tough Gets Going

No doubt, it requires a lot of stamina and courage to get into situations where you can actually be harmed by the person you are interviewing. We have already mentioned that Moore had helped Anne Bohlen and Kevin Rafferty on *Blood in the Face*, when he interviewed some of the most extreme right-wingers in America. In fact, Moore is fearless when comes the time to stand in front of a sociopath (or just a good old-fashion corporate monster). He goes where few reporters have ventured before and asks questions that no other American journalist is willing to ask about capitalism. In many ways, he is a kind of "war" correspondent on the battlefield of American political life. His camera is as close as you can now get to the "third cinema" camera proposed by radical South American filmmakers Solanas and Getino in their 1969 manifesto "Towards a Third Cinema." In his hands, cinema becomes a redoubtable weapon for concrete political action, as we have already demonstrated.

There is a scene in *Bowling for Columbine* where he meets with members of the Michigan Militia at a local training ground. He wants to inquire about that damn American vigilante attitude that had started with patriotic Minutemen, over a hundred years ago, and to link it to America's perception of itself as "One Nation under God" (but really divided on many subjects). In this segment, we notice that militia members are using bowling pins for target practice, something that might have also influenced the film's title. The pins, we are told by Frank, a militiaman, are supposed to be the rough average size of the region where vital organs on a human body are located.[55] As it is presented in *Bowling for Columbine*, the Michigan Militia is the scary symptom of a social illness, because it is about individuals who have decided to take the law into their own hands. Individuals so disenchanted by their government, army, and law enforcement agencies, that they've decided to organize community groups in order to fight "the enemy" which can even be the Federal Government for them. (This seems to be truer today with the Obama administration in office.) This form of "self-protection" is done without the official consent of the law apparatus and creates great tension between Washington and the states. It also stems from a profound hatred of illegal immigrants, especially those coming in from the southern border between Texas and Mexico. In *Bowling for Columbine*, one of the Militia members tells Moore that they are "not conspiracy nuts, racists or extremists, no terrorists or militants or other such nonsense," that

---

[55] The two teens that shot up Columbine, Eric Harris and Dylan Klebolt, were also practicing their shooting skills on bowling pins, as their private home video later revealed to the police. They were substituting these for people (until the day they actually get to shoot and kill for real).

they are "just *concerned* citizens." This man does not seem to believe that armed citizenry can exacerbate the frictions inherent to any community life. He does not understand that, when individuals with overblown egos take the law into their own hands, whether it is with guns, baseball bats or chains, any minor friction can turn into a major showdown on public streets. But then again, maybe armed citizenry also serves, in this case, as a test to unbridled American masculinity, or better yet, as a rite of passage to higher echelons of a society that has always been based on bloody rituals and bloodshed to begin with.

In the end, this paramilitary organization is trying to promote itself as a bunch of good American citizens practicing the Second Amendment with "fervor," the same way that many Americans often practice their religious beliefs with "fervor." However, the truth is that they are exponents of an extremist interpretation of the Bill of Rights. These people are definitely part of the problem, because they perpetuate the cycle of violence that has been such a plague to America since its colonial days. They see enemies where there are none. For Moore it simply borders on social psychosis. That being said, the problem of vigilantism is still very much present in the U.S. today. According to the Southern Poverty Law Center, there is a strong resurgence of these types of local groups all around the country as these lines are being written.[56]

Wackos

It matters not how strait the gate,
How charged with punishments the scroll,
I am the master of my fate,
I am the captain of my soul.[57]

On April 19 1995, almost to the day with the 1999 Columbine shooting, Timothy James McVeigh, Terry Nichols and the Fortier brothers bombed the Alfred P. Murrah Building in Oklahoma City, killing 168 people (including 19 children). This tragedy was obviously going to find its way into *Bowling for Columbine*, where Moore also puts in perspective McVeigh's background story. McVeigh was a decorated Gulf War veteran who came back to nothing but indifference once the fireworks were over in Iraq. He couldn't even get a low-income job because he was too "over-educated," as we find out in the

---

[56] Larry Keller, "The Second Wave: Evidence Grows of Far-Right Militia Resurgence," *Intelligence Report*, Fall 2009
[57] Excerpt from the poem *Invictus* by W.E. Henley that Timothy McVeigh chose as a last public statement before his execution.

film. Moore's contention is not that McVeigh was a victim, but that he turned on his own government who had left him completely disillusioned and ultra-patriotic. The deranged Indiana man had briefly joined the Michigan Militia, where he befriended the Nichols brothers, Terry and James, just before he resorted to an outrageous act of terrorism on his own people. McVeigh was executed on the electric chair in 2001, while Terry Nichols still rots away in jail to this day, thanks to a paper work mistake made by the FBI.

Interested in knowing more about what makes men like these tick, Moore interviews James Nichols, a tofu bean farmer who had been arrested but then released due to a lack of evidence in the case of the bombing. The nine charges laid against him were eventually dropped, and he walked back to his farm in Michigan. In the interview, Nichols admits that McVeigh stayed at his place for awhile, but that anything explosive near his house is just "normal farm stuff" (i.e. not connected to bomb-making). However, when we cut to the second part of the interview, inside his house, Nichols claims that federal agents were "scared to death" to search his home. According to him, the memory of Waco was still too fresh on their minds. He goes on to describe how his wife thinks that "he's a radical and a madman" with guns all over him and everywhere in his house. He even brags about it. In the film, Nichols nervously sits at his kitchen table while Moore is sitting at the other end.

Nichols:
If people found out how they've been ripped-off and enslaved in this country, by the government, by the Powers-That-Be… They will revolt with anger, with merciless anger. They'll be blood running in the streets… When the government turns radical, it is your duty to overthrow it.

Moore (off):
Why not use Gandhi's way? He didn't have any guns and he beat the British Empire. (*Notice how Moore does not disagree about the goal but about the means.*)

Nichols:
I'm not familiar with that.

Later, Moore asks him, "Do you believe it was right to blow up the building in Oklahoma City?"

Nichols:
No. But why was it blown up? That's a good question. *Why* was that building blown up? And who blew it up?

> Moore (off):
> But if someone did it, it would be wrong?

> Nichols (*hesitant*):
> Yeah.

> Moore (off):
> It is wrong to take the lives of innocent people?

> Nichols (*hesitant*):
> Yeah.

Later in the interview, we catch Nichols contradicting himself.

> Nichols:
> I use the pen, cos' the pen is "mightier than the sword." But you must always keep a sword handy, for when the pen fails... (*It cuts to Nichols standing up near his kitchen counter*) I sleep with a .44 Magnum under my pillow.

> Moore (off):
> C'mon, that's what everybody says... Is that true?

They both go to Nichols room where this one displays a piece, cocks it, and puts it to his head (loaded but "safe," according to him). This would be the only time when Moore would officially get sued in court (for actually having used this shot taken from outside of the room and describing in text, over the image, what was going on inside).[58] Then, we go back to the two of them sitting in the kitchen as they did before.

> Nichols:
> No one has the right to tell me I can't have it. It's protected in our Constitution.

> Moore (off):
> Where does it say that handguns are protected?

> Nichols:
> No, "guns."

> Moore (off):
> It doesn't say "gun..."

---

[58] *Bowling for Columbine*, supplements (DVD, Alliance Atlantis, 2002)

180

                    Together:
It says "arms..."

                    Nichols:
What is "arms?"

                    Moore (off):
Could be a nuclear weapon!

                    Nichols:
That's right! It could be a nuclear weapon.

                    Moore (off):
Do you think that you should have the right to have weapons like grey plutonium here on the farm? Should you have weapons with grey plutonium?

                    Nichols (*laughing*):
I don't want them!

                    Moore (off):
But should you have the right if you did want them?

                    Nichols:
Umm...That should be restricted.

                    Moore (off):
Oh, so you do believe in some restrictions?

                    Nichols:
Well, there *are* some wackos out there...

With this absurd but appropriate punch line Moore initiates a musical montage of different archival news reports relating to gun violence in America. The editing is synchronized to the last chorus and verse from the song 'Happiness is a Warm Gun,' extracted from the Beatles' classic *White Album* (1968). Appropriately enough the song is written and sung by John Lennon, who was killed with a handgun in New York City in December 1980, as we all know. It is surely not a coincidence that Lennon's widow, artist Yoko Ono, had a great interest in this film being made.[59] In the rhythmic montage, the filmmaker cuts in a variety of visual sources to create a feeling of insanity reigning over America

---

[59] Moore actually acknowledges her support in the final credits and she was subsequently a great defender of his next film, *Fahrenheit 9/11*.

today. Through his selection of material, Moore reminds us that gunplay is imbedded in politics and popular culture. For instance, we find out that in Virgin, Utah, the State government passed a law that required *every* citizen to own a gun. We see kids at a shooting gallery, as well as a young woman in a small bikini firing an AK-47, and of course tough guys branding their guns with macho energy. Towards the end, there is even a television report about a blind man who still managed to pass his shooting tests! This last sequence culminates in a crescendo of violence where people are shot on live television or whose murder was captured by amateur camcorders. The song ends tragically with the image of a black man receiving a bullet and falling hard on the street, which pretty much announces where Moore is going with all of this. He is going once more towards two fundamental notions required to understand the America ethos: ethnicity and class.

Monsters in the Making

Although the name of the school is in the title, Moore's inquiry does not limit itself to the Columbine killings. As an unconventional journalist, he often works around his main subject matter to include peripheral concerns, such as the effects of suburban life on the development of teenagers and the influence that industrial environments have on people's mental health. After the uncanny interview with Nichols and the ironic musical montage set to Lennon's raspy and eerie voice, the director interviews two young men who were approximately the same age as Eric Harris and Dylan Klebolt. He explains in voice-over that many warplanes departed from their hometown to fly to the Persian Gulf back in 1991. He also mentions that Harris' father flew one of these planes, as fate would have it. For Moore, there is no doubt about it: ethnicity and socioeconomic status play a key role in the fact that some kids are dealing in drugs and firearms in mid-town America today, but not necessarily in the way we might think it does. In this particular case, it is quite discomforting to know that we were dealing with middle-class individuals who had everything they needed, except attentive parents (e.g. a nice house, access to a BMW, fairly good grades, etc.). A more conservative look on the problem would probably have assumed that the Columbine killers were from a poor and/ or "ethnic" background.

If where you live and how much money your family is making are relevant data to the understanding of the gun problem in America today, so must be role-model identification. This is a notion intrinsic to American culture, with its Hollywood "artists" and prefabricated pop stars, actors, and presidents. Both Harris and Klebolt admired people like Charles Manson because their own parents were too busy paying the mortgage of their oversized suburban home, working two, sometimes three jobs at once. Be that as it may, it does not mean that the government and the media had anything better to propose to them either (i.e. as far as social values and a social agenda are concerned). The same could be said of the young man disappointed for not having made it to "Number One Troubled Teenager in Oscoda" in the film. Obviously, this boy is morally misguided and has the wrong role model to look-up to (i.e. the "Anarchist Cook Book"). On the outside, he appears like your regular guy-next-door, just another teenager hanging out at the local arcade, but then he goes and tells Moore that he's *"only* making *little* bombs the size of a tennis balls." When questioned further by the filmmaker, he reveals that the last thing he had produced was *"just* a 5 gallon-drum of napalm…"

Evidently, this *"Second* Most Wanted Teen in Oscoda" was bored. There was nothing for him to do in his crummy industrial/military town. He felt like a loser and his peers, government, television, radio, and Internet connection kept reminding him that losers are worthless in a society where being "Number One" is the only thing that matters. For this kid, to be able to make a bomb was "an ego thing," as he himself said in the interview. It served to define himself and to give him a sense of purpose. It also made him feel (the illusion of) being mighty and powerful in a society that emphasizes such "stupid white men" values. Essentially, the boy believed that guns would empower him, which is no different than government officials feeling mighty when sending young people to die in a war that should not have to be fought in the first place.

We Are Columbine

To discredit those who say that Moore is unaware of structure in filmmaking, the next sequence segues into a deeper look at the rampage by moving closer to the Littleton community itself. This is a very clever authorial decision on his part, because it allows him to move freely between the social, the communal, and the individual, managing to make us see their close ties. Moore introduces the next sequence with a close-up of a resident saying, "This is a great place to raise your children," a colloquial American expression that seems to be at odds with what we have just seen before. She adds that Littleton is "tight-knitted with good people," which is probably true. However, in spite of this optimism, we, like Moore, believe that there are other and darker undercurrents to this utopian vision of midtown America. Americans often choose to ignore problems by focusing on leisure activities or by popping all sorts of pills or drinking until bedtime. There is a large part of the population who has now decided to shut-off completely from the political reality, and who prefer to live in a cloud of illusions and make-believe. Again, what Moore does is to mock the head-in-the-sand attitude of some American adults who built themselves an ideal world and forgot all about their children shooting black-tar heroin in the park or hanging themselves in the basement of their cold suburban homes.

After introducing the community of Littleton to his audience, Moore interviews a home security consultant who starts breaking down in tears at the mere mention of the name "Columbine." The scene was funny until the consultant, used here by Moore as a scapegoat for those who make an industry out of fear, started sobbing on-camera. The filmmaker was setting out to use people of his kind to mock consumer paranoia, but winded-up with a sensitive man who was still traumatized by the tragedy that befell his community. "It changed how we talk," he says to Moore. "If I say 'Columbine'," he continues clearing his throat, "everybody knows what it means now." Moore seems surprised and changes his tone to accommodate the man's grief. In the editing, he includes the man's more enlightened comments about the tragedy, and what he actually says summarizes all of our worst fears about living in society: "There is something overwhelming about that kind of *viciousness*, that kind of *predatory action*, that kind of *indiscriminate killing*."

Always consistent with the ultimate message he is conveying to his audience, through his reflection about the material while sitting in postproduction, Moore pays a visit to Lockheed-Martin, the largest weapon manufacturer in the world. There, he meets with a public relation employee who says that 5,000 Lockheed employees have children attending Columbine. He explains that since the tragedy occurred the corporation started providing an anger management program for its employees and their families; even adding that the corporation made a 100,000 dollar-contribution "to deal with people's anger and frustration." Moore takes this comment as an opportunity to insert various shots of giant missiles inside the company lobby, which is reminiscent of the set for the weapon auction in *Canadian Bacon*.

Lockheed's P.R. man also believes that "What happened in Columbine is a microcosm of what's happening around the world." Still, he fails to make the connection between the mass-destruction created by the bombs produced by the company he works for, governmental destructive policies at home and abroad, and the mass-destruction at Columbine High School. "The missiles were designed and built to protect us from *somebody else* who would be aggressors against *us*," he concludes. Over the man's voice, Moore significantly cuts to an insert of a banner inside the lobby: "It has to be *foreign object free*," it says, which, taken in this context, seems to be again a cryptic reference to identity or ethnicity. The individual and the collective are linked through *webs of causality* in Michael Moore's films, and this editing strategy shows his attention to meaningful details which can eventually be used in favor of a more general argument that he is putting forth on screen. The editing itself is commenting on notions of normality and exclusion, two founding principles of modern American society by which an individual can be "made" or "broken" by his peers.

What a Wonderful (Ironic) World

One of the strongest moments in *Bowling for Columbine* is the montage sequence set to Louis Armstrong's moving ballad 'What a Wonderful World'. Like other gifted filmmakers, Moore instinctively knows how to choose a score for his films. There is great synergy produced here by the association of image and music on screen. The rhythmic flow of these sequences reveals his sensibility as a total filmmaker. These associations always convey more than what we see within the borders of the film frame. Today, 'Wouldn't It Be Nice' can never totally be disassociated from *Roger & Me*. If you have seen the movie, you can never truly get those images of Ben Hamper, derelict houses, and a growing rat population out of your mind when you hear this song. In the 'Wonderful World' sequence, we are shown stock footage from different eras highlighting U.S. military interventions around the world (refer to the Introduction of this book for details). Like Chomsky in his short but succinct book *What Uncle Sam Really Wants*,[60] the sequence illustrates the fact that the American government is afraid of the "good example" set by real democratic movements spontaneously emerging around the globe. Akin to Chomsky's discourse, perhaps (and unfortunately) less radical in its propositions, Moore believes that the U.S. always suppresses democracy where it can find it, in order to keep control of the New World Order.

As the song concludes, the filmmaker even pushes the irony of a contrapuntal use of sound, music, and footage by having American Airlines Flight 11 crashing into the first Twin Tower. It coincides cynically with the decrescendo of Louis Armstrong singing: "*Oh yeeeaaah!*," as if this was the outcome of decades of American aggressions around the world (i.e. in the end, it had to come back home in the shape of 9/11). Shortly thereafter, we can hear witnesses of 9/11 screaming over a shot of United Airlines Flight 175 crashing into the second tower, while the image chillingly fades to black. This punctuation epitomizes a nightmarish moment that will eventually

---

[60] Noam Chomsky, *What Uncle Sam Really Wants*, Odonian Press, 1992

become the point of departure for Moore's next feature, *Fahrenheit 9/11*. As it appears in both films, one where image and sound are at odds, the other where, as we will see, there is no image and sound predominates, Michael Moore gives to the actual events of September 11th 2001 a strong sense of fatality and even, perhaps, of doom.

Teenage Wasteland

The next segment opens with a fade-in and with a different, more upbeat score like shopping mall music. We see a low-angle shot of a monument made out of a plane that was once used for killing people in the Vietnam War. Under the plane, a plaque boasts of this sad accomplishment. Just outside of Denver, in Rocky Flats, Colorado, Moore tells us that there was once the largest manufacturer of plutonium in the world. Today it is just a mass burial ground for radioactive waste. A few miles away, buried under a mountain, is where NORAD is located. NORAD is a government facility that oversees America's satellite system and nuclear arsenal. These facts are of course reminders of the Atomic Age (which we are still living in today, but in a more pernicious way), but they also constitute the cornerstone of Moore's argument linking the behavior of the Columbine killers to greater ideological precepts and spheres of influences. The precepts advocated and promoted by the American government in its foreign policies. Thus, one of the greater statements made by the film is that American politics indirectly influence the mind-frame of its population on a day-to-day basis. Because, simply put: "If the government can use violence to impose its will, why can't we, those who have put this government in power to serve us?" Without short-changing *Bowling for Columbine*'s central hypothesis, we can certainly propose that one's opinion of a governing body influences one's standards and values almost every given time. Even believing that "government is useless," or that "big government is bad," is a political position in itself (usually in the far right end of the political spectrum). Still, it is not difficult to imagine how disaffected youth could resort to acts of violence simply because it is condoned by the Establishment and the government elected to serve it.

Moore then sets-up the events that were unfolding at the Columbine High School on April 20, 1999, between 11:08 a.m. and 12:08 p.m. An Eastern European television news report concerning American planes bombing Kosovo (with "precision targeting weaponry," a warped expression invented by ex-Secretary of Defense Donald Rumsfeld) is reminding us that this was the largest one-day bombing of the Bosnian War. Under NATO's supervision, American war machinery dropped twenty-two missiles on a residential part of the village, the reporter tells us. We see another clip of President Clinton addressing himself to the press. He explains that the U.S. is "striking hard against the Serbian's machinery of repression, while making a deliberate effort to minimize harm to innocent people." Moore crosscuts this conference with the previous report that cited local hospitals and schools as being primary targets of those bombings. Just like we are told in *Fahrenheit 9/11*, there is no such thing as a "precise bomb," especially on a moving target. When it explodes, a bomb has a radius of damage-inducing capabilities which is always underplayed by government and army officials. Soon after the report on Kosovo, a card indicates that the Columbine shootings are unfolding beyond the point of no return.

Moore cuts again to Clinton on national television asking his fellow Americans to pray for the parents, students, and teachers of Littleton. The President finishes his address by saying that the government "will *let the events unfold* and then they'll be more to say," revealing his impotence when the enemy comes from within (just like Oklahoma City, Waco, the L.A. Riots, 9/11, Hurricane Katrina, etc.). In this sequence, we can see Moore and Mark Taylor, a Columbine student, climbing the stairs in front of the now infamous high school. Then, in a series of slow lap dissolves, we are introduced to its deserted interiors. We notice banners, trophies, lockers, classrooms, the library...There is a strange vibe about this building that Moore manages to capture with a hand-held camera and a slow editing pattern. With a sound bridge, we are then shown the CCTV tapes of the shootings in a double-split screen format, which allows for multiplicity of point of views on the tragic event. Supported by Jeff Gibbs' ethereal guitar music, the screens depict students being gunned-down and bombed by the two demented teens (who blew their own brains out an hour later). It is a highly disturbing and emotional moment that affects everyone who sees it, because schools have never been associated with crimes of this magnitude (or with crime at all, for that matter). A school, much like a church or a hospital, is usually associated with the notions of learning, personal growth, health, and tolerance towards others; not with sociopathic behaviors such as those committed on that awful morning.

The Columbine sequence has a dream-like quality to it, just like the World Trade Center sequence will in *Fahrenheit 9/11*, two years later. In both instances Moore is using slow motion to dissect an alienating environment that might have been conducive to mayhem and murder. As the content really speaks for itself here, he allows himself to become meditative for awhile. Everything is unfolding in a kind of suspended animation, and we hear a soundtrack compiled from some 9-1-1 calls made that day to and from Columbine High School. On the soundtrack, we hear people calling to inquire about their kids (including Harris' father who speaks of the "Trenchcoat Mafia," which was basically his son and his friend), and there is even an example of the disturbing and inappropriate "want-to-know-it-all-ism" of specialized news networks like Fox News, CNN and MSNBC. One female reporter is actually heard asking for an "exclusive interview" with high school personnel (yes, even while kids were lying and dying in a pool of blood). As strange as this may sound, some victims found the time to compliment the reporter for the quality of her show, probably while they were crouched under a desk or hiding in a broom closet...waiting for the Grim Teenager to show up. If this does not say anything about America's fascination with media and its inability to think outside of the box, then what will?

When the rampage sequence ends, we hear a 9-1-1 operator whispering to a teacher caught in the crossfire: "Be very, very quiet," in a moment of absolute tension that Moore uses to great dramatic effect. The transitional shot, linking to the next part of the sequence, is one of a television being turned off. We then see various shots of students, parents, and teachers commiserating around Columbine, as impotent as Clinton, the FBI and the municipal cops behind the yellow ribbon were. The sequence seems to resurge from the past when a girl, who made it out of there alive, obviously and understandably hysterical, tells a reporter that one of the two killers decided to shoot a black student next to her in the face, "just because he was black." Moore decides to freeze-frame and fade out, which again is a clever authorial assertion on his part; because, from a creative point of view, this will allow him to open-up his narrative into a different line of questioning. It will eventually lead him to the heart and soul of America, to American "culture" in its broadest sense.

From His Cold Dead Heart

Halfway through the film, Moore introduces what will eventually become a symbol for the opposite view regarding gun-ownership in America. Why Charlton Heston? Simply because he was an icon who has benefited from, and perhaps even participated in that culture of fear and violence through the influence of his roles and the different texts he chose to serve. Heston embodied a certain old-guard philosophy whose political representatives are the Neocons in Washington today. It seems like the *persona of Heston* is used in *Bowling for Columbine* to simplify a greater and more complex sociopolitical dynamic at work in the United States. Moore shows us a clip of Heston at a N.R.A. meeting, the association for which he was then spokesperson. He is holding a gun in the air and screams out primitively, "From my cold dead hands," while an audience made out of paying members cheer in approval. On the voice over, Moore reminds us of the lack of empathy some people like Heston have, when we cut down the "Hollywood royalty bullshit" and get right to it. Once again, Moore utilizes an old technique of his, one which proved to be quite effective in the past, especially in the apotheosis of *Roger & Me*.[61] He crosscuts between Charlton Heston at the N.R.A. rally and Tom Mauser, a man whose son has been viciously killed in the Columbine library. This emotional sequence crystallizes the ideological factions at work in the U.S. today and serves Moore's discourse magnificently.

While Heston is reminding his friends that, "As Americans, we are free to travel wherever we want in our broad land," and telling them that even the Mayor of Denver could not appeal to his sense of decency, the editing cuts back to Tom Mauser at a very different kind of gathering.

Tom Mauser:
I am here today because my son would have wanted me to be here today. (*Applause*) If my son Daniel were not one of the victims, he would be here with me today. (*Applause*) Something is wrong in this country when a child can grab a gun so easily and shoot a bullet (*choking with sadness and pain*)…into the middle of a child's face, as my son experienced… Something is wrong… But the time has come to understand that a Tech-9, semi-automatic, thirty bullet-weapons like the one that killed my son is not used to kill a deer. It has no useful purpose. It is time to address this problem. (*Applause*)

Moore cuts to Heston at the inappropriate N.R.A. rally in Denver.

Heston:
We have work to do, hearts to heal, evil to defeat, and a country to unite. We may have differences, yes. We will again suffer *tragedy almost beyond description*. But when the sun sets on Denver tonight, and forevermore, let it always set on "We the People." Secure in our "Land of the Free" and "Home of the Brave." I, for one, plan to do my part. Thank you.

Despite the fact that Heston speaks in grand euphemisms and metaphors, he does not seem to reveal any kind of sorrow or regret

---

[61] This is in reference to the last sequence of *Roger & Me*, where Moore created a parallel editing between a poor black family being evicted and Roger E. Smith reading a poem by Dickens to the shareholders at the annual G.M. Christmas party.

concerning the tragedies which occurred because of firearm availability and full-access to cheap bullets in his "Land of the Free." He does not even acknowledge that there is a problem with gun violence in America in the final interview of the film, which has been highly criticized by detractors and supporters alike. Later on, we will have a chance to vindicate Moore treatment of that interview and explain why we think he might have acted the way he did with this "legend" of American film history.

Children of the Damned

After this sequence, where we are shown the validity of Mauser's rhetoric, Moore initiates a thematic that will carry the next hour of the film all the way to its open-ended resolution. It is his incursion into American popular culture, which seems to lie at the heart of the problem. This is a culture that caters to the desperation and neurosis of already-dead suburbia; to this bleak, homogenized landscape of never-ending streets, shopping malls, chemical factories, and weapon manufacturers. Moore meets up with Matt Stone, one of *South Park* co-creators, a revolutionary series in its own right. Stone explains that he was pressured to perform in high school like other kids and goes on to blame a system which does not allow for failure. A system that pins you as a "Big L," if you do not pass 10th grade math, according to him. Here again we are back to the "We're Number One" attitude, the one that has been pounded into Americans ever since they were infants. Until the day they recognize that there is no such thing as being "Number One" in math, as in politics or bomb-making, violence will always be threatening their fragile social order. Instead of trying to understand the nature of the problem as it truly is, and recognizing the failures of their under-funded educational system, adults started blaming their kids for what happened after the Columbine carnage. Moore creates another montage where he shows us various instances of school violence and shootings all over the United States. He also includes a long excerpt of a ludicrous marketing video for Garrett Metal Detectors that was "targeted" to school's administrators and PTAs around the country at the time. However, in *Bowling for Columbine* Moore also makes it appear as if kids are not responsible for their actions, since, after all, they are kids and highly subjected to adult influence. In the end, the film stresses the idea that Americans are dealing with their problems in a backward and illogical way. Instead of creating structures that would help their children evolve, and fostering a more active and creative life for them through community-based activities, for example, adults chose to install metal detectors, surveillance cameras and alarm systems in their institutions, something that only re-enforced everyone's alienation. In schools, where kids spend most of their time in a week, corporate-sponsored equipment and private security personnel are watching them as if *they* were the problem. Still, all of this technocracy could not prevent or deter attacks such as the one which occurred at Columbine in 1999, nor the other dozens of school shootings since then.[62]

Burden of Guilt

Michael Moore started wondering about who might be to blame for all this teen-violence after all. In the wake of the Columbine shootings, every media personality, psychologist, TV evangelists, and politicians had an answer to that question: angry heavy metal subculture, parents, violent movies, *South Park*, video games, television, entertainment, Satan, cartoons, toy guns, society, drugs, "shock-rocker" Marilyn Manson... Marilyn Manson? Who is he in the grand picture of things? Is he a cultural reference of a scope so great that he would have made two kids crack-up and go out on a bloody rampage on a school day? Was the image of rebel-without-a-cause James Dean alone responsible for sending the Starkweather/Fugace couple across the badlands in the 1950s? Probably not, but perhaps that a brutal or absent father might have sparked all that anger, though. Manson could not have been responsible for a drama of such origins and magnitude; since there are much more evil influences out there in the culture at large (even *he* recognizes that). He tells Moore that he understands the reasons why people pick on him, since he is a "poster boy for fear, and because he represents what everyone is afraid of" (what that is, is difficult to say). The shock-rocker goes on to remind Moore of the Kosovo bombings, and that fear is a great incentive to make people buy and consume "stuff" (in quotation marks here to signify "anything") in America. Essentially, Manson comes to the same conclusions as Michael Moore does in his film. When Moore asked Manson what he would have told Harris and Klebolt if he had a chance, the latter replied, "I wouldn't

---

[62] According to Wikipedia, from 2002 to 2010 shootings occurred at: John McDonogh High, Red Lion Area Junior High, Case Western Reserve University, Rocori High, Columbia High, Fairleigh Dickinson University, Randallstown High, Red Lake Senior High, Campbell County High, Pine Middle School, Essex Elementary, Orange High, Platte Canyon High, Weston High, Amish school, Henry Foss High, University of Washington, Virginia Tech, Delaware State University, Success Tech Academy, Louisiana Tech College, Mitchell High, E.O. Green School, Northern Illinois University, Davidson High, Central High, Henry Ford High, University of Central Arkansas, Dillard High, Henry Ford Community College, Wesleyan University, Canandaigua Academy, Harvard University, Larose-Cut Off Middle School, Skyline College, Atlanta University, Deer Valley High, Northern Virginia, Discovery Middle School, University of Alabama, Deer Creek Middle School, Birney Elementary, and Ohio State University.

have said anything to them. I would have listened to what they had to say, and that's what nobody did." These are words of wisdom, if there are any left nowadays; except it was later discovered by the police that these particular teens perceived themselves as demigods better than your average human being, as being Number One, all the way on the road to total perdition. Maybe what they really needed after all was to have a good talk "bashed" into them by a parent or an educator that actually cared, a kind of John Keating or Jaime Escalante in their lives. Perhaps that what they really needed (and wanted) was a more virtuous role model to beginning with, someone else than Marilyn Manson. Why is it that North America has no difficulty celebrating fools or sportsmen while forgetting the "smaller," more important heroes in their children's everyday life? Needless to say, television and the Internet have created role models that are insipid and utterly insignificant when compared to the teachers and civil servants working together to improve society.

Creative New Ways of Venting Out Anger

In a later moment from *Bowling for Columbine*, Moore stands next to two teenagers who are busy shooting up monsters on an arcade game at their local neighborhood cinema. They have just seen a film starring Arnold Schwarzenegger and seem to really enjoy their own destructive capabilities on the virtual zombies on screen. He asks if the picture they had just seen influenced them into playing this violent video game. Their answer is positive. In this instance, Moore does not try to make a direct link between Hollywood violence, video games and teen violence in schools. What he is trying to do is to tap into the collective unconscious of America, into the imaginary and thus symbolic representation of itself. His film is not about guns, but about what might be the reasons people use them on each other, and about the very *perception* of that "Other" that must be exterminated to be "Number One." Later on, in a similar type of interviewing technique, we learn from two students that Harris and Klebolt used to release their contempt for society by chucking balls down the lane in their favorite class: Bowling 101. Moore uses this seemingly trivial piece of information and runs away with it.

Moore (v.o.):

"So did Dylan and Eric show up that morning to bowl two games before moving on to shoot up the school? And did they just chuck the balls down the lane? Did this mean *something*?"

He goes on to ask "Why didn't anyone blame bowling for warping the minds of Eric and Dylan?" This seemed as plausible as Marilyn Manson, does it not? It is at this moment that the film starts using comparison as a didactic tool for reflection. While Moore ponders about different kinds of violence perpetrated in different countries, we hear Beethoven's '9th Symphony' on the soundtrack, a direct homage to the film *A Clockwork Orange* (1971) and its maker, the great Stanley Kubrick (one of Moore's idols). Through a musical montage, he takes us to Germany where they also listen to sinister Goth-Rock music. Moore then takes us to France, where people watch the same violent Hollywood movies as everyone else on this planet. Another case Moore chooses to talk about is Japan, a country where violent video games were invented but that does not have the same gun-murder rate as America. After, he even questions the conventionally expected explanations about teen violence, such as the breakup of the traditional family nucleus. He tells us that, in Britain, there is twice the amount of broken homes as there are in America, but this is still not explaining why Americans like to shoot each other at the rate they do. There surely has to be something else at work here.

The voice-over in the scene denies that only poverty and unemployment are responsible for gun murders in America. Joblessness leads people to criminal behavior and activities, like we have seen in *Roger & Me*, but surely not to arbitrary killings such as the ones perpetrated at Columbine High School. Anyhow, the shooters were just teenagers in this case...and it was not done out of economic desperation, they *were* middle-class kids... So, what did it all really mean? In a condensed sequence he cuts together different footage to tell us that some people explain this violence by using America's history of conquest and bloodshed. Still in voice-over, he goes on to add that most industrialized countries also have a bad record when it comes down to cruelty and domination, but that they do not go on killing each other the way Americans do. He ends a statistical sequence by revealing that in the United States in 2001 there has been 11,137 gun-related murders... Even for a population of 300 million individuals this constitutes a high rate of violence. These statistics speak volumes for Moore. They are too excessively disproportionate to be meaningless. This inquiry is still too fresh to draw any real conclusions yet.

A Bible and a Smith & Wesson

In one of the most incendiary sequences of *Bowling for Columbine*, Moore summarizes the history of the United States of America by using a cartoon figure (the "talking bullet" previously used to advertise Pistol

Pete in the *Awful Truth* series). This hilarious and quick-paced animation, evoking the *South Park* aesthetics (i.e. cutout characters and settings with no depth-of-field), is entitled "The Story of the United States of America," which in itself is a very bold move. It cuts pretty close to the bone as far as the place African-Americans occupy in the white version of American history, among many other things. Summed up, the plot of the animated sequence goes something like this...

The Puritans, scared of persecution from the Anglicans, left England and came to the New World, where they've exterminated Native-Americans, burned "witches," and finally got rid of their British rulers in 1776 with the help of a rag-tag army. These pilgrims then went on to abduct black people from their African homeland, enslaved them, brought them to the "Land of the Free," and made them work for nothing. By using free labor, they became so loaded with free money that they did not know how to spend it. The Civil War then freed the slaves who wanted to live in peace and prosperity, but this attitude scared the white man, so he invented and regulated the Colt six-shooter, founding the K.K.K. and the N.R.A. almost simultaneously. Whitey keep black people oppressed, politically and economically, by making sure drugs were readily available, and by giving them no choice but to burn their own ghettos down. This oppression lasted until Rosa Parks sat in that Alabama bus and galvanized the emerging Civil Rights movement. Then, white people created suburbia and went to hide in it, leaving behind city life and its many ghettos (in which it has now forced blacks and destitute immigrants of all origins). There in their gated communities, they believed they were free, safe, and untouchable. The fact remains that they are still as scared as when they left England 400 years ago, and that they are applying this philosophy of fear to almost everything they conceive and do today.

Here again we are confronted with two possible interpretations of American history. The one inscribed on a plaque at Ellis Island: America the great historical melting pot that welcomes with open arms the "tired, the hungry, and the poor;" and the one about the colonization and exploitation of an already occupied land: America with "a lot of blood on its hands." It could be argued that both versions contain elements of the truth. After all, as Canadian singer-songwriter-poet Leonard Cohen once sang, America is "the cradle of the best and the worst."[63] He might as well have been talking about the America Moore is showing us in *Bowling for Columbine*.

---

[63] Leonard Cohen, *The Future*, Columbia, 1992

Grey Flannel Suits

After this colorful animation sequence about how America came to be, Moore opens the last third of *Bowling for Columbine* by asking a simple question. It is in response to the last proposition of the cartoon character who said sarcastically: "And everyone lived happily ever after!" while showing us a happy family equipped with its arsenal (even the dog and the baby have high-caliber weapons). Moore's response, "Or did they?" is truly appropriate in this context since it is accompanied once again by footage from the 1950s, an era usually associated with peaceful times in the suburbs and an ideal lifestyle that White America had imagined for itself. But this era is also associated today to the fear of the Other, as we have established before, making it one of the most interesting and complex of the 20th century. To truly understand the 1950s in America, you have to consider its dual nature: people being extremely conservative on the surface and paranoid in the very depth of their collective psyche by the same token. In fact, the perfect icon for this ideal of "dysfunctional normalcy" in the emerging Corporate America is *The Man in the Grey Flannel Suit*, written by Sloan Wilson.

It is suggested in the previous chapters that in the 1950s Americans had a skewed look at the world and their own place in it (they still do to this day, less so under Obama, who is, if nothing else, a *moral guide* for more than 64 million Americans). It was a time when the American Dream, although unattainable for most, if only by credit, was forced down people's throat, basically, but there was also a whole stratum of society that was questioning its meaning and its purpose, very much like the man in the grey flannel suit. America and its allies had won WW II and it seemed so great to be American that they tried to make everyone on the planet American. All throughout the decade, people were repeated the same ideological mantra. The whole thing had a "Let's start anew" attitude, but with a kind of "Howdy Doody atmosphere" to it. It was a time when on the surface of things people were most naïve and forgetful of the horrors that had just occurred a few years before in the ovens of Bergen-Belsen, and on the bloody beaches of France. They were living in denial. Moore evokes the contradictions of a society that believes itself virtuous, free, and "clean," but which can only breathe on feelings of anger and mistrust for anything "foreign," constantly living in utter fear of the Bomb and of the unknown. Certain images in *Bowling for Columbine* and elsewhere in Moore's work are in direct link to what has been described above, not only because it is the context within which Moore himself grew up, but also because it shaped the imagination of those who control business and politics today.

Paranoid Android

In the following segment the filmmaker again uses footage from the 1950s. We see people watching their TVs and he asks us in voice-over if we remember the "Y2K Scare," the killer "Africanized bees" (as opposed to the kinder and gentler "European bees"), or again being told to be careful of razor blades in Halloween candies (something that rarely happens, as records show). In his editing scheme, he collages *faits divers* from nightly news reports, with stories of people being attacked by wild animals while mowing their back lawn and other such freak accidents. One local news commentator tells the viewer, "What you do not know might kill you!" There is even a report on the dangers of taking an escalator at the shopping mall entitled "Stairway to Danger!" One reporter reminds people "Not to draw attention to [yourself] as an American," while another reads from a report that states that "One in every five Americans suffers from *some form* of mental disorder…" Using the word "propaganda" does not seem inappropriate or too far-fetched here.

Hence, one of the main arguments put forth by the film is the tacit conspiracy between the different levels of government, corporations, and those who own media to keep people scared out of their minds, in order to better control them. In general, fear is an emotion that makes one act irrationally. It makes people more malleable, obedient, and responsive to orders. In essence, fear is a necessary reflex for survival and the superstructure learned to stimulate these feelings for behavioral purposes. Like it will be the case with his following film, *Fahrenheit 9/11*, Moore proposes the Orwellian theory of a futuristic totalitarian society to debunk the ultimate political fallacy of our age: that consuming will make you more apt to cope with "dangerous situations" (like the end of the world). In *Bowling for Columbine*, he inserts footage of George W. Bush's addressing himself to the military and to the American public on two occasions. These excerpts are there to remind us that sometimes it is so easy to scare people into doing things that "you do not even have to give them any reasons at all," like Moore says.

Determined to demonstrate that he is not afraid himself, the next sequence has Michael Moore roaming the streets of South Central Los Angeles, corner of Florence and Normandie (the epicenter of the 1992 L.A. riots). He trudges along with Professor Barry Glassner, who explains how TV news choose to cover what people want to see, not thinking that the ownership of TV news outlets create the agenda and leads the public taste. According to Glassner, what the public wants to see, and this is highly debatable as far as we are concerned, is a black man being wrestled to the ground by police officers (more specifically: with no shirt on his back). Moore then shows a sequence where black men are reported as having committed various crimes in different cities. The montage made out of TV news reports pertains to suspects usually described as being African-American. Moore shortens the shots' length and speeds up the sound bites to give the editing great momentum. He quickly and repeatedly cuts the words "suspect" and "black male" over various close-ups of African-American men doing casual activities. The intention here is to force a discussion concerning the white man's fear of black people in America. Moore is speculating about the reasons why so many white Americans are afraid and aggressive at the same time. Once again, he makes a giant conceptual leap through cinematic means by suggesting that whites are afraid that black people will someday rise and take revenge for what they had to endure in the past (slavery, oppression, permanent disenfranchisement, etc.). Implicit to Moore's editing is a kind of "return of the repressed" argument which says that Americans have armed themselves so that they'll be ready to defend what has been acquired through perhaps "uncivilized ways" or usurpation, through the exploitation of an entire people.

Going back home, Moore then interviews Arthur Busch, a County Prosecutor for the city of Flint. This one proposes that the black community has become entertainment for the rest of America. He tells Moore that African-American generally do not own guns, because they are "turned-off at the idea of owning one," according to him. Moore emphasizes the idea that it is rich suburban white kids that are most vulnerable to this kind of Scarface-lifestyle, not the black kids of America. Little white boys everywhere have too easily access to drugs and semi-automatic weapons to lay restless at home. They probably got around to all these adult "toys" by saving up the allowances or simply by stealing them from someone they knew (or that somebody else knew). Moore is curious about this link between gun violence, ethnicity and class, and he follows it in the narrative. At one point, after having established certain correlations between government action and individual action, between news and entertainment, between fear and consumption, Moore cuts back to another Oscoda teenager who explains how easy it is for minors to acquire weapons in America.

Moore (off):

How did you get a gun?

Oscoda Boy:

I stole mine.

Moore (off):

Where did you steal it from?

Oscoda Boy:
I stole it from a friend of mine. His dad owns a bunch of guns.

Moore (off):
What did you do with the stolen guns?

We cut to an amateur video of a transaction between a white teen and two young black teenagers in a project.

Oscoda Boy (off):
We went down to Detroit to try to sell them, cos' I can get 150 dollars a pop for a .9mm...

Moore (off):
Really?

Oscoda Boy (off):
Yeah.

Moore (off):
Who were you trying to sell them too?

Oscoda Boy:
Maybe gangs and stuff like that...

Moore (off):
Gangs in the city?

Oscoda Boy:
Yeah.

Moore (off):
Black?

Oscoda Boy:
Predominantly.

Colors

From what we know from social research, African-Americans who actually own a gun are a minority and stand at the most extreme margins of society. They usually are the gang-bangers, the dope dealers, and the pimps (usually young males from low-income and troubled homes). As we've already witnessed in *The Awful Truth*, a lot of black men are being shot at daily for handling such harmless objects as a wallet, a cell phone or a candy bar. So why would they want to casually carry a gun on them? To practice their right to the Second Amendment, like Mr. Heston himself? Moore is one of the few (white) media personalities who is actually interested in what this community has to say outside of its entertainment and sports exploits. In *Bowling for Columbine,* he shows no fear in visiting the most impoverished ghettos and neighborhoods in the country. In this instance, he walks through South Central as if it was Malibu Beach or Beverly Hills.

Later in the film, he is standing next to a young police officer on the sidewalk. The cop is mimicking the behavior he saw in a police movie, somewhere, or on a television show, somehow. It is obvious. He is obvious. By harassing him a bit, Moore goes after something that is crucial in understanding the phenomenon of violence in the United States of America today: American masculinity. He asks the officer if it is possible to arrest those responsible for the smog covering the Hollywood sign, but the young cop avoids interaction with Moore in a convoluted way, pretending that his attention is set down the street where a group of black people are hanging out. Actually, the viewer can see in depth of field that not much is going on in that direction, except a few kids playing skip-rope. Moore keeps asking him about his potential legal recourse regarding air quality in Los Angeles, but the officer starts walking away while Moore is talking, with his chest standing out, one hand on his club, the other on his revolver, obviously ready to rumble. Moore then uses a match-cut of a hand-held shot of the show *Cops*, where, from the exact same angle, we see the exact same action being replicated by a TV cop. Does TV imitate life or does life imitate TV? Is "TV Reality" really reality or is reality more real than "Reality TV?" Who knows about this stuff anymore? It got to a point where the line between both is too blurred for anyone to tell the difference. One thing for certain, every media representation is an intentional construction, whether it'd be a fiction or a "documentary" or "Reality TV," and it most certainly influences how we apprehend the world in the long run.

In that sense, *Cops* is not only about black men being arrested but also about the police officers who chase them down the alley, wrestle them to the ground, and handcuff them under a distorting lens. These officers are glorified by mass media while seemingly keeping order. What this glorification conceals, though, is that crimes committed in the ghetto are usually motivated by total economic despair, while those committed by white suburban people are often triggered by existential boredom and class malaise. The culture that *Cops* proposes is one that feeds from what people want to see, according to its producers and professor Glassner. However, experts like Glassner seem to forget that it is *distributors* who really dictate what people are watching, and there are only a handful of them. Those who own and control media rarely propose something enlightening to their potential viewers. They base their concepts on the lowest common denominator. They just give the masses what *they* think they want to see, not necessarily what they really want to see. Very much like Smiley and Panzer in *Canadian Bacon*, these men of power are sold on the idea that people want to see a hero protecting them from some absolute evil out there. Ultimately, this mainstream popular culture imposed by those who own and control the media influences how people think and behave, and, at the same time, gives them what they *seem* to want, in a downward circle of cheap thrills and illusions of empowerment.

Sometimes a Great Notion

In an attempt to understand the fascination with violence in American popular culture more profoundly, Moore pays a visit to one of the producers of *Cops*. His voice-over commentary mocks the idea of the so-called "melting-pot" in America.

>Moore (v.o.):
"For over a decade, there's been one show on American television that has consistently brought black and white people together, in an effort to reduce our fears and celebrate our diversity."

We see an excerpt from the show where three police officers nail face down a (shirtless) black man who has blood dripping from his forehead.

>Moore (v.o.):
"That show is *Cops*."

The theme song 'Bad Boys' starts beating up on the soundtrack.

>Moore (v.o.):
"I went to see a former Producer of *Cops* and Executive Producer of *World's Wildest Police Videos*, Mr. Dick Hurlin."

Hurlin is sitting in his L.A. office and Moore is facing him off-screen left.

>Hurlin:
Look up the word "liberal" in the dictionary and I think my picture is in there somewhere.

Moore (off):
So then, why not be compelled to do a show that, you know, focuses on, you know, what's *causing* the crime, as opposed to just chasing the criminals down?

Hurlin:
Because I think it's harder to do that show. I don't know what that show would be. Anger does well. Hate does well. Violence does well. Tolerance and understanding and trying to learn to be a little different than you were last year does less well.

Moore (off):
Does less well in the ratings?

Hurlin:
Oh yeah.

Moore (off):
Maybe because we, in the television business, tend to demonize black and Hispanic people. Then those watching it at home are going: 'Hey, I don't want to help these people, I'm not going to do anything to help them because I hate them now, because they *may* hurt me', you know what I'm saying?

Hurlin:
I know what you're saying, but I'm not sure that's what we're doing. I'm not sure we're demonizing black and Hispanic people…uh…particularly. I don't think we show black and Hispanic people as being criminals (*takes a breath*)… I'd like to say not more often, but probably they *are* more often…but, uh…I certainly do not think that… uh…We are certainly not trying to demonize black and Hispanic people.

Moore inserts another shot from *Cops* wherein, yet again, another young black man is being thrown to the ground, face down on the street.

Moore (off):
"We show them on the news as pretty scary people."

Hurlin (*repentant*):
Yeah, and I agree. I'd like to see that reversed as much as possible...I, uh...

Moore (off):
Start tonight.

Hurlin:
Well, the thing is that I don't know how to start tonight. I don't know how to do a show like that. If I was smart enough to do that...

Moore (off):
Okay, I'll pitch you one. Do a show called, not *Cops*, but *Corporate Cops*.

We see a quick excerpt from the intro to *The Awful Truth* episode where Moore is chasing a white-collar criminal down Wall Street.

Hurlin:
I love the idea. I don't think it would make very interesting "Reality TV." Unless we can get those people to get in their SUVs and drive really fast down the road away from the police.

Moore (off):
But I'm telling you, everyone in America who's got just your basic everyday job is gonna love watching the boss being chased down the street with his shirt off, thrown to the ground with a knee in the neck, I'm telling ya', that's gonna get ratings...

Hurlin:
...I'm with you. And if I could find a police outfit that would prosecute corporate criminals appropriately, and that would go after them appropriately... In other words, what you do to a man that just stole a little old lady's purse with 85 dollars, then you need to do an appropriate response to a man who just stole 85 millions from indigenous people, then, boy, were gonna be out there filming that... But as a matter of fact, when the police go after the guy who just stole 85 millions, they treat him as if he was a member of the City Council, as he may or may not be, and it's not *exciting television*. If you can get that guy to get his shirt off...

                    Moore (off):
Right.

                    Hurlin:
...and throw his cell phone at the police as they come through the door, trying to jump out that window...Then we'd have a show. You watch violence on TV in a place like Canada and you know it's not happening next door. You watch it here and you know it is happening next door... I don't know what the difference is, but there is a big difference...

                    Moore (off):
Yeah...Why isn't it happening in Canada? Why aren't there 10,000 murders a year?

                    Hurlin:
I don't know but I want to go to Canada and retire or something, cos' it sounds like where we wanna be... I'd like to find out what that difference is, wouldn't you?

                    Moore (off):
        Yeah, I'm trying to find out.

The 49th Parallel

Following on the producer's advice, Moore decides to head on to the Canadian side of the border to see if the Maple Leaf is more tolerant and less prone to violence than the Soaring Eagle. It is in conceptual continuity with his previous works, especially with *Canadian Bacon* that built its rhetoric on comparison. The first shot of the segment is one of a Taco Bell, something that already makes a subtle point about neocolonialism in itself. "Are we still in the United States?," the viewer might ask. As it turns out, we are in Sarnia, Ontario, Canada (population 75,000 and the "Kissing Capital of the World"). Moore asks three high school kids why they think America has so many murders committed with firearms. One teen tells him, "I do not know. People must really hate each other down there!" The two other kids claim that when a Canadian hates a Canadian, he or she does not pull the trigger on them but throws eggs or insults them verbally instead. Moore is no closer to understanding the difference, though.

While visiting the police commissioner of Sarnia, we learn that only one murder had been recorded there in the last three years. The director is well aware that the comparison does not hold with big

American cities, so he decides to pursue his inquiry in a larger Canadian town: Windsor, Ontario, which is five times the population of Sarnia (400,000). There, he interviews regular people in a bar and at a local shooting range. Those interviewed cannot even recollect the last time somebody was shot in their hometown. One police officer says that one gun-murder occurred in the last three years, and that a man from Detroit with a gun purchased in Minnesota had committed it. Moore concludes, too rapidly we might add, that there are just "no Canadians shooting Canadians" to be found. So he decides to have a poll with average Americans concerning "fun facts" about Canada.

In New York, he interviews people on the street who suggest that "Canadians do not watch as much violent movies as Americans do." This is a wrong assumption. Most movies distributed and shown on Canadian screens are made in Hollywood. American movies abound on television as well, and their advertising is everywhere in the Canadian environment. Another woman interviewed believes that there is no poverty in Canada like there is in America. This belief is again wrong, since the unemployment rate [was] higher in Canada than in the U.S., that is, before the subprime crisis of the last few years. Moreover, Canadian citizens have a lower annual income than their American counterparts, and they obviously pay more taxes. A third woman believes that most of Canada is white, when in fact it is a country constituted by 13% of visible minority, a rough equivalent to the United States. So, what does make Canuck different than Uncle Sam? Haven't we learned anything from *Canadian Bacon*?

Moore continues by suggesting that the reason why Canada has so few murders may be that it has so few guns. He informs us that there are 13 million guns in Canada (for a population of just over 30 million, this constitutes a high rate of ownership). Therefore, he goes to a Canadian K-Mart in order to prove that ammunition accessibility is easy there as well (even if you are from outside of the country, without a valid passport). Afterward, he asks people in an Ontario bar if they ever locked their doors when going to bed at night. All answer negatively, even if some had already been victims of a crime before. A man relaxing on a terrace says to Moore: "You think as Americans that a lock is keeping people out of your place. But we, as Canadians, see it more, like, when we lock the door we're keeping ourselves inside." Soon after, Moore decides to go unannounced to a downtown Toronto neighborhood to verify if people lock their doors or not. When he violates a man's front door, the latter explains that there was no reason to lock it, anyhow. Moore tells him politely, "Thank you for not shooting me!" Then, he makes a comment on what Canadians are watching on their evening news. He says that "it does not pump them full of fear and adrenaline like American TV does." He inserts footage from a Canadian MP saying to a reporter, "They're friends of ours.

We'll certainly listen to them courteously and carefully, but you do not make war just because someone says so…" referring to American pressures on Ottawa to participate in the second Iraq War.

Moore then drives the point even further by telling us that Canadian politicians talk "kind of funny." He inserts another television clip with the Mayor of Sarnia expressing what appears to be a socialist ideal: "We have to make sure that they [people] get better day care, have assistance for their elderly parents when they need to, when they are in an old-age home, that they have proper health care which insures that they won't lose their businesses or their houses because they can't afford medical bills… That's how you build a good society." Later, the same politician continues his reasoning: "No one wins unless everyone wins, and you do not win by beating up poor people who can't defend themselves. This has been the approach, unfortunately, that has been spreading in some of the *right-wing governments* all across North America. They pick on the people who can't defend themselves and, at the same time, they are turning around and giving financial support and tax breaks and tax benefits to the people who don't need them." Can anything more meaningful be added to this statement?

They Were Expendable

The most shocking fact permeating through *Bowling for Columbine* relates to the reality of children using weapons at a younger age in the United States. The narrative line jumps back across the American border to retell the story of little Kayla Rolland, a six year-old who had been shot by another six year-old at Theo J. Buell Elementary a few weeks after the Columbine massacre. Like in *Roger & Me*, Moore establishes many important links between socioeconomic status and violence in this later section of the film. As a matter-of-fact, these correlations are what make this film so precious from a sociological point-of-view. It puts back class issues at the center of the political discussion, an idea that *Fahrenheit 9/11* will pursue even further. First, the sequence opens up with a black image over which he lays the 9-1-1 recording of Jimmie Hughes, Buell's Principal, calling for help after Kayla had been shot. Not unlike the World Trade Center sequence in *Fahrenheit 9/11*, where we only hear the planes crashing into the towers and the screaming down below, this is an effective technique which also evokes the respect that Moore has for people he interviews (and sympathizes with, of course). This seems especially apparent when he interviews Principal Hughes. At one point, the woman is so overtaken by unresolved grief that they both have to turn their backs on the camera. On the soundtrack, we hear again Heston's N.R.A. rallying cry, *"From my cold dead hands,"* and then it cuts to the image of

Heston at the Flint rally that was inappropriately held just a few weeks after Kayla's death.

Moore also pays a visit to Michael Caldwell, a police detective who took under custody the boy who had shot Kayla. He had kept the boy occupied by giving him pencils and paper to draw on, and what the kid actually drew on that day, after shooting Kayla in the chest, was a rendering of himself and his home. As presented in the film, the drawing is without a doubt one of the most despairing mementos America has ever produced. At the height of this dramatic scene, Moore tells us that the boy had found the gun at his uncle's house where he was living, because his mother had been evicted and was forced to commute many hours a day to get her "Work-for-Welfare" check. She could not take care of her son because of a system that had been set up to exploit the poorest of the poor. In this sequence, we see shots of the classroom where Kayla was killed with soft piano music on the soundtrack. This is crucial to the dramatization process that Moore often relies on to create powerful emotions in the viewer, much like a fiction film would. Some accused Moore of making "docudramas," but one could reply to that: "Why not?" There is sometimes way more truth in fictionalized accounts of life than in films that purport to be documenting it without intervention. Moore's films are not documentaries in the common sense of the term. Again, they are nonfiction films that hybridize Direct-cinema techniques (handheld, wide-angle lens), television aesthetics (MTV, youth culture), news reports (with their "official journalistic tone"), public affairs (informative, didactic), animation (visual design and graphics), and the idioms of fiction film language (cutting in continuity, dramatic use of framing, editing, etc.). It is a completely original *amalgam of genres and modes of representation* that perfectly suits the chaotic, post-modern world we live in today. For many intelligent and sensitive viewers, it is not only what Moore says that makes a lot of sense, but his style of presentation as well. He has often been criticized for his "lack of objectivity," but in an image-saturated society such as ours, and given the fact that no media can be objective, how can anyone convey the highly dramatic nature of events such as the Columbine shootings or the killing of a 6 year-old by another 6 year-old?

After his interview with Ms. Hughes, he inserts a section pertaining to the coverage of Kayla's death by the national media. Here again we are clearly shown how news is turned into entertainment in America. A reporter from Fox is covering the shooting of Kayla as if it was a sordid affair, not the symptom of a greater social problem. The man seems more concerned about his sloppy hairdo than about the tragedy. As the alternative, Moore chooses to film the cameras and the crews around the reporters to illustrate the artificial nature and contrived aspect of the conventional journalistic apparatus. One assistant to the self-absorbed reporter is caught asking the latter: "Do you want hairspray?" after he completed his last unfelt question about the tragedy. As if this was where the real drama of the day was unfolding: in his 30 second soundbite and his bad 1980s haircut. In another conceptual leap, so frequent in his work, Moore explains that Flint has been destroyed by G.M. and ignored by government and national media alike. Everyone turned an eye on the tragedy of Flint, which can be understood as the tragedy of modern America itself. Over shots of derelict factories, bankrupted businesses, and abandoned homes, he goes on by saying that 87% of the students of Flint live below the poverty line. "Buell and Beecher, like Flint, did not fit in the accepted and widely circulated story-line put forth by the nation's media. The one about America and its invincible economy," he says in voice-over. Moore reminds us that Flint kids have nowhere to go, and that they live in a vicious circle of poverty, alienation and despair. Their community football field is even sponsored by…a local funeral home.

Moore pursues his sociological inquiry by striking the emotional chord even harder, like "the slaughtering of the innocents." He goes back to the glory days of high school life in the naive Eisenhower years. He tells us that Beecher High has won 13 state track championships in their history, but that all of these were actually won in other cities (i.e. since Beecher has a mud ring for a race track). These are not tenuous links that the filmmaker is establishing. These facts go straight at the top of the list of things that America is *not* about. Indeed, in the last 30 years, young Americans in every state were promised something that they never had and, for most of them, probably never will get: a brighter future. Moore explains that, "Years ago, someone named the streets in this part of town after all the Ivy-League schools (Princeton, Cornell, Yale, Harvard) as if they'd dream of better days and something greater for themselves." Obviously, what he is after here is some form of political understanding which is historically circumscribed. He is in the process of dismantling "the dream" by going back to the way America perceived itself in the post-war era. For him, this was a vision that was convenient to all, but which only benefited a few in the long run.

Behind Poverty

Structured like the back and forth swing of a pendulum, the section pertaining to Kayla's death segues into another one about gun control. Moore reminds us that the National Rifle Association does not have any shame when it comes to sell its one-track-mind ideology to the American people, regardless of their age. As mentioned before, a few weeks after Kayla was shot, Heston and friends held a big pro-gun rally in Flint, just to defend their right to bear arms (not to bring support to the family of the victim). As one angry Flint mom puts it: "How can they [N.R.A.] come here? To me it's like they're rubbing our nose in it." When asked by a reporter about the reasons why the N.R.A. decided to come to Flint after Kayla had been killed, and what this association had to say about 6 year-olds using guns on each other, Charlton Heston's reply was typical: "We spend 21 million dollars every year and we teach the 5-6 year-olds that, if you see a gun, do not touch it, leave the room, and call an adult." Three cheers for Eddie Eagle! He truly is the solution to all our problems! Where are Jay Martel and Pistol Pete when you need them?

Following this absurd clip with Heston, being the dialectician that he is, Moore goes back (in the editing) to see Flint's County Prosecutor Busch. He asks him if anyone proposed that the child who killed Kayla be trialed and judged as an adult. Busch tells Moore that people from all over the United States called or wrote to ask him just that.

Busch:
What's amazing to me, is that groups affiliated with the N.R.A., people that I call "gun-nuts," were writing me, telling me what a horrible thing it was that I had admonish homeowners in our country to be careful about bringing weapons into their homes... They wanted this little boy hung from a highest tree... I mean there was such an undercurrent of racism and hate and anger. It was ugly.

After interviewing the police officer who was holding the boy in custody, and in a far-reaching understanding of the problem, Moore engages in a segment concerning the boy's mother. The young African-American woman had to go on the program "Welfare-to-Work" in order to get food stamps to feed her children. This Michigan State program was a bureaucratic concoction designed to push people out of the welfare into total poverty and homelessness by making them work for nothing (the working poor). It was a way to "force them to work," so to speak, but at 5 dollars an hour and with no benefits (like the "welfare mothers" of *The Big One*). In effect, this plan was part of a greater one engineered by the Neocons to exploit poor people all the way and to destroy the notion of the "middle-class" in American society.

Moore insists on the correlation between the mother's predicament and Kayla's murder in the editing. He goes at great lengths, actually for more than five minutes of screen-time, to demonstrate how she had been unable to take care of him because of this form of pseudo-socialist program. Moore expands by telling us that the man responsible for the "Welfare-to-Work" program was also at the head of a movement that was looking to privatize the American health care system, a topic that he will address in greater details in *Sicko*. We also learn that this man's administrative skills were so great that even Lockheed-Martin required his help to privatize their own health care plan. Actually, we have came full-circle here. Moore is still after corporate crooks, only this time they are behaving badly in the political realm. Where's Crackers the crime-fighting chicken when you need him?

Grilling Dick

The shame of the current financial elite is that it fails to see the existing and afflicting rift between Wall Street and Main Street. A mogul like Dick Clark, another overvalued icon of popular culture, can only keep getting richer because he had money to invest with in the beginning. In the sequence pertaining to the *American Bandstand* host, we are shown a picture of him standing next to Bob Hope and Charlton Heston, a true framing of late 1950s superficial Americana. A trio made in Republican heaven. Clark's contemptuous attitude towards the down-and-outs seems obvious when Moore goes out to see him to inquire about the boy's mother, who was working at one of his American Bandstand Grill, 60 miles away from her home, at the time the tragedy occurred. He even asks one of his assistants to close the door on Moore's face, in a gesture of contempt for his fellow "entertainer." Moore tells us that restaurants such as the American Bandstand Grill and the Fudgery (where the boy's mother also worked, in double-employment, "temp-nation" style) profited from tax-cuts by hiring welfare recipients as cashiers. He expands by telling us that the boy's mother worked <u>70 hours a week</u>, at $5.25 an hour, making fudge for the rich, and that it still was not enough to pay for her rent. One week before Kayla's death, she had been told by her landlord that he was going to evict her, which forced her to place her boy with her brother (i.e. where he found the .32 caliber gun used to shoot Kayla). No doubt, if Dick Clark had known all of this he would have done something about it, right?

After the film came out in 2002, Moore reported on the boy's development: "Sadly, he's been permanently taken from his mother by the State of Michigan and he will never be returned to her. He has been put in a series of foster homes, and I've just heard that he was involved in a stabbing incident where he used a knife on another kid. He is, I think, horribly damaged. It's a terrible, tragic situation."[64] What Moore

---

[64] Michael Moore, *Guardian Unlimited*, Online Exclusive Interview, 2003

does is to set social problems in a greater chain of causality. This seems to be the only way to grasp the nature of this problem, since it is so multi-faceted. More than anything else that has been produced in American media in the last 30 years, the wheels of capitalism are well exposed in *Bowling for Columbine*, as they also are in *Capitalism: A Love Story*. The weight of corporate decisions is clearly illustrated by Moore's analytical lens, editing, and narration, just like it had been in his famous first film, made 13 years before as well. In all three cases, he manages to give a human face to the American economy.

Fear Mongers

The last 20 minutes of *Bowling for Columbine* foreshadowed Moore's next feature project, *Fahrenheit 9/11*, and encapsulates many themes contained in his entire body of work.

> Moore (v.o.):
> "In George Bush's America, the poor were not a priority. And, after September 11th 2001, correcting America's social problems took a back-seat to fear, panic, and a new set of priorities…"

The director cuts in a few shots of the 9/11 attacks and the pandemonium that followed. Then, we get footage of Bush dressed up in camouflage gear and addressing himself to a group of military personnel.

> G.W. Bush:
> One way to express our unity is for Congress to set the military budget, the defense of the United States, as a *number one* priority and fully fund my request!

The editing cuts back to other shots of people running the streets of Lower Manhattan. Moore resumes on his earlier claim that contemporary American society lives in utter fear of everything "foreign." We see television footage of a woman explaining how protection suits and gas masks are being sold daily (and in large quantity). Another woman tells a reporter that she is getting a suit and a mask for both, herself and her dog. On a different network, a man admits that he bought a large quantity of guns to be protected from an eventual terrorist attack. A sound-bite says that Wal-Mart had witnessed an increase in gun and ammunition sales in late 2001. As the montage progresses and gets its point across, we see other various shots of scared Americans, footage from an Ali-Baba film, and surveillance tapes of Arab-Americans being body-searched at airports around the country.

> Moore (v.o.):
> "In the months following the 9/11 attacks, we, Americans, were gripped in a state of fear. None of us knew if we too would die at the hands of the evildoers. Who might be sitting next to a crazy guy trying to set his shoe on fire? The threat seemed very real..."

There is then an excerpt from an interview with a man who explains that he is simply trying to protect himself and his family, and then the filmmaker mixes-in varied sources of visual material, which includes footage from reports concerning a considerable sales increase in home security systems. He also cuts in different close-up shots of ex-Secretary of Defense Rumsfeld, ex-Vice-President Cheney and ex-Attorney General Ashcroft, just to be sure that we get the point about who benefited from all this paranoia. Then, Moore goes back to the previous expert he had consulted on the issue of institutionalizing fear in America.

> Barry Glassner:
> Why are we afraid of all these things? It is because a lot of people are making a lot of money off of it, and a lot of careers off of it. So there's a vested interest, a lot of activity to keep us afraid...

> Moore (v.o.):
> "...And what better way to fight box-cutter terrorists than to order a record number of fighter jets from Lockheed? Yes, everyone felt safer, especially with the Army doing garbage detail on Park Avenue. And the greatest benefit of all, for a terrorized public, is that the corporate and political leaders can get away with just about anything."

In the editing, Moore inserts a shot of the Enron logo and a picture of the cover of *Time* that has the following headlines: "The Enron Mess: How Sticky Will It Get?" (over the White House gleaming in the twilight). Right after this we see footage of South Carolina Democrat Senator Ernest Hollings, a public official from the right, addressing the Congress.

> Senator Hollings:
> I've never seen a better example of "Cash & Carry" government than this Bush administration and Enron.

Following on Hollings' remark that the Republicans then in the White House are shameless thieves, Moore reminds us that the American economy was not doing too well before 9/11 anyhow, and that this instability had been affecting the American morale for quite some time.

> Moore (v.o.):
> "There were a lot of things I didn't know after the World Trade Center attacks, but one thing was clear, whether it was before or after September 11th, a public that's this out-of-control with fear shouldn't have a lot of guns or ammo lying around..."

This last sequence is cut in a knife-edge pattern and pulsating to Offspring's song 'Americana'. It also clashes various shots of Lower Manhattan streets in hand-held camera (constantly switch-panning). It is Moore at his most experimental, playing with editing, multiplicity of point-of-views, and near-abstraction. He is using film techniques to convey a greater idea than the smaller constitutive parts. He assembles images together to create a mosaic that represents an American state of mind. Ultimately, he wants to give the impression of what it is like to live in a culture such as his; where fear, suspicion, and animosity are the main ingredients to everyday life.

How K-Mart Was Won (without ever shooting a gun)

In one of the last sequences from *Bowling for Columbine*, Moore unites with two survivors of the Columbine massacre: Richard Costaldo and Mark Taylor. The filmmaker had requested their help in asking K-Mart to stop selling ammunition over the counter, because the bullets used by Harris and Klebolt had been purchased there...legally. Costaldo is now paralyzed and stuck to a wheelchair for life, while Taylor underwent numerous operations to dislodge the bullets incrusted in his body. These young men have grown old before their time because of the influence of corporations on law-making entities as much as the effects of capitalist values on two psychopath teenagers. As Moore sees it, they are the true spokespersons for gun control in America. Mark Taylor says in the film that "The kids at Columbine had to pay a penalty. We paid a penalty that day *for this nation*. The way we look at it...." At one point in the sequence, Moore even asked him to show his wounds for the camera (a request reminiscent of the "Funeral at a HMO" skit from *The Awful Truth* series).

Thus, both young men accompany Moore to K-Mart Headquarters in Troy, Michigan. Inside the HQ lobby, we see rapid inserts of banners asserting "Strategic Imperatives," "World-Class Execution," and other self-important corporate jingoism that conceals the truth about the reality of the American workplace. In true Moore infiltration-fashion, the three men (accompanied by Richard's mother) promptly request to meet with a corporate representative. An hour later, an executive finally comes down to talk with these victims about K-Mart's marketing philosophy. Costaldo reminds her that, "Since you've stopped selling hand-guns and all, it makes sense to stop selling bullets too." The woman replies that the company is only selling "sporting" firearms and "accessories" that come with regular hunting gear. Much later, a man responsible for buying the merchandise for K-Mart tells Moore "Still in trouble?" (referring to his reputation for creating havoc in the corporate world), to which Moore replies, "We are not the ones in trouble, guys."

After suffering a third rebuttal from an executive, they finally decide to go buy all the ammo available at local K-Mart stores and bring it all back to headquarters, but this time accompanied by the local media. They display the artillery on the reception desk, and Moore holds for the camera the type of bullet that still resides in Taylor's body. In what seems like a matter of minutes, a media relation employee came down and made an official announcement: K-Mart will stop selling ammunition across the U.S. within the next ninety days. It was a small victory for Moore on that day, but he knew that this commitment from one corporation was not exactly going to solve the problem either. What had to be done was to change the way Americans were thinking about issues of gun control, vindictive behavior, and how they perceived themselves as citizens of the world. He just had to go higher up the ladder, at the level of symbolic America, where all the ideas and dreams are concocted for the public. He had to go to Hollywood.

ced *Thou Shall Not Kill*…That Goes for You Too, Moses!

As noted earlier, Moore had to take on the mythical figure of Charlton Heston because the man embodied a certain ideal of what it is to be American; an ideal clustered around, but diverting from, the founding precepts of the country itself. He had to take on Heston because he is the kind of icon who has lived with the attitude that some of his characters have in his movies. He is the "Unreal America," a mere entertainer that had to be put back in its proper place by activists like Michael Moore. Let's face it, without the masses of immigrants, blacks, and women who went to see his movies in the last half a century he would not have been the rich and famous white person that he was the day he died. The final sequence of *Bowling for Columbine* starts with Moore standing in front of a Beverly Hills sign looking at a Star Map. He is looking for Heston's home address. Later, after having localized Heston's estate, he goes up to the wrought-iron gate and buzzes on the intercom to see if Heston would agree to an interview. Moore tells him that he too is a long-time N.R.A. cardholder to facilitate the infiltration. Heston agrees to meet him the morning after.

As Moore walks up to Heston's mansion, a day later, we can hear a version of *Mr. Rogers' Neighborhood* theme song on the soundtrack, which points to the fact that a) it is morning, and b) that Heston has been living out of touch with the world. The actor comes to greet him, obviously afflicted by old age and mobility problems, which did upset many viewers afterwards. Inside his pool house, after he shows him his own N.R.A. card, Moore soon starts to put into question Heston's sense of decency. At first, he is cryptic and suspicious of Moore's intention for interviewing him, but he eventually gets lost in his own digressions concerning the issues raised by the filmmaker. It is a pathetic moment that reveals that most Hollywood actors are clueless in regards to social policies, that, once they "made it," they lose touch with socioeconomic realities. An exhaustive transcription of this interview is necessary here to vindicate Moore's approach and his reasons to "pick on" Heston in the first place. Notice how their conversation switches to ethnicity halfway through.

> Moore:
> I assume you have guns in the house, here.

> Heston:
> Indeed I do. Bad guys take notice (laughs).

> Moore:
> So, you got'em for protection?

> Heston:
> Yeah, sure.

> Moore:
> Have you ever been a victim of crime?

> Heston:
> Nope.

> Moore:
> Never been assaulted?

> Heston:
> No. No.

Moore:
No violence towards you? You have guns in the house...

Heston:
Loaded.

Moore:
They're loaded?

Heston:
Well, if you really need weapons for self-defense, you need them loaded.

Moore:
Lemme ask you something. But why do *you* need it for self-defense?

Heston:
I don't...

Moore:
You've never been a victim of crime, you've never been assaulted here, you know? So why not...Why don't you unload the gun?

Heston:
Because...uh...the Second Amendment gives me the right to have it loaded.

Moore:
Oh, I agree! I totally agree with that. But I'm just saying, you know... the Second Amendment gives me the right...

Heston:
The Second Amendment is a *comfort factor*...You know?

Moore:
It gives you comfort to know that there is a loaded gun?

Heston:
Yeap.

Moore:
Comfort means…that…uh…It allows you to relax and feel safe…

Heston:
Not worrying about it…

Moore:
No worrying…and safe…

Heston:
I'm not really but… I'm exercising one of the rights passed on down to me from those **wise old dead white guys** that invented this country. If it was good enough for them, it's good enough for me…

Moore:
You can still exercise the right just by having the gun unloaded and locked away somewhere.

Heston:
I know… I chose to have it loaded.

Moore:
What sort of strikes me as interesting is that, in other countries where they don't have the murder rate, the gun-murder rate that we have, that…uh…you know, many people said "Well, it's because they don't have as many guns around"… "You can't get a gun in Britain or Germany or whatever…" But we went to Canada, and there are 7 million guns in 10 million homes…

Heston:
That won't be for very long…

Moore:
But hear me out, though…Canada is a nation of hunters, millions of guns, and yet they had just a few murders last year, that's it…for a country of 30 million people… Here's my question: Why is it that they got all these guns laying around, yet they don't kill each other at the level that we kill each other?

Heston:
I think American history is…uh…has…uh…a lot of blood on its hands…

Moore:
Oh, and German history doesn't? And British history?

Heston:
I don't think as much…

Moore:
Germans don't have as much blood on their hands?

Heston:
Oh, *they* do, yes.

Moore:
The Brits? They ruled the world for 300 years at the barrel of a gun. See, they're all violent people… They have bad guys, they have crime, and they have lots of guns…

Heston:
That's an interesting point that could be reduced… explored…and you're good to explore it at great length, but I think that…uh… That's about all I had to say…

Moore:
You don't have an opinion, though, as to why we are the unique country, the only country that does this, that kills each other on this level with guns?

Heston:
Well, we have probably more **mixed ethnicity** than other countries, some other countries…

Moore:
You think it's an "ethnic thing?"

Heston:
No, I don't…It's…I would not go so far as to say that…We had enough troub…problems with Civil Rights in the beginning…It's a…but, uh…I have no answer for that…

Moore:
But what do you mean you think it's a "mixed ethnicity thing?" I don't understand it.

Heston:
You said: 'How is it that there are so many Americans…uh… killing each other.' I don't think that's true, but…even…

Moore:
Oh, you know that! We know we have the highest murder-rate with guns… I mean it's way higher than any other country…

Heston:
The only answer I can give is the one answer I already gave you.

Moore:
Which is?

Heston:
Which is that we have a history of violence, perhaps more than most countries… Not more than Russia, not more than Japan…

Moore:
Not more than Germany…

Heston:
Not more than Germany, but certainly more than Canada.

Moore:
I come from Flint, Michigan. And last year a little 6 year-old boy took a gun into a classroom and shot and killed a 6 year-old girl. And it was really a tragic thing…

Heston:
These were kids, though?

Moore:
Yeah, did you hear about this? A 6 year-old shooting a 6 year-old?

Heston grunts a half-yes-half-no answer, communicated non-verbally, holding his lips tightly together.

Moore:
Well, here's my question, though. After that happened, you came to Flint and held a big rally…

Heston:
Uh-huh. So did the President...

Moore:
Yeah, but did you feel it was being at all insensitive to the fact that this community had just gone through this...

Heston:
Actually, I was not aware of that at the time we came... We came into the early morning rally and went on to... wherever we were going...

Moore:
You didn't know at the time you were there that this killing had happened?

Heston:
(*Grunting in the negative.*)

Moore:
If you had known...Would you have...?

Heston:
Would I have cancelled the...?

Moore:
Yeah.

Heston:
I do not ...pssss...

Moore:
It was not as if it had been already planned? The choice to come was made after this horrible killing took place? Had you known that, would you have come?

Heston:
I don't know. I have no idea.

Moore:
Maybe...maybe not?

Heston starts getting up from his chair. He shakes Moore's hand and looks at him, but somehow does not leave the room yet, perhaps expecting more "abuse" (because he knows deep down inside that Moore is right in his outrage).

> Moore:
> Do you think you'd like to, just maybe…apologize to the people in Flint for coming and doing that, at that time…or…

> Heston:
> You want *me* to apologize? *Me* to apologize to the people of Flint?

> Moore:
> Yeah. You know? or to the people of Columbine for coming after their horrible tragedy? Why do you go to places after they had these horrible tragedies? I'm a member of your group here and I…

> Heston:
> Well, I'm afraid we don't agree on that…

Heston now stands up and starts walking out.

> Moore:
> You think it's okay to just come and show up at these events?

Heston pats Moore on the shoulder in a way that means, "Nice try," and starts exiting the room.

> Heston:
> No.

> Moore:
> You *don't* think it's okay?

Heston leaves the pool house and goes outside, where Moore stops him and shows him a picture of Kayla Rowland, just in case he never saw who she was. Heston turns around, looks at the picture, and then continues to walk away.

> Moore:
> Mr. Heston?!! Just one more thing: This is who she is…or was…This is her… Mr. Heston! Please do not leave. Take a look at her, this is the girl.

We see Moore's imposing figure holding the picture and begging Heston to be more human-like, but to no avail... Sadden by the outcome of the interview with the living icon, leaving slowly the estate grounds, Moore decides to leave Kayla's picture next to Heston's garage door. Then he walks out towards the gated entrance of the driveway, while he offers his last thought on the issues raised by the film.[65]

>Moore (v.o.):
>"I left Heston's estate atop Beverly Hills and walked back into *the real world*. An America living and breathing in fear..."

"Trees of Green & Red Roses Too..."

In the very last moments from *Bowling for Columbine*, Michael Moore interviews a man at a firing range. The latter wears a baseball cap that has "Fuck Everybody" written on it. Moore asks him, "In your mind, when you imagine someone breaking into your house to harm you or your family...What does that person look like?" The man replies, "You," then pointing to Moore's assistant, "Her," then to camera-assistant, "Him," then to the camera-operator, "The camera guy, anybody...There could be a gun in the camera, I don't know." Then, Moore reprises his voice-over narration, but with a different infliction.

>Moore (v.o.):
>"Where gun sales were now at an all-time high..."

We see a quick insert of a man with a strong German accent demonstrating the merits of an automatic weapon and saying, "It can shoot as fast as a semi-automatic," totally enamored of the power this "tool" offers him.

>Moore (v.o.):
>"And where in the end, it all comes back to bowling for Columbine..."

Moore shows us another insert of a news report stating that the Colorado bowling alley where Harris and Klebolt used to hang out just

---

[65] On the supplements of the DVD edition of the film, Moore explains to a reporter what really happened after the camera stopped rolling: Heston's security tried to stop him from exiting the gated property in order to seize the film of the interview. Luckily, Moore and his director of photography had time to throw it over the gate to the rest of the production team waiting outside.

had a shooting. The filmmaker interviews a cashier who works there, but this one says he does not know anything about the tragedy. He "knows that just three people got shot and died," that's it... Moore concludes by telling him: "*Just* three people died," stressing his lack of empathy. His last sentence in the interview then meshes into his own voice-over narration to finally become one.

> Moore (v.o.):
> "...in Littleton, in a bowling alley... Yes, it was a glorious time to be an American..."

We then see a hand holding a G.I. Joe which in turn is holding an American flag in front of a map of the United States, and then Moore himself chucking a ball down a bowling alley. This symbolic gesture is perhaps a way for Moore to commemorate all of those who had died at Columbine High School, as well as those who will perish in the same manner in the upcoming years, in schools all over North America. Thanks to a lack of understanding regarding the real nature of the problem. Thanks to political inertia and corporate lobbying. Thanks to blatant conflicts of interests. Thanks to a generalized public apathy.

Getting your *isms* Confused?

Clearly, for Michael Moore, to understand the problem of gun-violence in America one has to question the collective unconscious of the nation. Therefore, one must also go back to when it all started, when the Puritans came off the Mayflower and started annihilating the indigenous population who greeted them with open arms and a more holistic understanding of life. According to the film's central thesis, it is fear itself that leads to the way of the gun. Hence, read in this context, *Bowling for Columbine* is not supposed to be interpreted as a nomenclature of facts about the reasons why Americans are so much in love with their guns. Such an endeavor would be an exercise in futility, anyhow. Rather, the film should be watched as an *impressionistic rendering* of what it is like to live in America today, in a perceivable culture of mistrust and anger, where the pressures of modern life have taken their toll on fragile and suggestible individuals.

In spite of all the prizes won around the world, *Bowling for Columbine* was still denounced at the time of its release by many American critics for its "narrow-minded," "one-sided" and "simplistic view" of politics and issues surrounding gun violence. Many of these critics saw the film as a crude and sensationalistic exploration of American society that did not fit with "their reality." Obviously, they were missing the point about the film and about Moore's work in general. As we have just seen, *Bowling* is not a documentary in the classical sense of the term. It is a work of nonfiction with a unique style of storytelling, as well as being a philosophical treatise in cinematic form. Like a dense painting that would vividly evoke a state of mind, the film is a transcendental experimentation in freedom of speech and freedom of the press in early 21st century. It is also a masterpiece of film writing, directing, and editing (as the Cannes Jury clearly indicated by giving it a special award).

Without a doubt, Moore tries to create an emotional effect at the reception level. He wants to jolt his audience out of its complacency. The Cannes Jury seemed to have caught on to it, and responded well to Moore's tactics, especially Martin Scorsese, whose career has been based on that same quest for the vernacular. The only ones who were not conscious of this aesthetic treatise were the people of mainstream media (with the notable exception of a few better acquainted with, and more sensitive to form and feelings) and condescending academics who bashed the film anyway for its obvious subjectivity. Foreign press representatives of teenybopper magazines and many Hollywood critics, for their part, read the film as being "anti-American" and "biased" in its discourse. Others even perceived it as an excuse for the international community to hate America even more vehemently. For instance, one Hollywood reporter claimed that she "was dismayed by the gleeful excitement of my international colleagues, their stupidest opinions of America confirmed by a large, unkempt, rambunctious *shlub* of a native who wears his gimme cap the way other stars favor sunglasses."[66] As if Moore did not hold a bit of truth about America and its materialistic culture in his film... In other words, what Moore was wearing and America's image abroad were more important than what he was revealing about the country's social, political and economical problems. This reaction seems by now typical when dealing with his work. American critics have always been more keen (and apt) at judging films by the maker or the actors' physical appearances (but more especially by the size of the budget), than by assessing the real value of a work. Obviously, Moore-detractors do not understand that he is more than just another entertainer on the map of cheap and mindless popular culture; that even though he might not fit the typical profile, he is a full-blown artist that has something to say and a style to articulate it, eloquently.

Other critics, who are considered part of the intelligentsia of film studies, were harsh on Moore and his brilliant picture as well. They were looking to see another film (probably theirs). Again, the fact that

---

[66] Lisa Scharzbaum, "Moore's 'Columbine's Provocative," *Entertainment Weekly Reviews*, Oct. 24, 2002

Moore puts himself in front of the camera truly disturbed some of these detractors. Jim Hoberman, for instance, wrote that: "As a movie, it's poorly structured, a half-hour too long and devotedly fixated on the filmmaker's persona. Preempting whatever appreciation the viewer might feel, Moore documents himself accepting gratitude for staging a successful protest against K-Mart's sale of bullets and hugging needy victims as though he were *Mother Teresa in a baseball cap*."[67] In other words, this cult figure of the institutionalized free press wanted Moore to a) get out of the picture, and b) shorten his film to give it "structure." But structure to what end exactly? And for what purpose? To be more entertaining? More didactic? How can you short-change the emotional impact of a topic this important just to make it "better structured?" It seems so trivial when compared to everything the film says about America and its sinister obsession with guns and violence. The effect *Bowling for Columbine* has had on millions of individuals around the world cannot be denied. Moore has delivered to his audience an extremely lucid and emotional piece of cinema. To deny this in order to prove some aesthetic or ideological point, in today's context, is old guard, to say the least.

Perhaps that Roman Polanski's prize was well earned as a personal "art film" masterpiece that year at Cannes (i.e. for *The Pianist*), but the one bestowed upon Moore had a different meaning altogether. It was a different film object requiring a different set of evaluative criteria for jury and public alike. In the end, the international praises it received were not about aesthetics or wits. It was honored because it made a statement. Because, as a film, it was in itself a statement. Even if *Bowling for Columbine* did not necessarily offer concrete solutions to the problem of gun violence, it still tried to address many of the unspoken issues that America is faced with today (even with a new President at the helm). It challenged our accepted views of what the nature of the problem of violence really is. It told us to look closely at how the White Angry Male thinks and behaves on a day-to-day basis. What his values, priorities, and goals are. In the end, it did give us a glimpse into a certain part of the American psyche. It also gave us a clue as to the reasons why America is so messed-up and why no one is willing to fix the problem.

However, time came now for Moore to turn up the heat a little, and directly target those who were responsible for making it worst than it already was, namely the Republican administration sitting in office between January 20th 2001 to January 20th 2009, eight miserable years for the entire planet.

---

[67] Jim Hoberman, "They Aim to Please," *Village Voice*, October 9-15, 2002

FAHRENHEIT 9/11 (2004)

In *Fahrenheit 9/11*, I wanted to deal with the mass fear and the mass hysteria that those in power often try to create, in part to distract the population from the real issues that we need to be dealing with, and in part to see that their agenda is enacted. There is no way that the Bush Administration could have had the Iraq War unless they first tried to scare the American people into believing that Saddam Hussein had something to do with September 11.[68]

Into the Fire

The follow-up feature to *Bowling for Columbine* is a crowning achievement in Michael Moore's career and a milestone in the nonfiction form. Akin to *Roger & Me*, *Fahrenheit 9/11* stems from a necessity to reveal the truth about important historical events and to express a personal point-of-view on politics and the way business is conducted in America today. It is about those who were directly and indirectly involved in the September 11th 2001 attacks, those who used this tragedy for personal gain, as well as those who subsequently suffered from it. Thematically speaking, *Fahrenheit 9/11* represents a cross between the two aforementioned films, in so much as it is set-up as a personal journey with a specific political goal: to change the course of the 2004 presidential election.[69] What Moore made us understand coming out of *Fahrenheit 9/11* is that, while the Bush Administration knew (or strongly suspected) that fundamentalist Muslims were going to perpetrate a terrorist attack on American soil in the Fall of 2001, it did nothing to prevent it from happening. Moreover, the film proved that these politicians, then in the White House, used this terrible tragedy as an excuse to go to war, reconfigure the geopolitical landscape in the Middle East, and re-ignite what might be a new version of the Cold War.

But the most scorching indictment made in *Fahrenheit 9/11* (whose title was inspired by Ray Bradbury's *Fahrenheit 451*), has to be the one dealing with the murder of young American soldiers and innocent Iraqi

---

[68] Michael Moore interviewed by Steven Applebaum, www.bbc.co.uk, 2004.
[69] In order to understand the film from all its angles, one should also read Moore's books *Dude, Where's My Country* (Warner Books, 2003), *The Official Fahrenheit 9/11 Reader* (Simon & Schuster, 2004) and *Will They Ever Trust Us Again: Letters from the War Zone* (Simon & Schuster, 2004). There are also numerous interviews with the director on the Internet about the film's broad-ranging implications.

civilians in an unjust war halfway across the world. The film shows us victims from both sides of this preemptive-turned-into-civil-war conflict (concocted by the Hawks) and tries to shed light on a monumental lie. We see American, as well as Iraqi pain, equally sharing screen-time. In the last half-hour of the film, Moore focuses on the effects this war has had on American families, and reminds us that Big Brother is already here and watches our every move.

A Cautionary Tale

No doubt, 2004 will forever be remembered as the year in which David took on Goliath on the big screen. It will also be remembered for being a time when a majority of American voters, knowing the facts concerning what their President did (or did not do) in his first mandate, allowed him a second term in office. As Moore reminded his fans in an email sent immediately after the election: "No President has ever been voted out in the middle of a war" (November 5, 2004). When history will finally weight the wages of American sin, Bush's re-election will probably go down as the great enigma of that emerging 21st century. Although, the 2000 election was the first real turning point in this revisionist version of American history, and lead the way to 2004, as we all know. Back then, Bush and Cheney took the White House against the will of the majority. They were rubber-stamped by the Supreme Court when the technology designed to help the voting process miserably failed (or was deliberately sabotaged). Moore tells us that never before have we seen an American President running for cover inside the White House on Inauguration Day. He does not utter the word, but for the viewer the images speak for themselves. It all seems so clear. It smells like a *coup d'état* perpetrated by domestic terrorists.

Like all of his other feature films, Moore wanted to start this one by framing it subjectively. Again, he uses a self-conscious voice-over narration and a myriad of visual sources that amount to a great impressionistic collage in the end. He begins his narrative by asking if Al Gore's temporary win was "just a dream." Then he breaks down the sequence of events, starting with all three major networks recalling Florida for Bush (as they followed Fox News' "lead" on election night, late into the night…). In fact, Moore will spend the next two hours telling us that what came after was more like a nightmare than anything else. Early on, we are told that we can only see the surface of things in American politics, and that the truth always lies beyond the perceivable. Moore seems to believe that only the analytical power of the camera lens and of film editing can better our understanding of what happened on that ill-fated night. For him, if one wishes to understand how 9/11 and the war in Iraq came about, one must also go through the ideological smokescreen created by powerful government agents and their contacts at the networks. However, one must first recognize the power and influence that media has in shaping both, political careers and public opinion. Without this prior recognition, the truth seems in effect unattainable.

Furthermore, in the first half of *Fahrenheit 9/11*, Moore rightly claims that it was old Reaganites that stole their way into the White House in 2000 (with the help of the Supreme Court and some of its Republican-appointed judges). In the 2004 election, when Republicans won out the majority of the votes strictly through fear and manipulation of the Christian Right, and when *Fahrenheit 9/11* failed in ousting Bush from office, Moore's first impulse was to send to 10 million people his afterthoughts of the results: a list of the soldiers who had lost their lives in Iraq.[70] By doing this he was reminding the American people of the weight of their bad decision in the voting booth. Then, in the months following the 2004 election, many voices rose to criticize Moore for having influenced the campaign negatively with his manifesto, since he also hadn't canvas for what might have then been perceived as the best alternative to the Bush fiasco: John Kerry. Because Bush/Cheney stayed in office for 4 more years, everyone became ready to dump on Moore and rehash previous reviews that had "analyzed" his film at the time it had come out.

> *Fahrenheit 9/11* is a sinister exercise in moral frivolity, crudely disguised as an exercise in seriousness. It is also a spectacle of abject political cowardice masking itself as a demonstration of "dissenting" bravery.[71]

Instead of perceiving Moore's filmic commentary as an unusual act of personal expression and courage, crypto-fascist critics such as Christopher Hitchens wanted his head on a stick. Actually, there has never been so many "journalists" from all sides showing so much venom as when Moore released *Fahrenheit 9/11* that summer; not even against Bush and his spin-doctors, we might add. How can anyone attack Moore on the basis of "moral frivolity" and "cowardice," considering that his film was shown on thousands of screens in the U.S. and around the world? Now, that's exposure and courage, is it not? In

---

[70] According to the Brookings Institution's Iraq Index, as late as June 2010, it was estimated that 4,409 soldiers lost their lives in Iraq, and that over 31,822 came back home seriously wounded.
[71] Christopher Hitchens, Unfairenheit 9/11, the lies of Michael Moore," *Slate Magazine*, June 21, 2004

any case, he certainly was not hiding behind his office desk and writing bad reviews of great films, something that has no political bearing whatsoever. On the contrary, Moore had the guts to get involve and he tried to communicate important information about the Bush dynasty, its links to Saudi money, and the errors committed in the prevention of 9/11. He took great personal and, yes, artistic risks to elaborate a piece of propaganda meant to shake people into political thinking, which is more than we can say about distant observers like Christopher Hitchens.

Send In the Clowns

When watching *Fahrenheit 9/11* those who were already familiar with Moore's work were reminded of the reportage from *The Awful Truth* where George Jr. and Jeb were fighting it out to see who "the toughest and meanest Bush" was. In the same way that W. could have fried a convict without losing sleep over it, he could have also seriously jeopardize the credibility of the presidency by putting his foot in his mouth or sending his army in a war that he, himself, might not have fully comprehended. And he did. His typical machismo energy and Texan-style circumlocutions, known as *Bushisms*, as well as his lack of competence, translated in the way he expressed himself to the press. His rhetoric, which was only a front for Cheney's rhetoric, was radical; more radical than Moore's rhetoric, anyway. He was almost always bound to be misconstrued by an audience, because he was so blunt, yet so inarticulate to the point of being almost unintelligible, especially when he diverted from the teleprompter and improvised on his own. Moore's film includes three excerpts of Bush confirming these assertions.

> George W. Bush:
> There are some who feel like, that, uh, if they attack us, that we may decide to leave prematurely. They do not understand what they're talking about, if that's the case. Let me finish. There are some who feel like that, you know, the conditions are such that they can attack us there. My answer is "Bring' em on!"

> George W. Bush:
> They're not happy they're occupied. I would not be happy if I was occupied either.

George W. Bush:
We wage a war to save a civilization itself. We did not seek it, but we will fight it and we will prevail.

What actually happened in the summer of 2004 is that a skilled artist turned a politician into an intellectually-challenged individual. To prove this, we just have to look at how Moore appropriates already existing footage of Bush to pervert its original meaning and to reveal his real essence. For example, in a typical photo-op of his, Bush stands behind the counter of a BBQ joint and asks if "anybody wants some grits?," evoking more than it really needs to because of Bush's provenance. The filmmaker even accuses Bush of playing cowboy, showing him at his dude-ranch, chain-sawing a tree or getting excited about his dogs and his horses (if not about his job, at least, not yet). Paradoxically, while acting as if he was just another typical working class American, with his baseball cap and running shoes (not unlike Moore, actually), Bush tries to emulate the lifestyle of a more sophisticated portion of his class (i.e. the filthy rich). He plays golf and, of course, practices his shooting skills at the firing range as though it made him sophisticated. He is the living proof that finance and intelligence are two different things, and that you do not need to be a grade A student to emancipate yourself in a society based on material wealth, personal connections, and, obviously, image.

The segment where the Hawks and Britain's Prime Minister Tony Blair are seen as *Bonanza* characters is only one example of his collage style of presentation and penchant for exaggeration. In this instance, he digitally collages disparate visual records into one powerful metaphor; inserting head-shots of the main Anglo-American architects of the war in Iraq within medium close-up shots of the corny television series from the 1960s. Moore is telling us that these decision-makers behave like cowboys, beyond the moral boundaries of civilization. Moore wanted to put W. and his friends in their "natural habitat" from the start, just to make us aware of his own power over them in the editing suite. Very much like Orson Welles taking on William Randolph Hearst in his days, the filmmaker from Michigan humiliated in public a man of great wealth and power with something more powerful (in the long run) than any man: motion pictures.

In effect, what will be remembered of 2004 in American media is a "little" film that took on gigantic proportions, even by American standards. Phenomenon is the word which should be used to describe *Fahrenheit 9/11*, because, historically, it became as important and as serious as its subject matter. Nobody wanted to ignore this film that summer; and nobody did. It seemed to have been vital for the survival of democracy, in a land that proclaimed to have re-invented it in the modern era.

Skull & Bones

Besides God and Dick Cheney, George W. Bush was then only accountable to his father, George H. W. Bush, ex-President of the United States of America (1988-1992), notorious Freemason, important board member of the Carlyle Group, and ex-Head of the Central Intelligence Agency (appointed by President Ford). A fact not generally known is that, once you are a member of the C.I.A., you are always a member of the C.I.A. Indeed this is a blood oath to be taken very seriously.[72] In fact, Bush Sr.'s "genius" lies in his skills that allowed him to bridge the business, the political, the intelligence, and the military worlds over a relatively short period of time, just like Cheney and Rumsfeld, two of his political allies. However, even George Sr. did not achieve all of this by himself. He had help on his way to the top from his own father, Prescott Bush, an oil tycoon who supplied everything for him and his offspring, and who also helped Nazi Germany to rebuild a decent army in the 1930s through the Thyssen family.[73] Surely, it must be disturbing for the American public to know that, while George Sr. was fighting the Japanese in the Pacific, his father was helping feed Hitler's ovens. Surely, the American public must be aware that this collaboration with foreign tyrants goes against everything they have been fighting for in the last century, is it?

Like the sketch from *The Awful Truth*, Moore shows us how Junior achieved by his name alone. His destiny to become president of the most powerful nation in the world was already carved out in the great book of American history, simply because he was part of one of the richest and most influential dynasties in the world. In a 1992 interview for ABC, while he was being investigated for the kind of stuff that put Martha Stewart in jail for half a year, Bush said without shame that, "It [does not] hurt when your dad is President of the United States." Yes. You can drive under the influence, take illegal drugs, avoid being drafted, become Governor, own a major-league baseball team, become yourself President of the most powerful country in the world, and order innocent foreigners to be *waterboarded* or killed with impunity...when your name is Bush. Now, when your name is Clinton, all you have to do is to get blown by a White House intern to face impeachment. There

---

[72] Ron Rosenbaum, "At Skull and Bones, Bush's Secret Club Initiates Ream Gore," *The New York Observer*, April 23, 2003

[73] Jonathan D. Salant, "Bush's grandfather was director of bank seized by government for affiliation with Nazi-funding German industrialist," *Associated Press*, October 18, 2003

is just no competition here. With his film Moore was dealing with the most sophisticated slime balls since Josef Stalin, and W. himself, not unlike his dad actually, greatly stained America's image around the world.

Endless Vacation

> This is an impressive crowd. The haves, and the have mores! Some people call you the elite. I call you my base. (*George W. Bush at a fund-raiser event in Washington in 2000 and as seen in Fahrenheit 9/11.*)

If the first proposition of *Fahrenheit 9/11* is that Republicans stole the 2000 election, the second is that once in power Bush was too busy golfing, fishing, chopping wood, and taking care of his dogs to deal with the real issues in Washington. What the viewer has to infer between the images and the text is the fact that Bush is an inexperienced puppet for the real decision-makers. These individuals, referred to as "The Hawks," always worked behind closed doors, and Bush was obviously a mouthpiece for their ideology. These good-old-boys knew all too well that the *out-of-sight-out-of-mind* ethos is a perfect way to conduct business and political affairs in this post-Watergate world. As a matter-of-fact, conservative politicians have learned to develop a sparse, almost enigmatic discourse over the years. A discourse which constantly conceals the truth, but which also exposes itself as an artificial construct of meaningless words and empty patriotic jingoism. The best example of this was Bush's State of the Union address on January 23rd 2007, when he managed to admit that America had lost control of the situation in Iraq without being booed-off the rostrum or being lynched by the media. Every cheer of approval from the Republican side of the House was carefully choreographed as to give his scripted words some sort of credibility.

Everyone who has seen the film knows that W. is honestly portrayed as the child-king that he really is. Moore presents him as a man whose ego has once been crushed by a bad sense for business, but who was later elevated by God, Daddy, and the Almighty Dollar. (In fact, Junior's big break came when the Hawks saw in him the only possible future for a waning Republican Party in the 1990s.⁷⁴) Contrary to Oliver Stone's *W.* (2008), we see him here as a stand-in, as a cardboard cutout of a President who has a hard time reading, and who can barely express himself in proper English. For instance, when a reporter asked him about allegations concerning his regular absences from Washington, he tried to reply something only he could understand: "[They] do not know the definition of work," he says. Even if it had been proven that he had spent over 40% of his time out of Washington in the first six months of his first term,⁷⁵ Bush still had the *chutzpa* to criticize his detractors all throughout his presidency. This Born-Again President went on by trying to rationalize his absence from Washington in that same interview: "It's amazing what you can do today with faxes and phones," completely betraying his contempt for the symbolic value of the White House, as an American institution representing what should be a democratically-elected figure. He then managed to sign a few autographs, and finally blabbed some convoluted, almost incomprehensible sentences when asked by an unidentified reporter what he will do with the rest of his day.

> George W. Bush:
> Karen Hughes is coming over. We're working on some things, and uh, she'll be over here, we'll be working on a few things, a few matters. I'm working on some initiatives… we're uh…you will see…*I've got made while I'm here*, and we'll be announcing them as time goes on.

Back in the winter of 2003, in an interview for the *UK Guardian*, Moore explained his intentions for the year: "I want him [Bush] paraded in handcuffs outside a police house as a common criminal, because I do not know if there's a greater crime than taking people to war based on a lie. I've never seen anything like Bush and his people. They truly hate our Constitution, our rights and liberties. They have no shame in fighting for their corporate sponsors."⁷⁶ Since those naïve years, when a majority of the American public still believed in Bush, a lot of things have been acknowledged by that same majority. It finally saw through some of the lies, it understood the cost of war, and the cost

---

[74] The Republican Party learned a lot from the 1992 presidential race, when George Sr. was not able to get the Christian Right to vote. Eight years later, when W. pretended to have "seen the light" and to stand ready to defend the idea that Israel is the Promised Land for all Born-Again Christians, he became an obvious contender for the 2000 elections. It coincided with a resurgence of exalted religiosity in the country and allowed him to get the vote of those who hadn't gone to the booth in 92.

[75] Charles Krauthammer, "A Vacation Bush Deserves," *Washington Post*, August 10, 2001

[76] Michael Moore, *UK Guardian Unlimited*, Exclusive interview, 2003

of an unregulated free-market. It was even able to measure the difference between two extremely different Presidents...

In the first quarter of the film, Moore also inserts footage of the House of Representatives when African-American representatives of Duval County, Florida, contested the Supreme Court's ruling which declared Bush the winner of the 2000 elections. The editing emphasizes how they were shunned by the House. We witness Congressmen Hasting and Jackson Jr., as well as Congresswomen Brown, Lee, Meek, and Mink in the Joint Session being told to shut up and to sit down by Gore (also acting out as President of the Assembly). Since the Senate would not certify the election results, the House was not able to contest the Court's ruling to put Bush Jr. on the throne. Moore reminds us that not one single senator stood up for African-American politicians on that day, and this is pretty consistent with the overall themes found in his work.

Operation Curveball

The first ten minutes of *Fahrenheit 9/11* are quintessential Moore in their style. The tone is upbeat and sarcastic, the pace is rapid, while the text is filled with innuendos and double-entendre concerning Bush's origins as a politician. It becomes more dramatic once the credit sequence starts kicking in. The tone is obviously more somber and sad then, because we are reminded of the weight behind the lost resulting from 9/11. What Moore does is a tonal shift, which is a figure of style that he often uses (e.g. going from comedy to drama). He is covering great many emotions in his work, and wants to make us think and, more importantly, make us feel concerned about the issues. Thus, after a compelling introductory sequence reminding the viewer of this unconstitutional and undemocratic coup perpetrated by the Republicans in 2000, Moore takes us into a very atmospheric credit sequence (without a doubt the most original and powerful of his career). It is made out of outtakes from television interviews with members of the Bush administration, as well as from the 19th of March 2003 television address, delivered hours before the nation went to war.

Moore's friend, collaborator, and co-producer Jeff Gibbs supplies again the music that accompanies the images. It is a simple but deep-resounding loop of sparse guitar notes, creating a mysterious aura over the stock images. This sequence is very grim and filled with evocative sound bites and suggestive silences. Anyone who sees it cannot help but to be captivated right from the start. To describe this moment more accurately, and with details that are more relevant to this formal analysis: We see different members of the administration just a few minutes before being interviewed by national media. Moore shows us various shots of Bush, Cheney, Rumsfeld, Rice, Ridge, Powell, Ashcroft, and Wolfowitz being prepared and groomed for the camera. The operator is making focus tests on them, with zooms and reframing, the lighting is off-key, there are buzzing sounds emanating from microphones and consoles, etc. In other words, the main architects of the Iraq War are not presented from their best angle. Instead they are shown in the awkward (and unpredictable) situation of being "made-up" by beauticians and TV crew people. Moore's editing makes these members of government appear like actors who are getting prepared to play a role, just long enough to convince the public of a major Shakespearian fiction. Overall, the credit sequence is appropriately irreverent and signals the dark satirical tone of the picture.

In it we see Vice-President Cheney being dusted like an old statue, ex-Attorney General Ashcroft telling a key-grip to lower the sound of his ear-piece so that he won't get his "head blown-off", ex-National Security Advisor Ridge laughing unconvincingly and wiping his sweaty forehead, Assistant-Secretary of Defense (and for awhile Head of the World Bank[77]) Wolfowitz using his own saliva to tame a recalcitrant hairdo, and finally Powell and Rice, the only two black people of this "wild bunch," being powdered in what appears to be an inverted minstrel-show. Nobody can do it like Moore. It is clever, funny, emotional, inspiring, but above all, truly disturbing. Moore's style of montage relies in footage selection, as well as in the viewer's capacity to really see what is going on in those set-ups and off-air situations. This is an example of subversive strategies that link him to the great rebel of compilation-filmmaking, Emile De Antonio. Like in *Millhouse, a White Comedy*, Moore shows the public something that the networks have never aired before (i.e. pre-broadcast material).

In *Millhouse*, De Antonio managed to portray Nixon as the control-freak and paranoid maniac that he was just by cutting certain footage together, and by using unreleased visual material in a certain order and duration. In Moore's instance, it is the head and the tail of a given television footage. He is telling us that those fragments of tape are more revealing than what we have seen in the official broadcast, between a car and a beer commercial, because they show the subjects in a more natural light. These sorts of compilation films made by De Antonio and later by Moore are in essence precursors to the YouTube phenomenon, where anyone who has access to a bank of images and editing software can "enunciate something" in "filmic form" (or editing), no matter how controversial or blasphemous it may be.

---

[77] Emad Mekay, U.S.: Wolfowitz Scandal Spotlights U.S. Influence Over World Bank, *Interpress Service*, May 16, 2007

As mentioned before, *Fahrenheit 9/11* relies on visual and aural manipulations to cement its overall look, which is not always an obvious thing to achieve when you are dealing with sources from different formats or of uneven quality (lighting, framing, blow-up transfers, etc.). Some sequences are organized around or built on the rhythm or meaning of a specific piece of music, while others are assembled as to support or contradict the voice-over commentary and the discourse of a given talking-head. For instance, in the introductory segment, the filmmakers uses mountain music on the soundtrack to clearly link Bush to a specific southern culture of social conservatism. He also uses this score to compare the 2000 election night to a "Ho-Down" of some kind. In the same sequence, he uses slow and reverse motion, as well as freeze-frames to give the images a certain expressiveness that we usually associate with the manipulations of fiction cinema. The following sequence also illustrates how Moore has great consistency of style and creative stamina across his entire body of work. It is set to the backbeat of the Go-Go's 'Vacation Time' and expresses its message again in montage fashion. Meaning is created here in the irony that stems from the song's lyrics, the choice of footage, and the rhythm of the editing (shot order and duration, and the movement within each image), as well as Moore's infliction on the voice-over).

Cantus

> Many families have been devastated tonight. This is not right. They did not deserve to die. If someone did this to get back at Bush, then they did so by killing thousands of people who DID NOT VOTE for him! Boston, New York, D.C., and the planes' destination of California - these were places that voted AGAINST Bush! Why kill them? Why kill anyone? Such insanity. Let's mourn, let's grieve, and, when it's appropriate, let's examine our contribution to the unsafe world we live in. It does not have to be like this.[78]

Moore revisits the 9/11 attacks in New York City in a very respectful and powerful sequence that gives sound predominance. Possibly inspired by Alejandro Gonzalez Iñárritu's contribution to the film *9/11/2001* (2002), Moore chooses to not show the tragedy, but to evoke it instead. Over a black screen, we hear the first plane/bomb hit the first tower of the World Trade Center. Soon after, we hear the second plane/

---

[78] Michael Moore's *Letter to New Yorkers*, September 12, 2001 (Visit www.michaelmoore.com to get the complete text.)

bomb hitting Tower Two in full surround effect. More emotional than the techniques used by Moore are the screams and cries of the crowd below on the streets around Lower Manhattan. We also hear a now recognizable noise, the one which emanates from the firefighters' emergency beepers, ghostly and chilling for anyone who knows its meaning. Once the image fades-in to fill the screen again, it is to show us television footage of people crying and praying for the unfortunate jumping to their death from the WTC. Then we see in slow motion from a low-angle shot a myriad of debris falling onto the streets of the financial district, creating a pattern of abstract matter.

This kind of manipulation forces the viewer to watch the ramifications of the attacks rather than the shockingly graphic impacts in themselves. Moore uses cinema as a tool, not only for political purposes, but as visual poetry. The flying papers and parcels of documents are reminders of the frailty of the system. None of these once important papers mean anything now. They are just particles, residues of a complex ideological warfare that has only just begun. But the WTC sequence in *Fahrenheit 9/11* is also about lost and absence. On the voice-over soundtrack, over the track 'Cantus in Memory of Benjamin Britten', composed by Arvo Pärt, Moore tells us that he too lost a friend and collaborator on that morning, Bill Weems (who had worked on *The Awful Truth*). Make no mistake about it, Mr. Hitchens, *Fahrenheit 9/11* was a personal and painful inquiry into one of the darkest days of American history, not the promotional document of a self-serving agitator you claimed it was.

Reading Makes a Country Great

> The public education system in America is one of the most important foundations of our democracy. After all, it is where children from all over America learn to be responsible citizens, and learn to have the skills necessary to take advantage of our fantastic *opportunistic* society.[79]

One of the most discussed and criticized moments from *Fahrenheit 9/11* is when Moore shows us a footage that network television reduced to a mere ten second-clip. It is the decisive moment when everyone would expect the American President to be strong, resilient, and sane. As it turned out, Bush was not any of this. At that particular moment, he became fragile, unsure of himself, introspective (if such a thing is possible for him – he just seems absent-minded). Moore shows

---

[79] George W. Bush, *Unknown source*, May 1, 2002

excerpts of W. sitting in that Florida classroom reading *My Pet Goat* with grade-level children on a special visit for Reading Day. He cuts away from that footage for more than 10 minutes of screen time and then goes back to it, as if Bush had been sitting there all along, even after the Barbarians crashed into the gate. There is also another obvious irony here (not due to Moore, but to the framing of the event by a local TV station) in the fact that Bush is sitting in front of a sign on which it is written "Reading Makes a Country Great." Elsewhere, Moore went as far as suggesting that the President's mom, Barbara Bush, initiated the "Get America Reading" program in the mid-1980s because she knew first-hand about child illiteracy.[80]

As the sequence begins, Moore reminds us that W. decided to go ahead with his publicity and photo opportunity, even though he had learned, just a few minutes before, that a plane/bomb had crashed into the first tower. Upon hearing the news that a second plane/bomb had hit Tower Two (i.e. when everyone on the planet knew it meant an attack), he stayed there for more than 7 minutes without doing anything but biting the inside of his mouth, looking pass the children into oblivion, and trying to keep the presidential front. Moore's critics accused him of taking out of context this particular excerpt. In fact, he shortened the 7 minutes in question with five elliptical dissolves, from the time Bush learns about the second crash to the time he decided to behave like the President of a nation under attack. The experimenter in him could have easily decided to keep the whole temporal integrity of the moment by inserting in the film a 7-minute long-take, but he did not, even if the overall effect would have made a much stronger point against Bush's administration in the end.

On the soundtrack Moore's particularly warm voice is telling us that, while he was sitting in that Florida classroom on the morning of September 11th, Bush was probably thinking if he should have showed up for work more often. Moore claims that Bush may have been pondering the quality of the crowd he was hanging out with, even perhaps of a "friend" (or someone related to a friend) who might have screwed him over. The voice-over suggests that W. was thinking about his (and his dad's) business rapport to the Saudis, and about what the dramatic events in New York and Washington would mean to this very special relationship. Stressing the fact that 7 minutes is too long to react to such a crisis, Moore pushes his criticism further by asserting that Bush had previously cut terrorism funding from the FBI and deliberately ignored a security briefing (with his head of counter-terrorism, Richard Clarke) in August 2001, a month before the attack. This briefing clearly indicated to Bush and his cronies that al-Qaeda

---

[80] Michael Moore, *Stupid White Men*, pp. 37-39

was imminently planning something on U.S. soil (perhaps with the support of the U.S. government itself, but this is never said). The director uses editing and voice-over techniques to create dialectics of credible speculations. He tells us that "Maybe he [Bush] was not worried about the terrorist threat because the title of the report was too vague," cutting right after an excerpt of Condoleeza Rice in front of the 9/11 Commission. The question she was being asked by Senator Benveniste regarded the title of the document handed out to Bush in that seminal August security briefing.

> Condoleeza Rice:
> I believe the title was '*Bin Laden Determined to Attack Inside the United States*'.

We are then shown a slow-motion wide shot of Bush throwing his fishing line in the water, all dressed-up like Arnold Palmer, and then to him again still sitting in that Florida classroom. On the voice-over track, while Gibbs' monochromatic piano chords sound as if it was child-like minimalism, Moore momentarily substitutes himself for W.'s consciousness: "Was he thinking: 'I've been hanging out with the wrong crowd...Which one of them *screwed* me?' We are quickly shown a rare footage of Rumsfeld "paying a cordial visit" to tyrant Saddam Hussein back in 1983. Over this last shot, Moore's voice-over goes on pondering: "Was it the guy my daddy's friends delivered a lot of weapons to?" (referring to the U.S. helping Hussein). We then see a still photo of a group of Taliban leaders visiting Texas: "Was it that group of religious fundamentalists who visited my state when I was Governor?" Moore cuts in an archival shot of Bush shaking hands with a Saudi prince: "Or was it the Saudis?," inserting another quick one of bin Laden firing an American-made M-16 that rhythmically coincides with the voice-over: "Damn! It was them... I think I better blame it on this guy," whereupon we are again shown a medium shot of Hussein (i.e. the scapegoat), dancing Iraqi-style with his posse.

These associations are swift and funny, filled with insights and well-measured sarcasm. They use rhythmical variations on the soundtrack and in the editing pattern and voice-over properties to propose a thesis about Bush's role in the whole 9/11 affair: the Bush administration knew about the imminent threat, but it did not act on it. How much clearer can you get? The question remaining now is "Why didn't it act on it?"

Air bin Laden

Soon after this moment of cinematic bravado, there is another tonal shift initiated by a shot of travelers stranded at airports around the country. Always in voice-over, Moore reminds us that in the days after September 11th 2001, all commercial and private airline traffic was grounded. In fact, no one could fly, including the President's father, George Sr., and has-been Latin singer Ricky Martin. The director asks the viewer mockingly: "But really, who wanted to fly? No one, except the bin Ladens," quickly inserting a brief shot of Osama sitting calmly at his son's wedding, cracking something that appears like a smile for an amateur camcorder (a rare sight to behold). Moore then straight-cuts to an airplane in full take-off action, while on the soundtrack we hear a few bars of The Animal's 'We Gotta Get out of This Place'... At that moment, the length of the shot and the music are synchronized to match each other retroactively, therefore creating meaning and humor in the viewer's mind as an afterthought. Moore's theory about Bush-bin Laden-the Saudis-9/11 comes out loud and clear in the first 20 minutes of the film. No one can accuse him of confusing apples with oranges here. The whole argument is right there, in the editing pattern, the meshing of voice-over with the visual and musical selection.

Even though the 9/11 attacks on America were (allegedly) orchestrated by one member of the bin Laden family, 21 other members of his extended family were the only people allowed to fly out of the United States in the days following 9/11. This disturbing fact, recalling the infamous "Rat Line" between post-war Germany and America in 1945-46, allows Moore to initiate his journey to the awful truth about American politics. First, he interviews Senator Byron Dorgan, member of the Senate subcommittee on aviation, who confirms that the "highest levels of our government" authorized this privilege. Then, Moore visits author Craig Unger.[81] This one claims that Osama bin Laden is still very much in contact with his relatives, even if he had been portrayed as the black sheep of the family. Later in the narrative, in an interview with ex-FBI agent Jack Cloonan, we find out that the bin Ladens were not even interrogated about Osama's whereabouts before they were courteously escorted to their homeland of Saudi Arabia (or to Europe, for a quick shopping spree, perhaps). Here, in typical post-modern fashion, the filmmaker uses footage from the TV series *Dragnet* to indicate how Bush and his intelligence agencies should have behaved with the bin Laden family after the attacks, allegedly perpetrated by one of theirs (i.e. tough and inquisitive, wisecracking *à-la* pulp novel,

---

[81] Graig Unger, *House of Bush, House of Saud: The Secret Relationship Between the World's Two Most Powerful Dynasties*, Scribner, 2004

etc.). Actually, Moore seems to be after the reasons that might have motivated al-Qaeda (or Saudi Arabia or the Illuminati) to attack America on its own soil, as much as on the effects of the tragedy. Those issues having been raised, a question remains. Why did the administration let the bin Ladens fly out of the country? Was it solely for political or economical reasons, or were there other motives behind this privilege?

Black Marker & Angel Investors

It is a well-known fact that elected politicians are, by and large, liars. Everyone interested in politics and in the truth knows that Bush lied about his administration's real agenda, and certainly about his past, to keep the American people in the dark for 8 long years. These lies have been documented in depth elsewhere, so no use in getting into them here. In *Fahrenheit 9/11*, Moore underlined how convenient it was for Bush to conceal the identity of James Reynolds Bath, a man who created a bridge between Bush's business ventures and his dad's political shenanigans (through the Carlyle Group – a conglomerate that makes most of its billions producing warfare technology). The filmmaker had already acquired W.'s military record at the time of *The Awful Truth* (around 2000, for the sketch "Affirmative Action"), so that when the White House officially released it in 2003, after Moore accused him publicly of having dodged the draft, he saw right away that certain names had been concealed with a black marker by the U.S. Government censors.

Moore's own inquiry revealed that Bath was one of Bush's intimate friends in the military. Both had been old drinking buddies who were lucky enough to avoid Vietnam because of their physical inaptitude for combat, according to their respective medical records. Moore also reminded us that, after the Vietnam War, in the mid-to-late 1970s, Bush went into business ventures that failed miserably over a short period of time. It was then that Bath became a "consultant" who made the connection between him and "angel investors," as writer Jim Moore calls them in the film. The linking of Bush and America to the Saudis is the most coherent and important one provided by the film, as far as its overall thesis is concerned. As a matter-of-fact, the second part of *Fahrenheit 9/11* is set-up as to shed light on the ways the American economy works, and how it is inextricably tied to the most sordid aspects of political life in Washington and on Wall Street (without ever getting into conspiracy theories concerning the role of the Federal Reserve or even the Bilderberg Group in shaping our world). The film is committed to expose the correlations between businessmen, politicians and dogma in the U.S.A. today, but without any speculations about the shadow government which obviously dictates policies. As we can see, at the center of it all, though, there was a bunch of orchestrated lies, starting with what really happened on 9/11.

Yellowcake (the Ultimate Loophole)

Perhaps that the greatest lie of all was the one told by W. during his State of the Union address in 2003. On that day, Bush and his posse clearly cheated the U.S. Congress, the American people, and the entire world. They used the rhetoric of apocalypticism to justify an unjustifiable war. The Commander-in-Thief spoke of a "smoking gun which could come in the form of a mushroom cloud," just to exploit our greatest fears. He made claims that were false, such as the one stating that Saddam Hussein was looking to acquire yellowcake (or enriched) uranium through an African connection in Niger (perhaps through Abdul Q. Khan, the father of the "Islamic bomb" in Pakistan). In fact, this information had been based on a report made by ex-Ambassador Joe Wilson who went to Africa (under the CIA's request) and who found nothing corroborating these allegations.[82] Moreover, and this is only one of the great political scandals of 2005, when Wilson refused to follow Washington's script, someone within the Bush administration, allegedly Cheney's right hand man, Gordon "Scooter" Libby, leaked information about his wife, Valerie Plame, an FBI agent who dedicated her life for her country.[83] *New York Times* journalist Judith Miller, who first wrote an article about it, had to go to jail for a few months in order to protect her source which came from inside the Oval Office (i.e. Cheney himself). Since then, the American public has discovered that nothing is too shameful for these people; even putting their intelligence services in danger and their journalists in jail.

Instead of admitting that Hussein did not have any military firepower or weapons of mass destruction, the Hawks asked the head of the Iraqi National Congress, Ahmed Chalabi, to fabricate a report based on unexacting proofs and tenuous links. This allowed the U.S. to declare war on the "guy who tried to kill my [Bush's] dad." The information in Chalabi's report was the one used by Bush's

---

[82] Joseph Wilson, "What I Did not Find in Africa," *The New York Times*, June 6, 2003

[83] In the opening statement of his defense, in January 2007, Libby declared that he had been a "scapegoat" for the administration, and that the leak really came from Bush advisor Karl Rove. Other sources suggested that Vice-President Dick Cheney leaked this particular information to the press.

speechwriter, David Frum, when he wrote the hyper-patriotic "soliloquy" for the infamous 2003 State of the Union address. The rest as they say is history. There were no weapons of mass-destruction in Hussein's backyard, as U.N. weapon inspectors had already confirmed before the war started (and even by Bush himself, in an interview for NBC in January 2007) and the Bush administration finally got what they wanted there: unlimited access to major oil supplies. In one moment from the film, Moore describes how members of the administration had previously told the American public that Hussein was incapable of producing weapons, and that Iraq had been under a severe embargo for the last decade (which essentially paralyzed its capacity to rebuild an army). The point is that, yes, Hussein was a dictator, but that, no, he was not the one to attack after 9/11. The proof of this still lies in Afghanistan, where Talibans are still ruling over the populace like some kind of invisible but omnipotent Mafia.[84]

Anyhow, Bush's war on terrorism was a pretext to intervene anywhere in the world at any time and for no reason at all. Since the attitude in Washington was to strike preemptively, who cares if any of this was true or not, right? Incidentally, Moore reminds us that the second Iraq War is more like a personal vendetta against the "Wacky Iraqi" than anything else. It was well advertised for years that George H. W. Bush's face was bracing one of Saddam's palaces in the form of a mosaic floor that Iraqis could "desecrate" by casually walking on it. The whole business between America and Hussein is, therefore, and according to Moore, an economic and symbolic one. It has no correlation to what happened on 9/11. It is the work of the Hawks who wanted to finish what they had started over a decade earlier, when Bush Sr. replaced Reagan. The precedent created by the second Bush administration, with its "preemptive war on terror" (an idea concocted by Cheney, Rumsfeld, Perle and Wolfowitz), cannot truly be assessed by Moore, or by anyone else for that matter. The consequences of this unilateral action to go to war against a great part of the Arab world is beyond any understanding if only perceived as a "normal reaction" to the 9/11 attacks. Needless to say that, in spite of the many conspiracy theories surrounding 9/11, the occupation of Iraq in itself will breed a new generation of Muslim men who feel nothing but hatred and contempt for America. We can almost certainly propose that there will be more fundamentalists holding a major grudge against America and Americans in the future. In fact, Islamic *Jihad* has only just begun, and 9/11 may very well have been the tip of the iceberg in that battle to stop the implementation of the New World Order.

---

[84] Obama's decision to send 30,000 more troops in Afghanistan by the summer of 2010 will probably not help to win that "war" in that sense either.

Screw *Habeas Corpus*

In this film, Moore also takes time to show that the Patriot Act, created in the aftermath of 9/11, served the administration well in its first term. For him, it gave Neocons in the White House an opportunity to spy on and to oppress the very people they are suppose to work for and protect. We are also told that this tragedy was dream come true for leaders with totalitarian aspirations, such as George W. Bush and Dick Cheney, puppets of a greater and more powerful body. The legislation within the Act made it possible for police and government officials to arrest and imprison thousands of individuals who had never broken the law before; simply because they were affiliated to some leftist organization, or because their names were Arabic sounding, or because they *looked* like terrorists.[85] There is even a whole segment dedicated to this kind of government abuse in Moore's thoughtful and provocative book *Dude, Where's My Country?*, which stands as one of the two companions to the film *Fahrenheit 9/11*.

No doubt, issues surrounding civil liberties have changed drastically since September 11, 2001, even under Obama's more "liberal" regime. They are now more closely tied to other issues, such as the right to privacy and civil rights. In one *Awful Truth* episode, produced a few years earlier, Moore had hired two cops to frisk innocent people on the streets of Manhattan. In that instance, regular folks were told to "spread' em and shut up," which is basically what Ashcroft told the American public in the months following 9/11. Nonetheless, what is truly amazing about this sketch is how people who were then arrested barely contested this symbolic rape. They bit the big one and did what they were told to do, just because the guy who was doing the frisking had a uniform and a badge. Leaning up against a wall, putting their hands behind their heads, waiting for the cops to find them guilty on some bogus charge and be sent to jail without a fair trial, these scenes showed how Americans are vulnerable to authority and authoritarian regimes in that sense. We found out since 9/11 that many Americans do not mind giving up their civil liberties, right to privacy and right to a fair trial as long as they believe it is for some "higher cause" (God and Country). They accepted all the "Whoppers" (as Moore calls them in *Dude*?) that the Republicans fed

---

[85] Briefly consider the case of Maher Arar, a Canadian citizen of Syrian origins who has been wrongly accused of terrorist activities and deported to Syria by request of the U.S. government. Arar spent a year in a Syrian jail being humiliated and tortured for nothing. His wife managed to get him back to Canada, an inquiry was lead according to Canadian laws, and the Canadian government exonerated him from all charges of terrorist involvement. Still, to this day, the U.S. refuses to take Arar off their list of "dangerous individuals" and even refuse to have his case heard by the Supreme Court.

them. They accept the silly restrictions imposed on air flights without ever questioning their legitimacy (lighters and matches = good, baby's breast milk = bad, as Moore demonstrates in the film); they accepted their personal records be investigated by intelligence agencies for no reason, without ever contesting or arguing the motives behind these police state actions; they let many of their fellow citizens be detained or imprisoned without a right to an attorney or a fair trial. And, in the end, they even bought the impossible association Bush made between bin Laden and Hussein, since it was based on one common element: they were both Arabs in a land far, far away.

The Visit

> The investigation should have begun on September 12, um, there's no reason why it should not have. 3,000 people were dead. It was *a murder*. And it should have gotten started immediately. (*Carol Ashley, mother of 9/11 victim as seen in Fahrenheit 9/11*)

Another disturbing fact Moore shows us in his film is the one pertaining to the administration trying to stop an inquiry in the following weeks of September 11th. Bush actually tried to short-circuit a process that certainly would have shed light on the reasons for these attacks to be committed in the first place. Later in the film, we are reminded that W. did "pay a visit" to the official 9/11 Committee, but that his appearance was not on record. It was all done behind closed doors, with Bush and Cheney telling the Committee anything they wanted (without having to take an oath). In one NBC interview excerpted in *Fahrenheit 9/11*, a journalist asked Bush if he intended to go to the 9/11 Commission. His answer was quite evocative of what he really believed and stood for: "*This* commission? I'll be glad to pay them a *visit*." At the press conference following his "visit," one of Bush's answers to a question concerning the nature of the discussion was: "I was impressed by their questions. I'm glad I took the time to *visit* with them." This use of semantic was obviously a way for Bush to disassociate himself from 9/11. After all, only strangers, tourists and outsiders can "visit" the Supreme Court, not the President of the United States.

After having made clear that the links between the Bush dynasty and Saudi money are real, Moore parallels W.'s utter contempt for the victims of 9/11 and their relatives, at least for those who were trying to get to the bottom of it all. Among these defenders of the truth was Carole Ashley, mother of a 9/11 victim, and Rosemary Dillard, a widow of 9/11. The filmmaker tells us that, in spite of these victims' grief, Bush and his cronies tried to stop both the 9/11 Commission and a private commission which was set on revealing what happened *before* the attacks. The ludicrous reason Bush gave the American public at the time had to do with "not giving the enemy information." Moore tells us that once the 9/11 Commission went under way and finally published a report about the events, the administration classified 28 pages pertaining to the Saudis and their ties to American businesses (and to the Bush family itself). Information that would have allowed people to connect the dots, to make this puzzle fit together in a grander and clearer picture was denied to them.

We are also reminded that 500 victims of the 9/11 tragedy filed a suit against Saudi royalty, and that the firm assigned to defend them in America was the firm of Bush's lawyer, James A. Baker III. On the DVD edition of the film, supplements were added where we can see and hear excerpts of Rice's testimony before the 9/11 Committee, as well as the complete press conference Bush gave after paying his "visit" to the Committee. The footage speaks for itself. Moore does not have to edit it in his own inimitable way. As we watch it, we understand that when Bush spoke of the "enemies of freedom," he was really talking about himself and his friends. Actually, W. trying to veto a commission on 9/11 is in many ways the same deal as Charlton Heston bringing his N.R.A. rally to Flint, Michigan, after 6 year-old Kayla Rowland was shot there, or to Denver, Colorado, after the Columbine rampage: it's in bad taste. Moore the Catholic and filmmaker/activist sees it as his mandate to bring to light this sort of petty and elitist behavior. For him, it seems to be imprinted with symbolic meaning.

Freedom Fries

Still in the first hour of the film, which is very dense information-wise, Moore goes back to his interview with Craig Unger, an expert on U.S.-Saudi Arabia relationships. Both men are standing at crossroads in Washington, at the middle of three symbolic buildings: the Kennedy Center, the Watergate Hotel and the Saudi Embassy. Unger tells Moore that Saudi Arabia owns 7% of the American economy, and that Bush himself has immensely profited from dealings with the Saudi political and financial elite (some of the richest people in the world, like the European aristocracy).[86] Right before this encounter with Unger,

---

[86] Read about Ibn Saudi, the legacy of his descendants, and the long economic relationship between Saudi Arabia and America, from F.D.R. onward, in Rachel Bronson's "Rethinking Religion: The Legacy of the U.S.-Saudi Relationship," The Center for Strategic and International Studies and the Massachusetts Institute of Technology, *The Washington Quarterly*, Autumn 2005

Moore had set up a montage in rhythmic time to R.E.M.'s 'Shiny Happy People' in which we saw Bush Sr. and other friends and members of his administration (Baker, Powell, Rumsfeld) shaking hands with half a dozen Saudi princes. At the beginning of the sequence, we can even hear George Sr. saying: "We've had a very nice reunion with friends." This special relationship is also mocked on the original poster of the film, where we see Moore holding hands with W. on the back lawn of the White House, as if they were the best of friends.

At the end of the musical montage, after the Bushes had "bought a lot of love" from Saudi oil-barons, Moore welds together two varied sources with an eye-line match-cut. We see a close-up of W. looking at something off-screen left, and then a very wide shot of a public square in Jeddah, Saudi Arabia, where two men are being beheaded in front of a crowd. The way the shots are cut in continuity makes it seem as if Bush is actually a spectator to the executions. Moore reminds us in voice-over that the United States are doing business with a country known for not respecting human rights, which is not very surprising, if we consider that Bush's America did not respect them either (Gitmo still being a form of "twilight zone" of human rights, even under Barack Obama's presidency). In his next feature film, *Sicko*, Michael Moore will bring his viewers to France to compare its health care system to the American one. By the end of that film, he will also ask his viewers if they know the reasons why the U.S. government wants its citizens to hate the French so much, over shots of kissing and hugging Parisians. The answer to this is clear: French people did not see or feel the need to bomb a country that was already in shambles, just like they do not enjoy celebrating tragedy while on vacation. It's a moral thing in the end.

Hawk Hunting

> Vice-President Dick Cheney's recurring wet dreams of a U.S. worldwide Roman Empire are, in and of themselves, the world's greatest single threat to the continuation of civilization in any part of this planet today. These facts demand that Cheney's prompt resignation be sought, and accepted.[87]

---

[87] Lyndon H. LaRouche, "Iraq Is a Fuse, But Cheney Built the Bomb," in *Executive Intelligence Review*, October 4, 2002

Fahrenheit 9/11 is not only a film about George W. Bush, as those who have seen it already know. It is also a film about other key-players of his administration, Saudi royalty, Iraqi civilians, American soldiers dying in Iraq (or forgotten once returned home), and their grieving families. In this list of people that Moore chose not to delve into, unfortunately, was hiding Dick Cheney, who is probably the most important and dangerous player in Washington, and will remain up until his death, since he still stands in the realms of the shadow government. Cheney was a Neo-Con who believed that the 21st century will be an American one, a philosophy in line with Leo Strauss' ideals of imperial supremacy (more details further down). His dream was one of a giant empire that will spread across the globe. He had been fancying this notion ever since he was a child, back in Nebraska then Wyoming, but more strongly since Communism started collapsing in the 1980s, under Reagan. From then on, he found a way to make money while creating enemies around the world. In essence, this is his heritage as it will go down in the history books.

Under the one-term reign of Bush Sr., along with two other "West-Wing Ghosts," Richard Perle and Paul Wolfowitz, Cheney managed to convince the American public to go after Hussein (whom they felt had "saddamized" them in Kuwait). These master-manipulators concocted a story that involved a military build-up along the southern border of Iraq, where Hussein had allegedly aligned his artillery, waiting for a showdown with the U.S. Army. However, since the American government controlled all of the informational output, reducing the coverage of the war itself to CNN alone, but forced to cover it from outside the battle zone, it was impossible to verify if these allegations had any credibility. Unless you were actually there or were able to have access to foreign satellites, even if you were smart and educated, you had to believe what you saw and heard on the severely handicapped American television news.[88]

Actually, the Florida-based *St. Petersburg Times* revealed that the whole story about the Iraqi build-up was fabricated by the White House.[89] A journalist there had managed to get access to soviet satellite photographs taken at the same time Bush Sr. announced the beginning of the war. These pictures clearly showed that Hussein did not have firepower gathered along the Kuwaiti border. (Not surprisingly, the American government used the same tactic in 1964 to justify its intervention in the Tonkin Gulf, and in late 2002 and early 2003 in

---

[88] John R. MacArthur, *Second Front: Censorship and Propaganda in the 1991 Gulf War* (Updated with a new preface), The University of California Press, 2004.
[89] Jean Heller, "Public Does not Get Picture with Gulf Satellite Photos," *St. Petersburg Times*, January 6, 1991

front of the United Nations Security Council to justify its intervention in Iraq.)[90] Contrary to Bush Sr., Quayle and Cheney's assertions about Hussein and his "great army," the satellite pictures revealed only one tank perched along a sandy cliff on the Kuwaiti border, decidedly not enough to intimidate to the entire American people and its all-mighty military. In effect, the whole "official" war lasted a few days. At the end of the first night of bombings, watching the "plot" of *Operation Desert Storm* unfold on a gagged CNN, we were expecting the end credits to start rolling upwards (accompanied by a John Williams score), with Bush Sr. and Quayle as producers, Cheney, as executive producer, and Schwarzkopf as (medal-winning) director.

The question remaining now is the following: How did such dangerous men acquire so much power? The answer lies, not only in *Fahrenheit 9/11*, but at the core of all of Michael Moore's work. Someone like Cheney, for instance, became powerful by being CEO of one of the largest corporations in America: Halliburton. This is what Moore has been telling us for two decades: big business and government are in collusion, and the Federal Reserve Bank is really in charge of policies in Washington. This has been the case since the Federal Reserve Act of 1913, but more intensely from the 1960s on, when corporations overtook the world. People like Cheney are first and foremost businessmen, and they apply the ethos of business to the policy-making process when they infiltrate government. When they are not sitting in government, they go back at running their business, in and out the revolving door, from high governmental position to private business, from private business back into high governmental positions. Considering the tautological aspect of this movement, and not unlike the unemployed worker of the Pay Day factory in *The Big One*, we might be tempted to ask here: "When is this gonna end?"

A Shot in the Face

> Well, let me tell you about Halliburton, the company I ran… I'm very proud of what I did at Halliburton, and the people of Halliburton are very proud of what they've accomplished. And, uh, I, frankly, uh, do not feel any need to apologize for the way I've spent my time over the last five years as the CEO and chairman of a major American corporation. (*Excerpt from a press conference given by Dick Cheney - circa 2000 - and as seen in Fahrenheit 9/11*)

---

[90] For an interesting article concerning U.S. tactics in justifying war, read Scott Peterson's "In war, some facts less factual," *The Christian Science Monitor*, September 6, 2002

After Moore's film *Fahrenheit 9/11*, Halliburton became a household name in America. It is now forever associated in the public mind with the oil industry and warfare technology. Cheney was Chairman of Halliburton from 1995 to 2000. He had to "step down" from this position because of his nomination to the vice-presidency in the 2000 election. In fact, nepotism has always been Cheney's game, because he still owned large shares of the company and kept close ties with people on its board of executives, even as V-P. When came the time to pick up the rubbles from the streets of Baghdad, after the American Army went through and blew it all to smithereens, a process that is now over, Halliburton was the very first company to be contracted for billions of dollars to go there and start digging. This is one direct association if any... In *Fahrenheit 9/11*, there is an excerpt of a conference to which Halliburton and other major American and British corporations participated, and one representative there reassured his colleagues regarding the potential of this mother lode we call Iraq.

> Youssef Sleiman:
> Now, lots of you are small businesses and you are struggling. "How do we get a piece of this big action? All of you big guys are going to get it and the rest of us that have subcontracting capability or none at all." USTDA[91] is for you. Once that oil starts flowing and money coming in, it's going to be lots of money. It's *the second largest reserve of oil in the world*, there's no question about how much money is there (...), and it's going to get better! Start building relationships, because it's going to get much better as the oil flows and their budgets increases, and the good news is, whatever it costs, the government will pay you.

Historically, Halliburton has been a dominating force on the American market for the last eighty years.[92] Therefore it does have some credentials, in so far as it has been involved in every aspects of American political life since WW II. In the 1960s, the corporation was closely affiliated to Vice-President (then President) Lyndon B. Johnson, who richly rewarded it with multiple government contracts, including the development of new war artillery that was used to kill more "gooks" in South Asia. Their good fortune lasted beyond the fall of Saigon, since they've also raked in the money from the insanity spilling over the Laotian and Cambodian borders, once President Ford had

---

[91] US Trade and Development Agency
[92] To know more, visit www.halliburtonwatch.org

declared the Vietnam War "over." In the 1980s, Halliburton hired Cheney who continued to entertain business relationships with Iran, which was then under severe U.S. and U.N. sanctions. What few people know is that Cheney managed to break American laws by trading with people he now considers his enemies. He was doing so by subcontracting the work to a Canadian company and by hiding the profits in a fiscal paradise. All throughout the 1990s, even when he became Halliburton's CEO, and under restrictive conditions laid-out by the American embargo, Cheney found a way to extirpate tax-money through government contracting of Halliburton in Iran and Iraq.[93]

Clearly, Dick Cheney, like Rumsfeld (who had to resign in December 2006 after the debacle in Iraq), is a master manipulator and expert at lies and propaganda. Over the years, whether it was his work with the Council on Foreign relations, the American Enterprise Institute, or with the Jewish Institute for National Security Affairs, he has learned to play individuals and nations against each other with skill and ingenuity. When he was not doing business with the Iranians against Iraqis, he was doing business with Hussein against Khomeni. Like other war mongers of his kind, Cheney went into overdrive when he got back into the commerce of war on that rainy January morning of 2001. Actually, beginning in 2003 Cheney's staff stopped filing reports of the vice-presidency to the National Archives and Records Administration. For him, there was no point in releasing documents because he had found a breach in the U.S. Constitution; one that allowed him to transform a democracy into a fascist regime. In the end, *Fahrenheit 9/11* would have certainly benefited from including Cheney's history and maneuvers into its critical discourse.

Old Men of (Long-Term) Vision

> I just met today with seven Iraqi businessmen who had their arms amputated by Saddam around '95 or '96 in order to blame them for the horrid state of his economy. They speak in a way that most Iraqis, 80-90% of them, speak about what a horrible regime it was and how glad they are to be rid of it. Does that mean they like being occupied? No. Does that mean they like Americans breaking down their doors? No. (*Deputy Secretary of Defense Paul Wolfowitz in an interview with Margaret Warner, 2004*)

---

[93] The Fifth Estate: *The Unauthorized Biography of Dick Cheney*, Canadian Broadcasting Television (CBC), aired in Canada in December 2004

The notion of preemptive wars have been laid out a long time ago in the Ford (and then later, in the Reagan) years. Although, it only hatched in the aftermath of 9/11, when the Bush administration decided to attack the already impoverished and defenseless civilians of Iraq, in spite of the United Nations and most of the world's opposition (minus the "Coalition of the Willing" that Moore mocks in his film). In this sequel to the Gulf War, the Republicans used the same tactics they had used in the first dramatic invasion of 1991. They relied on diversion of intent (and on the all-mighty levers of fear) to go drill oil wells in the Caspian Sea and to bring the black gold down to the Persian Gulf (the "magic pipeline" of Unocal, a subsidiary of the Carlyle Group, as we learn in *Fahrenheit 9/11*). For Michael Moore, these right-wing opportunists used the death of 3,000 American civilians to finally get their expensive program going. They milked it for all its worth by going after Afghanistan and Iraq (they already had Pakistan), and by keeping their own people clueless regarding the business shenanigans that had been going on in the last 30 years of American political history.

In *Fahrenheit 9/11*, Moore inserts a segment from a revealing NBC interview with Richard A. Clarke, who was Head of Counter-terrorism when the attacks on America occurred (and who later published a book about his experience[94]). Clark constitutes a reliable source of information, since he was a paid intelligence worker who had first-hand contacts with the Hawks before and after September 11, 2001. He even had worked under Reagan, Bush Sr. and Clinton before W. appointed him Special Advisor to the President on cybersecurity. He left the Bush administration in controversy in 2003, because he was highly critical of the ways in which the Iraq War was sold to the public by the Hawks in the last months of 2002.

> Richard A. Clarke:
> Well, Donald Rumsfeld said, when we talked about bombing the al-Qaeda infrastructure in Afghanistan, he said "there were no good targets in Afghanistan. Let's bomb Iraq." And we said, "But Iraq had nothing to do with this." And that did not seem to make much difference (...) and the reason they had to do Afghanistan first was that it was obvious that al-Qaeda had attacked us. And it was obvious that al-Qaeda was in Afghanistan. The American people would not have stood by if we had done nothing on Afghanistan.

---

[94] Richard A. Clarke, *Against All Enemies: Inside America's War on Terror*, Free Press, 2004

Clearly, the film *Fahrenheit 9/11* shows us that the Iraq War is a battle for land and oil, as well as a first step in the upcoming war for a total American hegemony in the Middle-East (and beyond, to Asia). It links Bush's business endeavors to the Saudis and to the Enron criminals (Kent Lay and friends). It foregrounds the connections between oil companies such as Unocal and countries that America has just finished raping, as well as those it plans to rape in the near future. Finally, and not unlike the Far-Right discourse, it tells us that sometimes the first enemy of a people is its own government. However, in the end, the blame does not only fall on George W. Bush's head. He is after all just a patsy for a whole group of wicked individuals, part of an invisible government. People like Cheney, Wolfowitz, and Rumsfeld served Wall Street, and went out of their way to convince the American public to attack and "liberate" Iraq. They have cleverly concealed the fact that Hussein was a former friend and ally to the United States against Iran, and that Osama bin Laden was also an ally in their own fight against soviet expansionism in Afghanistan. These birds of prey have used their connections with secret services, as well as their unlimited access to new media to convey lies, manipulate, and misinform the public. They have successfully brainwashed some people (at least for a short while) into believing that 9/11, bin Laden and Saddam Hussein were somehow related.[95] A lot of good people saw right away through the lies, but couldn't do much more than to protest on the streets of their city (along with millions of others around the world who were also questioning the legitimacy of this war). Today, we know that all of this was meant to rejuvenate the Anglo-American Empire, which is collapsing. It seems to have been a very temporary solution to a major crisis, if we consider the financial meltdown that followed in 2008.

Secret Kingdom

Here might be a good opportunity to break it down for the reader and to illustrate the clarity of Moore's argument about the Bush administration in his most unforgettable film to date. Like *Bowling for Columbine*, the links of causality established by this film are intricate and complex. The audience cannot possibly absorb the information conveyed in one single viewing. Some tried real hard to debunk Moore's arguments, but in the process only came up with "factual errors" that do not affect the

---

[95] How can anyone believe that an Islamic fundamentalist could actually get in bed with a dictator? A dictatorship is the epitome of individualistic and secular ideology. Even their respective hatred of America would not have made this one happened.

overarching theory presented by the film.⁹⁶ Again, his films are form of artistic expression, and to reduce them to inaccuracy of facts is to completely miss the point about their meaning in the first place. It is also to miss the point about what kind of effect Moore's art is having on intelligent and perceptive people all over the world. What he revealed in this case was accurate information. There is not one element in *Fahrenheit 9/11* that has been invented, recreated, or re-enacted by the filmmaker(s) for the camera. Most of this information was available to the public before he made his film, although it is not everyone's job to connect the dots like Moore does.

Fahrenheit 9/11 illustrated that the war in Iraq has to do with major corporations getting richer, and that Bush put the sons and daughters of the land in harm's way, just to allow his "base" to profit and to keep the structure of a decentralized plutonomy intact. Soldiers were sent abroad, not to defend the country, its geographical integrity, or its dominant ideology, but to allow certain corporations and banks to grow and prosper beyond anyone's wildest imagination. In essence, all policy-making in Washington is controlled by the Federal Reserve Bank, and the Fed is in itself controlled by the Bank for International Settlements, based in Switzerland (the "bank of all banks"). In the end, Bush/Cheney only enforced what was required from them by foreign, often European and Middle-Eastern interests. The enemies, as it turned out, were both foreign and domestic. The Bushes had close-ties with people that most Americans consider "opponents" (Nazis and extremists). The Republican government was using its own population as cannon-fodder for a war that only benefited the private sector.

Wages of Fear

> In this film I wanted to show Americans how they're manipulated with all of this fear, with these Orange alerts, and this thinking that we could be killed and attacked at any time. This is the essence of what Orwell was saying in *1984*: that the leaders needed to have the people in a constant state of fear. Because if you could convince them that the enemy was everywhere, anywhere, and could attack at any time, the people would willingly give up their freedoms in order to be protected. And that is what they have been attempting to do for the last two and a half years.⁹⁷

---

⁹⁶ In any event, Moore published a companion to his film, *The Fahrenheit 9/11 Reader* (Simon & Schuster, 2004) wherein he cites all the sources from which he got his information (pp.131-185)
⁹⁷ Michael Moore interviewed by Steven Applebaum, www.bbc.co.uk, 2004

Millions of Americans did not care if Bush and his cronies decimated the young men and women of America for a war that only benefited their likes, because for them the license to be President was a license to defend American capitalism. This is what Bush referred to when he spoke of a "war against a civilization." He referred to it as a war against the American Way of Life, against the very notion that the Empire has to economically survive, by any means necessary. People like the Hawks profited immensely from the trauma and mass-mental confusion of the post-9/11 world they created, through media and coercion. Disorder of the mind was their game and they were pretty good at it for awhile. They understood that the potential offered by the fear of punishment and restriction of individual freedom made it less likely that Americans would protest in public against a misuse of the political apparatus. The fear of dissent actually stemmed from the fear of punishment, as Machiavelli once taught us in *The Prince* (1532). This has never been as true as when Bush and Cheney were in power between 2001 and 2008.

When some people started protesting against the Iraq war, they were automatically perceived as being unpatriotic and immediately repressed with water-hoses and pepper-spray (or pulled-off the air). We see now that nothing had really changed in this G8 world since the Chicago riots of 1968. The tools of repression are as sharp today as they were 40 years before, under Nixon. Like in *Bowling for Columbine* two years earlier, Moore tied these tactics to the notion of instilled fear and how this helps to shape a national attitude. *Fahrenheit 9/11* can in fact be seen as a "D.I.Y. punk gesture" against a regime that ruled by fear. It was a big "fuck you" to Bush and Cheney's system of oppression. It was "flipping the bird" to a gang of sadistic and immoral "leaders."

In one brilliantly edited sequence, we see Bush saying that he does not spend a lot of time looking for Osama bin Laden, the original culprit who had started this whole mess (or so we were told in the days following 9/11). For Moore, "With the war in Afghanistan over and bin Laden forgotten, the War President had a new target: the American People." This serves to introduce this idea that the political establishment is using fear upon its own people to force them to accept their ideology of war mongering and relentless expansionism. The director inserts eight different excerpts from five different news media sources (Fox News, NBC, CNN, CBS, and a local station) where we are warned about "imminent threats" against America. The sequence begins with an intro clip made out of dramatic graphics created by Fox News. Something that seems to give artistic pretensions to its real purpose: "War on Terror," it says bombastically. The design evokes all the euphemisms that American media (under consultation with the

White House P.R. firm and Madison Avenue) has used in the past to describe American aggressions abroad. It also evokes the titles used by Smiley and Panzer's propaganda and war machine in *Canadian Bacon*, which only goes to show that a very thin line separates fiction and nonfiction in Moore's satirical world. One newscaster reads a headline which warns people to be careful about "poison pens," while other anchormen (who always have to project an air of authority and trustworthiness) speak of "high alerts" and even of a "possible terror threat as bad or worst than 9/11."

Moore is obviously after the same idea than in *Bowling for Columbine*, where "What you don't know might kill you" was a normal sound bite in mainstream American media. The filmmaker illustrates the Bush administration's schizophrenic discourse after 9/11, as far as "imminent threat" is concerned. He cross-cuts various excerpts where we see Bush, Rumsfeld, and Cheney sending two different messages at the same time, making people crazy, as Senator Jim McDermott suggests in the film. Moore plays with two different types of music, while cutting between the members of the administration: a dramatic military drum-roll and 'Hail to the Chief'. We first see Bush telling people: "The world has changed after September the 11th. It's changed because *we are no longer safe*," and right after, in an address to another group of people, "Fly and *enjoy America's great destination spots*." Following this, we see a shot of Rumsfeld who reiterates what Bush has just said before, "We have entered what may very well prove to be *the most dangerous security environment the world has known*," he says. Then, the editing goes back to Bush still being contradictory at a different address: "Take your families and *enjoy life*," followed immediately by Cheney saying, "Terrorists are doing everything they can to gain even *deadlier means of striking us*," again followed by Bush telling a crowd to "Get down to *Disney World* in Florida!" No wonder Americans are confused on certain topics. This is intellectual water boarding at its worst.

This last sequence segues into a more disturbing look at these "crazy-making" statements made to entertain American consumerism. When well-informed people speak of the "business of fear," this is the kind of thing they are usually referring to: You have to get people into the right mind frame so that they'll feel they have to buy equipment to better protect against "evil." In one sequence, we see an excerpt from a NBC morning show where a woman can barely put a "skyscraper parachute" on. Moore emphasizes this notion of instilled fear when he straight-cuts to a woman from Saginaw, Michigan, who believes that terrorists will attack her town. She is buying a large supply of survival material, which is the best way to keep the American economy going. What these sequences make us understand is that the American economy is not solely built on supply and demand, free market, and free enterprise principles alone, but that it is also based on the mental disarray of the masses. It has been proven that before 9/11 the economy was about to collapse. The Enron scandal was a sign of the times, an indication that things were not quite right in this post-industrial, technocratic, and hyper-corporate America. The U.S. Government needed a tragedy, something big that would justify the economy of war. Meanwhile, hundreds of thousands of American workers are been cheated out of their investments when the news broke out that corporations were milking their pensions dry and giving themselves indecent raises and bonuses.

Will anyone stand up and try to galvanized people into concrete political action? Will someone find a way to usurp political power to lay the seeds of destruction within the financial establishment? Can this war against social and economical injustice even be won? Is there any hope with this fresh new face in Washington called Barack? Can these new social networking tools help common people be heard, or do they only reinforce political inertia by keeping everyone separated, alone in front of a computer screen, susceptible to the New World Order? One day, we will have to understand the necessity of taking this fight unto the streets...again. By having his films on the big screen, Michael Moore succeeds in bringing people closer to their respective communities and engaging them in a political discussion. It's a start.

Shades of Orwell

> You get told things every day that do not happen. It does not seem to bother people. (*Donald Rumsfeld, in a Pentagon briefing, 2003, as presented in Fahrenheit 9/11*)

Even in our age of free access to digital and virtual technologies, the state apparatus systematically tends to repress the smallest hint of dissent. In mainstream media, newscasters and reporters alike have been known to retract from any "slip-ups" with polite apologies and regretful explanations. In fact, if it was not for some cable news networks and, more importantly, alternative media, there would not be any space left for different point of views in American media today. This is one amazing aspect of Michael Moore and his work: the ability he has to be in the mainstream media with an alternative political point of view, dissenting and being rewarded for it. In the year *Fahrenheit 9/11* came out, Moore was one of the only "journalists" brave enough to ask the right questions about the Bush administration's handling of the war. For him, questioning power is not a job but a duty. He does so at the risk of being labeled "anti-American" or "unpatriotic," and in spite of all the heat and threats that might come from Washington or from some right-wing nut out there; although he has not yet *really* attacked the powers-that-be, those above the puppets in service in Washington, the puppeteers, the financial elite of the Western world, even in his film *Capitalism: A Love Story*, which is disappointing for many left-wingers.

In spite of this criticism, we can certainly still admire Moore for having had the guts to bring forth certain images that would have normally been censored back in 2004, a year after the Iraq War had started. For instance, American mainstream media has never shown the heart-wrenching plea of an Iraqi grand-mother crying out for her dead grand-children, like the one we see in *Fahrenheit 9/11*. This elderly woman prays to her god, asking to avenge America's barbaric actions against her village in images that have never been seen in the West before (actually, Moore uses a lot of footage from Al-Jazeera, the famous Middle-Eastern answer to CNN).[98] Why do not American networks show these kinds of images, anyhow? Are they afraid the public would stop and realize the implications of a war such as this one? Are they worried the American people will find out that other nations have to suffer so they can drive their SUVs to the mall for cheap? Are they afraid they will care about the "Other?" *Fahrenheit 9/11* is the only American film that dared to show the point-of-view of the "other side" while the Iraq War was at its most intense. It included shots of Iraqi children suffering on hospital beds, with scars and missing limbs, images that would ignite most people's compassion. Yet, not once has the American media shown these images to its population on late-night news. Rather, what America media decided to focus on were unimportant *faits divers*. All of this is meant to turn people's attention from the real issues, those that affect our everyday lives, at home, at school, at work, at the grocery store, at the gas pump, at the hospital, etc. It also seems clear that the Iraq and the Afghanistan wars are being filtered through a perverted logic of negative concealment, and that major networks are not reporting the events they should be reporting on from the battlefield. The main excuse media gave for hiding the truth during the last 7 years is that it would have demoralized troops and public alike if they ever showed the effects of war on the ground. In reality media are owned by the puppet masters, and that is why they can't really say or show anything provocative.

In spite of all these lies and propaganda of the Bush era, and their effects are still reverberating today, more Americans started wondering

---

[98] In 2006, Al-Jazeera created an international version of its network but was not able to get a permit to show its alternative views on North American airwaves. The FCC denied its owners a license that would have put it in direct competition with CNN, Fox and MSNBC.

about the legitimacy of these two wars and the effects of imperialism on their lives, thanks in part to Moore. The awakening was slow, but it nevertheless led the way for Obama's election in November 2008, no doubt an historical moment. That being said, it remains to be seen if the Obama regime will be radically different than the one criticized in *Fahrenheit 9/11*. Many people doubt it, Moore being one of them, in his film *Capitalism: A Love Story*. The only thing one can really hope for is that Obama will be a more benevolent leader than Bush was. Americans expect from him a more thoughtful, transparent, and human conduct of political affairs. Acknowledging that he too was elected to defend American supremacy and the imperial affiliation that the U.S. has been entertaining for half a century with Britain and Israel, many people from the Left intend to give him a chance. What *Fahrenheit 9/11* couldn't have foreseen is that someone like Obama would soon emerge from state politics unto the federal scene and redefine the image of the United States presidency. But this could be a double-edged sword. On the one hand leftist are discouraged by right-wing policies and trust that Obama will carry through his campaign promises. On the other there is always a risk that he will step back and let the sharks of finance and the Pentagon get away with what they have been getting away since the Reagan years. In sum, will he be just another defender of the industrial-military-complex or a transformative leader? Only time will tell.

Goodnight Baghdad

> But why should we hear about "body bags," and "deaths," and "how many," "what day it's gonna happen," and "how many this" or "what do you suppose?" Or, I mean, it's, it's *not relevant*. So why should I waste my beautiful mind on something like that? And watch *him* [*George W.*] suffer.[99]

Fahrenheit 9/11 is showing us soldiers returning from the war in various V.A. hospitals around the country. Just like it was the case for Vietnam, thousands of young people were wasted in towns and villages of Iraq just to allow a few to get richer while the working stiffs pay the bill. So, in that sense, it is not a first in American history. Government did send soldiers to die in a profit-based war before. What changed from the time of Vietnam is that technology is different. For example, Moore's film illustrates how American tanks used in Iraq are equipped with top-of-the-line computers and digital sound-systems which allow

---

[99] Laura Bush on *Good Morning America*, ABC, March 18, 2003

soldiers to listen to their favorite heavy-metal piece while killing innocent people caught in the line of fire. 'Fire Water Burn' by the Bloodhound Gang acts as a soundtrack to women and children being blown to pieces, fathers holding their dead infants in their arms or crying over their dead wives. Through clever and sometimes painful editorial choices, Moore makes us see that Bush and his voracious friends have grabbed teenagers in front of their X-Box and sat them in the comfortable chair of a million dollar-high-tech piece of war machinery. For the young all you have to do is "shoot to kill" and "never surrender," but they do not seem to be aware that they'll never get a shot at a second life, because they have been so indoctrinated by the "We're Number One" ethos. No doubt, Lila Lipscomb, Cindy Sheehan, and so many other grieving mothers know this all too well.

Certainly, American media has been increasingly paralyzed in its capacity to report on American wars, whether it is in Afghanistan or Iraq. Before it could have covered an event on the ground, as it was unfolding in front of the lens. But the experiences of Vietnam, Grenada, Panama, and the first Gulf War have taught one or two lessons to the American political and military establishments (who dictate what you should or should not see and hear). Today news reports are slightly delayed in the control-room and almost always edited before being aired. The selection of what should or should not be seen on national television has gotten more rigorous when it comes down to the humiliating side of patriotism and the effects oil wars have on innocent people. Images of American soldiers returning in coffins were censored daily and had been replaced by a respectful "roll-call" on ABC's *This Week* and other shows like it.

Not only the mainstream media's performance in the lead-up to the Iraq war was a disaster, but there were actually very few instances where network news reported on the casualties with accuracy.[100] Neither did they report back with a desire to question the legitimacy of the war, which is worst. It is all about the sponsors and the ratings in the end. If it has a "narrative," you can make a show about it, but never doubt that your President is doing the right thing...because, after all, it would be "un-American" to do so, at least while Bush was in power. Only recently has American media started questioning what this war was really about and questioning the strategy of "embedding" journalists within ground troops in Iraq. In *Fahrenheit 9/11*, Moore reminds viewers that networks were at the service of the Bush administration during that year leading up to the war. The Hawks used media to distort the truth, misinform the public, and bend the facts for

---

[100] Dahr Jamail, "Another Casualty: Coverage of the Iraq War," *Foreign Policy In Focus*, March 23, 2007

their own personal interests. So why then scorn Michael Moore for having done a little "tampering" of his own? It all seems so out of proportion when we consider the weight of the lie on the other side of the ideological fence. It almost seems like rooting for the bad guys.

S&M Party at Abu Ghraib

No matter how television covered, covers or will cover war in the future, it will always be lagging far behind the Internet in reporting what is now considered newsworthy in general. The effect of Internet on television can be measured by the transformation of TV aesthetics into a pseudo-interactive interface. Pop-ups, scrolling headlines, screens within screens, and web links are only a few traits of this masquerade, when in fact television is a one-way medium that highly filters viewer-participation. The Internet is also a more personalized, immediate, and fragmented medium than television, thus allowing for a lot of "manipulations" and "tampering" indeed. It is also the appropriation of a large-scale distribution system, a network on its own, by the masses. This relatively new mode of communication is not yet under control by the Establishment and allows for "gatherings" of some sorts to happen all over the globe. It is a virtual public space. It probably helped in the election of Obama in 2008, and might also participate to his demise in 2012. In fact, there is no doubt that the Web helped bring awareness regarding the failures or the Iraq War during those awful Bush years. Moore himself was/is using this medium to communicate with his audience, as an extension of his television, literary and film career.

In this sense, the images of the Abu Ghraib prison are perhaps the best example of a new kind of "news," as well as a new kind of way of looking at reports from the frontline. Here in these images, posted all over the Internet, the link between war and obscenity was finally crystallized for all to see. These pictures of sexual humiliation and torture within the walls of the infamous Iraqi prison, after the invasion, caused a scandal from which we haven't yet recovered. American soldiers were ordered to "break" prisoners by using sticks and dogs, and by making these prisoners reenact seemingly homosexual orgies. All these images were entangled with others that showed hostages being decapitated on the Internet or Saddam Hussein's execution. In other words, it became an exercise in the grotesque that the Bush administration exploited to its fullest, proving that it did functioned by intimidation and fear. Blending "deviant" sexual iconography with violence, within the context of the war, became an explosive cocktail that no one has seriously dealt with, even the new administration. It's seems so…medieval. Bush did not have to utter the word "crusade," he just had to unleash all the nastiness that American foreign policy can unleash in times of financial crisis. First, it created the drama. Then it provided a biased and controlled spectacle of its effect to flabbergast a suggestible and gullible public. The orders from above were to "shock and awe" the enemy, regardless of any human morality or decency, and it also served to keep one's own population mesmerized and afraid to dissent.

The original *Fahrenheit 9/11* footage in Iraq and the Internet pictures of the Abu Ghraib prison are reminders that there is now such a thing as the *pornography of war*. It is not enough to torture and kill someone; you also have to humiliate that person at his/her very core before you do so (and put it out there in the mass media so that everyone can see it, like after school bullying on YouTube). The last portion of the film has Moore telling his viewers that, "Immoral behavior breathes immoral behavior," betraying what seems to be a profound sense of egalitarian outrage. At one point, we see hand-held shots of American soldiers making fun of a dead Iraqi soldier: "Ali Baba still has a hard-on," one teenage soldier says to his platoon friends. A small crew sent to Iraq by Moore, as well as footage from Al-Jazeera and European television, captured other graphic and shocking moments perpetrated by Americans on Iraqi civilians who had nothing to do with politics or with Hussein's regime. Mothers and children are rounded-up by foot soldiers on their way to Baghdad, in their very homes, at night, when they are at their most vulnerable. Of course, the excuse for these types of behaviors is to search for any man who might be associated to al-Qaeda or Saddam's discombobulated "army" (!) or part of an insurrection movement, but, if truth was told, it was only accomplished to create terror at the grassroots level. In fact, these are scenes that only a sadistic warmonger and expert in bringing fear and outrage can orchestrate; someone of Joseph Goebbels or Donald Rumsfeld's stature.

Smells like Nazi Spirit

As we can see in *Fahrenheit 9/11*, Iraqi families are all crouched on the sandy floor of their houses, crying, screaming for mercy to the invaders not to hurt or kill them, begging for their lives and the lives of their sons and daughters. They suffer at the end of a barrel that is held, after all, by American teenagers who know next to nothing. 18 year-olds who just graduated high school and who were told to fight for America's security. The treatment of war prisoners has been under the Geneva Convention since 1949, but it became apparent with Abu Ghraib and Guantanamo that cruelty and shock-value are essential elements to the spectacle of war as it was put-on by the previous Republican administration, and that they used young Americans as fodder. Nothing so moralistic (or historical) could have interfered with their plan of action, and we clearly see this in Moore's film. When all is said and done, today, in the wake of the Obama presidency, who told us that he intended to pull out of Iraq and shut down Gitmo, we know that it was their Nietzschean side that made them the arch criminals of our time.

To be sure all wars bring out the worst from people. However, the Iraq War will be remembered for its sheer cruelty and senselessness, just like the Vietnam War in hindsight is. Bush and his band of gangsters used the opportunity to "avenge" America for 9/11 and to further expand the Anglo-American dominion by the same token, we are told in Michael Moore's picture. They used soldiers to defend the interests of oil companies in the United States and they held Iraqi civilians as hostages of the New World Order. They are still putting at risk the lives of people who are trying to make a living by working for private companies in Iraq as well, like the young father we see leaving for Iraq at the beginning of *Sicko*. To this day the cash free-flows between the country they ran and the corporation they are now running. It is all the same in so many ways, since the Federal Reserve Bank (a private bank) controls every move of the political elite and the political elite only responds to the Fed's concerns and demands. If the Republicans win the next election, either with Jeb Bush, Sarah Palin or Newt Gingrich, there is always a chance that they'll resume their blood-sucking expansionism with more ardor than under Obama, finally bringing to fruition the disastrous One World Government, the one where less than 1% of the planet owns everything and everybody, like some sort of new and improved fiefdom for the 21st century.

To finally reframe *Fahrenheit 9/11* in its original context, Michael Moore was one of the rare public personalities who dared to stand up to the Bush administration while the war was still "officially" going on. He is the only nonfiction filmmaker who was willing to ask difficult questions and make precious correlations between those who profit from the war and those who claim it was necessary for America's survival to go to war. He is the only artist who had the idea to make a film about these important subject matters and brought it to light for the entire world to see...on the big screen. In hindsight, *Fahrenheit 9/11* definitely has to be the most important piece of filmmaking produced in America in the last two decades. Although, the only qualm one might have with this brilliant film is the absence of any mention of Leo Strauss, the Jewish-German expatriate who taught at Chicago

University between 1948 and 1973, and who is the main architect of the American neoconservative ethos.[101]

Along with Milton Friedman's economic theories, Leo Strauss' ideology is at the root of the problem in America, because he is the one who established the guidelines of right-wing political rhetoric in Washington today through his teachings on philosophy and politics. Leo Strauss was schooled by Carl Schmitt, himself a student of Martin Heidegger. Schmitt was the one who suggested to Hitler and his party to invoke Article 48 at the breakdown of the Weimar Republic back in 1933. This piece of legislation suspended all civil rights in Germany as Hitler was taking over a burning Reichstag with no one to stop him. It was a (martial) law which allowed for, and gave way to, a totalitarian state, not completely unlike the Patriot Act (part one and two) of the post 9/11 world. Needless to say that the resurgence of Carl Schmitt and Leo Strauss' ideology has been a worrisome trend for many liberal thinkers in the United States since the 2000 election.[102] It is leading us to believe that the fight for true democracy in the U.S. is not over yet, since Obama reinforced its continuity, investing it with an even more centralized type of power.[103]

To understand the essence of the Straussian school of thought, one has to go back to a specific understanding of pre-modern philosophers. In short, Strauss had esoteric views of philosophy and its share of well-known thinkers going back to Plato. He believed that philosophers could never write or say what they really wanted to write or say and, therefore, only a few "enlightened" people could decipher what they really meant in their writings (in a kind of perverted hermeneutics). According to Strauss, all the great philosophers refuted the existence of God and therefore of morality in itself. More importantly, Strauss' distrust of modern ideologies (such as liberalism and egalitarianism), as well as the infiltration of his disciples into American academia (like Allan Bloom, for instance[104]), paved the way for people like Paul Wolfowitz to get into the White House and acquire incredible power over the political world (and eventually reach the head of the World Bank).[105] Strauss was also the one who truly implanted the idea that America is "Number One" in the world. He believed that America's task was to fight evil and rule over the planet. Moreover, he sold the idea that only a strong myth about one's nation can keep it alive and

---

[101] Shadia B. Drury, *Leo Strauss and the American Right*, Palgrave MacMillan, 1999

[102] Barbara Boyd, "Carl Schmitt Revival Designed To Justify Emergency Rule," *Executive Intelligence Review*, January 19, 2001

[103] Michael B. Farrell, "Obama Signs Patriot Act Extension without reforms," *The Christian Science Monitor*, March 1, 2010

[104] Alan Bloom, *The Closing of the American Mind*, Simon & Schuster, 1988.

[105] Wolfowitz was a student of Strauss at Chicago University. The latter had a strong influence on him and other major players in and around the Republican administration.

thriving. Moore's film would surely have benefited from dealing with the ideology of people like Friedman and Leo Strauss and weight its influence in Washington today for the viewer. It would have put into greater perspective the seed that makes the Neocons so rootless and fierce, besides their love of money and power.

America's Broken Backbone

> We know what the real issues are which affect our daily lives, and none of them begin with I or end in Q. Here's what threatens us: 2 ½ million jobs lost since you took office, the stock market having become a cruel joke, no one knowing if their retirement funds are going to be there, gas now costs almost two dollars…the list goes on and on. Bombing Iraq will not make any of this go away. Only *you* need to go away for things to improve.[106]

The last 20 minutes of *Fahrenheit 9/11* focuses on a young soldier who just returned home, Corporal Abdul Henderson, and on the mother of another more unfortunate soldier who gave his life in Iraq, the tragic figure of Lila Lipscomb. After starting his film with conceptual statements about power, politics and economy, Moore brings it all down to a human scale in the end. He pulls it back to ground level, where "regular people" breathe, live, work, reproduce, retire and die. His artistic journey has to lead him back to the victims of the system, to the ones he devoted most of his professional life to. Moore first shows us the experience of Corporal Henderson, a young soldier who refused to go back to Iraq as member of the American Army. He saw first-hand that Iraqi people did not deserve the treatment they received from the U.S. government. Henderson is the conscience of America. He went there as he was told, but when he came back, he refused to serve again (at the cost of being a deserter and be sent to jail).[107] He must have learned something over there that all Americans would have learned as well, if only they had been in his boots for the right minute of his service.

As for Lila Lipscomb, Moore just had to follow on with her, although it was painful to see her being ripped apart by the lost of her son on a big screen, in a summer release... Her confusion about her own patriotic stance seems to have overwhelmed many viewers in the

---

[106] Excerpt from the letter Michael Moore wrote to George W. Bush on the eve of the war in Iraq, March 17, 2003

[107] The case of Private Ehren Watada, a dissident who refused to go to Iraq and got trialed for it, is also quite significant in this way.

last years. Many viewers I have encountered in the past appreciated Moore's film up to that point, when it became too "melodramatic" for their taste. However, what they seem to forget is that Moore did not create this tragic reality. He merely captured it with Miss Lipscomb's full consent. There is no way these scenes with her family could have winded up in the final cut if it had not been for a legal release signed by Lila herself and, most of all, if it hadn't made a strong case against the war and the administration, something that served both her and Michael Moore. The final scene where she goes to Washington is not only brutally touching but also stands as an appropriate counterpoint to all the patriotic, machismo, and megalomaniac discourses held by government, Neoconservatives and news media alike. The moments spent with Lila Lipscomb are an alternative view of the war, in a culture that romanticizes the concept of war. It only seems fair in this case to fully depict the ramifications of the decisions made by this administration on "regular people." After all, they are the ones who always have to pay the high price in the end.

More than anything else, the last portion of the film truly leaves a bitter taste on the viewer's buds. The amount of time spent with Ms. Lipscomb is never balanced by footage of Republicans consoling grieving mothers or disabled soldiers at V.A. hospitals around the nation. Now, the viewer has to wonder if it is Moore who did not want to redress the balance by showing us Bush as being repentant, helping victims, explaining to them why their sons had to die for profit, or if it was just that no visual records of such encounters between Bush and war victims existed at the time the film was being made. There is only one excerpt from a television interview where he says that he "can't imagine" what it would be like to lose a child or a husband or a wife in this kind of situation. The reason why he cannot imagine this is that he will never have to live it, because of his name, status, wealth, gender, language, and skin color; because he is part of a new monarchy.

When Moore concludes his film by quoting George Orwell from his classic novel *1984*, he reminds us that, all throughout history, the victims of war have usually been the minorities, the poor, and the disenfranchised, not the elites who have benefited from it. It is all so clear. Yet, so many people choose to remain deaf, dumb, and blind to these issues of class struggle and real democracy around the world. Many on the Left perceived it as being entertaining propaganda targeted against the dangerous policies of some of the most powerful men in the world. For us, in 2010, it remains as relevant as ever. It stands as a testament to the value of dissension in times of ideological repression, philosophical confusion, and spiritual turmoil. As a matter-of-fact, time has been good to this film and its makers. It resonates as deeply as ever today, at a time when the Republican Party is leader-less and in shambles, leaving angry "Tea Party" and Far-Right extremists with no other choice but to rely on Glen Beck or Rush Limbaugh, and show to the rest of America and to the world the violence and absurdity of their outdated Old Testament rhetoric.

In the resolution of *Fahrenheit 9/11*, Moore wraps it up by "paying a visit" himself to senators and congressmen on Capitol Hill. Along with Corporal Henderson, armed only with a few color brochures advertising the United States Army, a camera and a boom-mike, the filmmaker walks the beat in front of Congress, asking politicians if they'd be willing to enlist *their* sons and daughters in the war in Iraq. Obviously, they are scandalized by his proposition and prefer to run for cover, because they understand what is really at stake here…and so do we.

When the Lies Are So Big

Fahrenheit 9/11 did not open fresh wounds by making an American mother re-enact her grief for the camera's sake. Instead it zoomed-in on this maternal figure to make some sense, if such a thing is still possible, of the modern human condition. More akin to a visual manifesto than investigative journalism per se, mainly because it denies this naïve idea of objectivity and deliberately foregrounds a subjective treatment of the material, this feature film unveils a series of shady circumstances through a flashback and flash-forward "narrative" which almost seems like a dramatization of reality at times. It is those "formal manipulations" which many spectators have taken issues with since the film's release. And the debate has been going on ever since.

From a methodological point-of-view, the process which allowed for the achievement of this film went against every notion contained implicitly in the so-called Anglo-American ethos of journalistic practices. The reasons for this belief seem clear and obvious. *Fahrenheit 9/11* fully assumes its subjectivity and proposes that being "objective" will not help revealing the *awful truth* about the events of 9/11. For better or for worst, it defies instrumental reason and asks us to feel it in our hearts. It is asking us to trust our gut instinct on this one. More engaged in its interpretation of world events than conventional journalism, this film asserts that the attacks in New York and Washington were seized by a handful of ideologues, technocrats, and industrialists who felt it was their right to reconfigure the geopolitical dynamics of our world for profits. The main contention of *Fahrenheit 9/11* is that white-collar terrorists in America profited from that horrible tragedy by investing stocks in it, by gambling on its outcome with human lives – the most expendable of all commodities.

Furthermore, it asserts that this tragedy could have been avoided in the first place, which is probably the scariest of all thoughts for

Americans, since this proposition undermines their ideal of democracy, and irrevocably shatters their hope for a truly effective homeland security system in the future (which now translates into the so-called "preemptive war on terror" - an abstract project that has been sucking up tax-dollars since March 2003 and that will never end, even with Obama in office). Hence, *Fahrenheit 9/11* sheds a great deal of light on a monumental lie. But despite all these "illuminations" brought about by the authors of this film, many Americans refused (and still refuse) to believe that government and public officials, including their then President and Vice-President, could stoop so low as to send their children die in a corporate-sponsored war. If this did not do it, what can?

A Matter of Convenience

No question about it, *Fahrenheit 9/11* is an entertaining and disturbing picture. Yet it does not put on the spectacle so many of its detractors have claimed it does. Its creator went to great lengths to expose, granted through a subjective prism, the necessary information needed to think outside of the political box. But even though it cracked that lie wide open for all to see it remained ineffective as a weapon of mass-destruction whose main objective was to dethrone the Bush administration in November 2004. We will probably never fully understand the reasons why it did not achieve what it set out to do in the first place, since the effect that movies have on politics, and political understanding in general, has rarely been a topic of serious research and investigation.[108] However, what we do know is that it was most certainly convenient for the Republicans to be at war in electoral times. In spite of these unfruitful efforts to do away with a bad regime with too much corporate interest, let us not forget that *Fahrenheit 9/11* did address some disturbing facts about the state of democracy under a neoconservative agenda.

In short, the film retraced the rise of a king's son put on the throne through a well-orchestrated *coup d'état* back in November 2000. A little king made by proxy who has direct links to a dangerous and powerful prince and his rich relatives far, far away, beyond the sand dunes of Saudi Arabia. The film's narrator even goes as far as to claim that this little king and his entourage are criminals, since they have used the lives of 3,000 innocent people only to profit big business dealing in oil and warfare technology.

---

[108] For one example, read Robert Brent Toplin's *Michael Moore's Fahrenheit 9/11: How One Film Divided a Nation* (University Press of Kansas, 2006).

In parallel to this horrific political story, another, more important one is being told: An American mother loses her son in an unjustifiable war and realizes that her belief in her government was in vain. A young soldier returns home from Iraq and swears that he'll never fight innocent people again, realizing that his brand of patriotism was also in vain. Thousands of veterans who are coming home from Iraq and Afghanistan, poisoned by unknown substances, maimed, disabled, stigmatized by their own right-wing government. Wives, husbands, families, friends, and neighbors mourning the death of a loved one lost in a terrorist attack that might have been avoided in the first place...if the little king and his henchmen had taken the threat more seriously.

In hindsight, it would seem like the main plot of *Fahrenheit 9/11* did not only concern the doings of a "fictitious president" who has been chosen to create "fictitious wars" around the world, but it also dealt with the suffering and the courage of real people through adversity and flagrant injustice.

"The facts, ma'm, just the facts!"

Evidently, this humanist content of *Fahrenheit 9/11* which was smuggled in on American screens in the summer of 2004 was presented to us in a highly stylized and entertaining way. The bottom line is that if it had not been "manipulative" or "tampered with," most people would not have cared for it. But if there is one truth about cinema, and about media (and politics) in general, is that there is always necessarily manipulation and tampering involved. In documentary form, it is generally assumed that "objectivity" is the norm, or even a rule, and that a filmmaker has to suppress his or her point-of-view for the benefit of the subject matter. This is perhaps the greatest misconception of the film camera, as a scientific invention: its de facto "objective nature." If there is a framing of reality there also has to be some kind of subjectivity involved in the process. Any *framing*, whether literal or figurative, claims an intention, proposes a slant, is constructed for a purpose, because it has been *oriented or composed* to record or document a *chosen part of reality*. It represents a position in/on the world whether we like it or not.

In journalism, for instance, the mere fact that a publisher or an editor chooses one subject over another is already a kind of framing, since the selected news has already being "dealt with" even before being assigned to a reporter; whereas in cinema and television, techniques of editing and mixing have been developed to shorten and organize the spatial and temporal dimensions of recorded events, constantly along elliptical lines. In any given case the whole process of communication and/or creation is about *selection, organization, and interpretation of captured bits of reality*. It is about producing meaning where there might not be any for the naked eye or to the untrained ear.

Thus, a representation can never really encompass the entire reality of the world as we know it. It is almost always "biased" by definition. In philosophy, this essential nuance between objectivity and subjectivity dates back at least to Schopenhauer, while in the study of aesthetics it goes all the way back to Aristotle. Differently put: no media can ever be objective in the same way that no individual can ever be objective. We can certainly make abstraction of certain feelings about a given issue, but at the end of the day we also represent a walking point-of-view on the world. Therefore manipulation and tampering are delicate and necessary operations to produce art or entertainment or even a newscast, for that matter. With these kinds of formal manipulations, not only possible in the medium of moving images through editing and mixing, but also in the written press, by selecting and organizing information into a certain hierarchical order of relevancy and importance, the creator of *Fahrenheit 9/11* managed to produce cultural artifacts that reflect perhaps more than anything else the maddening reality of our times. Michael Moore helped a whole generation to better understand the world we live in by betting on the expressive properties of mass-media, not on its capacity to be, if not objective, at least detached, cold, and clinical, like it often is.

One More Day (Or Four More Years...)

Between *Fahrenheit 9/11* and his next film, *Sicko*, Michael Moore made available as a free download on the Internet *The Great '04 Slacker Uprising* (2007), a fly-by-the-seat-of-your-pants movie following him and a group of American dissidents on the trail of the 2004 presidential election. This film includes a series of speeches given by Moore on the College and University circuits and is supplemented by great musical performances by Eddie Vedder, Steve Earle, Michael Stipe and Joan Baez. Others came out to lend Moore a hand in his fight against the Neocons, such as comedian Roseanne Barr and legendary feminist activist Gloria Steinem. Even ex-Corporal Abdul Henderson came to tell his story to large crowds gathered for the "Slacker Tour." While shooting the film, Moore got into trouble with the Republican Party in Michigan for having "bribed" people into voting, by offering them Ramen Noodles and clean underwear. Moore wanted to sue as well: over the fact that someone had stolen the humor out of the Republican Party.

Slacker Uprising is a minor film in Moore's career, but it is still worth watching because of its extremely consistent discourse. A discourse he has been holding since the 1980's, when corporations took over every single aspect of our lives. In essence, it is about private interests in politics, lobbying forces and right-wing ideology being at odds with the founding principles of democracy. Overall, it is a pretty entertaining film and offers an insider look at Moore the public figure. As it opens with 'When Johnny Comes Marching Home' on the soundtrack, and a series of facts written on a black background, Moore tells us that by the end of July 2004 John Kerry had surged ahead of W. in the polls, but that Bush's people began a smear campaign to destroy his reputation; running ads from fellow Vietnam veterans claiming that "You can't trust John Kerry, because he is a traitor to our country." Kerry failed to respond to these attacks on time and the damages against his campaign were irreparable. Thus Moore, other artists and citizen groups went out on the road with their own 'shadow campaigns' to save the Democrats from themselves," the opener for the film tells us. One of the best moments from *Slacker* is when Moore chastises reporters at a press conference for having been the lapdogs of the Bush administration from 2001 to 2004.

Moore:
The propaganda that exists appears every night on the nightly news. Night after night after night, before this war started, "There are weapons of mass destruction! Saddam had something to do with 9/11!" and all of you [*reporters*] on TV, flying our flag all over the screen, told these misstatements and these untruths to the American people. How much are we propagandized by the Bush administration and by our mainstream national media? (…) What if you had done your real job? What if you had asked the hard questions, and demanded the evidence about this war? Because the great thing about the American people is, once they have the truth, that there weren't weapons of mass destruction, there was no connection to 9/11, they flipped! Because they got the truth, they got the information. What took so long? My movie [*Fahrenheit 911*] exists to counter the managed, manufactured news, which is essentially a propaganda arm of the Bush administration. My movies are the anti-propaganda. The only sad thing about that is that people have to pay 8 or 9 dollars to come to a movie theater, to get a babysitter, to learn things they should be getting for free, sitting on the couch, and eating Tostitos.

SICKO (2007)

> It is not my role to be a policy maker. I am a filmmaker and I make movies. I would like to talk about being a filmmaker, the process of making a movie. I am not writing a book. I am making a movie. I am very careful about the facts in the film. The facts are accurate. A fact is a fact. If I say there are 50 million people without health insurance, I am giving you a fact. Nine million children are uninsured, that is a fact. But if I say health insurance should be abolished, that is a conclusion I have researched, that is an opinion.[109]

This Might Hurt A Little

Michael Moore's next film, *Sicko*, was not only the long awaited follow up to *Fahrenheit 9/11*, a film which revolutionized nonfiction filmmaking and distribution as we know it, but also as its title suggested, a horror film (ref. *Psycho*). Many were wondering if Moore was going to live up to the hype and create news once again or if he was going to break his teeth on a subject matter so close to people and so sensitive for them that no one, not even him, could tackle it properly. As it turned out, *Sicko* was the film that perhaps captured the *zeitgeist* more than any other of his films, i.e. from an American standpoint. Moore was on the pulse of an entire nation, and this translated to all the other countries where the film was seen. Moreover, *Sicko* foreshadowed the health care bill that the Obama administration has managed to implement in 2010 for those 50 million Americans without insurance. Michael Moore, as a film artist, has a flair for choosing relevant contemporary issues and deal with them in a truly respectful way. The film is also dedicated to his mom, no doubt along ideological lines, as a wink to the first great "dragon-slayer" in his life.

Not surprisingly, *Sicko* was released with much less fanfare than its predecessor. We write "not surprisingly" because it would seem like Moore has been aware of the criticism targeted against him since the first edition of this book was published, and as far as having been overexposed during the time of *Fahrenheit 9/11*. He actually laid low for almost three years, changing his look, giving few interviews, except on certain alternative media outputs, and choosing to work on his next film in relative silence instead.

---

[109] Michael Moore interview, by Karin Luisa Badt, "Stay Well, or Else: Michael Moore's *Sicko*," August 2007 (visit www.brightlightsfilm.com/57/mooreiv.html)

In a nutshell, *Sicko* is a film about how American corporations benefit from people's illnesses and, yes, death. It came out at a time in history when more Americans were going bankrupt than ever before, precisely because of health care costs. As Moore says in voice-over at the beginning: "This film is not about the 46 million who do not have health insurance, but about the other 250 million of you who do," and this is perhaps the most disturbing aspect of the story, since being "covered" is not nearly enough to be assured of care in a right-wing America. In fact, what Moore traces with his picture is a series of personal and horrific stories about how patients were denied care on the basis of finance or because of so-called "pre-existing conditions" (like yeast infections or acne). In many cases patients died from a lack of care and the health insurance business made a lot of money on their backs, something that should shock any viewer with a conscience. As a matter of fact, *Sicko* can be considered as "part one" of *Capitalism: A Love Story*, where Moore unveils that many corporations are taking life insurance policies on their employees without them or their families ever knowing about it. Both films complement each other in the same way *Roger & Me* and *The Big One* did, or in the way in which many episodes from *The Awful Truth* were previews for *Bowling for Columbine*, one of his many illustrious films.

As far as an overall content analysis goes, Moore leads his viewer into asking many questions throughout the course of *Sicko*. We are led to ask about the causes for such violence against the common folks and why American conservatives do not see the clear and obvious links between social security and individual prosperity. Moore brings back here a central notion to his oeuvre, the one involving the duality of "Me vs. We," a philosophical conundrum which seems to have been resolved in other industrial nations but not in the U.S., apparently. How can anyone not see that health is as central to a society as other public services are? Right from the onset, *Sicko* exposes the facts surrounding the big squeeze of the American middle-class and the overriding power of corporations on social policies. We are taken from personal stories to more general statements about the current economic structure of the Western capitalist world in a parallel narrative pattern. Moore accumulates fact after fact describing how corporate decisions affect people in their every day lives and, once again, operates through comparison with other countries like Canada, England, France and, in a bold move, Cuba. From a formal angle *Sicko* follows on the trails of his previous films by relying heavily on voice-over, talking head interviews, fast montage sequences and *mise en scène*. It is once again a display of true cinematic genius.

Pray You Don't Get Sick

Sicko is one the most political films ever made mainly because it manages to personalize complex social issues without ever being overwrought. Moore starts on familiar grounds by including footage of George W. Bush being his usual unintelligible self at a local speech, as if it was in conceptual continuity with *Fahrenheit 9/11*. Some viewers will also recognize the classical score from the film *In the Bedroom* playing on the soundtrack, creating an atmosphere of doubt and romantic playfulness from the very beginning.

> George W. Bush:
> We got *issue* in America. Too many good docs are getting out of business. Too many OBGYN are not able to practice their love *with* women across this country.

As the opening credits introduce the filmmakers and set the tone for the next 2 hours to come, we are shown a home video of "Adam." Someone is filming him sowing back his own knee after a serious injury because he could not afford to go to the hospital. Moore makes sure to let us know that Adam did not have health insurance, and that it is the reason why he had to do this himself. In the same sequence, we are introduced to "Rick," a man who accidentally cut the top of two of his fingers with a table saw. We are told that Rick had to choose which one to save, since he also did not have health insurance and could not find the money to save both. We learn that his middle finger would have cost him 60K, while the ring finger, the one he decided to save, had "only" cost him 12K. We will soon find out that 18,000 Americans die every year because they are not insured. Moore again relies on footage from the 1950s to set into context this political and cultural problem, very much like he did in *Roger & Me, Bowling for Columbine* and *Fahrenheit 9/11*, and this preliminary exegesis serves to launch another one of his investigations into the damaged American psyche.

We are introduced then to Larry and Donna Smith, a couple in their late 50s who had to move in their daughter's storage room after a lifetime of working and saving. "It was not supposed to end like this for Larry and Donna," Moore tells us. They both had good jobs and raised six kids who went to fine schools; but Larry had a series of heart attacks and Donna got cancer, which left them bankrupted because of evil HMO and CEO policies. Needless to say, this is a sad fate to contemplate from a cinema seat, not at all the kind of entertainment Hollywood is used to feeding us in the summertime. Today, in North America, not only do young adults often have to go back living with their parents, but parents often wind up loosing their home and have to go live with their grown children. One of the most touching footage Moore chooses to include in this sequence is of Donna crying, but his voice-over undercuts the pathos of the moment by being extremely sarcastic: "They were bankrupt!," he says over the poor woman sobbing. Once they moved in with their daughter's family, they quickly get into a rift with one of their sons who popped in from across town. Tragically, the latter does not seem to understand his parent's situation, and we realize that this is a very delicate situation, and that the cost of corporate policies, in human terms, is almost impossible to assess. In fact, it can only be imagined from something which Larry says; that he gets the feeling he is bringing his problems with him wherever he goes, and that he does not know what to do about it. This segment about the Smiths ends with their grandchildren crying because their father is going to Iraq to work as a contractor, a sheer coincidence, Moore tells us in voice-over.

Donna Smith:
If somebody had told me 10 years ago this would happen to us because of health care I would have said it's not possible. Not in the United States. We would not let that happen to people.

The following story seems to be even more appalling. We meet Frank Cardill, a 79 year old man who has to work to pay for the drugs his wife and him need. Frank works for a low income grocery store job, picking up spillages, cleaning up bathrooms, and taking care of recycling with the help of a relatively dangerous piece of machinery. Frank is obviously too advanced in years to do such physical work, and we soon understand that for him there is no hope for a bit of rest in these so-called "golden years." He explains to Moore that his wife's painkillers cost over $200 a month, and that he works at the store only for the benefits which help to reduce the cost of their medication. Revealing a true American essence is the moment when Ms. Cardill tells Moore that she does not trust her conventional medication, preferring to chug a little shooter of brandy to numb her pain instead. We get here a glimpse of the good nature and resilience of middle-America, a place filled with modest, hard-working and decent people.

In the end, this is another fundamental aspect of Michael Moore's work: it showcases not only the inhumanity of American politics and economics in the particular, but the humanity of the American people in general.

Small Prints

> Understand, this is very personal to me. I'm thinking today about my mother. She died of ovarian cancer at the age of 53. She fought valiantly, and endured the pain and chemotherapy with grace and good humor. But I'll never forget how she spent the final months of her life. At a time when she should have been focused on getting well, at a time when she should have been taking stock of her life and taking comfort in her family, she was lying in a hospital bed, fighting with her insurance company because they did not want to cover her treatment. They claimed that her cancer was a pre-existing condition. So I know something about the heartbreak caused by our health care system.[110]

Laura Burnham got into a car accident. She tells us that she got billed by her HMO for the ambulance ride to a nearby hospital because it had not been "pre-approved." She wonders in front of Moore's camera about when she should have made the call to her HMO to inform them of her accident: before or after she got in the accident. This is only one of the many Machiavellian tactics used by insurance companies to not pay claims as presented in *Sicko*, a horror show for the modern age. We are shown how corporations will find any excuse to avoid paying benefits to needy patients; patients who had themselves paid for coverage for years. This sequence about Laura prompts a rapidly edited segment where Moore explains that he had asked for and received in his email an amazing amount of health care stories in a period of just one week.

One couple did not even wait for Moore to begin his attack on the health care industry. As soon as they learned he was planning a film, they used this information to challenge the decision of their insurance company, CIGNA, to pay for their 9 month-old girl's hearing implant in both of her ears, since it wanted to only pay for one. Their letter asked this corporation "Has your CEO ever been in a film before?" Here Moore's reputation as an anti-corporate muckraker led the company to allow for the implants in both of her ears, as it should have been from the beginning.

The next section opens with testimonies from Americans who wrote Moore to tell him about their stories. The director interviews a young woman who once worked for a major HMO where she was in charge of keeping sick people away. She tells him that the list of pre-existing conditions which render clients ineligible for claims can be

---

[110] Remarks of Senator Barack Obama, Asheville, North Carolina, October 5, 2008

wrapped around her apartment building many times over. Moore inserts a nomenclature of these conditions in the form of the *Star Wars* opening credit scroll. It accelerates and goes so ridiculously fast and becomes so unreadable that he decides to straight cut to the woman crying and telling how she declined hundreds of patients, and how her conscience now aches about it. Interestingly enough, this woman explains that she felt like she had to be a "bitch" over the phone in order to distance herself from the claimants. Read between the lines, we can measure how difficult it must be for some people to work at the lower echelons of a corporation. This is a good example of how the machine can make a good person alienated from his or her own feelings. It rationalizes why so many in the corporate world today are cold and detached; because acting out the opposite would involve too much humanity and too much grief and sorrow on their part as well. It would be an impossible way of life for all, except for those at higher corporate echelons, the "untouchables," who rarely feel anything for "little people," anyhow.[111]

Of the most insidious aspects of HMOs, as they are presented in Michael Moore's *Sicko*, is that they refuse to pay to claimants what these ones have paid for all their working lives; they refuse to provide a service paid for out of pocket. Thinking that they will be "covered" by a privately owned and operated company, millions of Americans learn the lesson the hard way: American laws are made as such that corporations have the same privileges as individuals, but not the same civil liability and civil responsibilities in return. This uneven relationship has given the business class the edge, the space to maneuver, to distort, and ultimately to conspire against their own "customers." How can it even be debated that once someone has paid for a service, one should be able to get the goods in return, no question asked, even along the most basic understanding of capitalism? Since health is considered a commodity in the United States, it can be argued that health services in the United States, if paid for, should at the very least be instantaneous and irrevocable, no question asked. Would anyone imagine paying for a loaf of bread and not getting that bread in return? How difficult would it be to defend this theft in a court of law in any state today? Why can't Americans get what they paid for in the case of the health insurance and pharmaceutical industries?

The answers are revealed in *Sicko* one step at a time. We find out that greed has permeated all American industries, including those who are supposed to have a public function. The very notion of a preexisting clause in an insurance policy is in itself ludicrous and should be illegal; because it is a breach in the *social* contract, something that is

---

[111] This is an expression now attributable to ex-British Petroleum CEO Tony Hayward.

not yet recognized by the rule of law in the United States. Moore develops *Sicko* around stories similar to President Obama's mother. In the first part of the film he includes a series of segments with different women who have been denied coverage. Moore tells us that some of them even died while they were waiting (and while he was filming). Maria was with Blue Shield, Diane with Horizon-Blue Cross, Laura with BCS, and Amy with Mega Life. They all had breast or brain tumors and all had to battle with their HMOs to get what they had paid for: a treatment. In some of these cases, HMOs were saying that a brain tumor is not life threatening. Moore uses parallel editing to make all of these stories coalesce into a greater picture of the problem. He puts square dance music on the soundtrack to express the absurd treatment of these women by companies who have become experts in giving clients "the runaround." As we can clearly see in this film, corporations are debating with medical expertise while people's lives are hanging in the balance. It is a crime. The case of Maria Watanabe versus Blue Shield is one clear example of this last proposition. Maria got a lawyer after a Japanese doctor confirmed she had a tumor and successfully sued Blue Shield. In *Sicko*, we get a glimpse of the trial through excerpts from a courtroom video. Dr. Glen L. Hollinger, Medical Director for GSMPA, and contracted for Blue Shield of California, is grilled by the prosecutor.

Prosecutor (off):
March 13, 2003. Let me direct your attention to Exhibit 1. Please describe for me what it is.

Hollinger:
It is a denial for referral to an ophthalmologist.

Prosecutor (off):
Is it your signature on the document?

Hollinger:
Yes.

Prosecutor (off):
I'd like to direct your attention to Exhibit 2.

Hollinger:
This is a denial of a request for referral for magnetic resonance imaging test of the brain.

> **Prosecutor (off):**
> And it has your signature on it?
>
> **Hollinger:**
> Yes.
>
> **Prosecutor (off):**
> Doctor, directing your attention to Exhibit 3, please read this document.
>
> **Hollinger:**
> This is denial for a referral to a neurosurgeon.
>
> **Prosecutor (off):**
> Can you explain for me how you came to sign the denial letter?
>
> **Hollinger:**
> This is the standard signature that's put on all denial letters.
>
> **Prosecutor (off):**
> Is that your signature or is that a stamp?
>
> **Hollinger:**
> That is a stamp.
>
> **Prosecutor (off):**
> Did you ever see a denial letter before your signature was stamped on it?
>
> **Hollinger:**
> No. But the denial letters are fundamentally the same... They're... The denial letters that are sent out...
>
> **Prosecutor (off):**
> The answer is "no."
>
> **Hollinger:**
> No.

This video then leads the way for the revealing testimony of Linda Peeno, a doctor and once medical reviewer for Humana, the same company which had declined Chris Donahue his pancreas transplant in the *Awful Truth* series. Ms. Peeno had left her contractual job because she was highly critical of the ways in which the company did business. In fact, her good conscience could not stand it any longer, as she walked out of the corporate world to become the most famous whistleblower on the health insurance scam. In *Sicko*, she tells Moore that the very definition of a "good" medical director is one where no claims are ever paid. She even says that "corporations look for a language where exclusions and so-called technical denials are the norm." According to Peeno, executives are rewarded for denying coverage, and the system rewards doctors with the highest rate of denials. In that sick, sick world of HMOs, any payment for a claim is referred to as a "medical loss." In effect, what she tells Moore is that insurance companies behave like banks and are misrepresenting their services. Another man interviewed in *Sicko*, only known as "Lee," had worked for big insurance companies and tells us that he hurt a lot of people too, and that he is glad to be "out of it." Lee reveals how language and small prints can actually kill somebody.

> Lee:
> We're going to go after this like it's a murder case. And I mean a whole unit dedicated to going through your health history for the last 5 years, looking for anything that would indicate that you concealed something and you misrepresented something so that they can cancel the policy or jack the rates so high that you can't pay them. And if we couldn't find anything that you did not disclose on the application, you can still get hit with a "pre-existing denial," because you do not even have to have sought medical treatment for it. They're supposed to be fair and even-handed, but with an insurance company, it's their friggin' money! So, it's not unintentional, it's not a mistake, it's not an oversight: you're not slipping through the cracks, somebody made that crack and swept you towards it, and the intent is to maximize profits.

Moore then continues by presenting the touching story of Julie Pierce, who was struggling to get care for her husband, Tracy, before he died from kidney cancer. Julie worked in the intensive care unit at St-Joseph's Medical Center in Kansas City, Missouri, which provided herself and her family with so-called "health insurances." She explains that every month doctors wanted her husband to use a new drug that might have cured him, but that letters coming from her HMO always managed to deny payment for these treatments. One generic letter was saying that this was "not a medical necessity," or that "it did not fall within the guidelines of your coverage." Other letters of this kind would simply deny coverage on the basis that "further clinical trials are needed" for these new drugs, or that this type of medical intervention is considered "too experimental." Furthermore, when doctors considered a bone-marrow transplant on Tracy, an operation which is known to be effective in stopping and sometimes getting rid of kidney cancer, the insurance company denied coverage once more. One of Tracy's brothers was considered to be a perfect donor match, and even then the company denied payment. Moore explains in voice-over that the Board of Trustees told Julie they were "sympathetic" to her situation, but like Chris Donahue, she replied that it is not sympathy she was looking for but to save her husband's life. In the end, Tracy Pierce died because of cruel corporate decisions and an unregulated insurance market.

Moore then cuts back to footage from Linda Peeno's 1996 testimony before the U.S. Congress over Samuel Barber's 'Adagio for Strings'.

Linda Peeno:
I am here primarily today to make a public confession. In the spring of 1987, as a physician, I denied a man a necessary operation that would have saved his life and that has caused his death. No person and no group have held me accountable for this. Because in fact, what I did was that I saved a company a half a million dollars for this. And, furthermore, this particular act secured my reputation as a good medical director, and it insured my continued advancement in the health care field. I went from making a few hundred dollars a week as a medical reviewer to an escalating six-figure income as a physician executive. In all my work, I had one primary duty, and that was to use my medical expertise for the financial benefit of the organization for which I worked. And I was told repeatedly that I was not denying care, that I was simply denying payment. I know how managed care maims and kills patients. So I'm here to tell you about the dirty work of managed care, and I'm haunted by the thousands of pieces of paper on which I have written a deadly word: *denied*.

Millhouse's Ghost

Linda Peeno's testimony marks a turning point in *Sicko*. Moore is now required to go somewhere else with this reality about American health care. First, he has to go back in history to discover how these practices were implemented and how they became legal. He asks his viewers in voice-over: "How did we get to the point where doctors and health insurance companies are actually responsible for the death of patients? Who invented this system? How did this all begin? Where did the HMOs start?" We then see a shot of the White House with the inscription "February 17, 1971, 5:23 p.m.," and Moore tells us that "Thanks to the wonders of magnetic tape, we know." Over stills of Richard Nixon in the Oval Office, we hear a conversation between the impeached President and John Ehrlichman, then Assistant to the President for Domestic Affairs. Ehrlichman was also a key figure in the Watergate scandal and convicted of conspiracy, obstruction of justice and perjury; not the best guy to take care of health care, we must admit.

Erhlichman:
We have now narrowed down the vice president's problems on this thing to one issue, and that is whether we should include these Health Maintenance Organizations like Edgar Kaiser's Permanente thing.

Nixon:
Now let me ask you...You know I'm not too keen on any of *these damn medical programs*.

Erhlichman:
This is a *private* enterprise one.

Nixon:
Well, *that* appeals to me...

Erhlichman:
Edgar Kaiser is running his Permanente deal *for profit*. And the reason he can do it...I had Edgar Kaiser come in, talk to me about this. And I went into some depth. All the incentives are toward *less medical care*, because the less care they give them, the *more money* they make...

Nixon:
Fine.

Erhlichman:
...and the incentives run the right way.

Nixon:
Not bad.

The editing then cut to Nixon addressing the nation on the following day, which shows just how much the officious political rhetoric can create a smokescreen to the real issues and decisions, or how Richard Millhouse Nixon basically lied through its teeth.

> Nixon:
> I am proposing today a *new* national health strategy. The purpose of this program is simply this: I want America to have the *finest* health care in the world. And I want *every* American to be able to have that care when he needs it.

It then cuts to a series of archival news footage from the 1970s, when America was in total distress, torn apart by the social and financial toll of the Vietnam War, the Oil Crisis and the bad trip that would become Watergate. One reporter indicates that 37 million Americans are without any form of coverage, while another asserts that the poor are obviously the ones who suffer the most from a privately-run health care.

> Moore (v.o.):
> "The plan hatched between Nixon and Edgar Kaiser worked. In the ensuing years, patients got less and less care."

> Reporter (v.o.):
> "Bigger logs-in at the nearby public hospital and less quality medical care..."

> Man waiting at emergency:
> I've been here for 18 hours...

> Reporter (off):
> 18 hours?

> Man waiting at emergency:
> Yes. 7 this morning...

> Reporter (v.o.):
> "What looks cramped and unsightly can also be dangerous..."

> Moore (v.o.):
> "While the insurance companies became wealthy, the system was broken."

> TV Reporter:
> 37 million Americans are without protection against catastrophic illness.

>Reporter (off):
>"The losers are the poor, who may now postpone urgently needed health care, until it's too late."

>Moore (v.o.):
>"This went on for years, until (this) man rode into town…"

Moore inserts pictures of ex-President Bill Clinton as a child, pony back riding.

>Moore (v.o.):
>"…Bringing with him his little lady…"

The image cuts to black in rhythmic funk time with the Staples Singers' 'I'll Take You There' (hence the reference to "little lady"), and Moore then starts admitting, publicly, his crush for Hillary R. Clinton by showing black and white stills of her in different pseudo-romantic moments.

>Moore (v.o.):
>"Sassy. Smart. Sexy. Some men couldn't handle it…"

To illustrate what type of men could not handle Hillary's grace and intelligence, Moore cuts in a shot of Newt Gingrich, a well-known Republican filibuster, also known for his hypocrisy and marital infidelity. Then we see footage of Clinton announcing a restructuring of health care under Ms. Clinton's guidance; a plan which miserably failed because of lobbying and "undemocratic" forces in Washington.

>President Bill Clinton:
>Today I am announcing the formation of the "President's Task Force on National Health Reform," chaired by the First Lady, Hillary Rodham Clinton.

Moore goes on to a series of clips of Hillary pushing health care reform on America with all her might. There is also great footage of Bob Dole criticizing President Clinton for putting health care in the hands of "his wife," and a heated debate between Representative Dick Armey, a Republican from Texas, and Hillary, in which she compares him to Dr. Kevorkian, the controversial right-to-die activist (and star of an episode from *TV Nation*). The sequence culminates with Clinton driving Washington insane. It seemed like, besides Ted Kennedy and his circle, no one else in America was quite ready to accept the idea of a state-control health care plan, and the debate was buried afterwards under other less relevant files. What Moore dwells on is the fact that, much like everything else in their culture, Americans have been scared into believing that universal health care amounts to dictatorial socialism. The Republicans are obviously behind this campaign of fear, and they got away with it for over 50 years, until Obama rode into town in 2008.

In *Sicko*, Moore shows how the American Medical Association used the voice and the image of then actor Ronald Reagan to produce propaganda against socialized medicine. We hear an excerpt from a record where Reagan tells the listener that socialized medicine is an infringement to personal freedom. There is footage of Americans burning effigies of Clinton and little by little Moore tells us that she got pushed out of the way by corporate interests, leading her into trivial photo-ops for the remaining years of her husband's presidency. Just around that time the U.S. slipped to number 37 in the World Health Organization's ranking, just slightly ahead of Slovenia, an ex-Soviet satellite. Moore inserts here an Eastern European comedy show where a poor man is having his legs sawed off by a team of incompetent doctors – combined with footage of the obscene profits of HMOs and disgusting bonuses handed-out to its CEOs, buying the Unites States Congress through the forces of lobbying, even rewarding Hillary Clinton herself with P.A.C. money.

From then on, the film tells us, the entire health care industry was put into the hands of corporations, insurance companies and pharmaceutical companies. These criminals were paying politicians to pass laws in their favor, as if such a thing was consistent with constitutional laws.

Mother...lovers

Moore picks on one of the main architects of the health reform debacle of the 1990s, Congressional aide Billy Tauzin. This one used the lowest common denominator to sidetrack public support of a reform of health care: accusing Democrats of not loving their mothers as much as Republicans did.[112] In front of a carefully-placed group of senior citizens, with a gigantic banner saying "Keeping Our Promise to

---

[112] This certainly recalls the absurd statements made by the so-called Tea Party while Obama was trying to pass his health care reform in the first incredible year of his presidency. Major hardcore right-wingers like Sarah Palin and Michele Bachmann were then trying to scare Americans out of Obama's health care reform by stating that, if it went through, there would be "death panels" and doctors around the U.S. would be allowed to "pull the plug on grandma..."(i.e. because of a legalized euthanasia program).

Seniors," and set to a variation on Pachelbel's 'Canon' on the soundtrack, we see W. signing a "historic" piece of legislation in favor of lobbying forces in Washington: the Medicare Prescription Drug Improvement and Modernization Act of 2003; which basically forced elderly American citizens to pay more for their medication in the long run. Pharmaceutical and private health insurance companies were buying out politicians in order to pass a bill which only served them, not their mothers at all. According to Moore, there were still 2/3 of senior citizens who had to pay over $2000 a year for their medication. Once again, like he had done in previous films, he ends the first section of this film by connecting the dots for the viewer. He explains that 14 legislators of the aforementioned bill went on to work for the health care industry after the bill was passed, including Billy Tauzin, "the man with the golden ticket," who winded-up CEO of Pharma for 2 million dollars a year.

Moore's cynicism regarding the American system finally leads him to look elsewhere for examples of successfully implanted universal health care. The first place he visits is a familiar one to Moore fans everywhere. He goes to the country to which he opposed American madness to, in both *Canadian Bacon* and *Bowling for Columbine*.

Looking at You to Find Out Who I Am

As the second act of *Sicko* begins, Moore accompanies 22 year-old Adrian Campbell, a Michigan resident, to Canada to see if she can get her cervical cancer treated. In the States her HMO had told her it would not pay because she was "too young to get cervical cancer." This non-medical and unacceptable explanation has forced her to cross over to Windsor with her young daughter in order to seek much needed medical attention. Adrian managed with the help of Kyle, her "Canadian friend," to get care in Canada but not without having creating a commotion at one clinic, where Moore's camera crew was detected by the employees. This created suspicion among the clinic staff and Adrian was forced to run with her daughter. Moore inserts many excerpts of TV "news" scaring Americans regarding the Canadian system, including a clip of Poppa Bush telling his audience that socialized medicine does not work, "just ask the Canadians;" which is precisely what Moore intended to do, anyway.

First he meets with Canadian relatives of his, Bob and Estelle, who choose to buy insurance before crossing the border to meet Moore and his family. The filmmaker is befuddled by this and believes that his relatives are just "anti-American" in their views. Estelle explains that a friend of hers once concocted a $600,000 debt in Hawaii, and that they cannot afford to be without health insurance even for a day in the U.S. as Canadian citizens. After sharing a fried onion with them at the local Sears, Moore meets another Canadian man, Larry Godfrey, who had an accident playing golf in Florida. He explains to Moore that if he had to be operated in the United States it would have cost him nearly $24,000, while in Canada it costed $0.

> Moore:
> I'm wondering: why do you expect your fellow Canadians who do not have *your* problem why should their tax dollars have to pay for a problem *you* have?
>
> Larry:
> Because we would do the same for them. It's just the way it's always been, and that's the way we hope that I will always be.
>
> Moore:
> Yeah, but if just had to pay for your problem, and do not pay for anybody else's problem… "Just take care of yourself."
>
> Larry:
> There are lots of people who are not in a position to do that, and somebody has to look after them.
>
> Moore:
> Are you, like, a member of the Socialist Party here?
>
> Larry:
> No, no.
>
> Moore:
> Green Party?
>
> Larry:
> No. Well, actually, I'm a member of the Conservative Party. Is that bad?
>
> Moore:
> Well, it's just a little confusing.
>
> Larry:
> Well, it shouldn't be. I think that where medical matters are concerned it would not matter in Canada what political party you're affiliated with, if any.

Moore:
But to us, as we look across the river here, you know, why don't you think we believe that? What's wrong on this issue with us?

Larry:
I guess the powers-that-be do not share our beliefs that health care ought to be universal. I mean, Canadians did not until we met up with a guy named Tommy Douglas who changed pretty much everyone's mind…uh…

Moore:
One guy?

Larry:
One guy, yeah. One guy did it.

Moore:
Can he come over and visit us?

Larry:
He's dead, unfortunately. In fact, he's just most recently been revered as "Canada's singular most important person."

Moore:
You mean in your history, in your whole history?

Larry:
In our whole history.

Moore:
More than your Prime Ministers?

Larry:
Yeah, even more than Wayne Gretzky.

Moore then moves along to London, Ontario, a place he has already been to in *Bowling for Columbine,* and encounters a man who cut his fingers and had to have an implant like Rick in the first minutes of the film. One doctor explains that a total of four doctors took care of this man's surgery. He tells Moore that he is glad he works in a system that does not refuse patients on the basis of financial concerns. Invoking class inequity, Moore tells his viewers that "It seems like nothing we were told about the Canadian system was true. Maybe I was just in the wrong part of town. So I went across the city to a crowded hospital waiting room." There he interviews patients who explain they have been waiting 20 minutes up to an hour in the emergency ward, that their treatment did not have to be "pre-approved," and that they could choose their own doctor if they want to (contrary to Republican propaganda in the U.S.). Moore explains in voice-over that, as it turns out, Canadians live three years longer than Americans, and that this data is not hard to believe when you meet Americans like Eric, a man obsessed with The Beatles and who dislocated his arm crossing Abbey Road on his hands.

Friends took Eric to the hospital in London where he only had to pay the equivalent of 10 dollars for drugs. This is for Moore the occasion to move onto Britain to find out how a hospital stay can be free and how drugs can be so cheap (i.e. in a capitalist country not that far off from his own). At a London hospital, he is told that drugs are almost always free and that no financial transaction is ever made in the context of medical care. Moore seems amazed that a state-run hospital can work so beautifully for British people and even for their visitors. One woman who is about to give birth tells him that she gets a year's pay for her maternity leave, something unimaginable in America. When he intercepts a couple with their new-born baby, asking such silly questions as: "How much did you have to pay for this baby?," they literally make fun of him. Moore finally discovers a cashier in one hospital hallway which turned out to be giving out money to cover a patient's transportation fees, and this is all done in accordance with National Health Services regulations. In fact, it is institutionalized and well interiorized by all British citizens, old stock and immigrant alike.

Later on, an American woman living in Britain tells him that the general American assumption regarding socialized medicine is one of a communist nightmare. Moore uses this as an opportunity to insert a clip from a Socialist Realist movie from the Stalin era, where we see actors portraying peasants who sing the joys of harvesting and collectivization. He also makes links with America and its share of socialized services: firefighters, teachers, postal services and libraries (but still not a socialized health care). As Moore stands in front of a marble bust of Karl Marx in Highgate Cemetery, there is a sound bridge to an interview with a long serving Member of Parliament and a central figure of the Left in England, Mr. Tony Benn.

Moore (off):
When did this whole idea that every British citizen should have a right to health care?

Tony Benn:
Well, if you go back, it all began with democracy, before we had the vote [*on universal health care*], all the power was in the hands of rich people. If you had money, you could get health care, education, look after yourself when you are old... And what democracy did was to give the poor the vote, and it moved power from the market place to the polling station, from the wallet to the ballot. And what people said was very simple. It said: in the 1930s we had mass unemployment but we did not have unemployment during the war. If you can have full employment killing Germans, why can't we have full employment by building hospitals, building schools, recruiting nurses, recruiting teachers (...) *If you could find money to kill people, you can find money to help people.*

Then he reads a historical document that marked the beginning of NHS in Britain.

Tony Benn:
This certainly flipped this issue, very very straightforward...

Moore (off):
What year was this?

Tony Benn:
1948. *"Your new national health service begins on the 5th of July. What is it and how do you get it? It will provide you with all medical, dental and nursing care. Everyone, rich or poor, man, woman or child can use it, or any part of it. There are no charges, except for a few special items. There are no insurance qualifications, but it is not a charity. You are paying for it mainly as tax payers, and it will relieve your money worries in time of illness."* Now, somehow a few words summed the whole thing up...

Over a series of stock footage from the Blitzkrieg, Moore reflects in voice-over about these "socialist practices" in Britain.

Moore (v.o.):
"I was amazed when he said that all of this started in 1948. The British had just come out of a devastating experience through WWII. The country was destroyed and nearly bankrupted. They had nothing. In an 8 month-period, over 42,000 civilians lost their lives. What we went through in 2

hours on 9/11, they went through nearly every single day. Remember how we all felt after 9/11? All of us pulling together? I guess that's how they felt. And the first way they decided to all pull together after the war was to provide free medical care for everyone."

Moore inserts a shot of a statue of James Keir Hardie in Benn's office. "Keir" was the first independent Labor M.P. in the U.K.

Tony Benn:
Even Ms. Thatcher said: "The National Health Service is safe in our hands." It's as non-controversial as votes for women. Nobody can come along and say 'Why should women have the right to vote now' because people would not have it. And they would not have it in Britain. They would not accept the deterioration or destruction of their National Health Service.

Moore (off):
You mean that, even if Thatcher or [Tony] Blair had said 'I'm going to dismantle health care...

Tony Benn:
There would have been a revolution, yeah.

Street Fighting Man

The film then cuts to a montage sequence organized around the riffing rhythm of the Rolling Stones' song 'Street Fighting Man', the powerful an unintentional anthem of the '68 movement. We hear reports about how Brits are healthier and live longer than Americans. A document is excerpted where we learn that hypertension, heart diseases, strokes, lung diseases and cancer are all more prominent in Americans than in Brits. As the classic Stones song fades out, Moore wonders what the financial effects of state-control health care on British doctors are, something which leads to an interview with a general practitioner. This one too explains to Moore that he would not want to work in a system which does not allow medical attention and care for poor people. This doctor goes on to show Moore that he is not suffering financially because of a nationalized health care. On the contrary, he earns close to $200,000 a year, lives in a million dollar home, drives an Audi, and can even afford luxuries and traveling many times a year; which seems to be enough for him and his wife. There is also the revelation that doctors are paid bonuses when they convince patients to stop smoking, a novel idea which surely has catch onto the rest of the world. After this interview, Moore cuts back in the editing to Tony Benn, who lays it out better than anybody else in the film.

Tony Benn:
I think democracy is the most revolutionary thing in the world. Far more revolutionary than socialist ideas or anybody else's idea. If you have power, you use it to meet the needs of your community. And this idea of 'choice', which Capital talks about all the time, that you need 'choice', well choice depends on the freedom to choose, and if you're shackled with debts you do not have the freedom to choose.

Moore:
It seems like it benefits the system if the average working person is shackled with debts…

Tony Benn:
People in debt become hopeless, and hopeless people do not vote. So they will say 'Everyone should vote', but I think if the poor in Britain or the United States turned out and voted for people who represented their interests, there would be a real democratic revolution. So they do not want it to happen, so they keep people hopeless and pessimistic. I think there are two ways in which people are controlled. First of all, frighten people, and secondly demoralize them. An educated, healthy and confident nation is harder to govern. And I think there's an element in the thinking of some people, we don't want people to be educated, healthy and confident, because they would get out of control. The top 1% of the world's population owns 80% of the world's wealth. It's incredible that people put up with it. But, they're poor, they're demoralized, they're frightened, and therefore they think perhaps that the safest thing to do is to take orders and hope for the best.

Hoping For the Best

Right after these insights into the trappings of modern political systems and the true meaning of democracy, Moore takes us into a sequence which satirizes classical documentary form entitled "Your American Life." In voice-over he rants about the fact that America has the highest infant mortality rate in the western world. A baby born in El Salvador has better chances of surviving than a baby born in Detroit, Michigan, he says. These statistics segue into the state of education in America, as a way for Moore to follow on human development potential. "65% of young American adults can't find Great Britain on a map," he throws in the pot of statistics. Going to college, he also says, is a decision that can put you into debts for the rest of your life, before you even started working (if work you can find). He inserts clips of interviews with young people who contracted high debts by going to college through rapid excerpts of footage from various eclectic sources. It is a clever montage sequence which pays tribute to Moore's ability with rhythm in film editing. In it we are told that the type of employee corporations are looking for has to be indebted because she or he will not cause any trouble. Moore rubs it in even more when he explains that, along with having to pay for health insurance, young workers are in a "big squeeze," domesticated and inoffensive, well-groomed for the dominating and daunting tasks of the corporate world.

In the background, we can almost smell the failure of unionization, something which is always implicit in his film work. There is also footage from factory workers, torture chambers and McCarthy-era B flicks of coercion and depravity. As he did in his previous films and TV series, Moore proposes the idea that a lack of job quality and having to work many jobs just to pay the bills is detrimental to a nation's mental health. This is a return to familiar themes from *Roger & Me*, *The Big One*, *TV Nation*, *The Awful Truth* and *Bowling for Columbine*.

Also in conceptual continuity with *Fahrenheit 9/11*, he shows us footage from a Town Hall meeting where President Bush "interacts" with a middle-age woman on a stage.

Woman:
I work 3 jobs and I feel like I contribute…

Bush:
You work 3 jobs?

Woman:
3 jobs, yes.

Bush:
Uniquely American, isn't it? I mean, that's fantastic that you're doing that…Get any sleep? [*Laughs*]

Following on Bush's insensitivity, Moore mixes in his own voice-over, which subsequently leads to a montage of different TV ads for tranquilizers and sleeping pills. This relates to many other themes found in his work, especially in *Bowling for Columbine*, where individuals are reduced to the mere state of drugged-out and violent automatons.

>Moore (v.o.):
"And if you're not getting enough sleep, take pharmaceuticals!"

>TV Ad #1 (off):
"You're tired all the time...you may feel sad, hopeless..."

>TV Ad #2 (off):
"If you suffer from excessive worry..."

>TV Ad#3 (off):
"...you could be suffering from generalized anxiety disorder..."

>TV Ad #4 (off):
"It could be adult ADD..."

>TV Ad #5 (off):
"Talk to your doctor..."

>TV Ad #6 (off):
"Ask your doctor..."

>TV Ad #7 (off):
"Ask your doctor..."

>TV Ad #8 (off):
"Ask your doctor..."

>Moore (v.o.):
"Yes, ask your doctor and ask him for more drugs! That should keep you pretty doped up until it's time to retire... Did I say 'retire'? Well, if you do make it to 80, I'm sure your pension will still be there, unlike the employees for (these) companies, who will never see a pension. But do not worry, I'm sure our kids will take care of us, considering the great life we've given them...Oh, and remember, let's defeat the terrorists *over there*, so we don't have to fight them *here*..."

This lesson in editorial manipulation of film leads to clippings from newspaper article announcing more pension freezes, as well as to footage from old movies where characters are caught up in concentration camp conditions. There is again a tonal shift when Moore is telling in voice-over the story of Darnell Keyes, a woman who had a policy with Kaiser Permanente, the biggest HMO in the United States. Her 18 month-old daughter Mychelle developed a fever of 104 degrees and had to be taken to South Central Hospital in Los Angeles. After checking with Kaiser the hospital told Darnell that it could not proceed with crucial testing and treatment. She had to take her daughter to an "in-network Kaiser-owned hospital," obviously to allow them to capitalize on Mychelle's condition. At South Central, her daughter got worst and even had a seizure. When the mother begged with doctors to ignore Kaiser's decision and operate on her child, she was considered a threat and escorted out of the hospital by security. She eventually managed to bring her daughter to the Kaiser hospital, where, because of time lapse, she went into cardiac arrest and eventually died in her mother's arms.

To sum it all up, a mother who *had* health insurance lost her daughter because of her bad health insurance policy, period.

Americans in Paris

At this point in the film the viewer starts wondering if there is any hope for Americans. Just as we are about to throw in the towel, Moore tells us about Carina, a graduate of Michigan Sate University and her young daughter, Zoe, who got a real nasty throat infection and developed a fever one night. She also had to be taken to the emergency. There, a team of doctors did everything to save her and she got much better, for no cost at all. The reason for this is that Carina and Zoe were actually living in France. Moore delays this information in the editing to mess with the American mind and to make everybody else even more depressed about American health care. The transition between South Central L.A. and Paris is done retroactively, as an ironic statement on the perception of the Other, "over there," i.e. across the Atlantic. Like he has done many times before, Moore plays with nasty stereotypes when dealing with the French, reducing them to their wine, their cigarettes, their fatty foods, and other clichés of French lifestyle; but this time he has something else in mind. It would seem like the days of *TV Nation*, where he was sarcastically proposing to bomb the French in order to show them good manners, are over.

Like Canadians and Brits, French people live longer and better than Americans. Moore presents another American man who had cancer and received the best treatment in France – he got paid vacation (a joint venture between employer and government, assuming the cost of treatment), and he was allowed time and resources to take care of himself. Moore also meets with the Head of Obstetrics at St. Antoine Hospital, who says that he is not in a position to make a judgment regarding the American health care system. America is a "great place," and that Americans are "great people," but adding that he prefers to be in France. In typical Mid-West, tongue-in-cheek humor, Moore says in voice-over that he cannot stand this doctor's "anti-Americanism" and instead joins a group of Americans living in France over supper. This varied group of women and men indicates that everything Moore was told about the French health care system is true. It actually considers people like patients, not clients, and put them at the center of the apparatus, which is basically a lesson in humanism to Americans.

This discussion over a meal leads to a section about S.O.S. Médecins, a service offered by the French government for people who are sick and cannot go to the hospital. Moore meets this time with Dr. Philippe Leminez, a house call doctor. He also seems amazed at this service where a doctor actually comes at your home to care for you, something inconceivable in the United States, except for extremely rich people like Warren Buffet. This system was created decades ago by Dr. Marcel Lascar, a professional who thought it was appalling that one could have a plumber doing home service 24/7 but not a doctor. Moore relies again on a musical montage set to 'L'Amour est bleu' sang by Vicky Leandros, which he lays over the sequence, and there is even a moment of *mise en scène* when Dr. Leminez and Moore are driving through town together or again giving each other a high-five coming out from a patient's home.

Moore returns to the supper with Americans in the editing, as a form of synthesis of all that was previously shown. He seems to be on to something, which will eventually be reiterated in the resolution: the French have more socialist values and this reflects in how society is organized and how individuals are living in a state of interrelationships and interdependency. In America, one of the main values is individualism. It is a much tougher country to live and to survive in than France or Canada. Anyone who has traveled to a city like New York has seen how tough you need to be to make it there. The fact is that the French, like the Canadian and British people, believe that public services should not be in the hands of private companies. For instance, accessible daycare is a fundamental right in today's world, because a woman has the right to have both children and a career if she wishes to. Since America is a rugged and macho culture based on competition and exclusion, public policies are regulated to reflect this intrinsic and institutionalized sexism: if a woman wants to have children, she will have to pay the high price for it. Therefore it is a vicious cycle of despair when a woman cannot find a job because she cannot afford daycare. It keeps those who have good, secure and high-paying jobs at the top of the game, able to afford what should technically be free or at least at a reasonable cost for everybody.

The supper with the Americans scene concludes with one of the funniest moments in the film. Moore is being told of all the benefits French citizens are allowed to have and is in total disbelief. We get a glimpse of the old Moore, at the time of *TV Nation* and *The Big One*, when he was still full of zest and wonderment. When he is told that French people get free health care, $1 a day daycare and educational services, that workers get minimum 5 weeks paid vacations (even for part-time workers), and that you are paid for your honeymoon, or when you move, or again, when you just gave birth and someone from the government comes to your house and does your laundry for you, he is shocked and blocks his ears out singing over his interviewees' comments, like a spoiled child who does not want to hear about eating his vegetables.

Next thing we know, Moore has "intruded" a French home where a government employee is assisting a middle-class working mom. She returns a question to Moore which must frustrate most American viewers of the film.

French Mom:
You do not have any associations, nothing like that?

Moore:
No. *Nobody* from the government *comes to your home* in America and does your laundry for you, if you're a new mother.

French Mom:
It's difficult…

Moore:
Yeah.

The sequence ends with Moore wiping the mouth of the infant she was holding with a little tissue and an American woman around the supper table telling Moore that she feels "guilty" for getting in France what her parents worked their whole life for and couldn't get in America. It is a very touching scene which explains in a simple way the real problem with America and its social policies. Another American woman across the table sums it up for Moore. As an exile, she clearly sees what is wrong with the dynamics of the so-called American democracy.

American Woman:
One of the things that keep everything running here is that the government is afraid of people, they're afraid of protest, they're afraid of reactions from the people. For as in the States people are afraid of the government, they're afraid of acting up, they're afraid of protesting, they're afraid of getting out. In France that's what people do.

Moore then illustrates this statement by his compatriot in exile by showing us again a montage sequence set to Nana Mouskouri's 'C'est bon la vie' (Simon & Garfunkel's *59th Street Bridge Song - Feelin' Groovy*). It includes footage from street protests by students and workers in France during the 2000s. He then makes the leap to asking how the French can afford all of these free public services and then concludes that they must be "drowning in taxes," a misconception that will subsequently be negated by the visit to a middle-class couple living comfortably. The links between social policies and quality of life are extremely clear in this segment, although the woman in the couple complains that food, especially fresh food, like fish or vegetables, is expensive and constitutes a financial burden on the household; which is something that everyone can notice about the globalization of essential markets today (where Coca-Cola and Monsanto are in total control). No debts and possessing two cars, as well as a 300 euros mortgage, this couple is even able to travel around the world every year. She shows Moore an art collection and sand gathered from some of the best beaches in the world and Moore, the snoop, even manages to get into these peoples' refrigerator and personal belongings to prove a point to his American audience.

Like the juke box from a French 1960's diner, the filmmaker concludes his holiday to Paris with the Birkin/Gainsbourg raunchy duo 'Je t'aime, moi non plus' and his voice-over coalescing on the soundtrack. We see him perambulating around town and the editing recreates his point of view, with shots of French citizens relaxing and young couples everywhere, kissing and enjoying life.

Moore (v.o.):
"After seeing all this, I began to wonder. Was there a reason that our government and our media want us to hate the French? Are they worried that we might *like* the French? Or like their *ways* of doing things? It was enough to make me wanna put away my Freedom Fries…"

Meanwhile, Back at Home

In his parallel editing scheme, Moore returns to America. He tells his viewers that in his own country hospitals found a way to deal with those who do not have any health insurance. The differences between Paris streets and American streets in the editing are truly shocking. Moore shows us homeless people and badly kept urban neighborhoods. At the Union Rescue Mission in downtown Los Angeles, we are told about the story of Carol, an elderly woman who was dropped on the curb by a taxi cab when she could not pay her hospital bill. Moore presents a surveillance camera tape which reveals how Carol was abandoned on the sidewalk confused and shoeless, by a system which ostracizes its most needy citizens. In this author's opinion, the moment with Carol is probably one of the most touching of Moore's entire career. We are clearly shown how an individual can be thrown to the street like dog waste, without any sense of decency or dignity for human life. Staff members from the Mission explain how Kaiser Permanente and their private hospital staff had decided to rip her identification bracelet before dropping her off, so that the origins of the crime would not be traced. They also tell Moore that other patients are dropped off regularly with IVs still lodged in their arms.

Moore then inserts an interview with James Lott, Vice President of the Hospital Association of Southern California who explains that compassion is not a choice in the private system.

> James Lott:
> The options are very few. We either open the front door and let them [*patients unable to pay*] out, which is not the humane thing to do, and that we do not want to do. Or we try to find some place for them to go. And right now, skid row is the best bet in town.

The tragedy of *Sicko* unravels fully when Moore and his crew follow another woman, seemingly Native American, who was left on the curb because she also could not pay her hospital bill. This drop happened the day they were shooting at the Mission and all the personnel there seem truly affected by it. We see in this scene dedicated staffers trying to help her, and any viewer with a heart can feel the inhumanity of such a system, where infants, women and senior citizens are as worthless as all the garbage thrown on the side by industry and commerce. When a man working there informs us that this patient has broken ribs and collar bone, sadness turns to outrage in the audience. Tears turn into frowning.

Moore (v.o.):
"May I take a minute to ask a question that has been on my mind? Who are we? Is this what we've become: a nation that dumps its own citizens like so much garbage on the side of the curb because they can't pay their hospital bill? I always thought and believe to this day that we're a good and generous people; people with a good heart and a good soul; neighbors who are quick to lend a helping hand to anyone in their hour of need. They say that you can judge a society by how it treats those who are the worst off. But is the opposite true: that you can judge a society by how it treats its best, its heroes?"

The Last Drop

This moving sequence is the cornerstone of *Sicko*, as Moore delves now into the last section pertaining to 9/11 rescue workers. He first presents us clips which show how the Bush administration and ex-Mayor Giuliani *talked* about the 9/11 firefighters, police and rescue workers, describing them as being heroes; but then he cuts to a small town bar five years later where a fundraiser for 9/11 rescue workers is being held (and where people are having raffles for one dollar a piece...). Outside in front of the bar three rescue workers explain that their work at Ground Zero made them sick, stuck perhaps for life with respiratory illnesses and overwhelming nightmares they cannot be treated for in the U.S. In voice-over the filmmaker explains that these heroes did not get the treatment they deserved because they were not "official city employees," or not on the payroll, or not paying union dues, and that the government had decided to drop them from coverage.

We are then introduced to John Graham, a volunteer from New Jersey who suffers from pulmonary fibrosis and who was denied benefits for his heroism. Earlier he had explained to Moore that he has to sleep in a chair since laying down stops him from breathing. Sitting at his kitchen table, he tells Moore that he gets the feeling that the public officials responsible for the 9/11 compensation fund are "waiting for him to die." This sounds strangely familiar in light of Moore's earlier work. We need only to remember the 'Funeral at an HOM' skit from *The Awful Truth* to know that things have not changed in America in the last two decades. Then we are presented with the case of William Mayr, a New Jersey firefighter who was one of the rescue workers at Ground Zero and who cannot stop grinding his teeth as a result of the trauma of having to dig up bodies and body parts from the WTC site. The 50 million dollar fund which was supposed to help the 9/11 rescue workers was sabotaged, according to Moore. He shows us a press conference of then NY Governor George Pataki explaining the long procedures to get help when you are an "unofficial" rescue worker, making it virtually impossible to get some assistance through the red tape of the so-called fund.

Right after this clip, Moore introduces a third rescue worker, Reggie Cervantes, a woman who got seriously ill from the toxic materials and substances she breathed in at Ground Zero. Too sick to work and with no income, she moved with her two kids out of the city. Meanwhile, Moore tells us that not everyone was ignored by the U.S. government as far as health is concerned: like the prisoners held at Guantanamo Prison, where alleged terrorist trainers, bomb makers, assistants to bin Laden, etc. apparently get better treatment than most 9/11 heroes. How can this be possible, that terrorists get better treatment than American citizens and taxpayers?

In another one of his big-time capers, Moore goes to Miami and rents a couple of boats where he leaves in direction of Guantanamo Bay, Cuba, with the three rescue workers, Donna Smith, as well as anyone else he could find who needed medical attention but could not get it in the U.S. on that day. It is perhaps the most controversial aspect of the film analyzed here, and we certainly have to wonder why Moore taking a bunch of sick Americans to Cuba can be so controversial after all, at least from a Canadian perspective. In this author's country, it is a well known and accepted fact that the American embargo against the Castro regime is as phony as the wars in Iraq and Afghanistan were/are. It has been going on since the Cuban Missile Crisis of 1962; a crisis initiated and entertained for all these years by the American Congress. As allies to the United States, Canada has decided to not participate in this form of economic terrorism practiced by the U.S. government on Cuba and has kept a close relationship to the large Caribbean island since the Revolution. As it is presented in *Sicko*, Cuba looks like a more civilized and humane society because it has understood that universal health care and education are fundamental rights for every citizen.

In this scene, we see Moore standing on the front of a small ship with a bullhorn. From the edges of the Caribbean Sea he is calling to the guards serving at U.S. Naval Base at Gitmo. This scene comes only after he made sure to show us a specially-made "government warning" stating that: "Homeland Security laws of the United States of American prohibit the filmmakers from revealing how they got to their destination." There is also a moment of definite *mise en scène* when Moore and his sick travelers all stand in front of the Guantanamo Prison sign, looking up at it as if it was some sort of shrine. Since they are in a place where they are not supposed to be, in a communist country, Moore controls the situation like a fiction film director would, and his guests/actors are playing along with him in what looks like a spontaneous re-enactment.

> Moore:
> Permission to enter! I have three 9/11 rescue workers! They need some medical attention! [*He takes a bullhorn.*] THESE ARE 9/11 RESCUE WORKERS. THEY JUST WANT SOME MEDICAL ATTENTION. THE SAME KIND THAT AL-QAEDA IS GETTING. THEY DO NOT WANT ANYMORE THAN YOU GIVE THE EVIL-DOERS, JUST THE SAME.

Moore and the three American heroes stand there, waiting for an answer from the Gitmo base.

> Moore (v.o.):
> "No one in the guard tower was responding, and then suddenly we heard a siren, and we figured that it was time to get out of here... But what was I suppose to do with all these sick people and no one to help them? I mean, here we were, stuck in some god-forsaken third world country, and communist, no less. When I was a kid, these people wanted to kill us! What was I supposed to do?"

In the following twist, Moore and the rescue workers are all near Havana. They are told by a group of young denizens that every neighborhood in Cuba has at least a doctor, a hospital and a pharmacy. As an American, Moore pretends like this does not impress him, but we know it is not the case.

> Moore (v.o.):
> "OK, OK, I know what you're thinking: Cuba is where Lucifer lives..."

In the editing is inserted a slow-motion head shot of old Castro in the middle of a speech, with some devilish gargles overdubbed on the soundtrack sounding like *The Exorcist*, and then a map of Cuba catching on fire.

> Moore (v.o.):
> "...The worst place on Earth. The most evil nation ever created. How do we know that? Cause' that's what we were told for over 45 years..."

There is then an insert of President John F. Kennedy addressing the nation on TV about the Cuban Missile Crisis back in 1962.

> JFK:
> A series of offensive missile sites can be none other than to provide a nuclear strike capability against the Western hemisphere.

We see quick shots of anti-Castro demonstrations in the United States and a "speech" by Chicken Little himself: George W. Bush.

> George W. Bush:
> I'm not going to yield until Fidel Castro allows freedom on the island. Uh, that, ah, uh, see, you can count on it! Put it in the bank!

The movie takes up pace again and thanks to a well-defined editing scheme allows for the filmmakers to expand on these ideas that are so well-embedded in America regarding Cuban socialism. As a Canadian viewer, it makes no sense that a filmmaker would have to go to these lengths to prove that Castro and Cuba are no longer a threat to the United States. If Americans had been allowed to go to Cuba in the last 50 years, it would make no sense for them either.

> Moore (v.o.):
> "It seems like what really bugged us about Castro is that he overthrew a dictator that we liked [*Batista*], and replaced him with a dictator we did not like: himself! And so now, after all these years, the one thing that Cubans do have is free universal health care. They'd become known around the world as having, not only one of the best health care systems, but as being one of the most generous countries in providing doctors and medical equipment to Third World countries. In the U.S., health care cost runs nearly $6,000 per person. But in Cuba, they spend only $251. And yet, the Cubans are allowed to have a lower infant mortality rate than in the United States and a longer average life-span than in the United States...They believe in preventative medicine and it seems like there's a doctor on every block. Their only sin, when it comes to health care, seems to be that they don't do it for *profit*..."

Muchos Gracias, Señor Moore

The follow-up to these great statements about the lies of the Cold War is Moore taking his three American heroes to a pharmacy where they acquire the same drugs than in the U.S. but at 1/10 of the price. Reggie Cervantes is appalled at the cost of inhalers and pills in Cuba, but in a good, cathartic way. Like Lila Lipscomb, she cries when she suddenly realizes that her patriotism is in vain, since her Republican government does not care about her (or about anyone else, for that matter). Later on at the Havana hospital doctors, nurses and staff take great care of these American heroes, whom they call "brothers and sisters." No bureaucracy, no unnecessary questions asked, no quagmire games about pre-existing conditions, just pure care with the main objective to cure, as it should be.

It is no doubt the final irony of *Sicko* that Americans have to find genuine and unconditional care in a country that has been so demonized by their leaders and their media for half a century. The final scenes in Cuba with the 9/11 rescue workers are some of the most touching ever put on film, in any documentary throughout cinema's history. It is no doubt an unusual American look at Cuban policies, but it is even more important than this, insofar as it is a human, lucid and open look at the Other, and how commonalities are more important than differences in this world.

But for extreme leftists in the audience the apotheosis of *Sicko* is the insertion of a short clip from an interview he did with Aleida Guevara, Che's daughter, who, like her father, is a doctor. It finally links Moore's endeavor with an ideological tradition which found its zenith in the 1960s, with human and civil rights, and with the struggle for decolonization. In the end, Moore explains that Reggie was diagnosed with a series of pulmonary and bronchial problems. Cuban doctors gave her a treatment plan to follow back home, "along with some of those 5 cent-inhalers." William received treatment for his back and had his entire front teeth replaced. John also received treatment and felt better than he had in years. As for Donna, the Cuban doctors properly diagnosed her cancer and eliminated many unnecessary pills American doctors had prescribed back home (in collusion with pharmaceutical companies). The last moment spent in Cuba is at a Havana firehouse. There, the three 9/11 rescue workers are finally received as they should be: as heroes, part of an international family, not as enemies in a convenient and "fictitious" imperialist war, fueled by a bunch of stupid white men.

"Me" versus "We"

For a film about health care, *Sicko* concludes on an unusual note. Moore first tells us that he sent an anonymous $12,000 check to JimK, one of the webmasters of Moore Watch, an anti-Michael Moore website that has been bashing him relentlessly since *Fahrenheit 9/11*. The filmmaker gave this virtual nemesis money to pay for his wife's operation because the latter could not afford to pay for it and keep his website running at the same time. Somehow the reality of having to pay so much for his wife's operation did not influence JimK into reconsidering his own political stance; never mind reassessing the validity of Moore's position on issues such as health care. It did just the opposite and propelled the website to greater heights, inducing it with ever more first-level readings of Moore's every word or move. Somehow this charity from Moore was answered with more venom. But this kind of small time nitpicking has now become a standard on the Internet. In the virtual/public world, everyone can pretend to be a scholar, a journalist, or even an "expert" on something, especially film. Every blogger or "tweet" can share an opinion and pass it as an argument. It is soft relativism at its most desperate and most despairing. It is the "illusion of a life lived" and an armchair-view of the world, disembodied from concrete experience and totally disconnected from the facts. But, as Reagan said: "Facts are a stupid thing," are they not?

The ending of *Sicko* is a plea to the American people. Moore asks them to shake-off their isolationist attitude and open up to the rest of the world. For him, if a culture makes a better wine, Americans should drink it, if a culture makes a better car, Americans should drive it, and so on. It seems like a corny ending when looked at through the prism of everything that occurred before in the film; all the pain, the suffering, the death, the sorrow and the guilt. But seen through the prism of the future, in reality, Moore is telling his home audience to cheer up and open up to the Others, something further stressed in the final credits by 'Don't Be Shy', the life affirming Cat Stevens song from *Harold & Maude* (1970). In the end, American viewers must understand that when they start thinking less about "Me" and more about "We" it will be a new and better day in America, for this is the meaning of real democracy: togetherness. In the final image we see Moore following on the French example by bringing to Capitol Hill his dirty laundry for his government to wash; for it was all that it was good for in those hawkish days that are now gone forever (we hope). It was one last "fuck you" to a sicko regime which believes that it is better to kill people than to heal them.

CAPITALISM: A LOVE STORY (2009)

It's not going to get fixed. There's going to be another crash. The commercial real estate bubble has not burst yet. That's going to burst. The credit card debt is so huge right now, it will never be repaid. That's a house of cards waiting to fall. So the crash of '08 is going to look like coming attractions. And we're in for a much, much worse time. That's how I honestly feel. But you don't want to hear that from me, do you? I mean, I'm only the guy who said that there weren't going to be weapons of mass destruction in Iraq and that we were being lied to. And I'm the guy who 20 years ago made his first film saying that General Motors was a piece of crap company that was going to slide down the hill and bring us all down with it. So don't listen to me.[113]

"Makes Me Wanna Sing 'Louie, Louie'..."

Michael Moore's most recent nonfiction film, released two years after *Sicko*, seems to have been once more right on the pulse of a nation. Perhaps some detractors will see this with cynicism, as a sign of the filmmaker's propensity to magnify social illnesses or of his opportunism and sense of self-promotion; but this would be to deliberately forget the timing of his past work. Always a step ahead on important issues, because he listens to the people around him who inspire his films, and these are meant to be seen and discussed by and with people, Moore is a sociologist with a camera and a microphone. This appeared quite clearly to a group of my students when we saw *Capitalism: A Love Story* together in a Washington D.C. cinema on a field trip during the Fall of 2009. We were amazed at the fact that what we were seeing on screen was exactly what we had seen outside of the theater during our excursion through the capital on that morning. And we were all pretty certain that everybody else who saw the film anywhere else in North America on that day felt the same way as we did. Somehow Moore managed to create some sort of osmosis between the world and the screen, much like he did during the times of *Roger & Me*, *Fahrenheit 9/11* and *Sicko*.

Capitalism: A Love Story was distributed by Paramount Vantage, the specialty film division of Paramount Pictures. Along with other extraordinary films like *Sicko*, *No Country for Old Men* (2007) and *There Will Be Blood* (2007), it was co-produced by The Weinstein

---

[113] Michael Moore interviewed by Cenk Uygur on *The Young Turks* in 2010

Company. Actually, as clever at spotting talent as they are, the Weinstein brothers, Bob and Harvey, only took Moore under their wing after the mammoth success of *Bowling for Columbine*. It is absolutely extraordinary that American film producers can support a discourse such as Michael Moore's in a context which is so rigidly controlled by a handful of distributors, usually hanging to the right. As we know, media concentration is a major enemy of democracy, and the fact that films such as *Fahrenheit 9/11*, *Sicko* and *Capitalism: A Love Story* can be financed, made and distributed for an American market only goes to show that some things might still be alright about capitalism after all, and that perhaps the establishment has not yet fully grasped the collateral implications of their own unrestricted free-market economy. Somewhere between the cracks of the major conglomerates, the Walt Disney Company, Time Warner, News Corporation and Viacom, there is a market for what Moore has to say; and even though this might play against their own image and power, it still makes money for them. In other words, they are so greedy that they are ready to cannibalize themselves (and each other). Could there be any other more perfect sign for how capitalism really works and self-destructs in the end than by allowing *a* Michael Moore to speak and reach millions on a big screen?

Like the opening credits from *The Awful Truth* and *Bowling for Columbine*, *Capitalism* opens with a warning: it should not be view if you have a heart condition. Then, we are aurally attacked by Iggy Pop's dynamite version of 'Louie Louie', with lyrics perfectly adapted for "Moore's Magnus Opus,"[114] even though this track was on a record released nearly two decades before.[115] On the image track we see a compilation of bank robberies from closed-circuit TV edited in typical Moore-style, full of rhythm and counterpoints with each edit. Content-wise it is already a commentary on the state of America in times of recession, but it is also a metaphor for things to come in the film; since many times throughout its two hour-course viewers will see robberies of another kind and on a grander scale. Then Moore establishes parallels between the respective decline of the American and Roman empires through clips from an old educational "documentary" produced by the University of Michigan. It emphasizes the idea of moral and political decay behind the magnificent facades. We are here reminded that Rome's economy was fueled by slavery (the working poor in American terms), and that there was a great disparity between rich and poor at that time as well. Moore and his team of editors are obviously having a blast cutting together shots of Roman landmarks with shots of buildings and monuments from the neatly organized heart of the

---

[114] Mary Corliss, "Michael Moore's Capitalism Goes for Broke," *Time*, September 9, 2009
[115] Iggy Pop, *American Caesar*, Virgin Records, 1993

American empire. Throughout its history, Washington architecture and urban planning has been organized as to reflect America's imperialist aspirations, and the filmmaker uses this fact to put things in an historical perspective.

This last sequence is a commentary on how the logic of contemporary capitalism resembles in almost every way the logic of old imperialist days, even if it is supposed to be compatible with so-called "democratic values." With its bread and violent games to keep the population well-behaved and subservient (in this case fast food, sports and entertainment), with its Emperor (then Dick Cheney) being above the law and ruling by decree, with its most "civilized" and sophisticated senators tolerating abuses of human rights, and with the irresponsible behavior of public officials, we can understand how Rome slowly corroded from within. The parallels between the two empires are too close for comfort. It has always been a known adage to compare them in the past, but when presented on a big screen like this we get a sense that the American empire really is on its way out, and fast. Nothing is eternal, especially when it is based on exploitation, whether it is Rome or Washington.

In fact, the references and links found within *Capitalism: A Love Story* are so well weaved together that anyone who takes time to look will realize how intelligently crafted Moore's films really are, including this one. For one thing, the fact that Iggy Pop's version of 'Louie Louie' is from a CD entitled *American Caesar* and that the second sequence of the film compares America to Rome's "splendor" is not a coincidence; just like how two different versions of 'What a Wonderful World' echoed each other at different points in *Bowling for Columbine* was not a coincidence. As to whether or not every viewer gets these cultural references is another question altogether; it can only give you as much as you bring to it in the end. Moore's films require multiple screenings to be fully appreciated as deep and complex cinema, no doubt about that; and *Capitalism*, along with *Bowling* and *Fahrenheit*, is certainly one of his most dense pictures.

Bottom Feeders

After the director's voice-over wonders over a black image. He begins with a question about how future civilizations will judge current American society: by meaningless YouTube phenomenons such as cats flushing toilets, or again, by how a system can allow for a bank to throw hard-working and humble people to the street on the basis that it "owns" their home through paper work and loans... This question leads to a home video taped by a young woman on the day her family were being evicted. We see the sheriff and his force breaking their way in the house while the whole family sits quietly on their living room couches. It feels like a modern retelling of Ford's adaptation of Steinbeck's *The Grapes of Wrath*, even though the way in which the first person video shows the police breaking in is more in line with Romero's *The Night of the Living Dead*.[116] Like *Sicko*, as it turns out, *Capitalism: A Love Story* is destined to become a true cult classic of the horror genre! Hence, when Moore's camera chooses to focus on inner city Detroit, where homes are being boarded up and citizens thrown to the street, sometimes because they only missed one payment of their mortgage, we understand that banks are the anthropophagous monsters of our age.

The film then cuts away again to a family losing their farm house in Peoria, Illinois, and whose name will be disclosed later on in the narrative. The family was told they had 30 days to move out, but when the sheriff comes the morning following the eviction notice to kick them out, in front of Moore's lens, we also understand that the bank wanted to strip away their dignity, as well as adding insult to injury.

Moore (v.o.):
"This is capitalism, a system of taking and giving; mostly taking. The only thing we didn't know was when the revolt would begin..."

The man from Peoria then says something to Moore which vindicates the catchy opening of the film.

Man from Peoria:
Everything, we've tried everything, except robbing a bank. I'm thinking of maybe doing that. Now, that's one way someone can get their money back. They did it to me. I don't know why I can't do it to them.

Following on this chilling statement, Moore decides to cut to the ramifications of a system which allows for different types of companies to profit from people becoming homeless. He zooms in on the Condo Vultures company, a self-described "bottom feeder" that specializes in "picking on corpses." Shot by a hand held camera, an agent takes us

---

[116] On September 21st 2010, Michael Moore received The John Steinbeck Award from the Steinbeck Family and Center for Steinbeck Studies. The statement from Thomas Steinbeck went as follows: "Courage is 75% of art. Michael Moore is a courageous man and a great selection for the John Steinbeck Award. My father would have loved him; my father was the Michael Moore of his time."

through a tour of a recently repossessed condominium, and later tells the filmmakers that this sort of business is not about "the killing" but about the "clean-up," making clear parallels, not only with great vultures in nature who do occupy a cleansing function, but between capitalism and a Darwinian conception of society, which defines the American philosophy today. The agent admits that "It's all about the taking right now" and contradicts himself by saying that he likes to "come in the action for the kill." Once again the contradiction is striking, simply because the man knows he entertains an unfair economic system and probably feels for the people who are repossessed, but his eyes are still gleaming with delight at the thought of making money on someone else's back. What is wrong with this picture? Are Americans united as their many anthems and slogans claim, or are they really and profoundly divided by a troubled past, an extremely shady present and a very uncertain future? This being said, if it really is the law of the jungle in the United States today, then, Condo Vultures will surely get its comeuppance one day.

"Inconceivable!"

As he did in almost all of his previous feature films, Moore returns to the 1950's conception of the "Promised Land," where every American could have its share of the pie. He includes more footage of old instructional films extolling the virtues of capitalism and free-enterprise, which finally gives way to reflections from actor and playwright Wallace Shawn. Shawn is also a friend of Moore, and he played the Canadian Prime Minister in *Canadian Bacon* (he unfortunately winded up on the cutting room floor because of studio interference). He is restituted here to explain fundamental notions of history, politics, and elementary economics. As a storyteller, Shawn uses a very effective figure of speech to describe what the free-market appears to be on the surface: a fair game of "who in the neighborhood has the best products for the best prices." But he also implies that the bottom line is different nowadays. Having bought out all the mom and pop stores in the land, conglomerates now rule over all markets and curb any attempt by small-time competition to penetrate larger ones. Today, no one is foolish enough to believe that the free-market is a competition between "little shops." The plain fact is that there is no competition, only an oligarchy.

This leads to the moving segment of Moore and his dad, Frank, visiting the lot where he had worked for 33 ½ years for AMC making spark-plugs. They are standing in front of a wasteland which used to be the center of an entire community. It is a wonderful moment where the two walk around together where GM factories used to be. These grounds once welcomed the most powerful and productive plants in the industrial world, but now it is just a pile of bent and rusty metal. The sequence is intercut with color Super-8 home footage from the same sources as *Roger & Me*. We see Moore as a boy at Christmas receiving a brand new baseball glove and he tells us in his familiar voice-over: "Boy, if this was capitalism, we wanted more of it!" This has become part of his style, and he obviously uses these archival sources to personalize his films. In fact, this sequence has a threefold purpose in *Capitalism*: it puts into historical perspective the American economy of today, it creates an impression for the viewer, and it is a stamp from the director on his film, bonding with his audience. The walk with his father allows in fact for an opening of the inquiry into America's duality: a land filled with good hard working people and a military-industrial complex defending an imperialist agenda, perpetrator of cruel and senseless acts of aggression and violence on its own people and almost everywhere in the world.

In this same sequence, Moore explains that during these post-war years, the quintessence of his dad's working days, the rich had to pay a tax rate of 90%, and that their money was used to develop infrastructures such as the Eisenhower interstate highway system. Everyone, owners and workers alike, was working for a common cause back then, he says, to make America productive and prosperous as a nation; a nation which had just won the war against fascism, granted, but which also "imported" some of the head Nazis after the war to be part of American military, government and corporations. In fact, there are theories outside of the film which corroborate some of its main contentions. It has been proven elsewhere that the model for contemporary capitalism and corporatism is the same as the one that was set in place by the Third Reich before and during WWII. Some went as far as to propose that "the Nazis really won the war" in the end, because their values can be found at the core of governmental and corporate policies, in America and elsewhere in the world today.[117]

With Beethoven's *9th Symphony* on the soundtrack, Moore expands on this golden age of middle-class culture, where job security was guaranteed and where even a middle income family could afford a house, a car and a vacation once a year. Germany and Japan's industrial structures were destroyed during the war, and thus no one else in the industrial world could compete with the might of America during its Baby Boom period. This relatively long montage sequence intercuts visual and archival footage from B-flicks, TV shows, advertising and instructional films. It is Moore at his post-modern best, like we have

---

[117] Noam Chomsky interviewed by David Barsamian, *Secrets, Lies and Democracy*, Tucson: Odonian Press, 1994, p.87-90

seen in *Roger*, *Bowling*, and *Fahrenheit*, three bona fide masterpieces of nonfiction filmmaking, as well as three incredibly successful films from a box-office point of view. While we see assembly lines, suburban homes, cars, shopping and leisure activities, baseball and a monkey going wild, Moore admits that the good life of yesteryears was only possible through the exploitation of others, at home and abroad, and that the lifestyle many could afford back then was a smokescreen for a cruel imperialist agenda in Washington.

                      Moore (v.o.):
"Yes, of course, not everything was perfect. We did not mind having to put up with a little bit of this [*African-Americans being hosed and brutalized in the South in the 1960s*], and little bit of that [*bombing Vietnam*], just a long as we could be middle-class. And we can count on our kids to have it better than we had it. It sounded like a good deal to us. Capitalism: no one ever had it so good."

Turning the Bull Loose

These golden times of American capitalism are cleverly interrupted in Moore's editing with a 1979 Presidential address by Jimmy Carter. He warns Americans about the changes in values and the over-emphasis on consumption and materialism. It is an amazing piece of footage unto itself, expertly chosen and included at the right moment in the film. Just when we thought Moore could not surpass the previous edit, he comes in with a segment about the Reagan era, opening up with footage from a western wherein we see Reagan riding on his horse as the town's sheriff. Moore tells us that Americans were weary of Carter's "soft manners" and needed a strong iconic and uplifting figure to get over the trauma of Watergate and the Vietnam War. All throughout the segment, he undercuts excerpts of social movements with clips from Reagan's B-movies, TV shows and ads. Moore explains that Reagan was a bad actor and that he quickly became a corporate spokesperson before winding-up Governor of California in the 1960's. As President, he took care of the unions as if they were the outlaws of corporate America; and he also took care of feminists. Moore tells us this by inserting a brief clip from *The Killers* (1964), one of his better movies, where Ron is violently slapping Angie Dickinson across the room.

      Further on, after telling us about Reagan's provenance and eclectic career, the filmmaker remarks that, on November 4th 1980, Wall Street found the man who would help remodel America into its negative half. As a matter-of-fact, the 1980's are a turning point not only in American history but in world terms as well. Everything started changing and many countries were afflicted by unimaginable debts and endemic unemployment and hunger. Everything became exclusively profit-based and extremely short-sighted. Social welfare took a major blow when the rich found a way to lobby for tax-cuts and corporations were allowed to crush unions and outsource production, liquidating America's commercial potential and white-washing the efforts of a labor force which had made them rich. It was not that different from what was going on before, except that the process of savage capitalism itself accelerated to reach a critical mass. People went from being mere consumers to being stretched to break-up point, like we saw in *Roger & Me*, the best film produced during the Reagan era about the Reagan era.

The following sequence allows for Moore to show how Reagan and his administration were not in charge back then, that there were forces much stronger than the political ones in Washington shaping social policies. In *Capitalism: A Love Story* Moore zooms in on Donald Regan, Chairman of Merrill-Lynch, telling the President to "speed-it up" in his opening speech on Wall Street. We are told that he later became Treasury Secretary and that this nomination put the last nail in an already closed coffin. Moore admits the country would now be run "like a corporation," passing the tax cuts for the rich and allowing Reagan to presided over "the dismantling of America's industrial infrastructure." We see footage of Reagan with Federal Reserve guru Alan Greenspan, passing laws which would be chipping away at what Americans had acquired, as far as civil and workers rights, since the 1920's.

A series of statistics appear over still shots of Reagan in the Oval Office. General Motors Profits: $24.1 billion and 100,000 layoffs; AT &T Profits: $9.6 billion and 40,000 layoffs; General Electric Profits: $20.4 billion and 100,000 layoffs. Over another graphic we see statistics ranging from 1980 to 2000 (illustrating the long-term effects of Reaganomics): Productivity was up 45% and working people's wages only up 1%; while the richest Americans got their taxes cut in half. Moore also explains that Americans were encouraged to live on borrowed money to keep up the illusion of the American Dream, Republican style; household debt went up 111% and bankruptcies up 610%; incarcerations increased by 355%; sales of anti-depressants went up 305%; finally, health care cost augmented 78%, while the Dow Jones Index has been up 1,371% and the ratio of CEO pay versus workers pay up 649%! An attack on America's middle-class. The start of a class war which is still going on today.

Revisiting Roger

In *Capitalism: A Love Story*, Moore inserts excerpts from his own first film, *Roger & Me*. Not only does his discourse come full circle but Moore himself, as a film artist, became self-reflexive. He uses a clip from his meeting with Tom Kaye, then P.R. man at G.M. (read section about *Roger & Me*), and expands once more on what has happened since then. As we can see in the film, the rapid and brutal deindustrialization of Flint was a microcosm of what would happen to the country over the next 20 years. Flint's economic "model" had been replicated in hundreds of towns and cities across the land. Once more, the filmmaker decides to go to Detroit and GM's general HQ. He is received the very same way he had been 20 years before, by suspicious guards at the entrance who stop him from meeting with executives. Moore goes on to take Germany as an example of where unions have a say in hiring or firing CEOs, and the same goes for Japan, where the public makes sure that "even the most conservative politicians are not allowed to destroy the Japanese middle-class."

Linking the past with the present, Moore clearly illustrates that history has a tendency to repeat itself in America. He now focuses his attention on the case of Republic Doors & Windows, a company set in Chicago, Illinois, where the entire unionized work force had been given a 3-day notice before being fired in December 2008 (right at the time when Wall Street received its 700 billion bailout). Since Bank of America would not provide the company with a line of credit, it had decided to close down without any consideration for its employees; not even paying wages which were owed to the 250 workers. This allows Moore to revisit one of his favorite targets: the infamous 43rd "President" of the United States of America. He shows us clips that could have been in *Fahrenheit 9/11*, such as W. trying to dance like a Zulu, fishing or riding his bike while his last year in office was passing him by. But according to Moore, he could not hide any longer and was forced back in the public eye to sell the system, because everyone saw and felt the economy was crumbling. Commenting on Bush's comments about capitalism, Moore has an "exchange" with him via the editing scheme.

George W. Bush:
Capitalism is the best system ever devised.

Moore (v.o.):
"Uh, really?"

In another clip, W. is in front of a Manhattan Institute crowd, shoving more propaganda at a crowd which is already sold to it.

>George W. Bush:
>There (is) voices from the Left and Right equating free enterprise system with greed, and exploitation, and failure...

>Moore (v.o.):
>"Um, greed? exploitation? failure? Go on, I'm listening..."

>George W. Bush:
>Capitalism offers people the freedom to choose...where they work...what they do...

Moore then inserts a clip from a news report where a woman is looking for work in the classified section of a newspaper. She says there is nothing to find except sleazy jobs like being an escort,.

>George W. Bush:
>...The opportunity to buy and sell products they want...

Again, Moore cuts in another excerpt from a news report about a man whose business produces "Foreclosure" and "Bank Owned" signs, words that now make up half of his sales.

>George W. Bush:
>If you seek social justice and human dignity, the free-market system is the way to go.

>Moore (v.o.):
>"And for those seeking justice in Pennsylvania, free-enterprise is definitely the way to go..."

The Cost of Free Enterprise

This selling-out of America by the Right leads into a scandalous type of free-enterprise in Wilkes-Barre, Pennsylvania, where teenagers were for years funneled into a privately-owned youth detention center for profit.[118] This sordid case has been documented elsewhere, but it seems to take on a whole new proportion in this film's context. It evokes the black and poor youths being used as statues for the *Roger & Me* elite party, and the young and poor being railroaded into jail in Nevada County, California, in the segment from *The Awful Truth*. What this story says is that the American people, regardless of their age, are commodities. In this case, the "products" are teenagers who committed minor offenses, such as talking back to a step-parent or putting up a web site mocking their high school principal, nothing that could really be considered dangerous or seditious. As Moore says in voice-over, "The good people here employ the practices of capitalism in dealing with their wayward youth."

PA Child Care was an evil company concocted by extremely deranged minds. It was owned and ran by two businessmen, one of whom was Robert Powell, an attorney at law and entrepreneur. Powell had found "good friends" in Judges Michael Conahan and Mark Ciavarella to milk the system with these cruel, unusual and unfair methods of incarcerations. He had actually found a way to have the public juvenile home closed and to have an $8 million private prison built for teenagers (which was later leased to the county for an outrageous $58 million). After exposing the main players in this scandal and what they had bought with the profits (planes, boats, etc.), Moore presents the kids who had been victims of the scheme. First we meet Maggie (who smoked pot at a high school party), then Matt (who got into an argument at the diner table with his mother's boyfriend), Jamie (who had gotten into a fight at the shopping mall with her best friend), and finally to Hilary (who had made a MySpace page poking fun of her assistant-principal for being strict and having no sense of humor). Again, as we can see, there is nothing here that would have justified radical measures such as being put into prison. Moore tells us that these kids got their "First lesson in American capitalism" when they went to Judge Ciavarella and were sentenced to up to a year, even though probation officers then often objected to detention.

Moore (v.o.):
"Not only PA Child Care paid off the judges to fill their cells, but their employees were the ones who got to decide when a child had enough rehabilitation. But that makes sense, because anytime a governmental unit turns over to a profit-making corporation the duties it should be performing, what do you expect to happen?

---

[118] Michael Rubinkham and Maryclaire Dale, "Pa. judges accused of jailing kids for cash:," *AP Worldstream*, February 11, 2009

It seems like Michael Moore is going from one outrageous example to another in *Capitalism: A Love Story*. After shocking his audience with the PA Child Care scandal, a local story that the nation might not have been aware of, he pushes another button, on the national level this time, by starting his next segment with the heroic exploits of Chesley Sullenberger,[119] the pilot who managed to avoid a major crash by landing US Airways Flight 1549 in the Hudson River, off Manhattan, on January 15, 2009. After reminding us that Sullenberger was honored left and right, attending the State of the Union address, gracing the cover of major newspapers and magazines nation-wide, throwing a pitch at Yankee stadium and even being honored at the Super Bowl, he went to Congress to testify about the extremely bad wages and working conditions of airline pilots in the United States today.

In this scene, Moore uses extra-diegetic and pompous fanfare music on the soundtrack while he describes how this hero was honored, but when he cuts to Sullenberger's Congress hearings, the music skips and winds-down, as if to say that Sully had just ruined the party thrown in his honor by speaking the truth about government deregulations and the abuses of corporations. After the heroic pilot had stated that he "did not know one single pilot who wanted his or her children to follow in their footsteps," Moore brings back the fanfare music but at a higher volume, completely burying his testimony. Obviously, playing with sound and mixing is a standard procedure in documentary and non-fiction forms. It is one of the main devices a filmmaker can use to alter the meaning of images or to orient the spectator's reading of them, but Moore pushes this device to its extreme here, almost to the point of alienation. At the end of this segment about public safety breaches due to corporate malfeasance, he interviews pilots for regional and national airlines, and we find out through "Joe" that a pilot who has just started flying often has to rely on credit cards, food stamps and even giving plasma to make ends meet.

Moore (v.o.):
"I do not know about you, but I want the pilot that's got me 30,000 feet in the air to be paid really well, and not sitting up in the cockpit digging through the pilot seat looking for loose change."

Later in this sequence, one young airline pilot who had recently started flying tells her story, which seems to be a familiar one for many in the audience. Her professional life has barely started and she is in a financial hole. This is symptomatic of millions of young people in

---

[119] According to Wikipedia.com, Sullenberger is a registered Republican.

North America today, where the system has found a way to make you prisoner of the sharks at banks and credit companies even before you start your working adult life. They have your PIN number, alright.

"Susan":
I took out $100,000 [*of student loans*]. And by the time I pay it back, at this rate, It will probably cost me well over half a million with interest, and fees and penalties... I mean, it's something that I do not like to spend a lot of time thinking about because it is abysmal. It's one way that I get down really quickly about my chosen career field, just to think about how much I owe...and how little I make.

"Joe" and "Susan" are not atypical in this sense. There are millions of Americans who have been denied the possibility of working well and living well, even with a higher education diploma, as opposed to working in order to survive (never mind aiming for the American Dream). It would seem like capitalism has found a way to create a psychic and financial prison for all generations since Gen-X. It has created a dog-eat-dog world where airline pilots, no less, have to juggle many jobs to simply pay their bills, even though serious responsibilities are in their hands (literally). Financial preoccupations have no doubt an effect on these people's ability to concentrate on their job, which is to take-off, fly, and land a plane without anyone on board getting even as much as a scratch. Anyone who ever had financial worries will tell you: it occupies most of your thinking time in a day, and it even stops you from sleeping at night. This particular piece of information in *Capitalism* creates a tension as far as our understanding of security in public transportation is concerned. How can we seriously expect a professional airline pilot who makes minimum wage to take us safely to our destination? Should we all be scared that one day a plane flying over our cities will crash unto our homes?

Moore's argument regarding poor wages in the commercial airline industry is far-reaching because it explains clearly how corporate greed on Wall Street has now put public safety in jeopardy. The case of the crash of Flight 3407, near Buffalo, New York, in 2009 is an example which the filmmaker uses to conclude the first third of his film. The two young pilots flying the plane were discussing their "careers" when they crashed on a residential district, killing 50 people aboard and on the ground. And the casualties could have been much worst if the plane had fallen over a major city such as Buffalo on that night. No one likes to imagine a tragedy like this, but it can be inferred when watching Moore's last picture.

Moore (v.o.):
"The media focused on the actions of the pilots. 'Careers' was a euphemism, for what the pilots were really talking about was how little they were paid and how overworked they were. There would be no discussion in the media about why we have an economic system that allows a pilot to be paid less than a manager at Taco Bell (...) How are these companies able to get away with this? I guess that's the point of capitalism, it allows you to get away with anything...Like making a profit off the death of an employee."

Dead Peasants

Next in all of these atrocious horror stories of capitalism gone mad, is the case of Dan Johnson, who worked at middle-management level for Amegy Bank in Houston, Texas. Dan had died of cancer leaving behind his wife, Herma, and two sons, and unbeknownst to them was the fact that Amegy had taken two insurance policies on his life. When he died the company reaped a total of $5,000,000 and left Herma Johnson and her kids out in the freezing cold with nothing but funeral bills and debts to pay. This is perhaps the turning point in *Capitalism: A Love Story*, from a human point of view. If the viewer has not been completely marked by indignation at this point, then we can assume that nothing will succeed in engaging him or her into a truthful discussion about this flawed system and its many dens of inequities. From there after, Moore explains that Ms. Johnson had hired Michael D. Myers, an attorney known to look into these unethical practices. Myers tells Moore that "Certain companies are actually hoping that their employees will die" so that they can collect life insurance policy money, sometimes even commiserating about the fact that "not enough employees are dying." Moore then exposes some of these blue chip corporations which have so-called "dead peasants" policies on their employees' lives (Bank of America, Citibank, Wal-Mart, Hershey's, Nestle, Proctor & Gamble, American Express, etc.), and tells the viewers that a policy on their own lives could have been taken as they are sitting in the theater, watching his film, without them knowing about it.

As if this was not enough crap to prove his point about the white collar mafia, Moore goes on with the story of Paul Smith, an ex-Wal-Mart employee for 18 years whose late wife, LaDonna, had also been an employee of that same corporation. She was a cake decorator there, for only 18 months. Unbeknownst to Paul, the company had taken a $350,000 insurance policy on his wife's life, knowing that she suffered from severe asthma. The corporation even made more money because she was young, we also find out in the film. Her children crying to the camera makes it extremely difficult to watch.

> Paul Smith:
> I was left with over $100,000 in medical bills and a $6,000 funeral, and Wal-Mart did not offer a penny to help with that. (...) I did trust them. Never in a million years would I've ever thought that somewhere on a profit statement it says "Dead Associate: $81,000" ...Wal-Mart does not care about you.

Holy Crap

At this point in *Capitalism* Michael Moore needs to go back to his own roots, so to speak. He has to return to fundamental and moral questionings. It only seems natural that he would eventually move into the area of religion and spiritual concerns to address the evils of a materialistic world, the one created by the U.S. Government and private companies like the Federal Reserve Bank and, more recently in history, Wal-Mart. At 48 minutes into the film, Moore interviews two Catholic priests from two parishes. He asks them about the current economical and political system which allows for such crimes to happen and be left unpunished. It is an amazing moment which encapsulates his whole career in many ways, since it has been based on the idea of exposing the truth and keeping America on a moral track, in spite of Social Darwinism and the propaganda coming from the Right.

The first priest he visits is actually the one who married Moore and his wife, Kathleen Glynn. Like most sit-down interviews in Moore's films, the framing is in medium close-up with significant details in the background of the composition. Often these are caught with rack-focusing and reframing motions.

> Moore:
> Is capitalism a sin?

> Father Dick Preston:
> Yes. Capitalism, for me, and for many of us, at this present moment, is an evil. It's contrary to all that's good. It's contrary to the common good. It's contrary to compassion. It's contrary to all of the major religions. Capitalism is precisely what the holy books, our holy book in particular, reminds us is unjust, and in some form and fashion, God will come down and

eradicate it, somehow. Capitalism is wrong, and therefore has to be eliminated.

In voice-over, Moore tells us "Eliminated? That might be a little harsh…", so he decides to meet with another, perhaps less radical man of the cloth. This time it is the one who married his sister Anne and brother-in-law, believing that he would have a "more balanced" approach to the issue.

> Father Peter Dougherty:
> It is immoral. It is obscene. It is outrageous. Yeah. It is really "radical evil." It's radically evil.
>
> Moore (v.o.):
> "Wow. Does their boss know that they're talking like this? I thought it best to go and check this out with the bishop [*Archdiocese of Detroit*]."
>
> Bishop Thomas Gumbleton:
> The system does not seem to be providing for the well-being of all the people. And that's what makes it, almost in its very nature, something contrary to the Jesus who said '*Blessed are the poor, woe to the rich*'; that's right out of St. Luke's Gospel.

Moore goes back in the editing to Father Dougherty, while seemingly asking a question to Bishop Gumbleton.

> Moore (off):
> How have we put up with this system for so long? I mean, it's, they thought us…
>
> Father Peter Dougherty:
> The system has built into it what we call propaganda. I'm in awe of propaganda: *the ability to convince people who are victimized by the very system to support the system and see it as good.*

This statement of interest, as far as the endeavor of this book is concerned, is followed by some capitalist propaganda, as Moore cuts in an excerpt from an "educational film" from the 1950s. On the soundtrack, he lays out the gruesome but yet sublime tonalities of Bernard Herrmann's score for Hitchcock's *Vertigo*, as if this was an investigation into America's troubled identity and many phobias.

Talking Head:
We know that American capitalism is morally right, because its chief elements: private ownership, the profit motive, and the competitive market, are wholesome and good. *They are compatible with God's laws and the teachings of the Bible.*

On the soundtrack, Moore loop this last sentence but with a distorting and hypnotic effect, while showing us different clips from old Hollywood horror movies. He synthesizes the previous 20 minutes of the film in order to bring us to a chilling hypothesis about American capitalism, one that reinforces every other film and TV show he has made in the last 20 years.

Moore (v.o.):
"As long as I can remember, I've been told that competition and profit are good things. And if increasing profits mean locking up a few kids or cashing-in on the death of an employee, it is morally right to provide for the stockholders. Deaths, evictions, and exploitation. What were we really pledging allegiance to? And so, all good Americans came to act as if they believed that our capitalist economic system was compatible with the teachings of the Bible."

It is at this moment that for the first time on film Moore admits he once thought of becoming a priest. This confession is supplemented by church music and great color Super-8 movies of him coming out of his confirmation.

Moore (v.o.):
"When I was a kid, I wanted to be a priest. It was not because of the fancy get-ups and the Knights of Columbus escorts, or even the groovy nuns, who were so good to me. It was because of the priests who went on the march in Selma [*Alabama*], or tried to stop the war, or devoted their lives to the poor. They told me quite clearly what Jesus said: *that the first shall be last, and the last shall be first; that the rich man will have a very hard time getting into heaven; that we will be judged by how we treat the least among us, and that there are no more important people to God than the poor.* Since that time, it seems like Jesus got high-jacked by a lot of people who believe that the Son of God was sent here to create heaven on Earth for the well-to-do. I must have missed that part of the Bible, where Jesus became a capitalist."

This makes way for a perversion of an excerpt from Zeffirelli's *Jesus of Nazareth*. The character played by Robert Powell is overdubbed by another voice with a British accent mocking a right-wing understanding of his famous but often misunderstood teachings.

Man #1:
Please tell me, master, what must I do to have eternal life?

Jesus of Nazareth:
Go forth and maximize profits.

Man #2:
You say the Kingdom of Heaven is at hand, but when exactly will it come?

Jesus of Nazareth:
When you deregulate the banking industry.

Man #3 (*strapped to a stretcher*):
Help me. I've been this way for 20 years!!!

Jesus of Nazareth:
I'm sorry but I cannot heal your pre-existing condition. [*Then to the crowd*] He'll have to pay it out of pocket!

Moore goes on to remind us that Jesus did not come to Earth to ring the bell at the NY's Stock Exchange, whereupon he superimposes Christ on the cross over the NYSE floor. We see clips from the Senate where former US Senator Phil Gramm is saying that, for him, Wall Street is a "holy place," and right after this an excerpt from the CNBC show *Kudlow & Company* where the host claims that the war in Iraq and the "war against terrorism" have made the economy better. Moore wonders about this angle, where one can see Wall Street as sacred grounds, and goes back in the editing to Bishop Gumbleton.

Moore (off):
(They) think Wall Street is a holy place. What do you think Jesus would say about capitalism?

Bishop Thomas Gumbleton:
[*Laughs*] I think he would simply refuse to be part of it.

Riding the Gravy Train

This exchange between Moore and the Bishop leads into yet another disturbing segment about Citibank Inc. memos issued internally from 2005-2006, wherein the corporation says "it wants to rule the world." These documents from one of the main beneficiaries of the 2008 Wall Street bailout were in fact leaked by a disgruntled insider, and they reveal just how crooked American corporations and banks really are today. It also reveals their philosophy and sense of purpose for the years to come, if nothing is done about it. With his omnipresent voice-over covering CGI reproductions of the aforesaid documents, Moore unveils one of the cornerstones of the New World Order, set by the likes of the Bilderberg Group and "consultants" like old Zbigniew Brzezinski and Richard Perle. Perhaps for the first time in a direct fashion, he addresses the issue of the current class warfare head on.

> Moore (v.o.):
> "Back in 2005 and 2006, Citigroup wrote three confidential memos to their wealthiest investors about how things were going. They reached the conclusion that the United States was no longer really a democracy but had become a *plutonomy*. A society controlled exclusively by and for the benefit of the top 1% of the population, who have now more financial wealth than the bottom 95% combined. The memo gloated about the growing gap between rich and poor, and how they were now the *new aristocracy*. And that there was no end in sight for the gravy train they were on. There was, though, one problem. According to Citigroup, the most potent and short-term threat would be *societies demanding a more 'equitable share' of the wealth*. In other words, *the peasants might revolt*."

The film director goes on to explain that the notion of "one person, one vote" is threatening for this plutonomy, a form of highly concentrated power, reminiscent of a dictatorship in many ways. He tells us that this is what really scares the new financial elite: the fact that 99% of the population can vote, arguably the most important of all democratic acts. And here is perhaps the most important aspect of *Capitalism: A Love Story*, a detail within Citibank's memos that cracks the whole thing wide open, like a walnut filled with maggots. Moore tells us that Citigroup believed the reason why the 99% of the "bottom" population is accepting this new form of tyranny is that they too believe they will reach the top 1% one day. Thus, it is imperative for this plutonomy to take and keep control of *popular* culture, and it does so by owning imaginary stocks on something which should really belongs to the many: airwaves, networks, monopoly of cinema chains, etc.

This idea links back to the introduction of this book, where we claimed that popular culture was now the ploy by which the elite controls the masses, making them think like they do, with the same right-wing and archaic ways of conceiving society and the roles individuals play in it. The reality is that the top 1% has absolutely no intention to share the wealth with anyone, and that the masses are mistakenly led into aspiring to an unattainable lifestyle, the one edified in all mass media today. Michael Moore never really came out to say that media was the channel by which this plutonomy stayed in power, though. That the true reason why the masses are so inert and apolitical is that they do not see the correlations between media ownership and thought-control, between their favorite "reality shows" and their discontent with the current political systems, the "real reality," the "political reality." After having used once again video clips from YouTube culture and advertisement about dogs doing tricks with a chewy-bone, obviously symbolic of Americans' willingness to be good and obedient and to believe the great lie told to them, he interviews Steven Moore (no relation), a columnist and editorial board member for *The Wall Street Journal* who breaks it down in layman's terms. It is the antithesis of Tony Benn's comments in *Sicko*.

Steven Moore:
I think capitalism is a lot more important than democracy. I'm not even a big believer in democracy. I always say that democracy can be two wolves and a sheep deciding on what they'll have for dinner (…) Now, look, I'm in favor of people having the right to vote, and things like that, but you know, there are a lot of countries that have the right to vote that are still poor.

Moore then cuts in a shot of the U.S. Capitol building as *one* example of a society where one's right to vote does not guarantee his means to subsist on a daily basis.

Steven Moore:
Democracy does not always lead to a good economy or even a good political system. With capitalism, you are free to do what you want, to make whatever you want out of yourself. It does not mean you're going to succeed. Remember the U.S. Constitution does not guarantee happiness.

This last sentence prompts Moore to perambulate through the National Archives in Washington, D.C., looking at the various historical documents, such as the Declaration of Independence and the U.S. Constitution.

> Moore (v.o.):
> "Ah, the Constitution! All my life I've heard that America is a capitalist country. So I went to see the original Constitution and check out if it was true."

The voice-over mixes with the live sound inside the National Archives, where Moore is wondering where, within the Constitution, it says that America *must have* a capitalist economy.

> Moore (v.o.):
> "There was no mention of the 'free market' or 'free enterprise', or 'capitalism' anywhere. In fact, all I saw was '*We* the People' and something about 'a more perfect *Union*' and 'promoting the general *Welfare*'. Welfare? Union? We? That sounded like that other *ism*... But no, that's democracy. And I began to wonder what it would be like if the work place was a democracy?"

A Novel Idea: Fairness in the Workplace

This question leads Moore to Isthmus Engineering & Manufacturing, a Wisconsin company owned by its workers, as a cooperative, not something like "bullshit stock options," he tells us in voice-over. It was founded in 1980 and specializes in automated assembly and machining systems. Following on the comment made by one of the owner-workers, that there has always been a schism between how the country is ran and how the work place is ran, Moore underlines the disconnection between America's "professed love of democracy" and "how it is willing to accept dictatorship, every day it shows up to work." In fact, this question could have been asked more directly by the director: How did Americans let corporations take over their country? It would seem like America's revival, if there is ever to be one in the future, will only occur through people's ingenuity and ability at creating and managing their own work, by providing services and products they, as workers, will have control over, and reaping the benefits from production, distribution and sales.

Moore brings forth another factory based on the cooperative model, Alvarado St. Bakery, located in Petaluma, California. This company has been a leader in producing healthy, organic whole grain breads which is sold across America. It is the opposite of monstrous conglomerates like Monsanto (perhaps the most dangerous of all corporations out there today), because it keeps essential food real and tasty. The General Coordinator and CEO of the company, Joseph Tuck, explains to Moore that sharing the profits turned out to be extremely lucrative for everyone involved, and Moore himself adds in voice-over that an assembly line worker at Alvarado St. Bakery earns in average over $65,000 a year there; three times the amount made by a starting pilot at American Eagle.

> Joseph Tuck:
> I'm just hoping that people take notice of this type of organizational activity and start considering it as an alternative (…) Why do you want to get rich? How many cars do you really need in life?

Moore takes this piece of information to tell us that not everyone is interested in making profits. There were some inventions that have been given to the public "for free" in the past, such as the polio vaccine, discovered by Dr. Jonas Salk in 1955. Moore tells us that Salk thought his talents should be used to "a greater good," not only to serve him and to make him a millionaire. In his life Salk made a decent salary as a researcher and professor which allowed him a comfortable living for him and his family. When asked by Edward R. Murrow on his television show about the ownership of the patent for the polio vaccine, back in the 1950's, Salk simply replied: "The people, I would say, there is no patent…Would you patent the sun?" This allows Moore to come to terms with America's transformation over the last five decades; these are operated and controlled by the 1% discussed in the previous section.

> Moore (v.o.):
> "Yes, we've come a long way since the days of Dr. Salk, because today our best minds are used for something else."

From an interview with Professor William Black, we realize that *Capitalism*, much like *Bowling for Columbine*, tries to unearth something fundamentally embedded in the American psyche. He tells Moore that many of the best minds coming out from Universities today are sent to work for Wall Street, not to further the common good. Moore rationalizes this new reality by reminding the viewer that many students come out of college with overwhelming debts, so they feel like the field they choose must be overwhelmingly profitable at the outset, and they wind up working for the banks to which they owe money to instead. Thus, they contribute to a vicious circle where they are both victims and perpetrators at the same time.

> Professor William Black:
> We've taken people that could be enormously productive, just what we're short of in America, and we take them and we put them in an activity that is not simply less productive, but where they are actually destructive. Where they actually, every day they work, make the world worst.

Deregulate This!

This sad reality prompts Moore to ask about *what* these so-called "best American minds" are working at today, and the answer he finds drives him through the second half of his film to Wall Street, with its Mad-Hatter type "derivatives" and "credit default swaps," two financial subterfuges which eventually led to the near destruction of the capitalist structure as we know it. The words confuse Moore and he decides to ask NYSE brokers for definitions and explanations, right there on Wall Street. Needless to say that they do not take his presence lightly. They either run away from him and his camera or tell him bluntly to stop making movies. Moore finally gets in touch with Marcus Haupt, an Ivy-League educated engineer who was once Vice-President of Lehman Brothers and who worked on Wall Street for 15 years, concocting what they call "complex financial instruments."[120]

Even this expert could not explain what a derivative was to Moore, beyond the fact that it is "privilege for the stockholder" and an "opportunity for the broker." The director pushes this gag further by inserting an excerpt of an interview with a Harvard University professor, actually the Former Chief Economist of the International Monetary Fund, Kenneth Rogoff; who is also at pains in explaining what these new and twisted Wall Street "instruments" are.

> Professor Kenneth Rogoff:
> Yeah, uh, the, uh, the, uh, the ump, uh, the buyer, so the seller holds the loan and it might default, and they sell off, uh, uh, somebody, somebody else, uh, uh... Sorry, let me, let me just back off, I'm, I, I apologize (...) These are pretty exotic...

---

[120] "Former Lehman Brothers V.P. Marcus Haupt Talks About *Wall Street* vs. Wall Street," *New York Magazine*, January 12, 2009

Moore takes over and after doing his research explains to the viewer that "derivatives" are nothing more than complicated betting schemes. He even shows us what a derivative's equation looks like on screen, and it is filled with complicated algebra and trigonometry icons, incomprehensible for the everyday person.

Moore (v.o.):
"[*To the viewer*] Can't figure it out? That's OK, you're not supposed to. They made them purposely confusing so that they can get away with murder."

Marcus Haupt then tells Moore that if you work for the government and you can actually "make out what is going on in these books" (i.e. filled with derivative formulas), chances are that Wall Street will hire you for more money than Uncle Sam. In the editing Moore dissolves pan shots of the NYSE floor with the interior of a Las Vegas casino, indicating that there are no lines between the two any longer. As a transitional device used to take us into the next section of *Capitalism: A Love Story*, Moore zooms in on Alan Greenspan, American economist, Chairman of the Federal Reserve Bank from 1987 to 2006, and surely one of the people responsible for allowing the deregulation of Wall Street under Reagan, and then intensely under Clinton. Moore cuts many sound bites gathered from different sources to probe the conditions which led to the big financial meltdown of 2008. There is even one clip of Tom Brokaw comparing Greenspan to (of all people) rock-God Mick Jagger.

"Tap your home equity," was Greenspan's favorite saying in the late 1990's, and he is no doubt one of the main architects of the system which allowed for the subprime crisis to occur. As these lines are being written, 6,000 American families are losing their homes everyday because of policies conceived by the "genius" of Greenspan while he was at the Fed (a *private* company in spite of its name, we might want to repeat here, for the sake of our readers). Greenspan also fostered a culture where elderly couples are led into refinancing their homes after having paid for them for decades, just so that they can borrow more money from the bank to invest in other retirement activities. It was a way, in so many words, to get senior citizens out of their houses so that banks can get a hold of them and resell at a profit, according to the monetary policy dictated by the Fed.

Moore (v.o.):
"The scam to swindle the people out of the homes they already own was masterful. Here's how it worked: First, tell these home-owners that they own a bank, and that bank is

your home. So if your home is worth $250,000 that makes you a quarter millionaire. 'You're sitting on a goldmine! You own your own bank: *the bank of you*! And you can use your bank to get more money. Just refinance, everyone's doing it! Of course, hidden in the dozens or hundreds of pages of fine print our tricky clauses that allow the bank to raise your interest rate to a number you didn't know about, perhaps so high that you won't be able to repay your loan, but that's OK, if you can't repay it, we'll just take your house'."

While his sarcastic voice-over explains how the "home refinancing fiasco" came to be, with small prints and false pretense, and while his voice is gaining in speed like some old-time advertising technique meant to bamboozle consumers, Moore rapidly cuts together many different TV ads from specialized home equity firms, definitely a booming industry prior to the subprime crisis. This gives way to the section dealing with the deregulations of Wall Street in the late 1990s, but more intensely in the W. years, with the Annual Report of the Federal Deposit Insurance Corporation of 2003. The FDIC's mandate is to "provide deposit insurance" and to "guarantee the safety of deposits in member banks," its website declares. Moore is asking Professor Black about the identity of four individuals found on a photo he saw in that document. It tells him that it is a picture of John Gilleran, Head of Office of Thrift Supervision, "which is supposed to regulate savings and loans. He's the guy with *the chainsaw…*" he says in the interview. He goes on by saying that "the four other *grinning idiots* in the photo are the three leading lobbyists in banking and the deputy director of the FDIC…"

In hindsight, it is a powerful picture that foreshadowed the shape of things to come. The four men are poised over a pile of documents supposed to represent regulation forms. The chainsaw is meant to be used to destroy these regulations, and, as we can see it in *Capitalism: A Love Story*, they have succeeded in doing so. The effects were catastrophic and led the way for the most shameful abuse of banker-power in stock exchange history and the greatest financial collapse since the Great Depression. In March of 2010, Moore appeared on MSNBC's *The Rachel Maddow Show*, one of the few intelligent news commentary shows on air in America today, to talk about this scene in relation to another 2008 clip of Mitt Romney pledging for deregulation in the midst of the financial system collapsing.

Maddow:
What does that make – what does that say to you about the sort of way the rhetoric and the politics do not change with the – they can even tell the impact of them [*deregulations*]?

Moore:
Well, it –they are – they are blind and they are deaf to all of this. And it's – I'll tell you what's going to happen here. Because not one single regulation or rule has been reinstated on the banking industry, on Wall Street, you know, they're back to dealing with their crazy derivatives and credit default swaps and all that – Trust me, the next collapse or crash is right around the corner, because they're doing the same stuff they were doing leading up to that first crash of '08. And it's amazing that nobody's doing anything. It's amazing that the Democrats in Congress haven't forced this issue in a very strong way, because they would have the support of the American people. Nobody wants the other shoe to drop here, and it's getting ready to drop. And I just do not understand, well, I guess I do understand, because those banks and the people on Wall Street are lining the pockets of our members of Congress. So…

Maddow:
But on the right of course they're caricaturing reform as socialism. Everything is socialism.

Moore:
Yes. Everything is socialism to them. Boy, that is so tired, isn't it?

Maddow:
I know.

Moore:
It's, you know, as I said in my film, to me, everything they call socialism, wanting to help people when they're sick, wanting to provide, you know, jobs for people when they do not have work, these are all – are not these the Christian, Jewish, Buddhist, Muslim, even atheist principles that we all grew up with? That we are told that we were to be good to those who were without? And then we were to share the pie?

Here again is an example of Moore relying on questions of morality and spirituality to discuss politics and social policies. It seems clear as we progress throughout this analysis that he is trying to use the opposite view's perspective to convince his audience. He had already told his viewers in preceding films and TV shows that religious beliefs have no place in politics, but here he is telling people that politics do have commonalities with religion, that both realms offer a position on the world and affect the way things are done in everyday life. It also seems clear that there is a difference between morality and spirituality (or even religiosity), and that Moore himself might be struggling with this difference.

In many ways this filmmaker could be here perceived as a "closet priest" with a camera, a man of faith who gives sermons to his audience about America's moral misguidances. Perhaps this is the reason why so many people do not appreciate him or his work; because he is in fact lecturing and maybe even sometimes pontificating to his audience. We cannot stress enough the fact that his Irish Catholic background makes it such that he has to fight for what he perceives as being "right," and in doing so has to confront the brute, the insensitive, the ignorant and the bigot along the way. Moore's films are lectures in this new age of darkness, where simulacras have replaced reality, and where corporations, profiting from financial deregulations and corrupt civil servants, have become our worst nightmare.

Dark Days

After taking us to Wall Street Moore goes back again, in the editing that is, to an earlier "character" whose name has been withheld from the viewer until now, Randall Hacker and his wife, Donna, in the middle of clearing out their family home. Randall explains that Citibank took everything away from him: his home but also all his life savings with "the stroke of a pen, a lawyer and a judge." "In a final humiliation," Moore says, the Hackers winded up accepting a $1,000 check to get rid of their own stuff by throwing it in a bonfire, like some sort of black ritual imposed on an innocent. Of course, Randall is completely bitter about this life-altering situation and can barely contain his hatred.

Then Moore himself goes out of his mind when he finds out that the foreclosure letter send to the Hackers came from his hometown of Flint, Michigan, one of the most desperate places in the United States. How can this be? It turned out that some people are working in Flint after all. On the voice-over, Moore reveals that a company subcontracted by Citibank employed Flint workers to mail foreclosure notices to the rest of America. It would seem like the incapacity of corporate executives to fully empathize with their fellowmen has reached a new low in American capitalism. We are now way beyond "Compassionate Conservatism" and into the realms of just good-old sadistic behavior. If we recall the sayings of Tony Benn in *Sicko*: someone that has been shackled with debts will obviously be discouraged, and discouraged people do not usually vote.

And here we have perhaps the missing link to understand the recent financial crisis that rocked the Western hemisphere in 2008. The economy is planned by the 1% in a way as to artificially and cyclically create recessions and depressions. This has been the case since the J.P. Morgan-organized Banker's Panic of 1907 (which led to the creation of The Federal Reserve in 1913, perhaps the darkest day in American history). By allowing deregulations of Wall Street, the self-described plutonomy knew that Main Street would suffer, but they just didn't care. Like all the recessions of the 19th and 20th centuries, millions of people suffered and only a few profited from these complex financial instruments like "bilateral netting," "derivatives," and "credit default swaps." As it turned out, these bankers also left scum into their trails for Moore to follow on. They almost always do.

Angelo's Friends

At this point in the film we understand that Moore will eventually box-in the ones who are responsible for such a downfall of the economy and expose them for the viewer. With the help of Robert Feinberg, a man who used to be an employee for the largest and perhaps most crooked mortgage company in the United States, Countrywide Finance, he will open the last third of his film with a myriad of elements and details regarding the subprime crisis. Feinberg tells him that he was in charge of the V.I.P. loans for Countrywide, and that favors were made to important "friends of Angelo (Mozilo)," the CEO of the company. He adds that he was responsible for taking care of top political leaders who received hand-outs and gifts from Mozilo, and that paperwork was waved. What Feinberg actually reveals in *Capitalism* is that politicians on Capitol Hill were on the payroll, and that they were essentially bought out by corporations.

On the Friends of Angelo payroll were the Head of Fannie Mae, Jim Johnson, Senator Kent Conrad and Chairman Max Baucus of the Finance Committee, U.S. Special Envoy for Afghanistan and Pakistan, Richard Holbrooke, Secretary of Housing and Urban Development, Alfonso Jackson, and various Wall Street deregulators. But the most scandalous aspect of all this is that some of recipients of Mozilo's payoffs where senators who themselves had been lecturing in public about corporate handouts, such as Senator Christopher Dodd, a Democrat. Moore's film reveals that partisanship had nothing to do with these special favors, that both parties were guilty of corruption at the highest level. It confirms what he has been saying for years, that Republicans and Democrats are in fact one party: the Republicrats. As we can see it in the film, Feinberg was involved in a complex structure of bribery and even feared for his own security while he was working for Countrywide.

Although, the man who has been the most threatened by the Wall Street mafia is William Black, who uncovered the savings and loan crisis in the 1980's. At the time, Charles Keating Jr. was head of the "Keating Five" and had sent company memos to "Get Black" and to "Kill (him)." In *Capitalism*, Black's interview is perhaps the most revealing and informative. He reminds Moore that the FBI had issued a public warning about "an epidemic of mortgage fraud" as early as September '04, and that when 9/11 occurred the Bush administration transferred the FBI assigned to white collar crime to another kind of terrorism, the one attributed to foreigners, like those members of al-Qaeda. Like Moore said two years before in *Sicko*: "Let's defeat the terrorists *over there*, so we do not have to fight them *here*…"

What is confirmed at this point in *Capitalism: A Love Story* is that these frauds were perpetrated and controlled by those at the top of the organization, not by smaller fish or by those who aspire to reach the top within. Moore finally asks Black how can the American public let CEOs get away with it, and the latter replies that they *are* letting them get away with it. The explanation for this can be found in the collusion which exists between government and big business. In other words, as long as Americans are willing to accept/tolerate that their elected representatives are bought out by private interests, they will always be considered Number Two. What they need to do is require Washington to clean up its act and/or to vote for representatives who do not come from (or have direct ties to) the corporate world. They also have to change their ways of thinking about the role of federal government.

For instance, many do not believe in "big government" and that Washington has no right to "interfere with" (i.e. regulate) commerce or to pass laws relating to health care, which are necessary interventions for democracy to really function. In opposition to this, many of the same people believe that government should be big and intervene in people's bedrooms and make gay marriage illegal, or should be able to stop a woman from having an abortion; which is ridiculous since, like a man, a woman is entitled to own and control her body. Those are definitely areas where a government should not have any form of power. Why is it okay that Bush gets America involved in preemptive and unjustified wars, costing American taxpayers billions of dollars, but not okay for Obama to take taxpayers' money to help revive the moribund economy or help the needy? Once again, and unlike Canadians, British, French and Cubans, right-wing Americans seem to believe that it is better to spend money on killing people abroad than to spend money on healing people at home.

Moore concludes this section of *Capitalism* with great footage from a silent film where we see bourgeois characters stealing silverware in a store, intercut with clips of Senator John McCain, being interviewed in 2008 by Reverend Rick Warren for the Saddleback Civil Forum, where he qualifies someone as only being "rich" when he or she has over 5 million dollars. This sort of contempt for working people explains why a majority did not vote for McCain in '08, because most Americans are not "rich" but are perceptive enough to know when someone is putting them down or leading them on. As if it was not enough that neoconservatives participated in bankrupting Americans when they were sick, they also distracted them from the real issues with "good old fashioned fear," as Moore says on the voice-over. But what else is new, since fear is the whip that makes anyone jump through any hoop of fire?

The Sky is Falling

Capitalism: A Love Story is by no means a funny film. Even if Moore uses his conventional sarcastic and tongue-in-cheek humor, it is very difficult to point to a scene which generates genuine and deep laughter, like in *Roger & Me* or even *Fahrenheit 9/11*. There is one moment obviously meant for comic relief but that barely makes it. It is when W. addresses the nation at the time of the financial meltdown and is oblivious to everything crumbling to pieces around him inside the White House (a metaphor for America here). The CGI animation of this sequence is of high quality and the tone is reminiscent of Terry Gilliam's animation in *Monty Python's Flying Circus*. After every line delivered by Bush, Moore has his animators adding an extra effect: a lightning perceived through the window, a thunder bolt striking a chandelier, the walls and the ceilings cracking wide open, a hurricane bringing a mighty wind that even makes a cat fly, fires starting everywhere, a man going insane running in the background, etc. The discrepancy between Bush's "Chicken Little" attitude and the damages around him is an excellent allegory for his entire mandate, but still the whole thing does not work as a comedy interlude. The destruction and mayhem only reinforces the viewer's indignation and hatred regarding Bush and Cheney's legacy. After witnessing the horrors previously shown in his film, there is nothing Moore can do that will put a smile on our faces. So, might as well go the other way now.

At the end of this scene, the filmmaker tells viewers that in reality Bush was too late when he admitted there was a crisis; for "the media had already drunk the Kool-Aid." This segment is supported by many TV news sources where the meltdown is compared to a financial Armageddon. Again, because Wall Street was on the verge of collapsing on itself, as a consequence of its own greed, everyone else was supposed to be scared out of their minds. And they were. Thus, the Republicans' 700 billion dollar bailout (of taxpayers money) seemed justified, and it was effectively carried over to the Obama administration. At this point in *Capitalism*, Moore returns to ask Professor William Black: "What the fuck happened?" The latter describes it as being like a dam failing, where a small crack gets bigger without ever being noticed, leading the dam to erosion and, finally, explosion. Black stresses the fact that everything played against it, especially the structure of the economy set in place by the Fed and the deregulation of Wall Street, as mentioned before. It started out with the free fall of the market and with Fanny Mae & Freddie Mac losing 11 billion dollars and the rest just came tumbling down with it, like a stack of tricked cards badly piled up together by a bunch of corporate crooks.

Here Comes the Flood

In *Capitalism: A Love Story*, Michael Moore and his team did a great job at editing and mixing a wide variety of images with rock, folk and classical music, but nowhere better than in the 2008 meltdown sequence. It is a great work of synthesis, a characteristic which seems to describe better than anything else Moore's style in later years. The sequence basically illustrates the fact that it can take only two minutes to bring down 200 years of capitalism, because it was rotten at its very core, i.e. instead of resting on solid "bedrock" (Black) of positive and humanistic values. One of the evidences backing up this statement in the film is the section pertaining to two of the architects of the fall, the deregulators-in-chief, Robert Rubin and Larry Summers. As members of Congress, both men had worked for either Citigroup or Goldman Sachs. Rubin was US Treasury Secretary from 1995-1999 and championed a change in the law so that commercial banks could get into new areas of investment, like "exotic insurance products." Under his term Citicorp and Travelers Group merged, a deal which was reported to be in excess of 70 billions dollars: creating the world's largest bank. Moore suggests that this is not a coincidence.

After leaving the Clinton administration, Rubin worked for Citigroup, earning 115 million dollars over a relatively short period of time. What he did to merit such a salary, no one can say. One thing is certain, though. Some individuals who have interests in both the financial and the political world are merging both shamelessly and getting mega rich doing it; making the economy only about politics and politics exclusively concerned with unscrupulous financing. Should there not be an oath taken by these people regarding a certain ethical practice once they are elected? What about Larry Summers, who took over from Rubin as US Treasury Secretary, from 1999 to 2001, and who made money as a "consultant" and for giving speeches, sometimes at $10,000 a pop? He also made 5.2 million dollars advising a hedge fund, one of the schemes by which the elite got richer on the back of the working-poor. Can he really get away with it? Of course he can. He did.

And so did Timothy Geithner, who "screwed his job at the Fed," according to Professor Black, and who then went on to occupy the Treasury Secretary position within the Obama administration. How can this register with American viewers? Who can explain the reasons why people like Rubin, Summers and Geithner are allowed to be rewarded for damaging the economy and the very fabric of their society? How can anyone have hope when even a democratically-elected President is forced to include people like this in his administration? Black tells Moore that this is nothing new in Washington: people who have the wrong answers are hired because they did absurd things in the past, such as deregulating the financial markets. For Moore, it is not surprising either that in this process the rich became richer and the poor poorer, because the entity known as the "Federal Government" has permanently been usurped by private interests and is not working for the people like it used to before (in Frank Capra films, perhaps).

Differently put, laws and policies are voted on and carried out for the benefit of the few, while the many suffer the dire consequences. We are then reminded in *Capitalism* that the bailing out of Wall Street in '08 was voted on by the House and that the nays had won; in fact, thousands of letters from angry taxpayers made it clear to their Representatives that banks didn't deserve the bailout money, and as a result the stock market plunged to depths which had not been reached since the Great Depression. A day later, after Henry Paulson had run into Bush's office to ask him to apply veto power on the vote, the bailout was approved.[121] State capitalism was saved on that day, and even Paulson appeared as a little boy about to receive a gift as he

---

[121] In 2008, *Time* called Paulson "The face of the current financial crisis," but in reality this ex-CEO of Goldman Sachs was just an (expensive) executive for the entire superstructure of the financial elite.

walked out on the steps of the Capitol with Bush Jr. to announce the reversed decision.

Moore goes at great lengths to show that this decision was undemocratic, or at least influenced by forces that were not democratic. It confirms that there is another level of power above the White House, the Congress and the Senate. A sphere of influence not restricted by the United States Constitution and beyond public scrutiny, like a secret society or a cult of the occult. As he stands on Capitol Hill he intercepts democratic representative Baron Hill from Indiana, who was talking to his wife on his cellular phone. "Honey, I'm standing with Michael Moore, the filmmaker!," he says to her over the line. Moore manages to get out of him that Representatives were "cornered" into voting for the bailout in '08, something confirmed by both, Elijah Cummings, a true Democrat from Maryland, and Marcy Kaptur, a true Democrat from Ohio.

This whole segment of the film is edited rapidly and with clever parallelisms. We are first told by Rep. Kaptur that the controversy surrounding the bailout was justified, as she accepts Moore's idea that a *coup d'état* had been perpetrated on the U.S. government. Originally, the failure of the bailout was due to 12 votes (and to public pressure), but Paulson made a back room deal with some Democrats (Christopher Dodd, Barney Frank, among others) and there was an about-face from the Congress, not to mentioned pressures from the President that changed the original vote, in a second vote, which resulted in passing the bailout. Kaptur tells Moore that this was not happenstance, that it was carefully planned, "like an intelligence operation." Then it is to Rep. Cummings, who says that all reps were told that the economy would collapse if Wall Street did not get the bailout. Even martial law was branded as being a way to keep social order if the bailout failed. Again, the argument from the Left leads to the fear mongering coming from the Right, and there is something to be made out of all of this, especially when one considers Moore's films *Bowling for Columbine* and *Fahrenheit 9/11*. Fear is the great incentive, while the use of force is the great menace. Politicians and business people alike now use these coercive methods to get whatever they want. And they do.

The strongest moment of the bailout sequence belongs to Rep. Kaptur, when in the House she tells American citizens who are being evicted on the basis of payment default to be "squatters in their own home." It is a very powerful indictment of all the abuse from banks, credit card and insurance companies, one that Moore can probably endorse wholeheartedly. She tells the public over C-Span to ask for papers proving that the bank owned their house, and that it would not be able to find any document proving that it did, "up there, on Wall

Street." She also reminds her representative colleagues that they all took an oath to protect the American people from attacks by *all enemies*, foreign and domestic. Finally, she equates bankers to "criminals who can shut down the democratic institutions of the United States of America," a definite allusion to, and accusation of the highest sphere of influence: the invisible Fascist one-world government. (If only there could be more politicians like Kaptur, full of empathy and passion, working for the people and not for banks, America would be a much better place.)

This segment of *Capitalism* concludes dramatically with another bold statement from Dennis Kucinich, the eccentric Democrat Representative from Ohio. He is asking the Chairman if the members of the House are working for the American people or for the Board of directors of Goldman Sachs. The answer to this seems clear by now, even for the neophyte to Moore's political art.

"Troubled Asset Relief Program" (or how to steal the poor to feed the rich)

When in the following section Moore visits Elizabeth Warren, Chair of the Oversight Panel on the Bailout, and asks her "Where's our money?," she cannot answer and explains that the Treasury has had a "don't ask, don't tell" policy on this issue. Quite simply put, the government gave Wall Street banks 700 billion and told them they did not have to say what they would do with it. As it turned out, 6 billion dollars were handed-out to the CEO and executives of Goldman Sachs, and 73 people received one million each at American International Group (AIG), and this was all condoned by the all-mighty Fed.[122] When Warren suggests to Moore that he could get better answers to his questions from actually calling Paulson himself, he was obviously going to follow on it.

Moore (*over the phone*):
Hello, yes, this is Michael Moore and I would like to talk to Henry Paulson, please.

Receptionist:
Michael Moore?

---

[122] Daniel WAGNER, "Treasury, NY Fed to defend AIG 'backdoor bailouts'", *Associated Press*, January 10, 2010

> Moore:
> Yes.

She hangs up on him.

> Moore:
> Hello? Hello?

As we can see, gone are the days of *Roger & Me*, when Michael Moore could infiltrate the most privileged quarters of society, film it, and ridicule rich and insensitive people on the big screen for all to see. Today everyone in America knows who he is and what he does, and they tend to give him more of a hard time; although there are many instances where being a public persona helped him to get what he wanted, such as K-Mart stopping selling bullets in their stores in *Bowling*, or again, the couple getting the insurance company to pay for their daughter's hearing aid in *Sicko* pretending that its CEO would be in Moore's next film. It is with this recognition in mind that he rented out an ice cream truck to read to senators on Capitol Hill some sections of the Constitution in *Fahrenheit 9/11*, and it is with the same recognition of his public persona that he rented out an armored truck to go to Wall Street and recuperate the bailout money in the name of the American people in *Capitalism: A Love Story*.

The final two parts of this film could not be any more diametrically opposed, insofar as one is based on comedy and the other on tragedy. In a way, it synthesizes all of the elements in the film into one clear proposition: There exists two very different Americas, one where a few stand in their ivory tower and exploit people and resources; the other where many stand on their rooftops crying for help and getting none when their homes are flooded and their lives are shattered.

But the first segment is Moore going to Wall Street to make a citizen's arrest and to get back the money, at least the one which had not yet been spent. He walks out from his armored truck straight to Goldman Sachs and AIG's headquarters in a way which recalls his old pranks from *TV Nation* and *The Awful Truth*, just for the show. He confronts security guards and lobby-level corporate personnel as he once did, full of vitality and humor. At the Goldman HQ he bangs himself against a tough and zealous security guard; while at the Citibank HQ, the guard tells him that he will have to talk to his supervisor, upon which we see the man in question coming down the escalators and Moore asking the guard: "Is he the one with the white shirt, the blue tie and the receding hairline?," describing a common type of corporate stupid white male that we are all supposed to recognize.

In the end, the whole "Let's get our money back from Wall Street" operation did not work. Moore was reduced later in the final scenes to put a "Police Line Crime Scene Do Not Cross" ribbon around Wall Street buildings, for the show and maybe even for the laughs…a little. But before he decides to return to Wallace Shawn, who tells him that today there are hints that "the unimaginable can occur," that "people can actually become angry at the wealthy"! According to Moore, this discontent was the equivalent of a great noise, the one emanating from a collective voice, the voice of the millions who voted for Barack H. Obama, a black man, and a politician of supreme intelligence and refinement.

Even though it would be premature to assign to President Obama all the virtues, since he has not yet delivered on certain important campaign promises, such as closing down Gitmo and putting Wall Street on a leash, we can be certain that Moore's endorsement and perception of the man is right. There is a great emotional moment when from Obama's headquarters we see people cheering and crying on election night. That moment surely represented, as Moore said in the film, a farewell to the old America and the beginning of a new America, filled with hope and even perhaps a glimmer of chance for a brighter future.

In any case, the way Obama appears in *Capitalism: A Love Story* is similar to the way he appeared in our lives, via his election in November '08: totally out of the blue. Since the film was mainly produced during and immediately following the 2008 Presidential election, Moore could not yet see what the first year of Obama's presidency would be like; although it seems in hindsight to have been quite prophetic. In *Capitalism*, the sequence pertaining to Obama is ambiguous, to say the least. It seems to hesitate at times between hope and cynicism, and it seriously takes under consideration the fact that people like Robert Gates and Timothy Geithner are still in the picture. For the first part of this sequence, Moore compiles moments from the 2008 campaign with "special appearances" from Obama's opponents John McCain and his running-mate, the unintelligible and self-described "bulldog with lipstick," the "maverick" ex-Governor of Alaska, Sarah Palin. There is even a clip from the encounter between Obama and "Joe the Plumber" (Samuel Wurzelbacher): the most obvious Mr. Redneck Public Republicans could have come up with. In it he argues with Obama about Constitutional law, when he is supposed to be a plumber, just a regular working-class kind of guy; not knowing that Obama himself is a Constitutional lawyer and expert who graduated from Harvard University.

All of these Republicans were obviously putting down Obama as being a socialist, and this relates to earlier sequences in the film as much as to what will come afterward.

As the sequence progresses Moore avoids falling into too much details regarding Obama's opponents, as colorful as they may be, and however tempting this might have seemed for him; simply because the subject matter is too complex and requires editorial precision. Moore cannot afford to open up his inquiry into the ramifications of Obama's historical election either, so for a while he goes back to America's general understanding of "socialism." According to him, the more Republicans were trying to scare the American public by saying that Obama was a socialist, the more they became interested in finding out facts about it. The filmmaker even interviews Bernie Sanders, an Independent from Vermont and the only socialist in the Senate. For him, and this is certainly close to our understanding of the term, democratic socialism represents low and middle income people, just regular working folks; nothing un-American about that, if we look at the history of the United States.

With the help of more graphic charts, Moore then explains that there are changes in values at the grass root level, for 37% of young Americans described themselves as being for capitalism, while 33% said they believed in socialism. This would have been unthinkable only 5 years ago, before Obama came into the picture. We can thus infer from the film and what it exposes that the American population is rapidly changing. With the aging baby-boomer population and the massive input of new immigrants, we can almost bet that a major ideological shift is laying ahead in the not-so-distant future. It seems like the sound of the people will finally be heard in Washington (and beyond, towards the invisible government). Obama might just be a precursor.

In the scenes preceding the resolution of *Capitalism*, Moore unwinds his narrative by reminding us that common folks are still fighting for what is right in corporate and inhuman America. One example is Benny Napoleon, the Sheriff from Wayne County, Detroit, who refused to evict people from their homes on moral grounds. In an interview he tells Moore that "the free-market has failed the country and made it look like Third World," and also suggests that people will eventually revolt against this system. This leads the filmmaker to logically cut to the Trody family in Miami, Florida. They are trying to regain their home with some much needed help from the Low-Income Families Fighting Together Association, whose main goal is to go around and "liberate homes" that have been taken away by banks in destitute neighborhoods. Moore organizes the sequence as to say that a revolution has already started in the United States. He then goes back to the workers at Republic Doors & Windows in Chicago, and reveals the outcome of their sit-down strike: as President Obama was in agreement with them all down the line, Citibank decided to finally pay the workers what was owned to them.

FDR's Dream

The resolution of *Capitalism: A Love Story* allows Moore to return to Flint, something he had already done earlier in the film by including an excerpt of *Roger & Me*, as well as a scene where he walks on GM's old grounds with his father. He stresses the fact that when united and protected by their government, as they were in the Great Flint Sit-Down Strike of 1936-37, workers can accomplish quite a lot and have their rights finally respected. Although, the situation today seems to be different, since the later stages of state capitalism are much more virulent and damaging to the common working folks than they were before, under industrial capitalism. According to Moore, it got to a point where workers have to fight to just get the basic things in life, which is in line with accepted theories regarding the erosion of the middle-class in North America since the mid 1980's.

In a conceptual leap common to his other feature films he inserts footage of President Franklin D. Roosevelt at the time of World War II, and tells us in voice-over that this great politician was looking into passing a Second Bill of Rights into the United States Constitution. Roosevelt was too sick from polio and had to address the nation via radio; but in a later part of the speech, he asked a film crew to come in the Oval Office to immortalize the moment visually as well.

> President Roosevelt:
> In our day, certain economic truths have become accepted as self-evident: a second Bill of Rights, under which a new basis of security and prosperity can be established for all, regardless of station or race or creed. Among these are the right to a useful and remunerative job, the right to earn enough to provide adequate food and clothing and recreation, the right of every farmer to raise and sell his products at a return which will give him and his family a decent living. The right of every business man, large and small, to trade in an atmosphere of freedom: freedom from unfair competition and domination by monopolies at home or abroad. The right of every family to a decent home, the right to adequate medical care, and the opportunity to achieve and enjoy good health, the right to adequate protection from the economic fears of old age, sickness, accidents, and unemployment; the right to a good

education. All of these rights spell security. And after this war is won, we must be prepared to move forward in the implementation of these rights, to new goals of human happiness and well-being. For unless there is security here at home, there cannot be lasting peace in the world.

Roosevelt died a year after this speech and did not live to see an enactment of his new bill of rights, Moore tells us. But luckily, the latter's film revived a moment in history which properly informs the present. It proves that the backbone of America is indeed community-based, and that the American government has been usurped and destroyed by corporate-minded fools in the last 40 years. In an extremely moving and final sequence, perhaps the saddest of Michael Moore's entire career, he says that if Roosevelt had lived all the rights contained in the Second Bill could have been available to every single American citizen without any questions being asked. He shows black and white stills of Roosevelt's funeral and pictures from the civil rights era, and this sequence is on par with some of the best work from Ken Burns, the PBS documentarist. But the most condemning moment of *Capitalism* is when he reminds the viewers of the Katrina tragedy, full of unresolved grief and anger for the rich elite who rules his country.

Moore (v.o.):
"The people of Europe and Japan got everyone of these rights. How did that happened? After the war, the people of Roosevelt's administration went overseas to help rebuild Europe. During this time, new constitutions were written for the defeated nations of Germany, Italy and Japan. The Italian Constitution guaranteed all women equal rights, and this was 1947. The German Constitution said that the state has the right to take over property and the means of production for the common good. And here's what we wrote up for the Japanese: all workers have a right to organize into a union and academic freedom is guaranteed. For the next 65 years, we would not become the country that Roosevelt wanted us to be. Instead we became this [*we see aerial shots of New Orleans at the time of Katrina*]. I remember thinking during the Katrina flood: Why is it always the poor who have to suffer the misery? Why is not there ever a Bernie Madoff up on the roof screaming for help? or the Head of Citibank? or the hedge fund guys at Goldman Sachs? or the CEO at AIG? Never is these guys, is it? It's always those who never got a slice of the pie, because these men took it all and left them with nothing, left them to die."

Like Moore was reminding us in *Sicko*, by adapting one of Jesus-Christ's teachings of the New Testament, a society is judged on how it treats its weakest and poorest people. *Capitalism* offers another example which shames American society. While we see African-American families stranded on their rooftops asking for help, the soundtrack is set to a touching version of 'The Last Rose of Summer', sang by Deanna Durbin. The fade out at the end of this sequence, as Moore pronounces the last words of voice-over commentary, is effective and quite powerful from an emotional viewpoint. Over what is now a black image, he says that he refuses to live in country like this and that he is not leaving, a good news for his millions of fans around the world. He claims that decent jobs, health care, a home, and a good education for all, what in fact was to be FDR's dream come true, are now inaccessible for millions of Americans, and that this is a crime committed against them. For Moore, capitalism as it is now (and as it has been since the 1970's) is evil; and "since you cannot regulate evil, you have to eliminated it and replace it with something better: democracy." The music for the end credits can be faintly heard and the editing cuts back to Moore on Wall Street, putting a police crime scene ribbon around it. He tells viewers that he is tired of doing this alone and asks them to come and help him in his quest for justice, equality and human rights.

In another final "fuck you" to the current system and to those who run it, he puts Tony Babino' swinging version of the 'The Internationale', the communist-socialist-left-wing anthem, and Woody Guthrie's "commie" song 'Jesus Christ' over the final credits. These are supplemented by quotes from famous American politicians and businessmen in between the filmmaker credits. Thomas Jefferson: "I sincerely believe that *banking establishments are more dangerous than standing armies* (1816)". John Adams circa 1765: "Property monopolized or in the possession of a few is *a curse to mankind.*" Finally, a quote from Benjamin Franklin: "No man ought to own more property than needed for his livelihood; *the rest, by right, belongs to the state,*" as well as a quote from the World's Richest Person in 2007, Warren Buffet: "It is class warfare, my class is winning, *but they should not be.*" Essentially, what Michael Moore brings out is the truth regarding some of America's founding fathers: they were in fact the forefathers of...socialism.

Other noteworthy elements of the final credits should be mentioned as they attest to Moore's positive effect on corporate policies. First, we find out that Wal-Mart no longer takes out "dead peasant" policies on their employees, even though they still call them "associates." Secondly, the viewers are asked to give generously to "Pennies for Pilots" so that airline pilots all over America will be able to eat properly and fly passengers to their destinations. Third, we are reminded that a home is foreclosed every 7 ½ seconds in America, and that the company which had sent the foreclosure letter to the Hackers has now moved out of Flint, leaving only a PO Box and more unemployed workers behind. Lastly, eight months after taking back their own home in Miami, the bank gave up on trying evicting the Trody family, and they are still living in it.

Get Off the Dime!

As it has been noticed many times before throughout this book, and contrary to Wallace Shawn's assertions about the coming "revolution against the rich," the reality of today's culture is that the rich (and the famous) are still very much admired by the millions who do not seem to mind "elevating fools into rich heroes."[123] Some would probably say that Michael Moore fits the description, but this would be a terrible mistake, more specifically from a social and cultural point of view. Moore did get rich from making movies that communicated important political messages to the masses, but he did not force these down people's throats like advertisement. People wanted to see and paid to watch. When detractors accuse him of criticizing a system which made him wealthy they deliberately underplay the fact that he did not make his wealth by scamming the general American public like the government, big banks or Fox News do daily. He did not tell them to come see his films claiming there were about one thing and then show them something else once they were in the cinema, after they had paid, like insurance companies do with their "customers" through unfair (and now illegal) business practices.

The plain fact is that Michael Moore is an artist even though he might not look or talk like one; and this is only valid if he is perceived in a classical frame of what an artist should look and talk like in the first place. The refusal to admit that what he does is art comes from both sides of the isle, and this schism only became wider after *Capitalism: A Love Story*. First there are the voices of some cinephiles, who cannot accept that Moore is an intelligent American who manages to make entertaining and well-crafted films that are seen and appreciated by the general film-going public. There is a snobbism there which defeats the very purpose of film going and film criticism. Strangely enough, if you ask a cinephile, especially those older than 40 years old, if she or he enjoyed watching Michael Moore films, the answer will be 'yes'; if you ask the same people if they agreed with

---

[123] Charles Bukowski, "Dinosauria We," from *The Last of the Earth Poems*, Ecco, 2002

what Michael Moore said in his films, the answer will also be 'yes', but if you ask them if they like Michael Moore, the answer will often be 'no.'

Undoubtedly, the fact that he creates filmic sermons has something to do with this, and unfortunately so does his image. Film criticism can be so petty and narrow-minded at times that we wonder if it is even worth writing about cinema at all. In today's world, making important statements is not nearly enough; you also have to look like George Clooney or Angelina Jolie to be respected and admired for making these statements. This is in fact America's double standard: it boasts that anyone there is entitled to the Dream but it excludes anyone who does not fit the Hollywood/Madison Avenue crypto-fascist paradigm. Moore just doesn't fit the model. But this could really be his burden in the end: to have been a Catholic moralist in a Protestant libertarian culture based on appearances. It is a shame, because America as a whole has so much more to offer than just surface studies and a superficial appreciation of culture. At its best, it blends all the northern and southern influences into one original and powerful statement about contemporary forms of living; telling the world that human beings from all walks of life can be free to express whatever they feel is right, and that "a book should not be judged by its cover." In the end, most of the controversy around *Capitalism: A Love Story* came about because the film made money at the box-office. Those who accused Moore of getting wealthy by profiting from the very thing he criticizes are missing their target. Moore became wealthy because he has offered cinematic "products" which register with an audience in a direct and honest way. His work does not address itself to intellectuals or journalists or critics; it is meant to be "consumed" by a general public who is into what is real, smart, funny and, yes, tragic. It proves that all of this is, not only possible in creative terms, but desired by most film viewers as well.

This being said, Michael Moore's films are about something which truly matters. His vision and consistency, by first studying the problem locally in *Roger & Me*, then nationally in *The Big One*, *Bowling for Columbine* and *Sicko*, and finally to the superstructure of it all in *Fahrenheit 9/11* and *Capitalism: A Love Story*, can truly be perceived as one life-long endeavour which seeks to shed light on the failing of the American Dream. Time has now shown that Michael Moore is a one-of-a-kind film author who deserves to be heard and respected because he synthesizes complex socio-political issues better than anyone else in cinema today. To illustrate this has been the main goal of this book all along, and we hope that we have succeeded in convincing some unbelievers of the relevancy, the meaning and brilliance of Michael Moore's political art.

EPILOGUE
REBEL, REBEL

The Art of Turning Kings into Fools

> We worked hard on creating a work of cinema that would move people not just politically, but on an emotional and visceral level as well.[124]

The place known as "Ground Zero" has been cleared for a decade, but the psychical wounds created by the 9/11 events and its aftermath have yet to be healed. This is a familiar story because it is what mainstream media has been covering and discussing every night of the week since September 11th 2001. We know that 9/11 is not over because we are told daily by those who profit from it, whether it is from the political angle or the spectacular one. Every year since then, on September 11, the media coverage about the commemoration is about showing in real time the events which happened in New York on that morning. It is never about trying to understand it by analyzing it, by proposing introspection. Now, follow on Michael Moore's trail and question the reasons which might have led to such a frightful event at home, not thousands of miles away, but on the very shores of America's glorious East Coast, right there on the front porch of the empire, and you will certainly find answers that might shock you, like those found in his films *Fahrenheit 9/11*, *Sicko*, and *Capitalism: A Love Story*.

Indeed, all of us saw in total synchronicity the brutal causality of political affairs on that day, but perhaps none of us fully comprehended what it truly meant or felt like we could do anything about it, except being afraid. At least Michael Moore showed us a way of looking at it, through his framing and his editing, from an analytical perspective. He showed us that 9/11 might not be about terrorists *over there* coming to America like Barbarians at the gate, but about domestic and more dangerous enemies. How else can we explain that Wall Street profited from 9/11? Why else would "terrorists" attack the World Trade Center instead of the Federal Reserve Bank or Wall Street itself? If it really was an outside job, as perfectly executed as it was, would it not have hit the *right target*? Whoever was responsible for it, it did was it was supposed to in the end: it helped to trigger America's downfall as an empire. It destroyed it politically, financially and emotionally because it opened the can of worms of all that is bad about the military-industrial complex. It either initiated a self-destructive process or prompted over reactive actions which revealed America's true nature.

These facts became even more obvious when we started considering the proportion of that belligerent response to what we were told were nineteen terrorists high-jacking planes and crashing them into

---

[124] Michael Moore, *The Official Fahrenheit 9/11 Reader*, pp.xv

three buildings with symbolic meaning. In fact, the conflation of 9/11 and Iraq by the Bush administration is something which is still being questioned by a large part of the American public and by the rest of the world today; but the new President in the White House told everyone to "turn the page," so what now? Should we really turn the page? What about accountability, does it count for something? What about those 5,000 soldiers who died in Iraq as a consequence, why was their blood really shed for? And the half a million Iraqi civilians?

This tragedy being played out live on television, in newspapers and on the Internet, subsequently creating war and misery in its wake, war and misery that are still going on today in Iraq and Afghanistan, proved that we are all trapped in this intricate web of *realpolitik* and world domination by a small elite group, an invisible government of royalty, bankers and industrialists; we are mere witnesses to and victims of a situation where the chickens came home to roost. Perhaps it was discomforting to be reminded of 9/11, 2 ½ years later, and in a summer movie to top it all off, but it also offered us the distance and an opportunity to deconstruct and try to understand the event.

A film like *Fahrenheit 9/11* took us out of the isolation created by our television sets, personal computers and other electronic gadgets, and brought us closer together at the cinema instead, like in times gone by. In fact the most interesting and fascinating aspect of *Fahrenheit 9/11* is that many viewers did not leave with the end credits upon its initial run in the theaters. People stayed for minutes on end discussing with strangers what they had just seen and heard. They were debating with each other when they should have been off to sleep or to the closest bar for a nightcap with friends.

No matter what those Moore critics might say, it did have a public effect.

Burn, Freedom, Burn!

As we know, freedom and justice are two concepts that never came naturally to human beings. It would be foolish to think that they ever did anywhere in this world. These principles were invented by the "better angels" of our nature and always had to be fought for in the past. It seems that it will always be that way. Like so many of us, Michael Moore is aware of this endless struggle against greed and apathy and puts it at the core of his work. This platform is simple, and maybe it is the reason why some intellectuals have so much trouble recognizing the genius of his (popular) work. Since it is simple, it has to be simple-minded as well. What they do not hear and see in between the images seems obvious to many others in so many different ways. What Moore is really telling us echoes the rallying cry of an entire generation. It tries to resuscitate, perhaps quite naively, given the reality of politics in this corporate world, the golden mean of all liberal ideologies: *"Believe in yourself, live a good life, respect your neighbor and try not to pollute along the way."*

At the end of the day, all he ever produced for television, for film and in books is about this simple, but not simplistic, premise: *Peace, love, unity, power to the people, not to those who should serve them.*

But what is more unusual and interesting is the way in which he proposes this philosophy: with a lot of guts and an irreverential attitude, which could only be described as being "punk" (in its 1970's incarnation). Unlike his detractors we believe that Moore does not necessarily preach his humanistic messages overtly and explicitly. He hides behind broadside comedy and satire because he knows Americans despise syrupy feelings and are more willing to listen when it is entertaining and light, even though he sometimes relies on melodramatic devices to stress the drama of a given situation (the killing of Kayla Rowland, for example). But by and large, he chooses to provoke in comedy, which is probably the only way to make people react nowadays. This seems especially true of the younger crowd who seems *blasé* about everything that truly matters: education, politics, history, philosophy. Moore manages to reach and engage them in thinking about the world, how it is ran, and what are their responsibilities to it.

As a college professor of cinema, I have the opportunity to notice every year how 17-20 year olds are affected by Michael Moore's films. It speaks to them in formal ways that MTV or YouTube might do, with a lot of humor and a major attitude. For them Moore has style, self-determination, and moxie. He believes in something, and that something is very similar to their virtues and aspirations. For them, and beyond this point, often lies total disillusionment or even cynicism and nihilism; all negative viewpoints which Moore manages to circumvent in his work, preferring to "keep hope alive" for future generation instead. Thus, not only does an appreciation of Moore's work requires a certain class awareness, but it might also have something to do with age (and with being hip or not). No doubt, his work is the product of popular culture, but contrary to most popular culture out there today, it is about human rights and political emancipation, not about narcissism and mindless consumption. Michael Moore is a master at the art of turning kings into fools, and this provides relief and comfort for intelligent and sensitive people all over the world, especially the ones who are young at heart and who wish to better understand the political world that we live in today.

Won't Get Fooled Again?

On another more popular level, the very notion of "art" is being relinquished to the realms of pansy, pseudo-intellectual, college professor discourses. Art does not interest the common folk because it is not presented as being important to a society controlled by conglomerates and corporations; a society where the rich white man values are presented as the norm, as the model to be emulated by everyone who believe in the Dream. The keepers of that model rather make people ignorant but beautiful and "well built" than to have them smart and curious. Basically, what Moore should be saying aloud in his work is that media has rendered Americans (and Canadians) inept at thinking outside of the box, that it has bet on our most base fantasies and has allowed us to be lost, looking at life through a window; a window looking out onto an American Dream lived by others (money, power, success, beauty, popularity, social networking, etc.).

Even some left-wingers and liberals now succumb to the trappings of shows like *American Idol* and *So You Think You Can Dance?* They do not seem to notice that all of these shows are based on competition, inclusion and exclusion; even if on the surface it all seems inoffensive or simply "entertaining." The premise of this kind of show is to vote in order to "eliminate" or "celebrate" the contestants, but the real fun for the viewer at home is to watch judges critique their performance and to "let them have it," as they say in the corporate world. It forces and entertains a certain type of rapport to the Other, and shapes a conception of life based on negativity, pettiness and jealousy. It shifts the attention from white collar and political crimes to flaming, meaningless and insignificant spectacles. No doubt, the day the American public starts seeing the relationship between what they consume as "culture" and their predicament in a divided society ran by the few will be the day it reaches adulthood from a cultural studies point of view. We cannot wait for the day when Moore finally tackles this issue in a clear and informative way for all to reflect on it.

Although, many individuals from the Left, the Right, and in the Rear-End of the political spectrum (where Christopher Hitchens is hiding) argue that Moore is a "sell-out," that he is nothing but a rich bourgeois who secretly seeks fame, fortune and power, and that his whole project is just self-serving in the end. But the question they should be asking themselves is the following: Why would Moore continue doing what he does if he has now so much money that he would be able to afford an early retirement and therefore avoid confrontations with second-rate corporate professionals and minor security forces at lobby level? Would he not prefer to go and hang out in the Cayman Islands with Dick Cheney if he really was a sell out?

We should insist here: some got it all wrong about Michael Moore. His rhetoric is one of enlightenment in an age of great darkness, where people get most of their information via *Access Hollywood* type of shows, yellow journalism, blogs, tweets, or just plain gossip around the water cooler at the work place. He is constantly trying to shine a light on a cancerous growth which has only gotten bigger since the 1980's, and that cancer is the marriage of government and big business. He explains the wheels of capitalism in a synthetic way and reveals how they spin. He expands on what are the consequences of living in a system which privy rich people who already own everything, even things that don't exist yet.

Furthermore, he reminds the American people of the cost of these reckless actions taken by their leaders to push the New World Order project further, one brick at a time; like sending a generation of young people to war on the basis of financial interests and ideas of world domination. He wants to underline how politicians like Nixon, Reagan, Bush and even Clinton affect families, neighbors, and community, pillars of our society now under attack by other greedy and despotic people within the executive suite and on Capitol Hill, the ones who come from the corporate world and pretend like they really are civil servants.

But Moore is also aware of his own contradictions, such as having his book at number one on the *New York Times* Best Seller list while chasing down corporate criminals he might even be working for on that given day. He includes this paradox in a movie that he is making at the very same moment, proving his awareness of context and his knowledge of where he fits in it. Some get and appreciate this self-reflexivity and self-negation, others do not. We hope that this literary effort will have converted some unbelievers in Moore's cause and complex ways of thinking and talking about such difficult social and political issues. This was one of our primary aims to begin with.

What *American Dissident* has demonstrated is that Moore is not only an intuitive journalist but also a gifted communicator who produces important politically minded art for the masses. One may be tempted to ask at this point: "What is political art?" The definition seems to vary from person to person, from book to book, or from website to website, but generally a lot of people seem to believe that these two things should not go together, because politics and "entertainment" (if not art) are not on the same plane of importance.

This is actually untrue, because art can have influence on politics or can be the result of politics (or at the very least the result of a political context or specific political atmosphere). In cinema's history, many masterpieces were created under certain oppressive regimes. *The Battleship Potemkin* (1925) from Sergei M. Eisenstein and Leni Riefenstahl's *Olympia* (1938) are only two examples. Then there is the political cinema of the European film *auteurs* like Alain Resnais, Bernardo Bertolucci and even Rainer W. Fassbinder, who did not help the 1960's struggle for liberation at all, but who did reinforce the brooding bourgeois white male stereotype for those who already hated the "artsy-fartsy" Left. The logical conclusion to this kind of political cinema is *Salò: the 120 Days of Sodom* (1975) from Pier Paolo Pasolini. It has been so misunderstood and so shocking (even as a metaphor for fascism/capitalism) that it had its director killed after its release. That was probably the day real "political cinema" died, but still a lot of other voices joined in afterwards to express their own political reality, in niches which convey their personalized agenda, as subgroups of society.

In film studies, the expression is usually associated with propaganda or agitprop, but it also refers to the meaningful avant-garde or the revolutionary art of the Soviets, Spaniards or South-Americans in specific decades of the 20th century (20's, 30's, 60's). Other times it evokes a kind of production which serves to question preconceived truths about the nature of politics, art, culture and power in all its dimensions (political, sexual, etc.), like the film work of Jean-Luc Godard. However, who knows what political art means today, in a world that only believes in money, and where old Godard is dating pornographic starlets?

What's Wrong with the Left, Anyhow?

Seen from a moderate left-wing and civil libertarian perspective, it is hard to imagine that a great part of the American thinking Left dislikes Michael Moore as much as the Right does. For a lot of us Moore's dissident stance transcends political art to reach a higher level of media consciousness. In a land made out of double standards and plastic icons, it seems to us like Moore is using the intrinsic power of media with enthusiasm and skill, with intent and purpose. How can a liberal be against virtuous acts such as saving the life of a man from imminent death because of a bad HMO clause? Or again, how can a self-proclaimed leftist criticize Moore for putting an end to a chain-store selling bullets over the counter, the same kind of bullets which were used in one of the most tragic school shoot-outs in American history? How can anyone claim that Moore is unpatriotic when everything he has done in the last 20 years has been about bettering the state of democracy in his country and abroad? Are we that desperate for a good argument or what?

Just like everything else which could be tagged "controversial," Americans are divided 50/50 regarding Moore and his work. In the case of *Bowling for Columbine*, critics were ready to attack his appealing "populist approach," while some ultra-left-wingers deplored Moore's on-screen persona and pseudo Man-of-the-People icon as some sort of "disjunction," that is, in spite of everything he was uncovering about the problem of America's predisposition for violence in the course of the film. Still, many of these critics, even though they might have perceived the truth of what Moore was saying, lingered on his case, attacking him on what appears to us to be petty issues. What many critics and armchair academics did not appreciate, or so it would seem in the so-called "serious readings" of his films, is the idea that Moore does not present the facts objectively as a documentary filmmaker should do. Instead, he informs us with the idioms of a fiction film, with a lot of creative freedom and expressiveness. Ultimately, that this brand of low-budget intellectualism is disconnecting left-wing Moore-bashers from the true meaning and function of activism in society.

Left and right of the ideological fence the argument against Moore predictably lies around his derisive tone, which is considered to be condescending to his audience. For instance, some critics find that Moore "talks down" to the public, but this seems to be the opposite of what he does (he is also often accused of "demagoguery," meaning that he tells people what is appealing to them, which does not seem to be the case either, even along partisan lines). So there is confusion here as far as understanding the tone of his work. His messages call upon a certain sense (or not) of possible human decency and dignity in the viewer. "You are what you watch," some say. This has never been as true as when watching a film or a show produced by Michael Moore and his talented accomplices.

In fact, what some detractors cannot fully grasp is that his films, books and TV shows are not common show business but a sophisticated form of *meta*-show business which manages to circumvent the conventions of the industry. His work is alive and conscious, informative enough to be considered relevant in this age of predetermined plots, generic formulas and prefabricated truths. It deliberately inscribes itself in the "Machine" because he is aware that it is where power resides. He picks up where mainstream media and academia usually quit: in action, in exercising what is expected from a breathing democracy. This to us is a noble cause and should be encouraged, discussed, dissected, analyzed, inscribed in its historical context, and even challenged by the opposing view. In the end, Moore's controversial films are not to everyone's taste, certainly from an aesthetic point of view, but they should be at least allowed to be produced and enter the public arena to stimulate the debate and questioned the status quo.

Rolling Stone Gathers No Moss

Jean-Luc Godard was one of the detractors of *Fahrenheit 9/11*. He once told a European reporter that "Moore does not distinguish between text and image. He does not know what he's doing" (he said without having seen the film). The first point to be made here is that Moore does understand the power of images/sounds and how to weave a discourse with them, and this was recognized by other gifted filmmakers like Lynch and Scorsese. The second is that he does put in perspective all these political images in *Fahrenheit 9/11*, but in a self-referential and necessarily post-modern way. If Godard had seen the film he would have found out that Moore cleverly substitutes to his own discourse Orwell's not-so-fictional account of a futuristic totalitarian society at the film's conclusion. Text and image are being differentiated by a well-know statement on class struggle throughout history, respecting a dialectical and diachronic argumentation, laying facts and commenting on them with parentheses, quotation marks and sub-thematic digressions.

Actually, what critics like Godard wanted from Moore's 2004 film was a more "radical" stance towards the United States government, but expressed through constructed means which would have foregrounded the apparatus of filmmaking, thinking the subject completely outside of the box like the great American thinkers Noam Chomsky and the late Howard Zinn. Moore definitely knows about these "alienating effects" that Godard is so good at (and which come from Brecht's epic theater), but chooses to go the other way by creating a more plot-driven, and therefore more "predictable" media product, to the great dismay of intellectuals. Although, the language of cinema is brought forth in his films when he uses ploys such as voice-over, slow-motions, fast-forwards and freeze-frames; and he uses these in order to illustrate cinema's intrinsic capacity to analyze a subject matter, something that television is never allowed to do, we might want to add.

In the end, one should remember that, formally speaking, Moore is a self-deprecating satirist before anything else. His use of stylization is most of the time targeted at mocking popular culture and the viewer's perception of it. In other words it has to look like every other product out there but with a marginal sensibility, closer to the Situationists International. His work provokes thoughts in the viewer, but also very strong emotions. His films are fast and loud, filled with the fury of good and necessary agitprop. They hit the right people at the right time and right where it hurts. When was the last time Godard achieve this, at the time of *La Chinoise*? When he was asked about Godard's comments regarding *Fahrenheit 9/11*, Moore had only this to say:

> I felt bad that he made a comment about a movie he hadn't seen. I think he has the right to make those perverse, weird comments. Always admired him. The only way people in Flint were able to see his films is because I brought them there. I ran my own little art house every weekend, on Friday and Saturday nights for close to ten years. I showed everything by Godard, Fassbinder, Truffaut, and Bergman.[125]

Obviously, and sadly, Godard's rhetoric is congealed in a form of historical past; a past which determined where we are at today (in trouble, because of the failure of 1960s liberal ideologies to come together against right wing ideologies and corporate control). In contrast, Michael Moore's ways of conceiving and making movies are set in the present-day, with a resolute mind-set, fired-up by a true determination to change, if not the world, at least America's mentality about its role in the world. Even though they might have the Situationist link in common, Moore aim is unlike the so-called "68 Generation," who was rather self-serving with its own political strength and who went on to participate to corporate crime or to make cryptic art videos that few in the world have seen.

What does all of this pettiness against Moore mean at the end of the day? It means that he will probably never be fully appreciated within the borders of his own country in spite of the awards he might receive there. Because his country is not really one country, but two countries; because he dares to practice in public what Ron Reagan Jr. called "the most deeply cherished American freedom: the right to dissent."[126]

Furthermore, because his work does not correspond to preconceived templates or aesthetic dogmas, like those of Godard, Moore will never be fully appreciated by his fellow leftist filmmakers abroad as well. A short but coherent overview of the criticism against him reveals that in America there is always a cost when you use the language of the people to read against the grain; while in Europe, there is always a high price to pay when you try to speak the language of the people but can only re-enforce the one spoken by the intellectual elite.

The Right Side of the Left

Admittedly, Michael Moore works from within a commodity system which allowed him to prosper both as an individual and as an artist. But by saying that Moore is part of the system and a sell out, one is

---

[125] *Film Comment*, July/August 2004
[126] Ronald Reagan Jr., "The Case against George W. Bush," *Vanity Fair*, August 4, 2004

deliberately killing the messenger. Perhaps against his own will he finds himself at the center of a debate about the value of art (only if we can still consider cinema as an art form today) in capitalist societies. In effect, he is able to distribute and show his work because of a superstructure which lies at the very heart of his criticism. Some might even claim that he embodies the inherent contradictions of an artist who creates in a consumer-based world, but for many left-wingers everywhere, taking this angle is to make abstraction of his importance as a strong alternative voice in American media today.

Moore's films are successful but they also transcend box-office values once the storm in their wake has ceased existing. His films, books, and TV shows might appear like commodities to some, but the many examples of Moore's living activism found in these films and shows seem to prove otherwise. At times it actually brought some results. It is well-worth noting here that Moore was not only financially rewarded for what he produced over the years, but that numerous nations around the world rewarded him critically, by praising the originality and importance of his work. For these non-Anglo-Saxon cultures, a person who stands for anti-poverty, anti-social despair, anti-corporate crime and anti-government crime should be seen as a light in the dark, not as an agitator to be silenced.

This book has demonstrated that objectivity is not the main characteristic of Michael Moore's work; even if it is entirely based on research, social interactivity and the editorial summary of this material, which has subjectivity involved at every step of the way. The subjective quality of what he produces is the most interesting aspect of what he does in creative terms, because it represents a personal account of historical events, seen through a specific sensibility. Is this not what we do when we want to understand an era: turn to its artists, whether they are painters, novelists, playwrights, composers or filmmakers? At the end of the day, Moore's work is a record of a certain society at a given time and place in history; through its vicissitudes, its accomplishments and its failures. It is like a family picture book with happy memories to be cherished together and painful ones to be nursed alone.

This being said, it does not mean that Moore's subjectivity is the only one represented in his work either. The canvas which he has created with his collaborative team allowed for other voices to be heard as well. *TV Nation* and *The Awful Truth* had moments where Moore changed things for the better only because he had collaborated with other talented people who shared his point of view on the world. Maybe they had to manipulate people and bend the facts along the way, but perhaps this was the only way to operate in a culture which is all about manufactured lies, counterfeited truth, and outright manipulations; a culture which elevates fools like Bill O'Reilly and Rush Limbaugh at the top of the television and radio game.

Moreover, if Moore really was so self-centered, would he have created a forum on his Internet site to consult the public for its opinion or co-founded the Traverse City Film Festival to re-inject some life into Flint's culture? Would he have gone to Mississippi and Louisiana after the great flood of 2005 to bring comfort and goods to the bereaved? If nothing else, Moore's strong iconic presence will always be a reminder that there are people with alternative modes of thinking, even in that homogenized wasteland we call American popular culture. Now, will the mass tune-in when he again battles *American Idol* or some other form of mindless entertainment for Nielsen's ratings on television? Will there be anybody there to listen to what he has to say, like those millions of people who watch the *Glen Beck Show* daily? Of course there will be. Because there are two Americas, the hardcore Old Testament crowd of the South and Center, and the more liberal and egalitarian body who descends from the millions of immigrants who reached the American shores in the last century and a half; those who believed and still believe in the American promise.

Louder Than Bombs

In the summer of 2004 the Chinese government imposed restrictions on American film quotas, but it did so only in relation to most American films, not all of them. There were in fact two American films (actually one was a movie) allowed in China that year: *The Day After Tomorrow*, a run-of-the-mill blockbuster wherein America is destroyed by cataclysmic natural forces that it cannot comprehend, and *Fahrenheit 9/11*, Moore's extraordinary pamphlet against the Republicans and the New World Order. This alone should speak volumes as far as Moore's reputation outside of the United States is concerned. Christians, Jews, Muslims, Buddhists, atheists and agnostics alike support his endeavor, his call for reason and unity. This cross-cultural breakthrough should be considered a great accomplishment for any artist, regardless of his origins and his looks.

People from everywhere have surely felt and understood what Moore was saying with his film concerning Bush and his posse. It *communicated* something to them, no doubt about that. Now, the reason why it did not help to oust Jr. is now known: people were afraid to replace those who led them in two wars in the Middle-East. They thought that by replacing the Bush/Cheney administration, America would not be able to conquer who they were led to believe was responsible for 9/11. To this day, millions of Americans still cannot grasp the meaning of their leaders' decisions and actions around the world and they prefer not to worry about it, tuning-in to see who will be the next instant idol instead. Unfortunately millions blindly bought these false claims about Hussein and his alleged weapons of mass destruction without losing any sleep over it, and now they are more susceptible than ever to be victim of a terrorist (or government) attack because of their refusal to dissent.

To nuance what might appear like a series of over-generalizations to some, it would be unfair (and untrue) to suggest that all Americans were duped by this half-baked rhetoric of the Republicans from December 2002 on. All of these lies and deceitful statements did not go unnoticed by a variety of intelligent and sensitive Americans as well. Moore is only one example here, but there were numerous others who openly questioned the validity of the link made between 9/11, bin Laden and Iraq in the led-up to the war. Most of them were told to shut up, though. The ones who did challenge Bush's foreign policy were lynched in public by right-wing media pundits, especially at the Fox network, where people like O'Reilly, Hannity, Beck and Coulter are acting as lap dogs of the Republican Party and the hate mongers of the American religious Right.

It might be interesting here to recall how politicians and celebrities alike went on national television or public tribunes to speak openly against the war and how they were hammered by the Right and their ultra-conservative media fiends. People like (Senator) Al Franken, Bill Maher, Susan Sarandon, Tim Robbins and Sean Penn were perceived as being unpatriotic when they claimed their right to dissent against the war, and their career seemed to have suffered from it in certain cases. From then on, Bush's administration would have a strained relationship with a great part of Hollywood, which leans anyway to the left. The conflict boiled out of the pot when Bush himself claimed in the primaries of the 2004 election that "Hollywood [is] not the heart and soul of America, but that *regular people* are," as if he could personally relate to them, and as if he was not only himself a "fictitious President" hired to create "fictitious wars."

Spanking the Bully

One of the main points made by Michael Moore in his most memorable film, *Fahrenheit 9/11*, is that war will never end because for people like the Hawks and the invisible government behind them it has to be perpetual to be profitable. The whole notion inspired by Leo Strauss, that a state is allowed to do anything to its population under certain "emergency situations," had eventually reached for them its full potential in the aftermath of 9/11. With the Soviets weakened by the fall of Communism, these (old) men of long-term vision had to find a new "evil" to be defeated, a new "threat" to national security that would justify the suspension of some civil liberties, and that would allow America to finally fulfill its imperial destiny. No matter how hard you might try to defend these reckless interventions in the Middle East, whether it was in Iraq, or it is in Afghanistan or on the Pakistani border, or even in Iran, a fact remains: the terrorist attacks in New York and Washington in September 2001 only served that purpose for them. No matter who back it up, it made some people a lot of money and opened the door for all kinds of government and corporate abuse.[127]

As for the rest of the world, well, there is nothing like seeing the bully getting spanked for once. Both 9/11 and *Fahrenheit 9/11* were such a spanking. For at least 50% of the American public and for American mainstream media in general, this seems to be a hard pill to swallow. With the belief that the United States are the "World's Police" and the "Great Exporter of Democracy & Freedom" should also come the humility to admit that there is a margin of errors and that mistakes can happen sometimes. The war in Iraq is only one of the many errors that will have to be pondered by Bush and his gang of thugs when they finally get to the gates of hell.

It is also a well-known fact that American leaders, regardless of their political leanings, have understood the power of fear to keep, not only its own citizenry, but everybody else around the world subservient and well-behaved. In fact, they have extended the American/Israel/Great Britain empire by oppressing and killing millions of individuals, through organizations such as the International Monetary Fund or the World Bank, and by supporting dictatorships or backing-up covert operations which included raping, torturing and killing of hundreds of thousands of men, women and children. To find out more about these facts, i.e. based on research, one has only to consult the work of intellectual Noam Chomsky, perhaps a reference for Michael Moore.

Given all of these facts, is it even necessary to mention or even to worry about the consequences of those terrorist policies?

Since when did bullies stop to think about anything or anyone else but themselves, anyhow? Isn't their job to go out and beat up some frail kid in the schoolyard anyway, like Nicaragua, El Salvador or Guatemala? Maybe are we expecting too much from a military-industrial complex which uses sheer brute force to spread its flawed understanding of "freedom" and "democracy" all over the world? American governments since Truman sure have shown us that actions speak louder than words. They have ruled over the planet by using

---

[127] Matthew Goldstein, "After 9/11, Wall Street Reborn," (the street.com), September 8, 2006

coercive and sadistic methods to achieve their ultimate goal. Will Obama really be different in that sense?[128]

Like Moore, we believe these facts to be irrefutable. Beyond the history written by America herself, there are many factual accounts of American imperialism and expansionism existing in libraries and archives all over the world. It is only a matter of time before a greater part of the decent American public discovers the truth about their corrupt system and its overpaid executives. Following on Moore's example, and like he says at the end of *Capitalism: A Love Story*, we hope that they will do something about it. Neither should all Americans forget the hard and cold lessons of history, especially the ones taught on September the 11th 2001. On a national level, not much insight came from this costly lesson, though. A few weeks later, while the ashes at Ground Zero had stopped smoldering, and while their President was "bombing a country whose name he could not pronounce," many went back to their old ways, to afternoons of soap operas and an endless parade of pregnant teens and desperate housewives. Left with no analytical map to follow on, stopped from being introspective, they went back to Jay Leno and David Letterman making their tired old jokes on late-night television. Even if they claimed it changed their perception of the world, Americans rarely questioned what ultimately went wrong abroad to lead to such a frightful event at home, whether it was accomplished by foreign or domestic enemies. It seemed much easier to fabricate a boogeyman, to bring him out of his cave and to "smoke him out of his hole," than to engage in an unavoidable *mea culpa* regarding hostile aggressions around the world in the last 100 years.

This is a political attitude which can only lead to self-destruction in the end, and it probably will in the next decade or so. In this regard, America might learn a few lessons from the failures of the ex-Soviet Union, that other "superpower" of the 20th century. When the Iron Curtain suddenly ripped open and fell on the Russians' head, thanks to *glasnot* and *perestroika*, as well as to 70 years of bureaucracy and government corruption, they finally understood that the "Union" in question was only a chimera. The same could be said of the "United" in the United States of America, the *two* countries under analysis by Michael Moore. If we consider that those responsible for the Oklahoma City bombing and the high-jackers of the 9/11 planes came or had help

---

[128] Can we trust Obama when he made in his victory speech the following statement: "And to those watching tonight from beyond our shores, from parliaments and palaces, to those who are huddled around radios in the forgotten corners of the world, our stories are singular, but our destiny is shared, and *a new dawn of American leadership is at hand*"? Is this a sign of opening and compassion or is it a call for the last stages of the New World Order to take place?

from within, and that the neo-Nazis, the Tea Party, the "Birthers," and the Michigan Militia are all American citizens, we can almost be certain that America's real enemies are domestic, not foreign ones.

These are only a few examples illustrating the inner tensions which may eventually burn a hole in the nation's delicate social fabric; because marginal groups on the loose can be as dangerous as a total mass upheaval or anarchy. All it would take is a Timothy McVeigh-type to bring a dirty bomb into New York or Washington and that would be the end of the demonization of the foreigner. But this stigma against the Other goes deep in American culture. The wounds of the Civil War have apparently not been healed yet. The election of Barack H. Obama is incredibly significant in this sense. It might be the beginning of a new chapter in American history or it could really be the end for American "democracy." Good people everywhere want to believe that he is a benevolent and transformative leader. They intuitively feel that he is a good man who will defend the interests of the working and (quickly eroding) middle-class. As these lines are being written, he and his administration are about to pass another bailout…for Main Street. This being said, it would seem like Americans suffer from amnesia, because a majority decided to vote for a Congress on the right in the mid-term election in November 2010.

Redeeming the Bully

So, finally, what is it that all those harsh critics of American policies like Moore and millions of others around the world want from America? We want from America an entrepreneurial spirit which can lead the world into a brighter, more prosperous, and more secure future for everyone. We want America to start respecting Mother Nature and to get involved in stopping global warming. We want from America an understanding and openness to others outside of their culture and value-system. We want from America a more benevolent attitude when their help is required, asking nothing in returns but respect (and maybe some admiration…why not?). We want America to stop putting its fingers in everybody else's pie and start fixing the problems on the home front, with jobs, health and a good educational system. In the end, we also wish that Americans were more sympathetic to other people's grief, because what goes around must eventually come around, as 9/11 proved.

All of the above is not a neo-Marxist dream or a left-wing utopia impossible to achieve. It is not a Good Simon fairy tale or a naïve interpretation of human nature. It is actually within a possible reach. It just requires the guts to care for others and the humility to admit one's own fallibility.

We believe that Americans are good people, but that they are being misled by a handful of ideologues, capitalists and plutocrats who denatured the American Dream to suit their needs. Michael Moore can probably describe them better than this author can, since he is himself an American.

> The majority of our fellow Americans are liberal and progressive when it comes to the issues. That's not just me saying this or wishing it to be true. Every poll shows that the majority of Americans believe in women's rights. The majority of Americans want stronger environmental laws. The majority of Americans are pro-labor. Put down the whole list of issues, Americans, whether they use the label or not, and most Americans do not like labels, but most Americans in their hearts are liberal and progressive. It's just a small minority of people who hate. They hate. They exist in *the politics of hate*.[129]

This statement about the politics of hate became more relevant than ever on November 4, 2008, when 64 millions Americans voted for a black man from modest origins for the first time in the history of American presidency. The air was unusually warm and still for an autumn night, which was perhaps foreshadowing the shape of things to come: a better and more benevolent America. Like millions around the globe, Canadians also watched with amazement and held their breath. Some even shed a tear and realized that what was happening was indeed historical and revolutionary, and that America could not be reduced to one single identity. Since that day many also wondered if Barack Obama will be redeeming the bully he represents or if he will just be another puppet of the New World Order like George W. Bush was before him. Only time will tell.

American Dissident

Michael Moore seems to truly believe that television and cinema should be used to the betterment of society. This was obvious when I saw *Roger & Me* as a young adult back in 1989, when my girlfriend and I saw *Fahrenheit 9/11* in 2004, as well as when I saw *Capitalism: A Love Story* with a group of my college students in 2009, two decades after my first encounter with the man's work.

---

[129] Michael Moore in a speech made at the Democratic Convention, Boston, July 2004

Moore is an artist who chooses to emphasize the poetic properties of the film making and film-going experiences by using it as a tool for change, and in spite of intense pressures on him and his work. He is working to remind his world public that there is a new form of apartheid going on in the U.S. today. He tells us that his country is an unfair and brutal empire abroad, and sometimes even more unfair and brutal with its own people (by forging a greater cleavage between rich and poor, and by ignoring the true will of the people). Of course, to deny these facts would be the same as claiming that the world is flat like a pancake, or that Dick Cheney is a benevolent man in his own right.

Besides acting out on his most profound convictions, one of Moore's goal is to share uncommon knowledge, which is always a good way to initiate discussion and propel political action in our world. Beyond what can be said of him as an activist or as a muckraker, Moore went on to create some of the most compelling films and TV shows ever made along the way, as an American artist. His work leaves no one indifferent. You may love him, you may despise him, but you cannot really ignore him.

Whether we like it or not, American dissident Michael Moore is here to stay. And this is a fact.

MICHAEL MOORE
WORKING

Directing
Capitalism: A Love Story (2009)
Sicko (2007)
The Great '04 Slacker Uprising (2007)
Fahrenheit 9/11 (2004)
Bowling for Columbine (2002)
The Awful Truth (1999-2000)
And Justice for All (1998)
The Big One (1997)
Canadian Bacon (1995)
TV Nation (1994-1995)
Pets or Meat: The Return to Flint (1992)
Roger & Me (1989)
Rage Against the Machine "Sleep Now In the Fire" and "Testify"
R.E.M. video "All the Way to Reno (You're Gonna Be A Star)"
System of a Down video "Boom"

Film & TV Writing
Capitalism: A Love Story (2009)
Sicko (2007)
The Great '04 Slacker Uprising (2007)
Fahrenheit 9/11 (2004)
Bowling for Columbine (2002)
The Awful Truth (1999-2000)
Big One (1997)
Canadian Bacon (1995)
TV Nation (1994-1995)
Pets or Meat: The Return to Flint (1992)
Roger & Me (1989)

Producing
Capitalism: A Love Story (2009)
Sicko (2007)
The Great '04 Slacker Uprising (2007)
Fahrenheit 9/11 (2004)
Bowling for Columbine (2002)
The Awful Truth (1999-2000)
Better Days (1998)
Canadian Bacon (1995)
TV Nation (1994-1995)
Pets or Meat: The Return to Flint (1992)
Roger & Me (1989)

Acting & Performing
The Fever (2004)
Michael Moore Live! (2002)
Bon numéro, Le (2001)
Lucky Numbers (2000)
Edtv (1999)
Canadian Bacon (1995)

Appearing
Capitalism: A Love Story (2009)
The Great '04 Slacker Uprising (2007)
Fahrenheit 9/11 (2004)
Orwell Rolls in His Grave (2003)
The Corporation (2003)
Stupidity (2003)
I Love the '80s (2002) (TV)
Bowling for Columbine (2002)
Last Party 2000 (2001)
Fever Pitch (2001)
Trade Off (2000)
The Awful Truth (1999-2000)
I Think I Cannes (1997)
The Big One (1997)
TV Nation (1994-95)
Pets or Meat: The Return to Flint (1992)
Blood in the Face (1991)
Roger & Me (1989)
Sherman's March (1986)

Guest Appearing
Countdown with Keith Olbermann (2010)
Larry King Live (2008-2010)
Moving Pictures Live! (2010)
Hannity (2009)
Daily Show, The (2004)
Tavis Smiley (2004-2010)
Real Time with Bill Maher (2003-2010)
Jimmy Kimmel Live! (2004-2010)
Late Night with Conan O'Brien (1993, 1998, 1999, 2004)
Comme au cinéma (1998)
Johannes B. Kerner Show, Die (1998)
Simpsons, The (1998)

Book Writing
Adventures in a TV Nation (with Kathleen Glynn), N.Y.: HarperCollins, 1998.
Downsize This! Random Threats from an Unarmed American, N.Y.: Random House, 1996.
Dude, Where's My Country?, N.Y.; Boston: Warner Books, 2003.
Stupid White Men and Other Sorry Excuses for the State of the Nation, N.Y.: HarperCollins, 2001.
The Official Fahrenheit 9/11 Reader, N.Y.; London; Toronto; Sydney: Simon & Schuster, 2004.
Will They Ever Trust Us Again?, N.Y.; London; Toronto; Sydney: Simon & Schuster, 2004.

Awards (a non-exhaustive list)
Academy Awards, USA, 2008, Nominated Best Documentary for *Sicko*, 2003 Won Oscar Best Documentary Feature for *Bowling for Columbine* (2002) Shared with Producer Michael Donovan.
Amsterdam International Documentary Film Festival, Holland, 2002, Won Audience Award *Bowling for Columbine* (2002)
Aspen Filmfest, USA, 1997, Won Audience Award Audience Favorite Documentary for *The Big One* (1997)
Atlantic Film Festival, Canada, 200, Won Audience Award for *Bowling for Columbine* (2002)
Australian Film Institute, 2003, Nominated Best Foreign Film Award for *Bowling for Columbine* (2002). Shared with Charles Bishop, Jim Czarnecki, Michael Donovan and Kathleen Glynn
Bergen International Film Festival, 2002, Won Audience Award for *Bowling for Columbine* (2002)
Berlin International Film Festival, 1990. Won Peace Film Award - Honorable Mention for *Roger & Me* (1989)
Bodil Awards, 2005 Nominated Best American Film for *Fahrenheit 9/11*, 2004 Won Best American Film for *Bowling for Columbine*
Cannes Film Festival, 2004, Won FIPRESCI Prize Competition for *Fahrenheit 9/11* (2004); **Golden Palm** for *Fahrenheit 9/11* (2004); Won 55th Anniversary Prize for *Bowling for Columbine* (2002) – Unanimously; Nominated Golden Palm for *Bowling for Columbine* (2002)
César Awards, France**,** 2003, Won César Best Foreign Film (Meilleur film étranger) for *Bowling for Columbine* (2002)
Denver International Film Festival, 1997, Won People's Choice Award Documentary Film for *The Big One* (1997)
Emmy Awards, 2001, Nominated Emmy Outstanding Non-Fiction Program (Reality) for *The Awful Truth* (1999). Shared with Kathleen Glynn (executive producer), Michael Donovan (executive producer),

Dave Hamilton (co-executive producer), Charlie Siskel (supervising producer), Tia Lessin (supervising producer), Rob Huebel (producer), Marc Henry Johnson (producer), Nick McKinney (producer); 1999 - Nominated Emmy Outstanding Non-Fiction Series for *The Awful Truth* (1999). Shared with Kathleen Glynn (executive producer), Ellin Baumel, Dave Hamilton (supervising producer), Tia Lessin (senior producer), Ann Cohen (head writer), Francis Gasparini (writer), Jay Martel (writer), Nick McKinney (writer), Henriette Mantel (writer); 1996 -Nominated Emmy Outstanding Informational Series for *TV Nation* (1994). Shared with Kathleen Glynn, Jerry Kupfer (supervising producer), Annie Cohen (writer), Jon Derevlany (writer), Francis Gasparini (writer), Jay Martel (writer), Jeff Stilson (writer) and Louis Theroux (writer); 1995 - Won Emmy Outstanding Informational Series for *TV Nation* (1994). Shared with Kathleen Glynn, Jerry Kupfer (supervising producer), Eric Zicklin (writer), Stephen Sherrill (writer), Chris Kelly (writer) and Randy Cohen (writer).
Independent Spirit Awards, 2003, Won Independent Spirit Award Best Documentary for *Bowling for Columbine* (2002)
International Documentary Association, 1998, Nominated IDA Award Feature Documentaries for *And Justice for All* (1998); 1990 – Won IDA Award for *Roger & Me* (1989)
Kinema Junpo Awards, 2003, Won Kinema Junpo Award Best Foreign Language Film Director for *Bowling for Columbine* (2002)
San Sebastián International Film Festival, 2002, Best Film for *Bowling for Columbine* (2002)
Sudbury Cinéfest, 2002 Won Audience Award for *Bowling for Columbine* (2002)
São Paulo International Film Festival, 2002, Won Audience Award Best Documentary for *Bowling for Columbine* (2002)
Toronto International Film Festival, 2002, 3rd place People's Choice Award for *Bowling for Columbine* (2002); 1989 – Won People's Choice Award for *Roger & Me* (1989)
U.S. Comedy Arts Festival, 2003, Won Freedom of Speech Award
Vancouver International Film Festival, 2002, Won Most Popular Film for *Bowling for Columbine* (2002); 1989 – Won Most Popular Film for *Roger & Me* (1989)
Writers Guild of America, USA, 2003, Won WGA Award (Screen) Best Screenplay Written Directly for the Screen for Bowling for Columbine (2002); 2001 - Nominated WGA Award Documentary - Current Events for *The Awful Truth* (1999). Shared with Nick McKinney for the feature "Holiday Inn Attempts To deport Its Mexican Housekeepers For Organizing A Union." 2000 – Nominated WGA Award Documentary - Current Events for *The Awful Truth* (1999). Shared with Annie Cohen, Francis Gasparini, Henriette Mantel, Jay Martel, Nick McKinney for the segment "Funeral at a HMO"

Websites

www.michaelmoore.com

www.myspace.com/americandissident_book

ABOUT THE AUTHOR

Cover illustration & photo: Tina Carlisi

François Primeau is a professor of cinema and communication in Montreal, Canada. He has been teaching film and video production at university and college levels for over a decade, as well as lecturing extensively on such varied topics as film history and aesthetics, journalism and television. Primeau wrote many articles and reviews for various cinema magazines and journals. He is also an independent filmmaker whose first feature has been recognized by the Canadian Guild of Film Producers and Directors in 2003.

American Dissident: The Political Art of Michael Moore is his first book.